# the TOMORROWS

>> REALITY dEAD

TIME BROKEN

WARN EVERYONE

oNLy

TOMORROWS CAN

SAVE US

/// END Transmission. >>

# the TOMORROWS

/// Story

Curt Pires

/// Art

Jason Copland

Alexis Ziritt

Ian MacEwan

Andrew MacLean

Liam Cobb

Kevin Zeigler

/// Colors

Adam Metcalfe

/// Lettering

Colin Bell

///Cover Art

Jason Copland

 <DH Slug®>

<Dark Horse Books>

/// publisher
Mike Richardson

/// editor
Dave Marshall

/// associate editor
Aaron Walker

/// assistant editor
Rachel Roberts

/// design
Dylan Todd

/// collection designer
Justin Couch

/// digital art technician
Christina McKenzie



This volume collects issues #1–#6 of the Dark Horse comic book series *The Tomorrows*.

Published by
Dark Horse Books
A division of
Dark Horse Comics, Inc.
10956 SE Main Street
Milwaukie, OR 97222

DarkHorse.com

First edition: September 2016
ISBN 978-1-61655-914-4

10 9 8 7 6 5 4 3 2 1

Printed in China >>

associate editor
Aaron Walker

assistant editor
Rachel Roberts

design
Dylan Todd

collection designer
Justin Couch

digital art technicians
Christina McKenzie

The Tomorrows © 2015, 2016 C... Pires. All rights reserved. Dark Ho... Books® is a trademark of D... Horse Comics, Inc., registered... various categories and countries... rights reserved. No portion of... publication may be reproduced... transmitted, in any form or by... means, without the express wri... permission of Dark Horse Com... Inc. Names, characters, places,... incidents featured in this publica... either are the product of the auth... imagination or are used fictitio... Any resemblance to actual pers... (living or dead), events, instituti... or locales, without satiric inten... coincidental.

This volume collects issues #1... of the Dark Horse comic-book se... *The Tomorrows*.

Published by
Dark Horse Books
A division of
Dark Horse Comics, Inc.
10956 SE Main Street
Milwaukie, OR 97222

DarkHorse.com

10 9 8 7 6 5 4 3 2 1

Printed in China

"WRITE YOUR WAY OUT OF THE DEAD FUTURE."—ALDOUS ELLIS

## /// BEGIN **FOREWORD.>>**

It's the first week of 2016 and the Chinese stock market is already convulsing like a Pentecostal minister. I've just returned from picking up groceries in my hometown, where the tidemark from the recent unprecedented flood caused by climate change is chest high in some areas. My Twitter feed is exploding with images of starving Syrian children with xylophone ribs and canceled eyes, so I turn on the TV. *Great.* There's blurting offal boulder Donald Trump, pouting again because some hack noticed the seam in his human suit. Stop the century, I want to get off.

All communication is marketing.

Our heroes have all been bought.

If you're born poor, then you'll almost certainly die poor.

Culture is something done to us by the children of hedge fund managers.

And another thing.

In short, the crisis is at our door.

*But so is tomorrow.*

I don't mean tomorrow in the quotidian sense: that gray certainty most of us greet with a bone-snapping sigh at six a.m. I mean tomorrow the way Curt Pires means it: an effulgent realm of possibility viewed through the keyhole of a thick dungeon door. This is why the globe-hopping techno-thriller you're very wisely about to read might equally be called *The Hopes.*

Claudius, Sasha, Jiro, new recruit Zoey, sentient AI Warhol, and absent founder/father Aldous Ellis could have been cyberpunk caricatures in less capable hands than Curt's. You know what I mean: a bunch of earnest cheekbones in fetish gear taking on the forces of slightly blander conformity with their secret blend of eleven revolutionary herbs and spices. Curt's too smart to fall for that garbage. He understands that *real* power gets to control both sides of the argument—the thesis and the antithesis. So, please don't read what follows in the expectation of empty us-versus-them pyrotechnics. They may be comforting because hey, we all like to identify with the underdog, but the reality is that we're part of a system so smart it's succeeded in monetizing our resistance as well as our participation. That contradiction, which can only be resolved through ceaseless creative exploration, is the humming you can hear under the hood of *The Tomorrows*. Curt's asking us a question, see: *Is it possible to tunnel out of a nightmare if the only tools to hand are part of the nightmare?*

Then there's the art. I don't know how he did it, but Curt managed to assemble a dream team to handle the rotating art chores—names you'll have seen before in the pages of breakout indie hits like *Space Riders*, *Pop*, *Sex*, *Silica Burn*, and *ApocalyptiGirl*. Although they're all radically different and unique, the art styles of Jason Copland, Alexis Ziritt, Ian MacEwan, Andrew MacLean, Liam Cobb, and Kevin Zeigler complement each other beautifully when *The Tomorrows* is inhaled in one sitting. I suspect this is entirely down to both the painstaking design work of Dylan Todd and Adam Metcalfe's woozy, dystopian colors. Throw in my dear friend and frequent collaborator Colin Bell on letters and you have a guerrilla network of the finest talent on two continents.

Ultimately, *The Tomorrows* is a book that feels absolutely right for its time and place. Curt has a tremendous sense of mission, God help him, and that's why this book doesn't shy away from asking the tough questions. As Bob Dylan once so aptly put it, "Let us not talk falsely now, the hour is getting late."

You know, Bob Dylan: that guy from the IBM commercial.

Alex Paknadel
Lancaster, England
January 2016

*Alex Paknadel is the writer of* Turncoat *and* Arcadia *from Boom! Studios. He's way grumpier than this in person.*

/// part one

# REALiTi

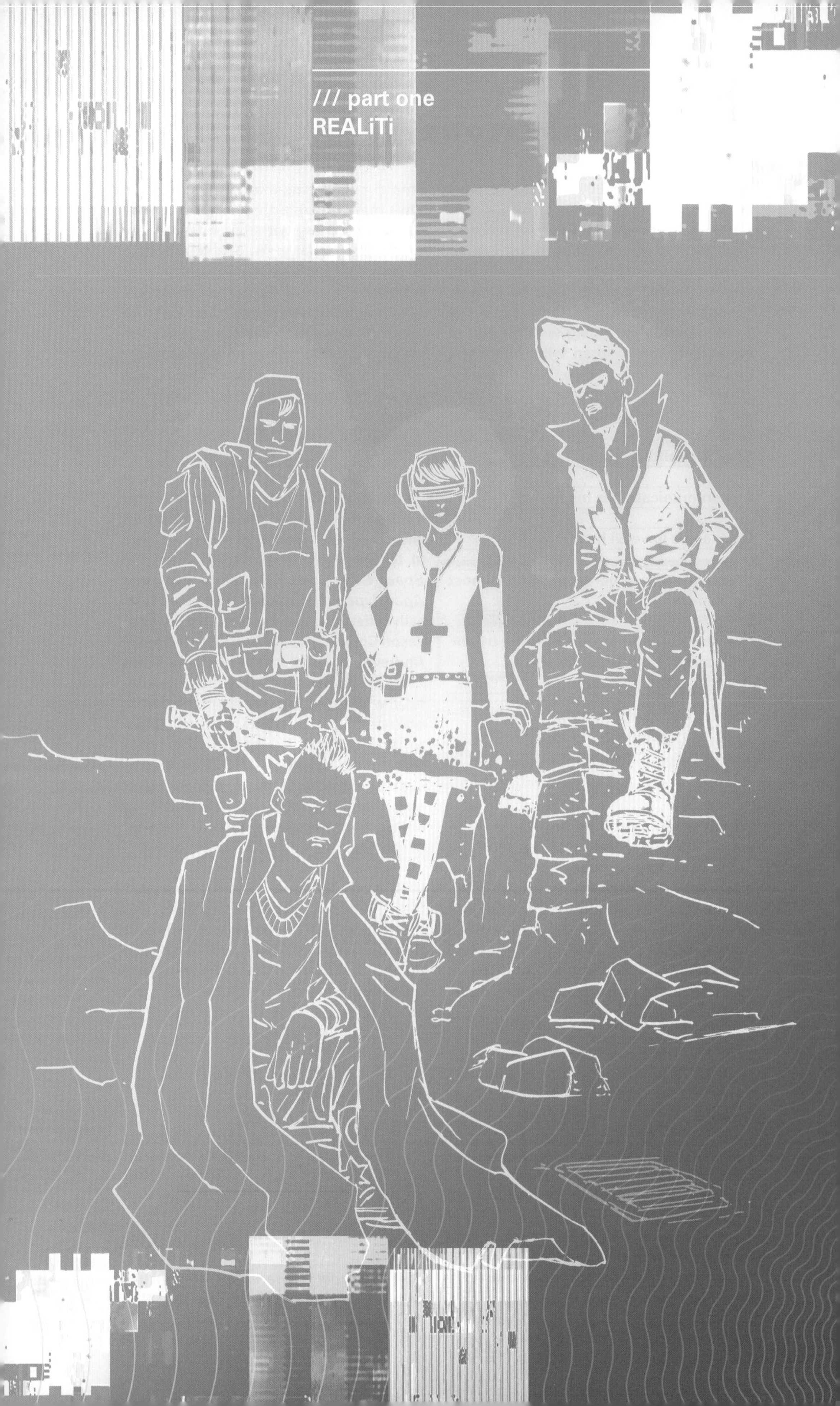

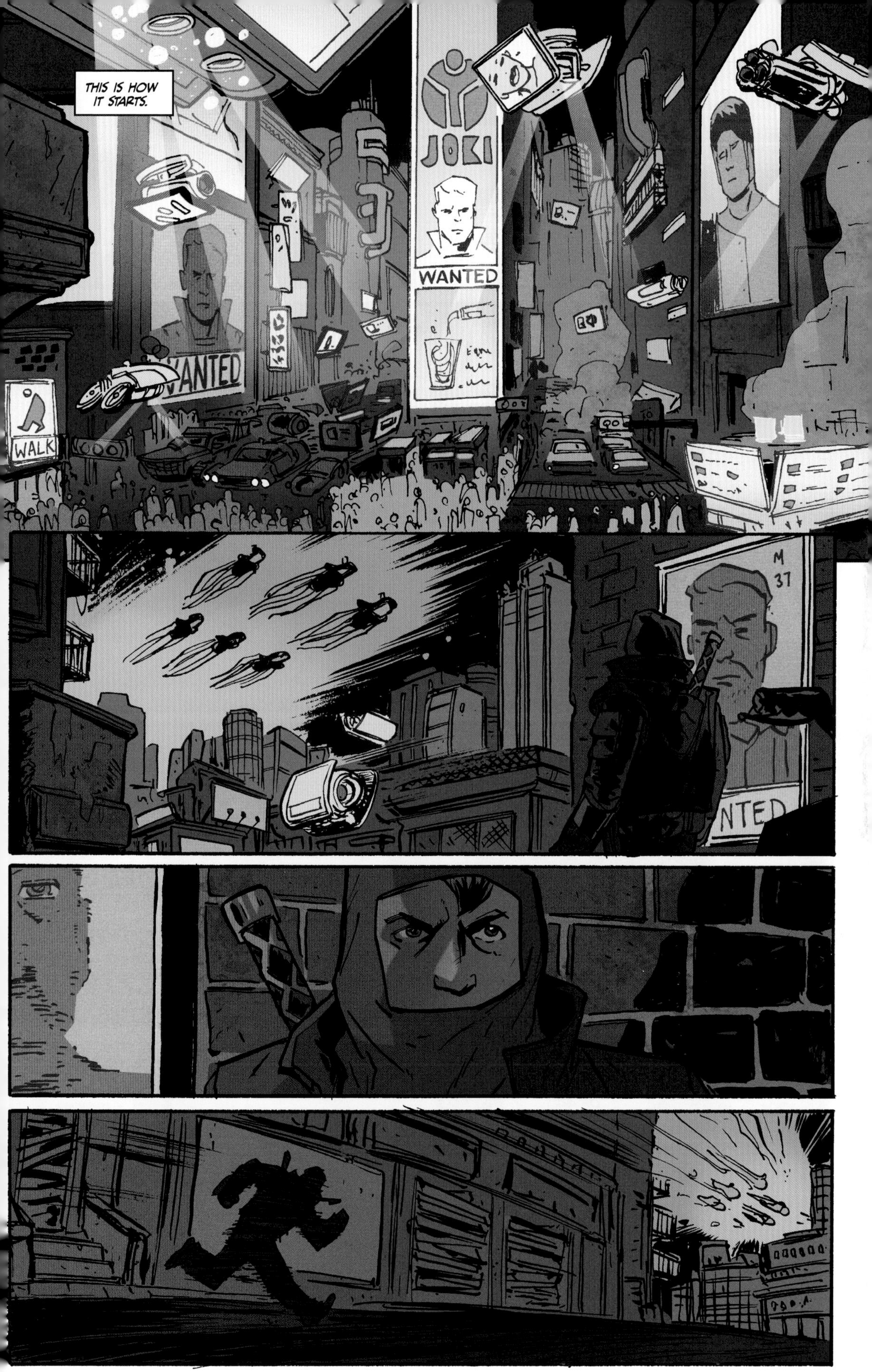

THIS IS HOW IT STARTS.
JOKI
WANTED
WANTED
WALK
M 37
NTED

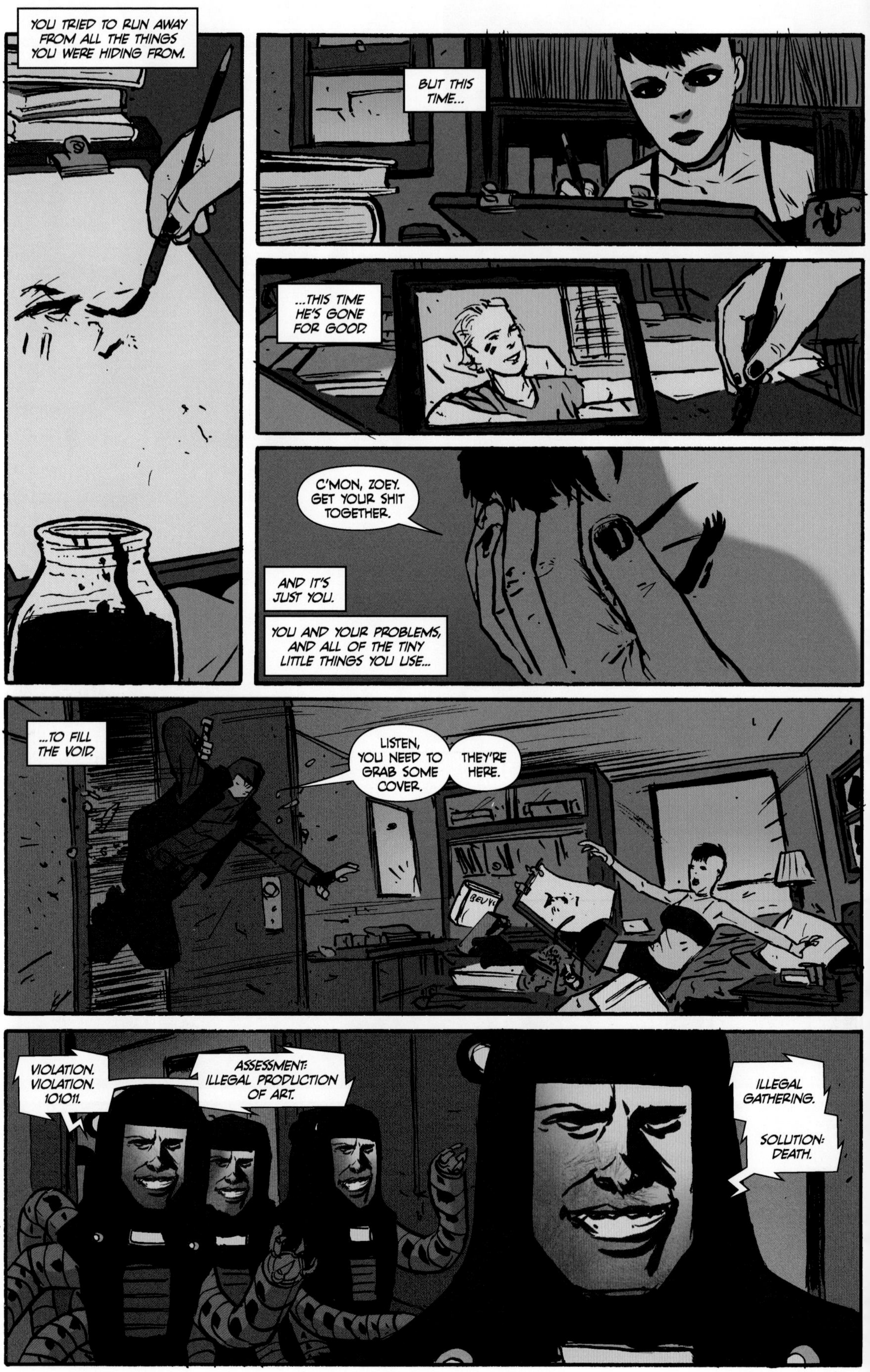
YOU TRIED TO RUN AWAY FROM ALL THE THINGS YOU WERE HIDING FROM.
BUT THIS TIME...
...THIS TIME HE'S GONE FOR GOOD.
C'MON, ZOEY. GET YOUR SHIT TOGETHER.
AND IT'S JUST YOU.
YOU AND YOUR PROBLEMS, AND ALL OF THE TINY LITTLE THINGS YOU USE...
...TO FILL THE VOID.
LISTEN, YOU NEED TO GRAB SOME COVER.
THEY'RE HERE.
VIOLATION. VIOLATION. 101011.
ASSESSMENT: ILLEGAL PRODUCTION OF ART.
ILLEGAL GATHERING.
SOLUTION: DEATH.

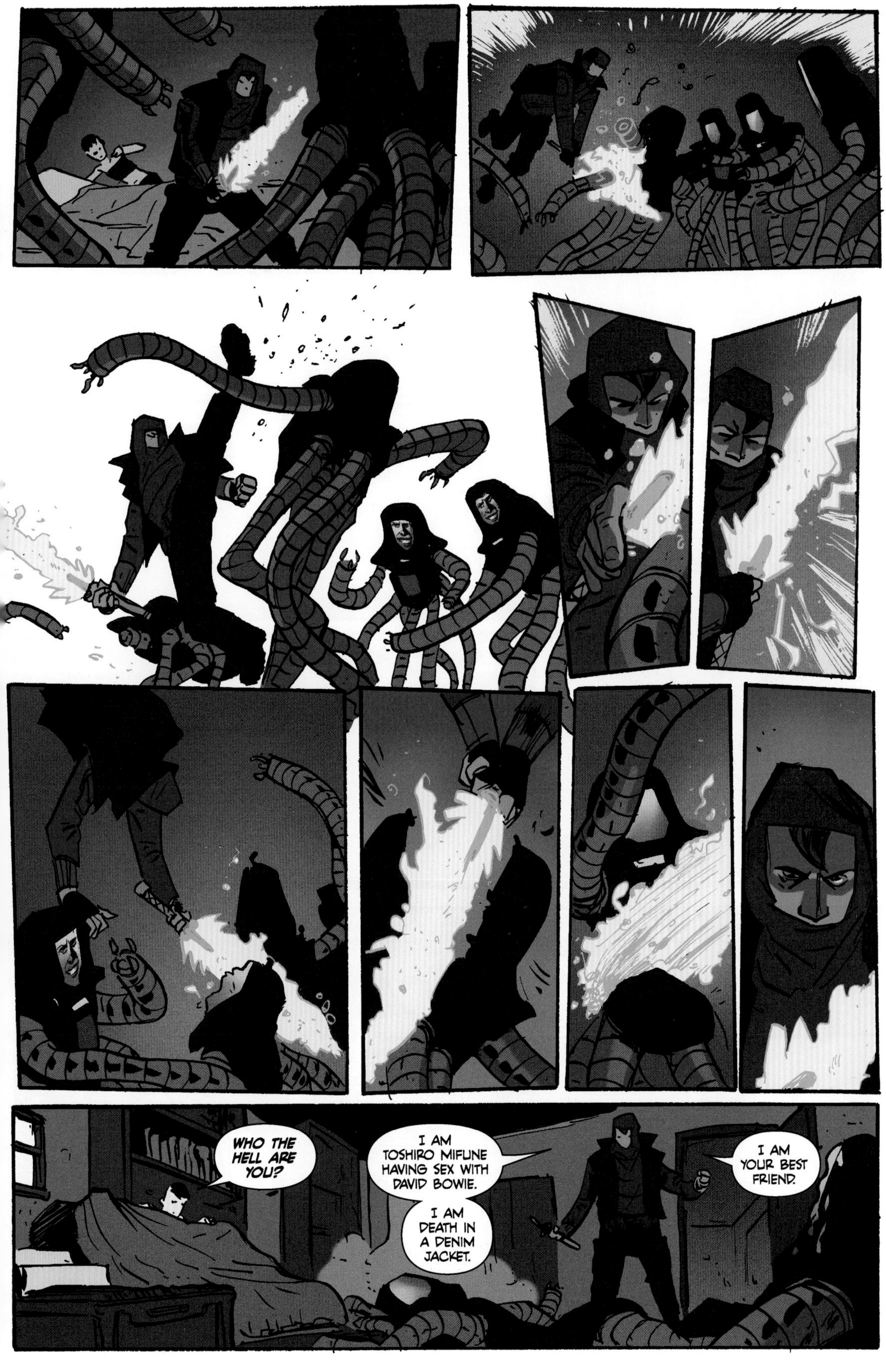
WHO THE HELL ARE YOU?
I AM TOSHIRO MIFUNE HAVING SEX WITH DAVID BOWIE.
I AM DEATH IN A DENIM JACKET.
I AM YOUR BEST FRIEND.

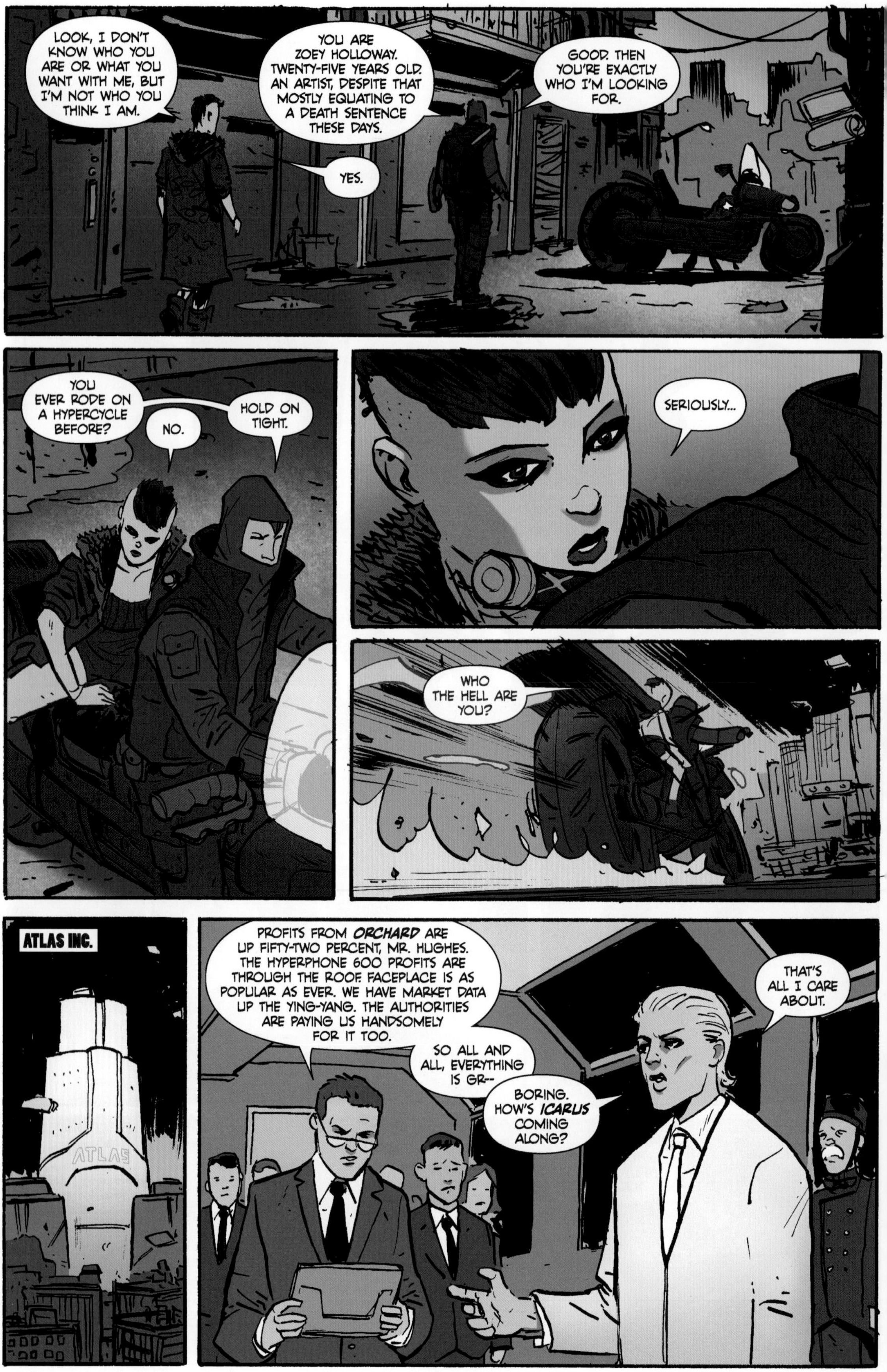
LOOK, I DON'T KNOW WHO YOU ARE OR WHAT YOU WANT WITH ME, BUT I'M NOT WHO YOU THINK I AM.
YOU ARE ZOEY HOLLOWAY. TWENTY-FIVE YEARS OLD. AN ARTIST, DESPITE THAT MOSTLY EQUATING TO A DEATH SENTENCE THESE DAYS.
YES.
GOOD. THEN YOU'RE EXACTLY WHO I'M LOOKING FOR.
YOU EVER RODE ON A HYPERCYCLE BEFORE?
NO.
HOLD ON TIGHT.
SERIOUSLY...
WHO THE HELL ARE YOU?
ATLAS INC.
ATLAS
PROFITS FROM ORCHARD ARE UP FIFTY-TWO PERCENT, MR. HUGHES. THE HYPERPHONE 600 PROFITS ARE THROUGH THE ROOF. FACEPLACE IS AS POPULAR AS EVER. WE HAVE MARKET DATA UP THE YING-YANG. THE AUTHORITIES ARE PAYING US HANDSOMELY FOR IT TOO.
THAT'S ALL I CARE ABOUT.
SO ALL AND ALL, EVERYTHING IS GR--
BORING. HOW'S ICARUS COMING ALONG?

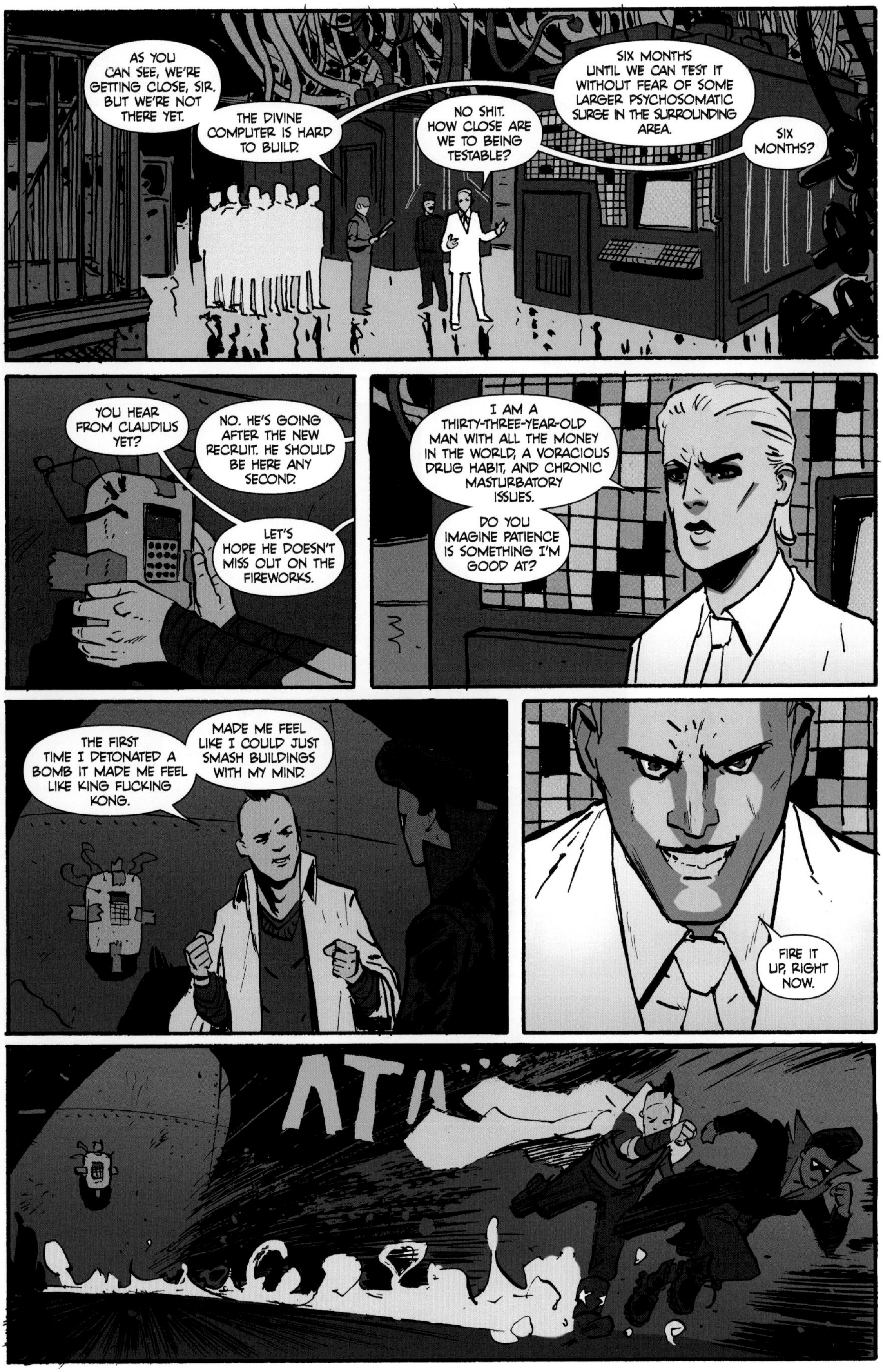
AS YOU CAN SEE, WE'RE GETTING CLOSE, SIR. BUT WE'RE NOT THERE YET.
THE DIVINE COMPUTER IS HARD TO BUILD.
NO SHIT. HOW CLOSE ARE WE TO BEING TESTABLE?
SIX MONTHS UNTIL WE CAN TEST IT WITHOUT FEAR OF SOME LARGER PSYCHOSOMATIC SURGE IN THE SURROUNDING AREA.
SIX MONTHS?
YOU HEAR FROM CLAUDIUS YET?
NO. HE'S GOING AFTER THE NEW RECRUIT. HE SHOULD BE HERE ANY SECOND.
LET'S HOPE HE DOESN'T MISS OUT ON THE FIREWORKS.
I AM A THIRTY-THREE-YEAR-OLD MAN WITH ALL THE MONEY IN THE WORLD, A VORACIOUS DRUG HABIT, AND CHRONIC MASTURBATORY ISSUES.
DO YOU IMAGINE PATIENCE IS SOMETHING I'M GOOD AT?
THE FIRST TIME I DETONATED A BOMB IT MADE ME FEEL LIKE KING FUCKING KONG.
MADE ME FEEL LIKE I COULD JUST SMASH BUILDINGS WITH MY MIND.
FIRE IT UP, RIGHT NOW.

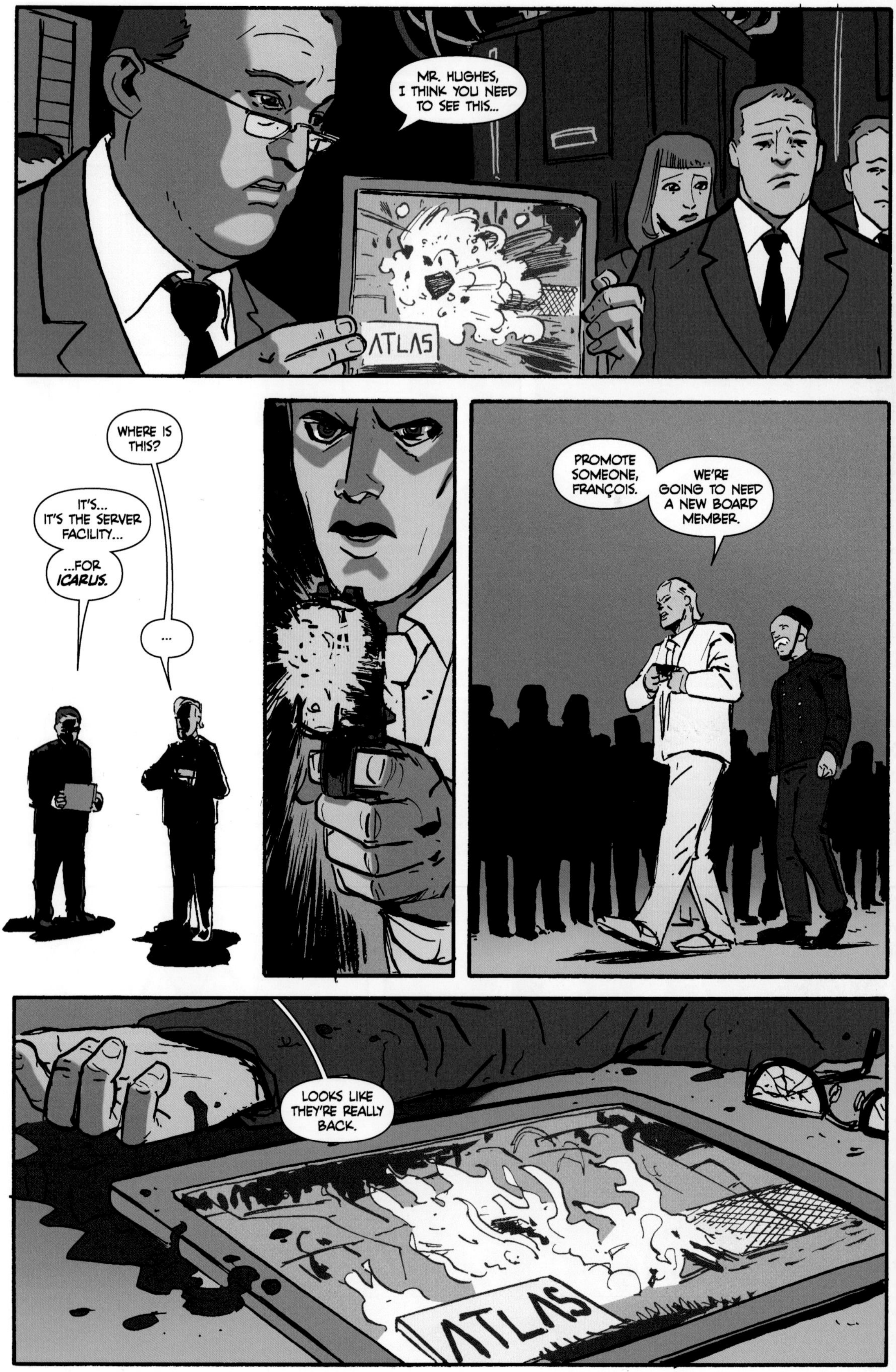
MR. HUGHES, I THINK YOU NEED TO SEE THIS...
ATLAS
WHERE IS THIS?
IT'S... IT'S THE SERVER FACILITY...
...FOR *ICARUS.*
...
PROMOTE SOMEONE, FRANÇOIS.
WE'RE GOING TO NEED A NEW BOARD MEMBER.
LOOKS LIKE THEY'RE REALLY BACK.
ATLAS

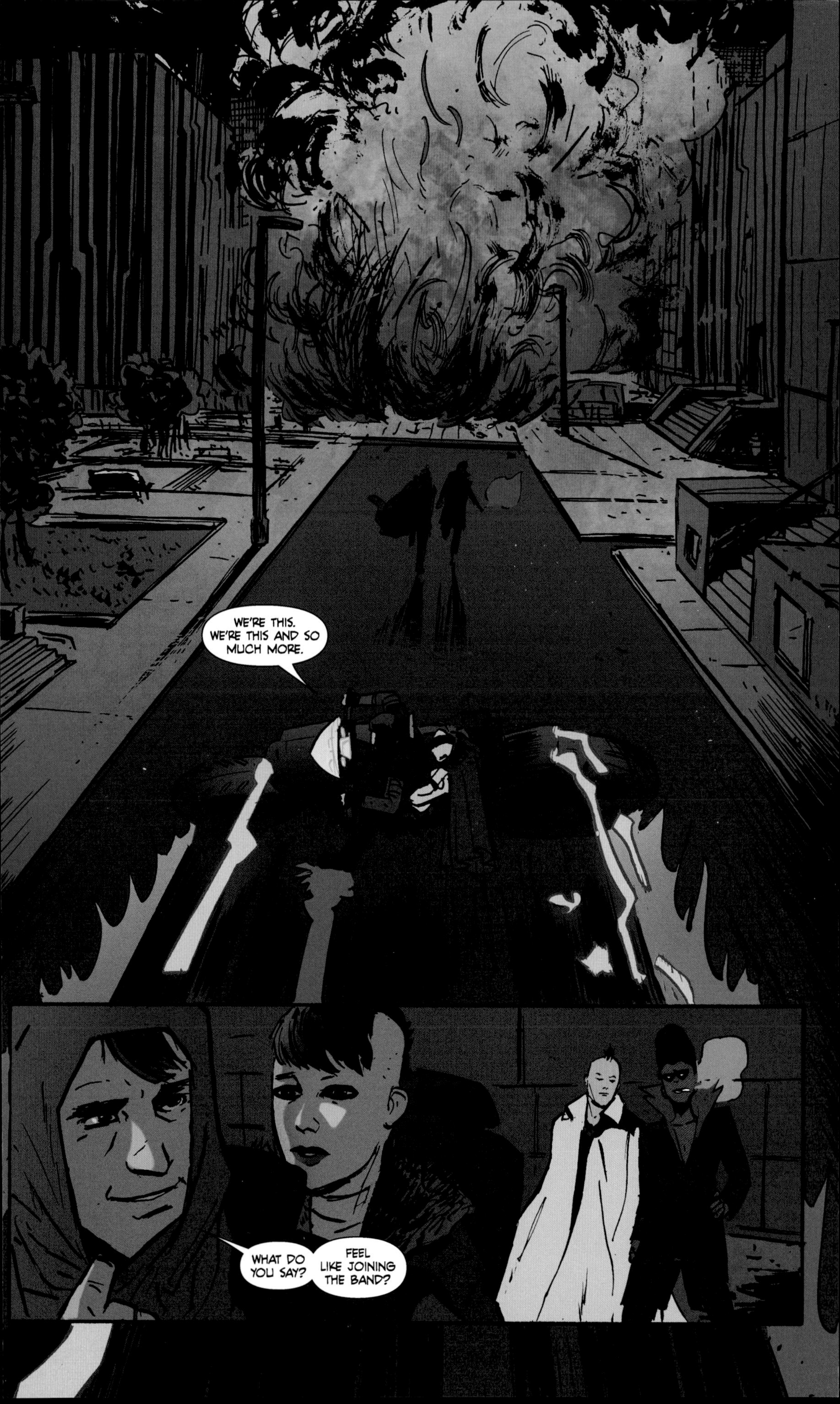
WE'RE THIS. WE'RE THIS AND SO MUCH MORE.
WHAT DO YOU SAY?
FEEL LIKE JOINING THE BAND?

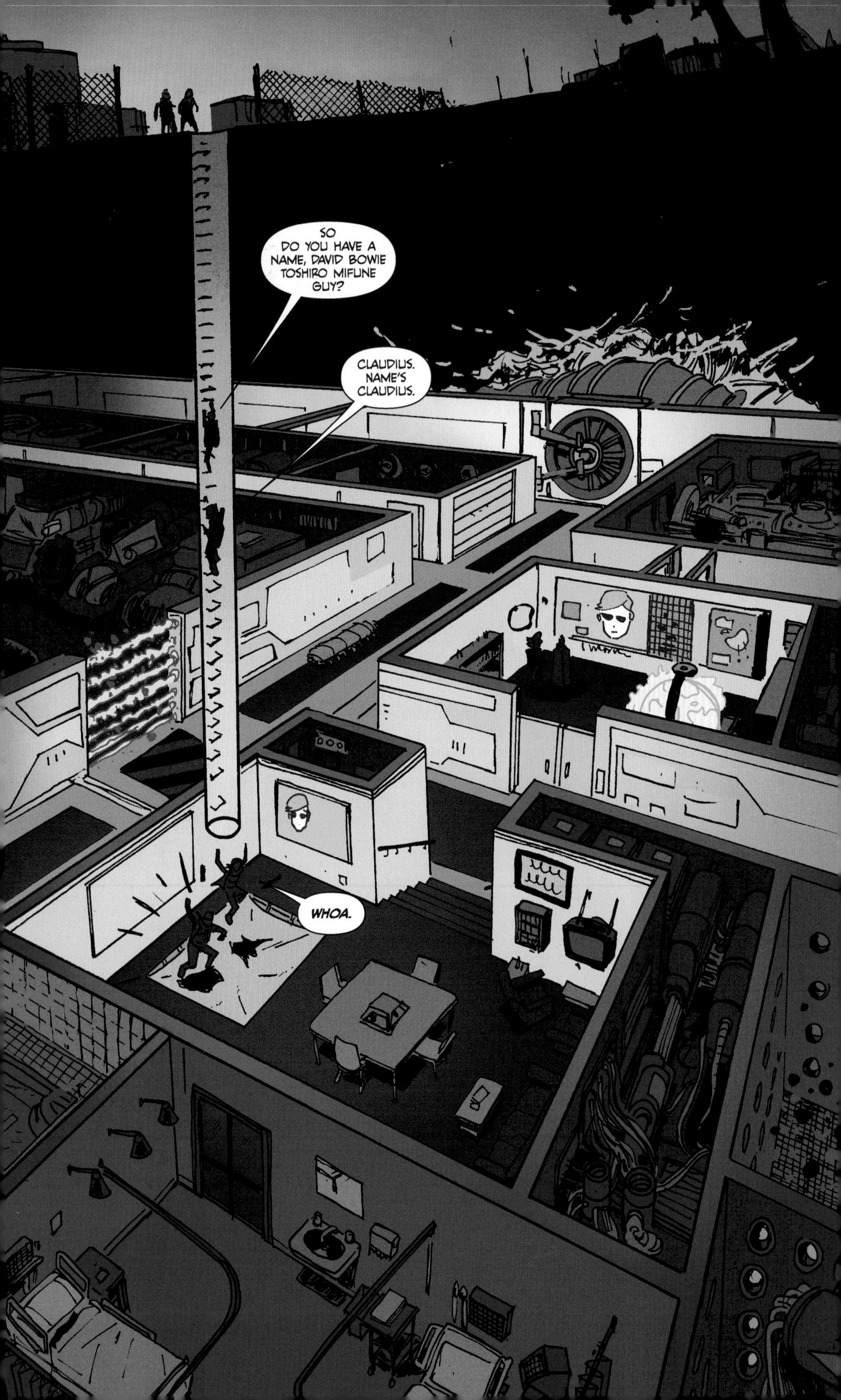

SO DO YOU HAVE A NAME, DAVID BOWIE TOSHIRO MIFUNE GUY?
CLAUDIUS. NAME'S CLAUDIUS.
WHOA.

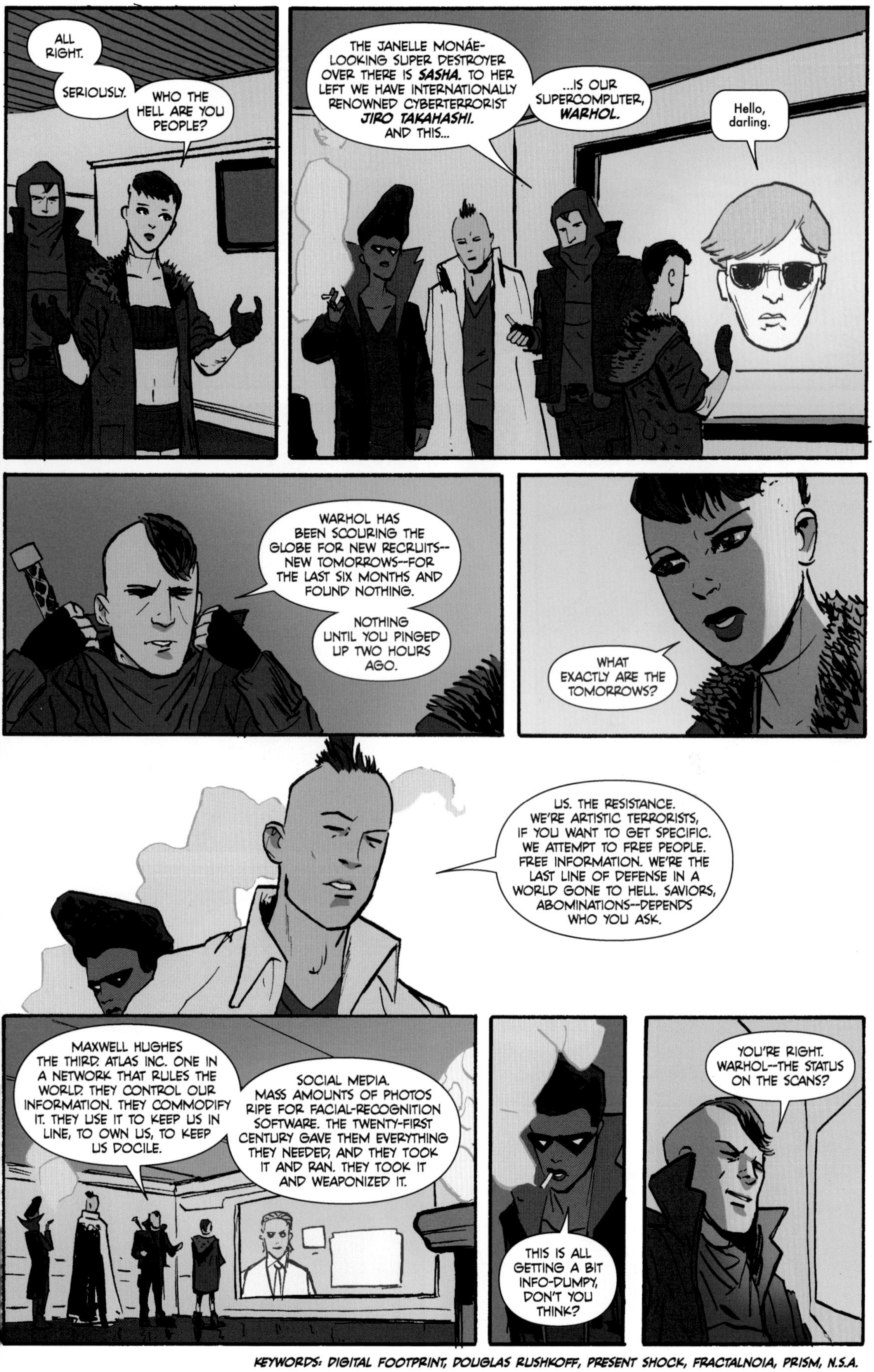

ALL RIGHT.
SERIOUSLY.
WHO THE HELL ARE YOU PEOPLE?
THE JANELLE MONÁE-LOOKING SUPER DESTROYER OVER THERE IS SASHA. TO HER LEFT WE HAVE INTERNATIONALLY RENOWNED CYBERTERRORIST JIRO TAKAHASHI. AND THIS...
...IS OUR SUPERCOMPUTER, WARHOL.
Hello, darling.
WARHOL HAS BEEN SCOURING THE GLOBE FOR NEW RECRUITS--NEW TOMORROWS--FOR THE LAST SIX MONTHS AND FOUND NOTHING.
NOTHING UNTIL YOU PINGED UP TWO HOURS AGO.
WHAT EXACTLY ARE THE TOMORROWS?
US. THE RESISTANCE. WE'RE ARTISTIC TERRORISTS, IF YOU WANT TO GET SPECIFIC. WE ATTEMPT TO FREE PEOPLE. FREE INFORMATION. WE'RE THE LAST LINE OF DEFENSE IN A WORLD GONE TO HELL. SAVIORS, ABOMINATIONS--DEPENDS WHO YOU ASK.
MAXWELL HUGHES THE THIRD. ATLAS INC. ONE IN A NETWORK THAT RULES THE WORLD. THEY CONTROL OUR INFORMATION. THEY COMMODIFY IT. THEY USE IT TO KEEP US IN LINE, TO OWN US, TO KEEP US DOCILE.
SOCIAL MEDIA. MASS AMOUNTS OF PHOTOS RIPE FOR FACIAL-RECOGNITION SOFTWARE. THE TWENTY-FIRST CENTURY GAVE THEM EVERYTHING THEY NEEDED, AND THEY TOOK IT AND RAN. THEY TOOK IT AND WEAPONIZED IT.
THIS IS ALL GETTING A BIT INFO-DUMPY, DON'T YOU THINK?
YOU'RE RIGHT. WARHOL--THE STATUS ON THE SCANS?


KEYWORDS: DIGITAL FOOTPRINT, DOUGLAS RUSHKOFF, PRESENT SHOCK, FRACTALNOIA, PRISM, N.S.A.

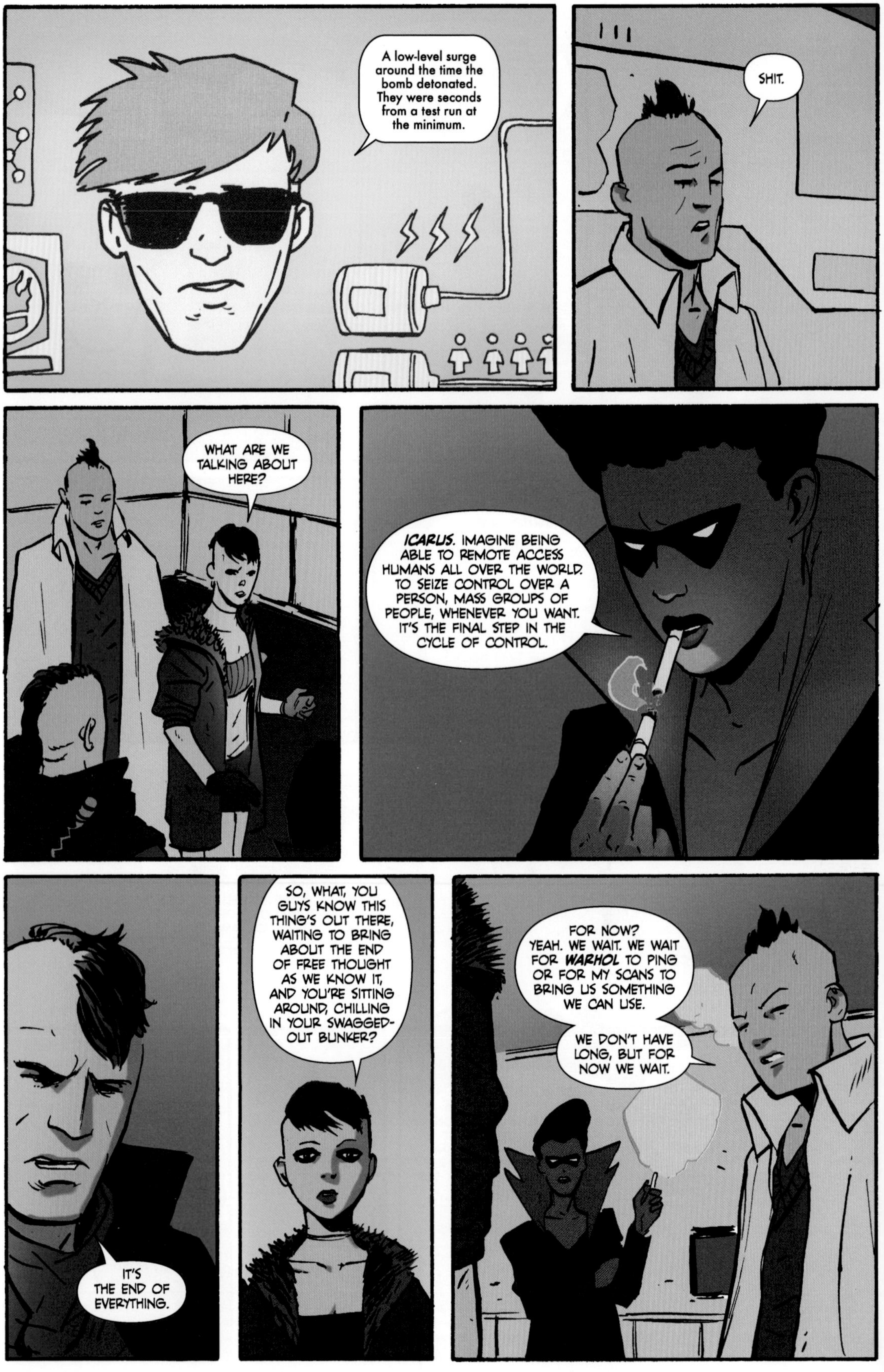
A low-level surge around the time the bomb detonated. They were seconds from a test run at the minimum.
SHIT.
WHAT ARE WE TALKING ABOUT HERE?
*ICARUS*. IMAGINE BEING ABLE TO REMOTE ACCESS HUMANS ALL OVER THE WORLD. TO SEIZE CONTROL OVER A PERSON, MASS GROUPS OF PEOPLE, WHENEVER YOU WANT. IT'S THE FINAL STEP IN THE CYCLE OF CONTROL.
IT'S THE END OF EVERYTHING.
SO, WHAT, YOU GUYS KNOW THIS THING'S OUT THERE, WAITING TO BRING ABOUT THE END OF FREE THOUGHT AS WE KNOW IT, AND YOU'RE SITTING AROUND, CHILLING IN YOUR SWAGGED-OUT BUNKER?
FOR NOW? YEAH. WE WAIT. WE WAIT FOR *WARHOL* TO PING OR FOR MY SCANS TO BRING US SOMETHING WE CAN USE.
WE DON'T HAVE LONG, BUT FOR NOW WE WAIT.

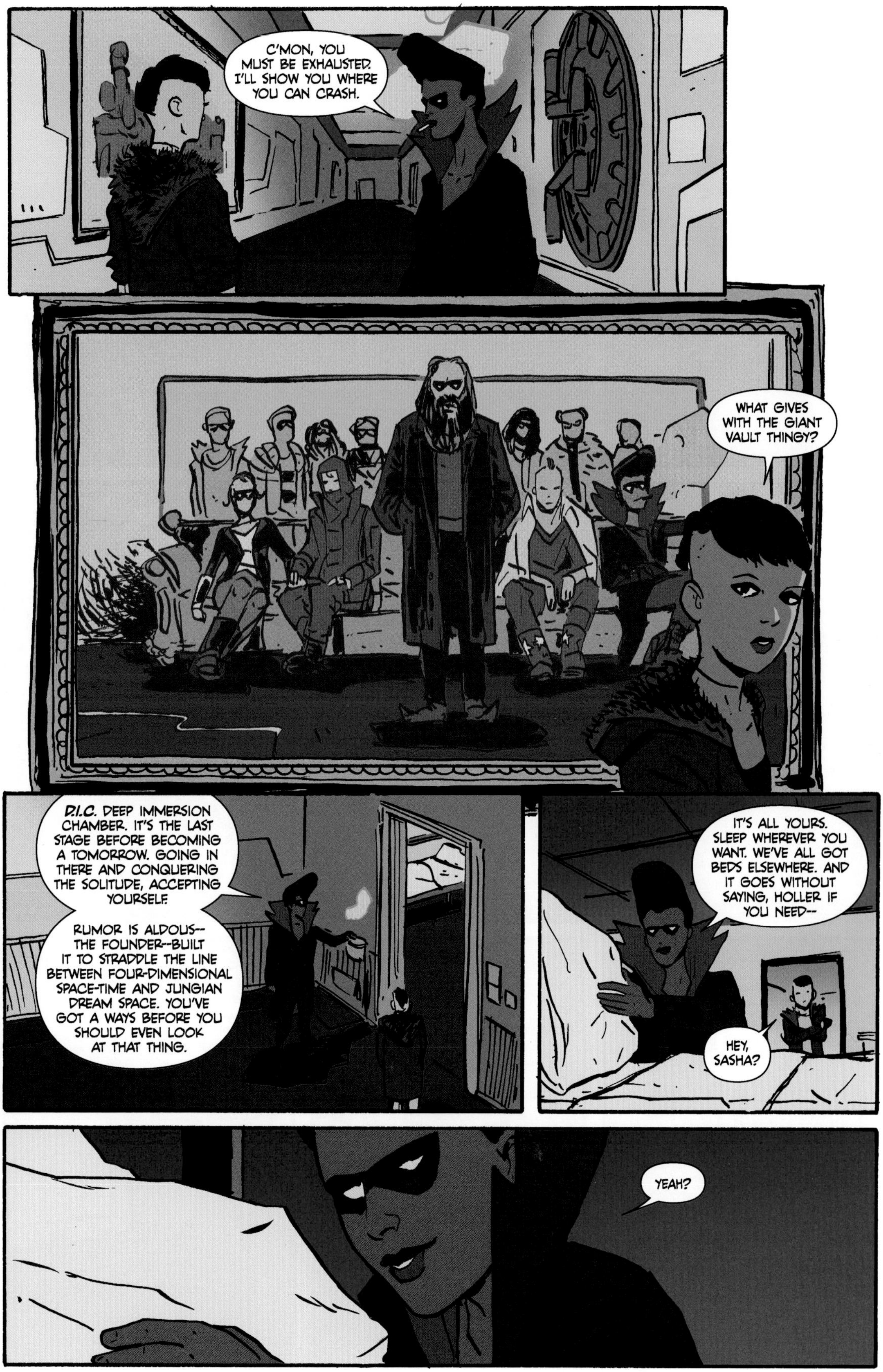
C'MON, YOU MUST BE EXHAUSTED. I'LL SHOW YOU WHERE YOU CAN CRASH.
WHAT GIVES WITH THE GIANT VAULT THINGY?
D.I.C. DEEP IMMERSION CHAMBER. IT'S THE LAST STAGE BEFORE BECOMING A TOMORROW. GOING IN THERE AND CONQUERING THE SOLITUDE, ACCEPTING YOURSELF.
RUMOR IS ALDOUS-- THE FOUNDER--BUILT IT TO STRADDLE THE LINE BETWEEN FOUR-DIMENSIONAL SPACE-TIME AND JUNGIAN DREAM SPACE. YOU'VE GOT A WAYS BEFORE YOU SHOULD EVEN LOOK AT THAT THING.
IT'S ALL YOURS. SLEEP WHEREVER YOU WANT. WE'VE ALL GOT BEDS ELSEWHERE. AND IT GOES WITHOUT SAYING, HOLLER IF YOU NEED--
HEY, SASHA?
YEAH?

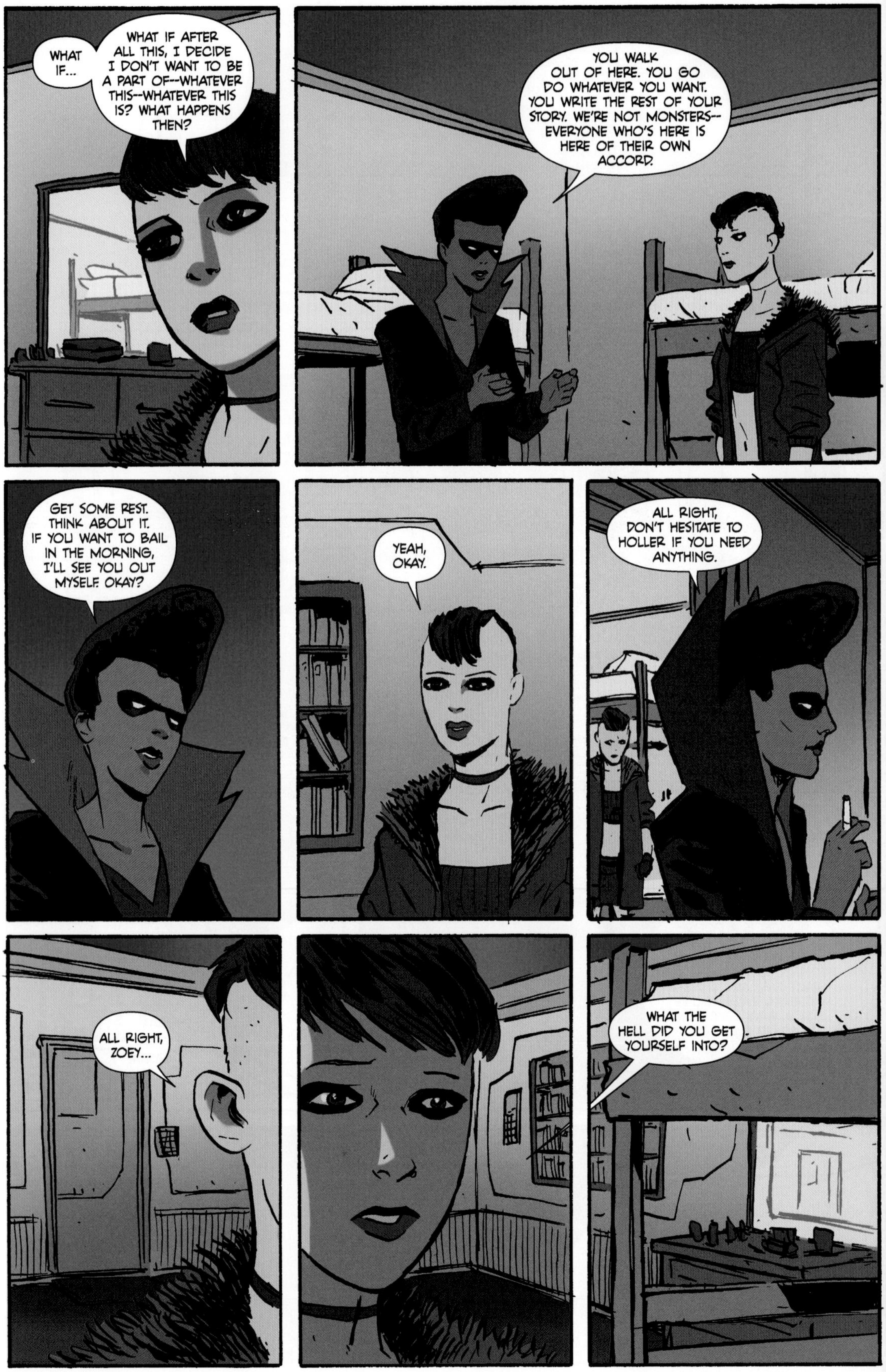
WHAT IF...
WHAT IF AFTER ALL THIS, I DECIDE I DON'T WANT TO BE A PART OF--WHATEVER THIS--WHATEVER THIS IS? WHAT HAPPENS THEN?
YOU WALK OUT OF HERE. YOU GO DO WHATEVER YOU WANT. YOU WRITE THE REST OF YOUR STORY. WE'RE NOT MONSTERS--EVERYONE WHO'S HERE IS HERE OF THEIR OWN ACCORD.
GET SOME REST. THINK ABOUT IT. IF YOU WANT TO BAIL IN THE MORNING, I'LL SEE YOU OUT MYSELF. OKAY?
YEAH, OKAY.
ALL RIGHT, DON'T HESITATE TO HOLLER IF YOU NEED ANYTHING.
ALL RIGHT, ZOEY...
WHAT THE HELL DID YOU GET YOURSELF INTO?

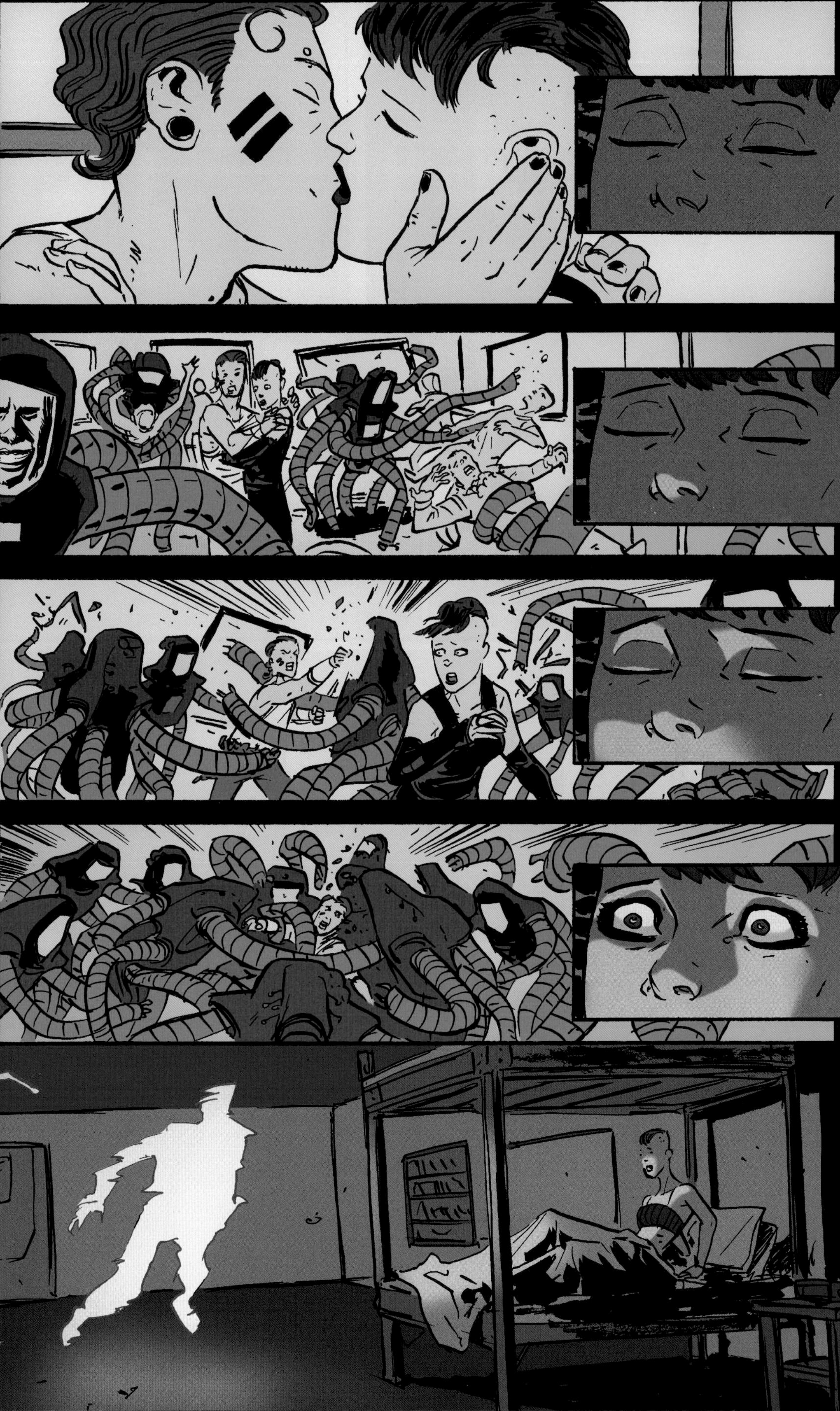

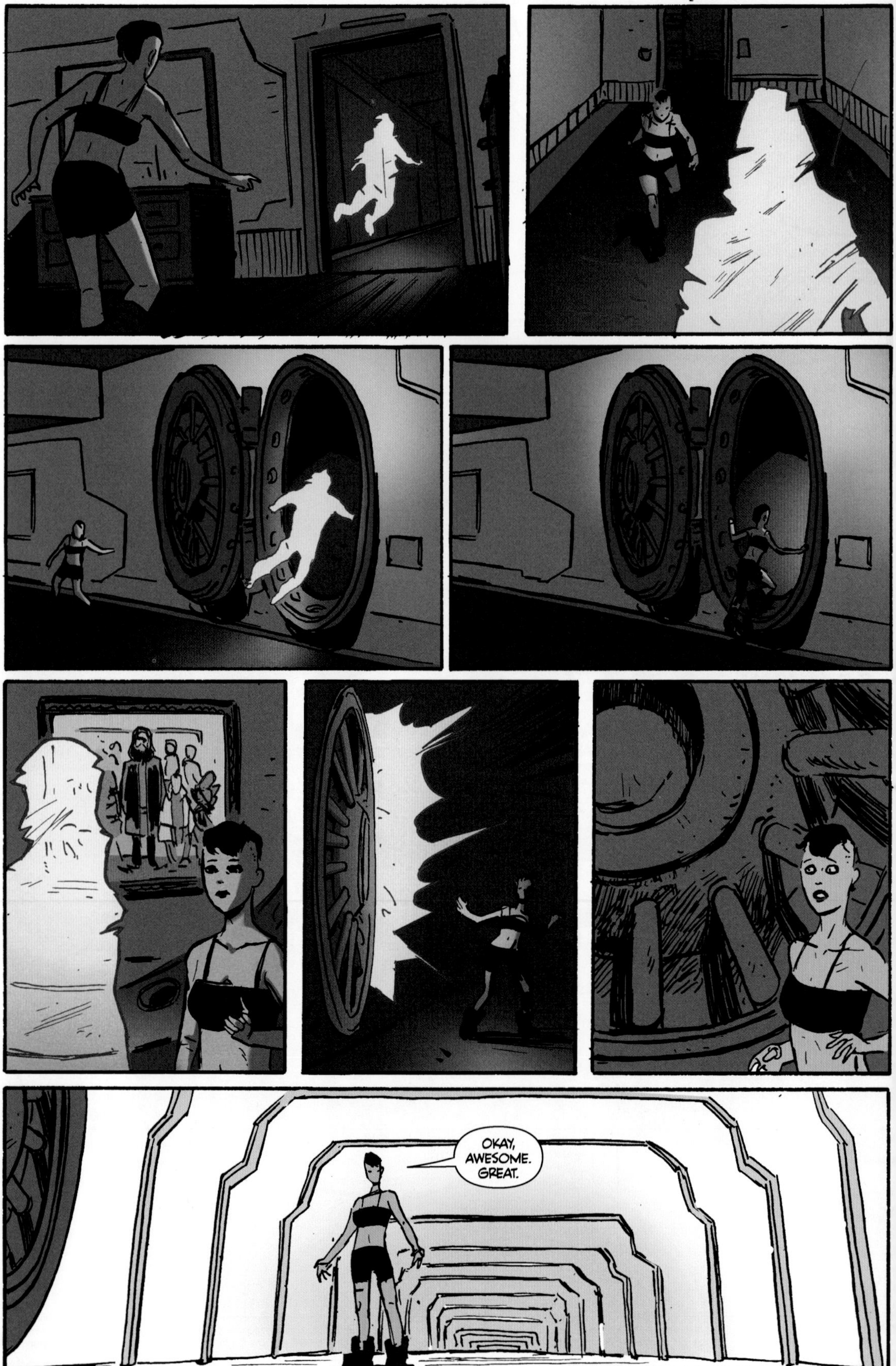
OKAY, AWESOME. GREAT.

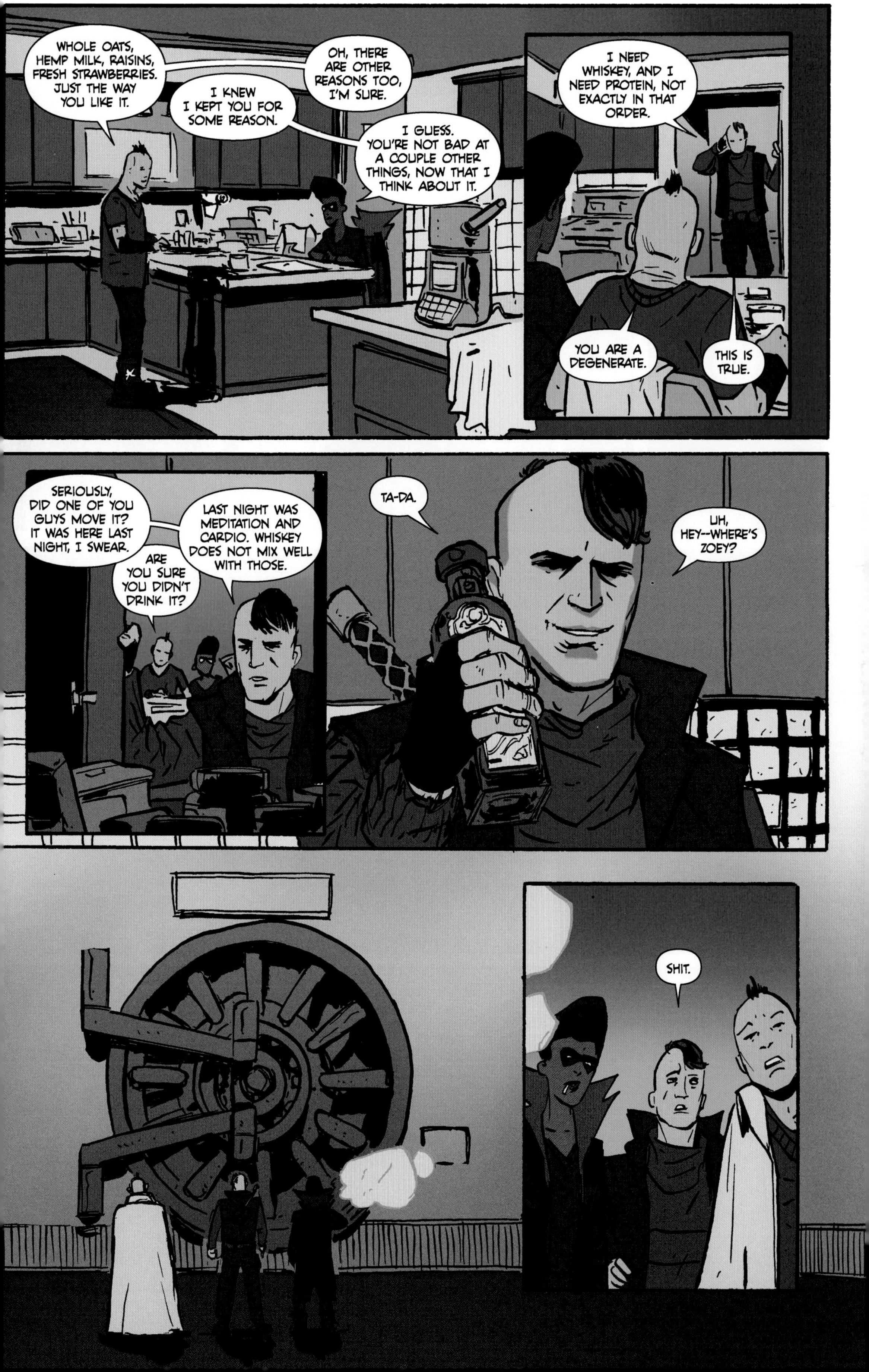
WHOLE OATS, HEMP MILK, RAISINS, FRESH STRAWBERRIES. JUST THE WAY YOU LIKE IT.
I KNEW I KEPT YOU FOR SOME REASON.
OH, THERE ARE OTHER REASONS TOO, I'M SURE.
I GUESS. YOU'RE NOT BAD AT A COUPLE OTHER THINGS, NOW THAT I THINK ABOUT IT.
I NEED WHISKEY, AND I NEED PROTEIN, NOT EXACTLY IN THAT ORDER.
YOU ARE A DEGENERATE.
THIS IS TRUE.
SERIOUSLY, DID ONE OF YOU GUYS MOVE IT? IT WAS HERE LAST NIGHT, I SWEAR.
ARE YOU SURE YOU DIDN'T DRINK IT?
LAST NIGHT WAS MEDITATION AND CARDIO. WHISKEY DOES NOT MIX WELL WITH THOSE.
TA-DA.
UH, HEY--WHERE'S ZOEY?
SHIT.

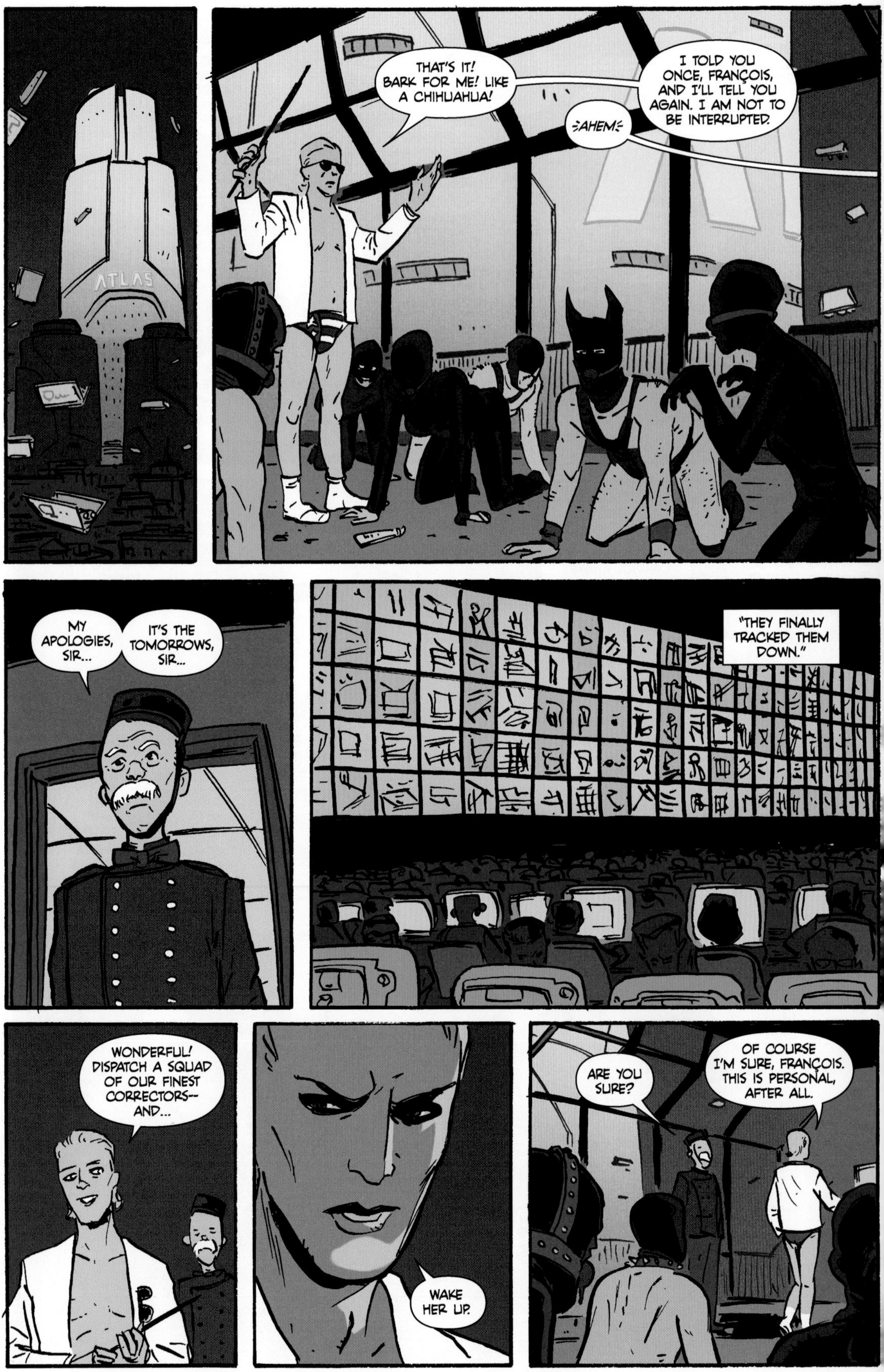
ATLAS
THAT'S IT! BARK FOR ME! LIKE A CHIHUAHUA!
I TOLD YOU ONCE, FRANÇOIS, AND I'LL TELL YOU AGAIN. I AM NOT TO BE INTERRUPTED.
AHEM
MY APOLOGIES, SIR...
IT'S THE TOMORROWS, SIR...
"THEY FINALLY TRACKED THEM DOWN."
WONDERFUL! DISPATCH A SQUAD OF OUR FINEST CORRECTORS-- AND...
WAKE HER UP.
ARE YOU SURE?
OF COURSE I'M SURE, FRANÇOIS. THIS IS PERSONAL, AFTER ALL.

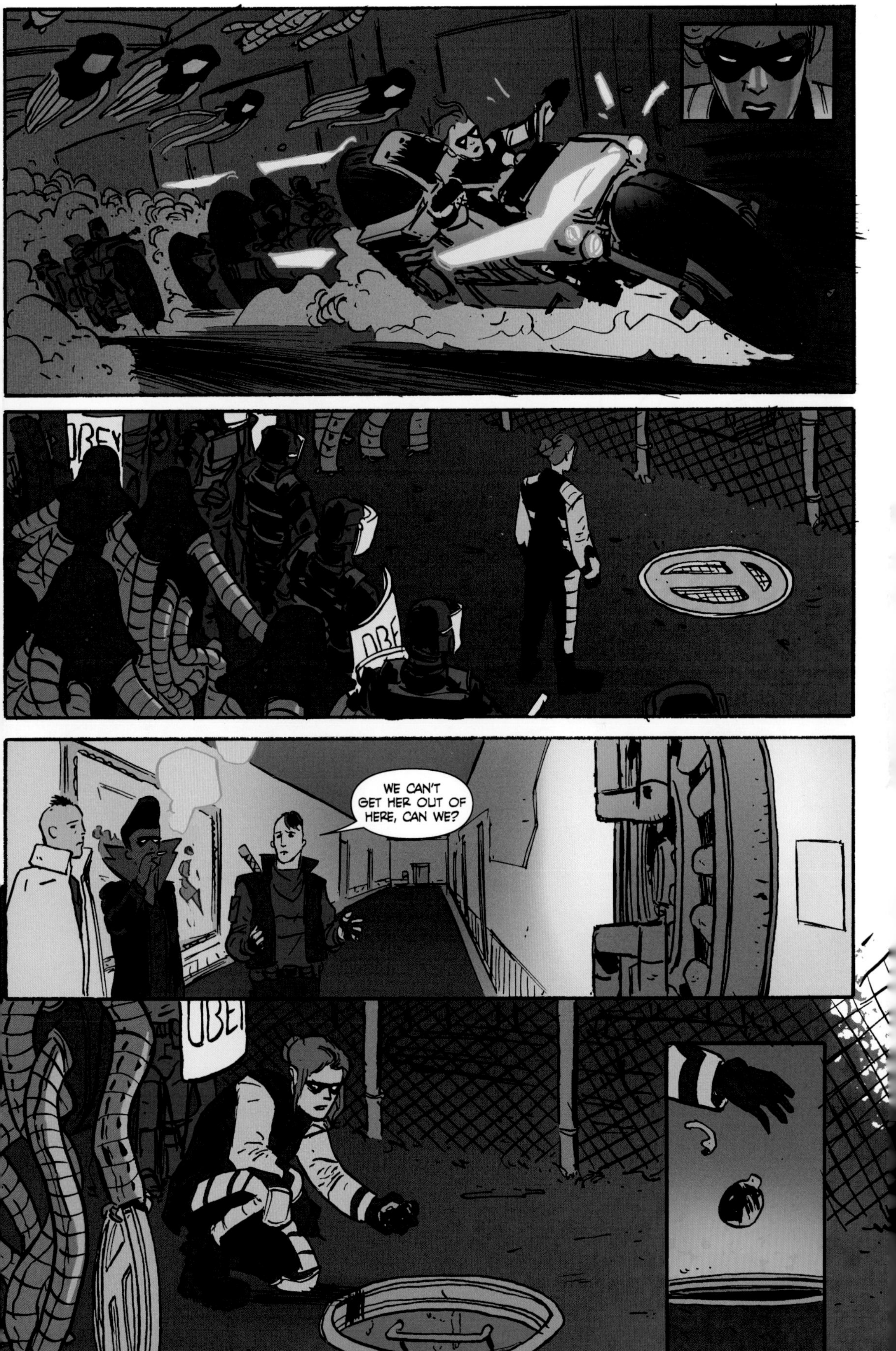
WE CAN'T GET HER OUT OF HERE, CAN WE?
OBEY

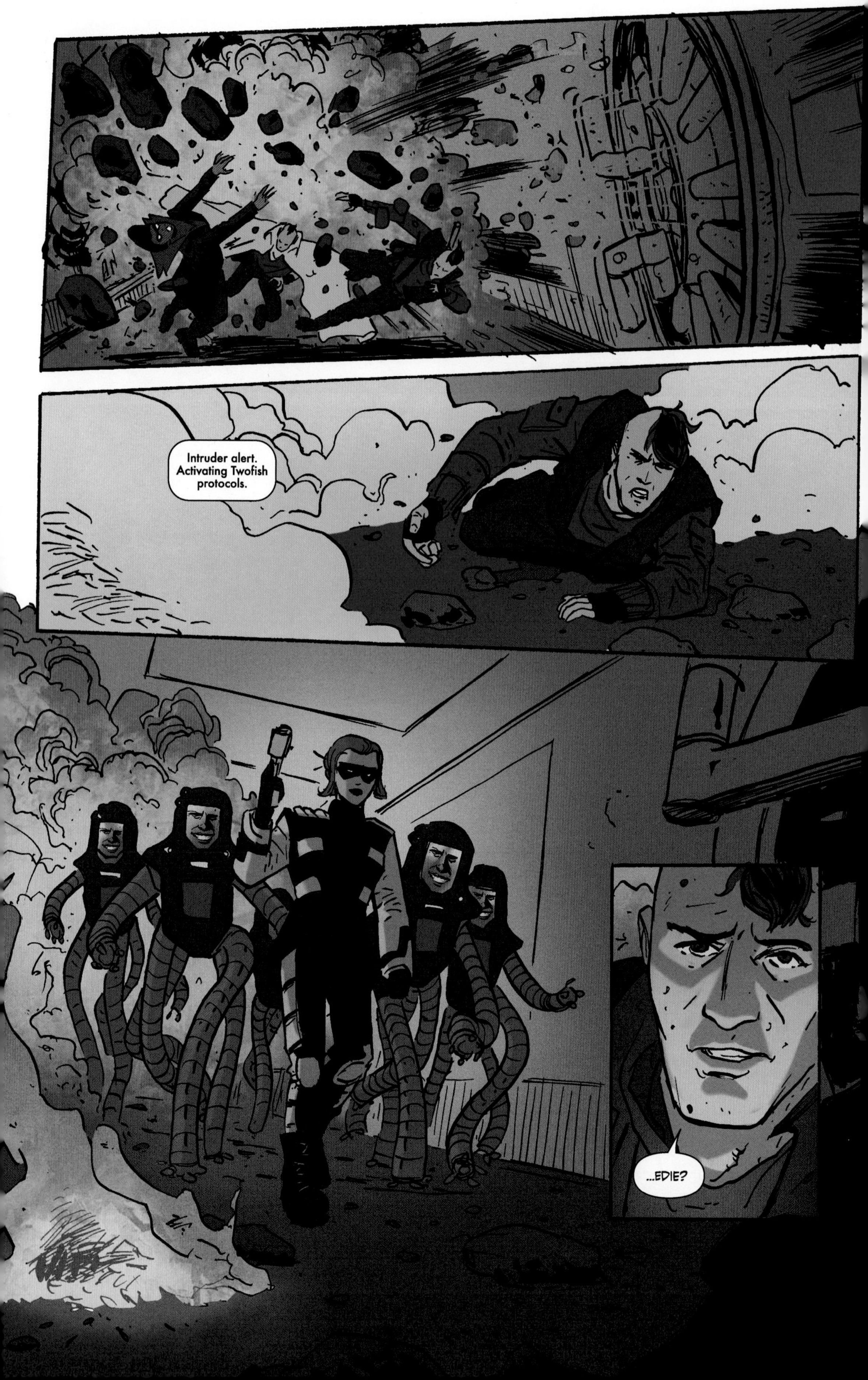
Intruder alert. Activating Twofish protocols.
...EDIE?

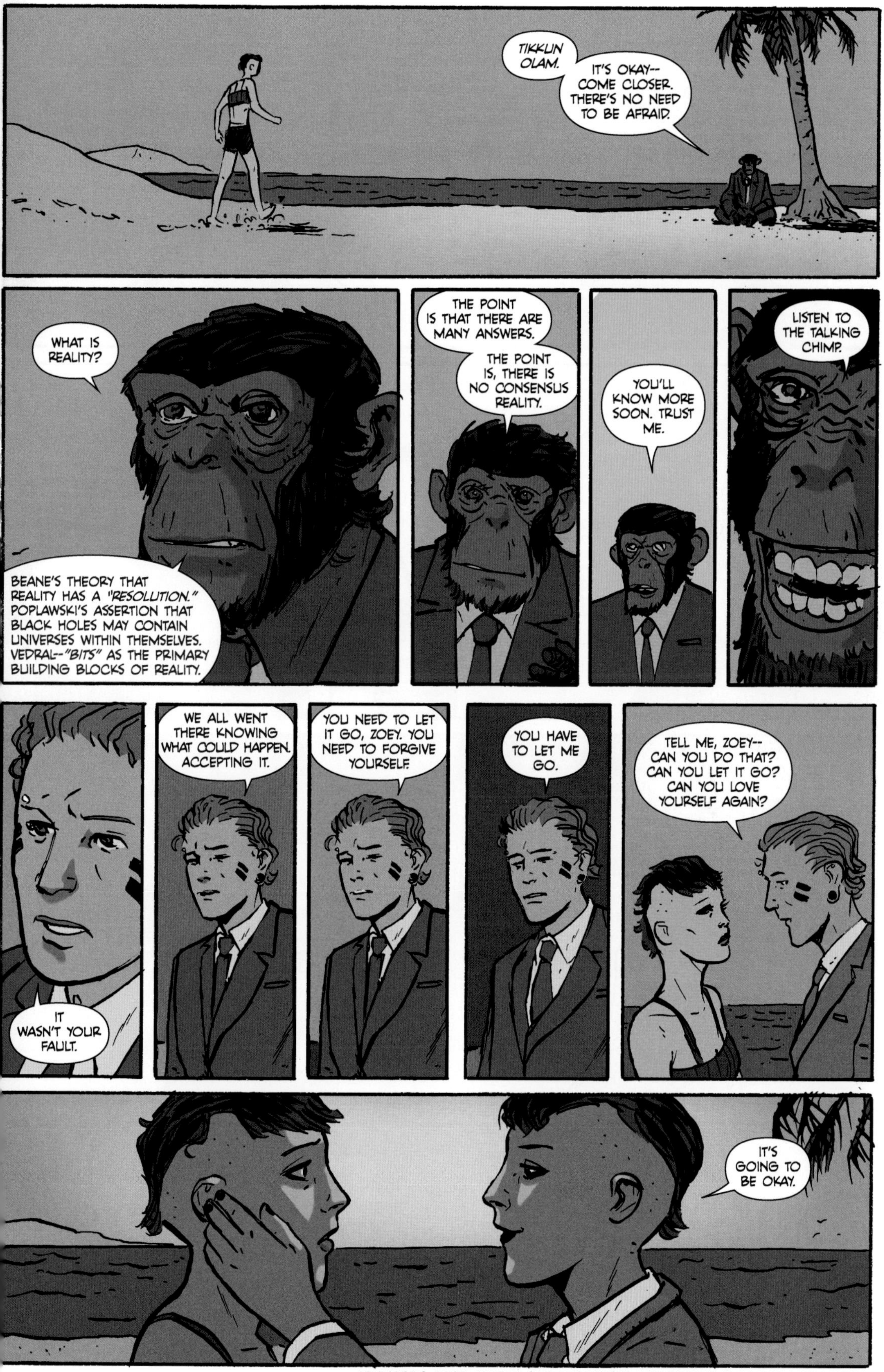
TIKKUN OLAM.
IT'S OKAY-- COME CLOSER. THERE'S NO NEED TO BE AFRAID.
WHAT IS REALITY?
BEANE'S THEORY THAT REALITY HAS A "RESOLUTION." POPLAWSKI'S ASSERTION THAT BLACK HOLES MAY CONTAIN UNIVERSES WITHIN THEMSELVES. VEDRAL--"BITS" AS THE PRIMARY BUILDING BLOCKS OF REALITY.
THE POINT IS THAT THERE ARE MANY ANSWERS.
THE POINT IS, THERE IS NO CONSENSUS REALITY.
YOU'LL KNOW MORE SOON. TRUST ME.
LISTEN TO THE TALKING CHIMP.
IT WASN'T YOUR FAULT.
WE ALL WENT THERE KNOWING WHAT COULD HAPPEN. ACCEPTING IT.
YOU NEED TO LET IT GO, ZOEY. YOU NEED TO FORGIVE YOURSELF.
YOU HAVE TO LET ME GO.
TELL ME, ZOEY-- CAN YOU DO THAT? CAN YOU LET IT GO? CAN YOU LOVE YOURSELF AGAIN?
IT'S GOING TO BE OKAY.

*KEYWORDS: DAVID PEARCE, "THE HEDONISTIC IMPERATIVE," SIMULATION HYPOTHESIS, COMPUTATIONALISM, JEAN BAUDRILLARD, BLACK HOLE.*

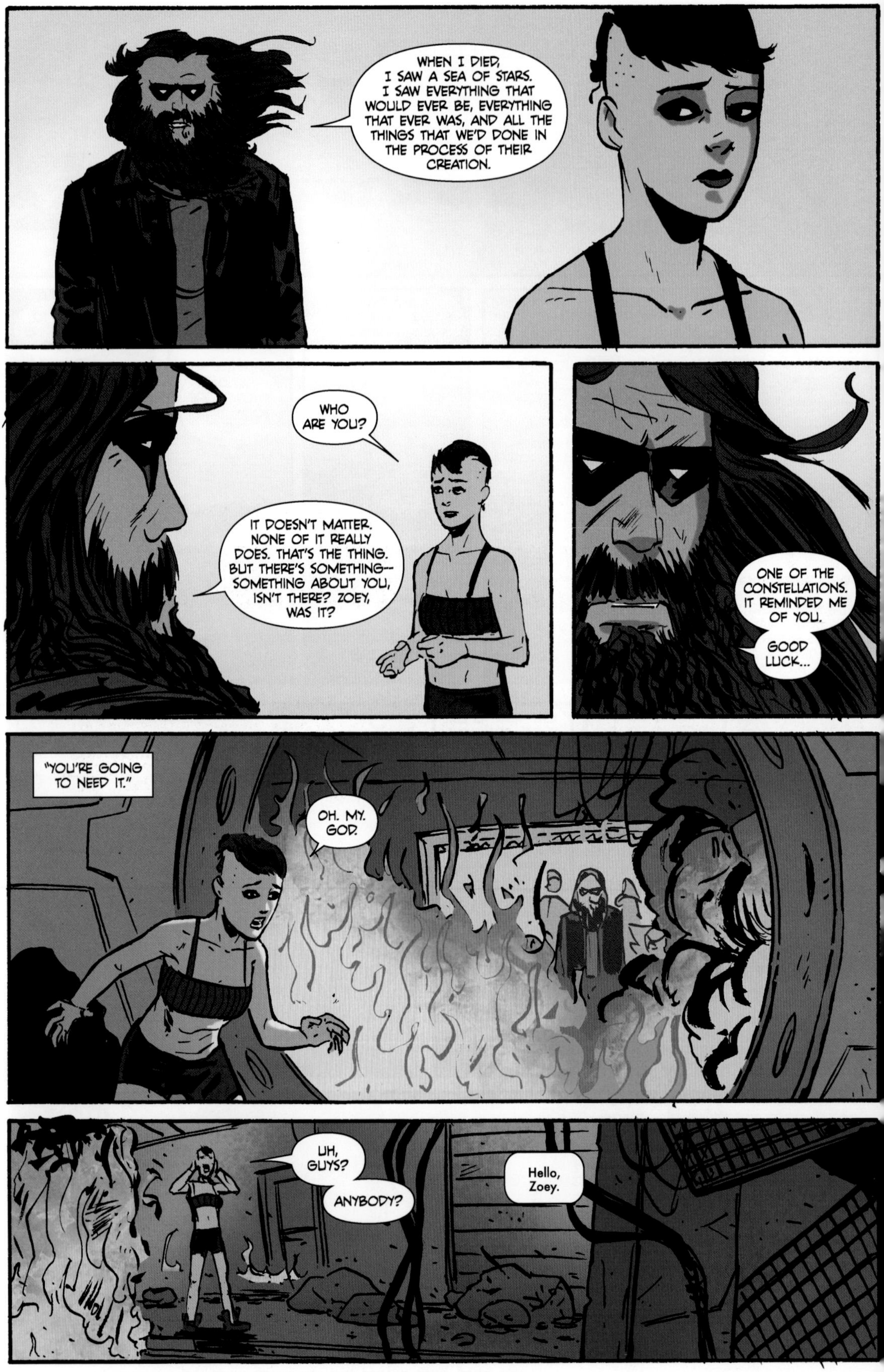
WHEN I DIED, I SAW A SEA OF STARS. I SAW EVERYTHING THAT WOULD EVER BE, EVERYTHING THAT EVER WAS, AND ALL THE THINGS THAT WE'D DONE IN THE PROCESS OF THEIR CREATION.
WHO ARE YOU?
IT DOESN'T MATTER. NONE OF IT REALLY DOES. THAT'S THE THING. BUT THERE'S SOMETHING-- SOMETHING ABOUT YOU, ISN'T THERE? ZOEY, WAS IT?
ONE OF THE CONSTELLATIONS. IT REMINDED ME OF YOU.
GOOD LUCK...
"YOU'RE GOING TO NEED IT."
OH. MY. GOD.
UH, GUYS?
ANYBODY?
Hello, Zoey.

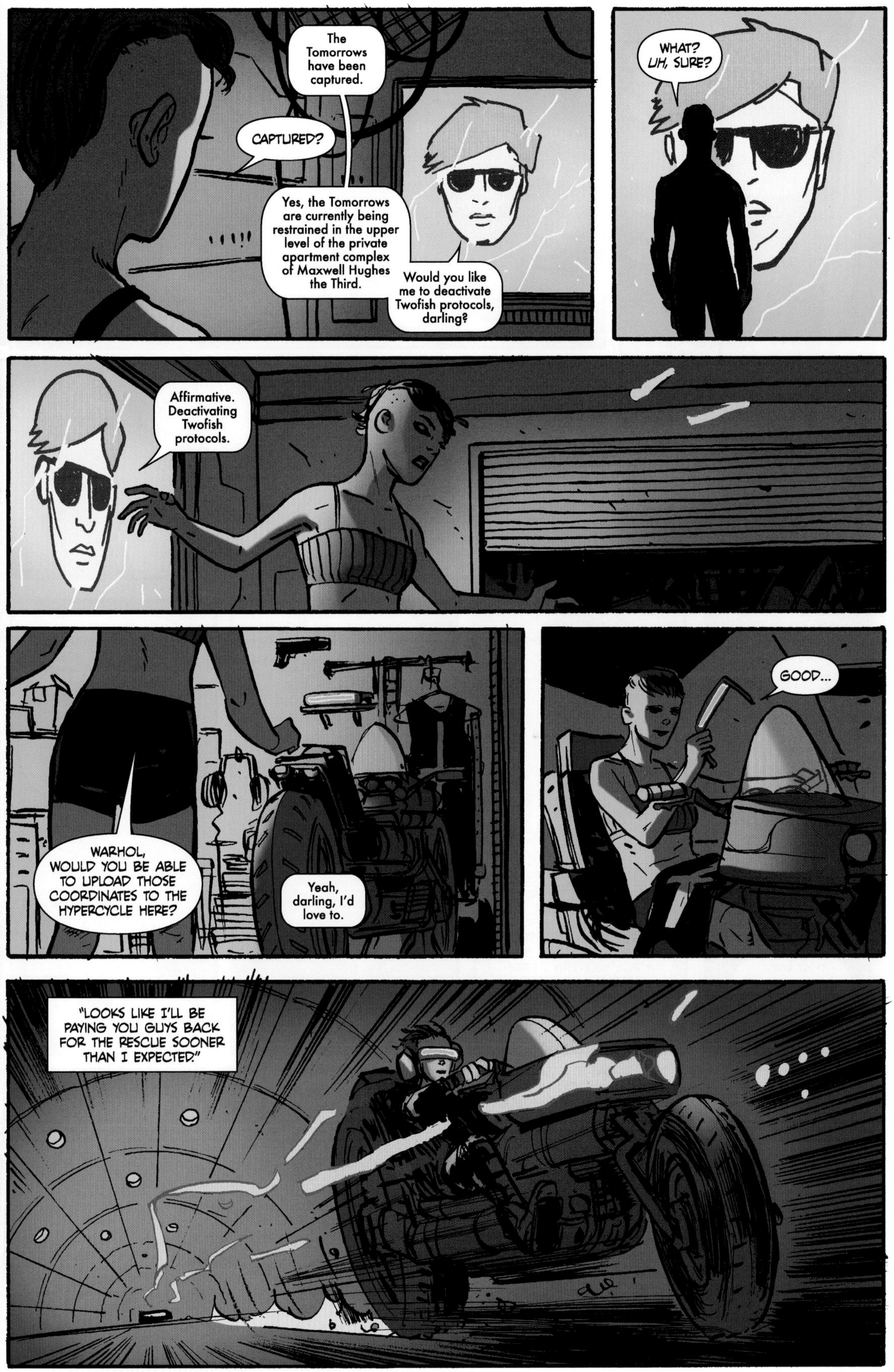

The Tomorrows have been captured.
CAPTURED?
Yes, the Tomorrows are currently being restrained in the upper level of the private apartment complex of Maxwell Hughes the Third.
Would you like me to deactivate Twofish protocols, darling?
WHAT? UH, SURE?
Affirmative. Deactivating Twofish protocols.
WARHOL, WOULD YOU BE ABLE TO UPLOAD THOSE COORDINATES TO THE HYPERCYCLE HERE?
Yeah, darling, I'd love to.
GOOD...
"LOOKS LIKE I'LL BE PAYING YOU GUYS BACK FOR THE RESCUE SOONER THAN I EXPECTED."

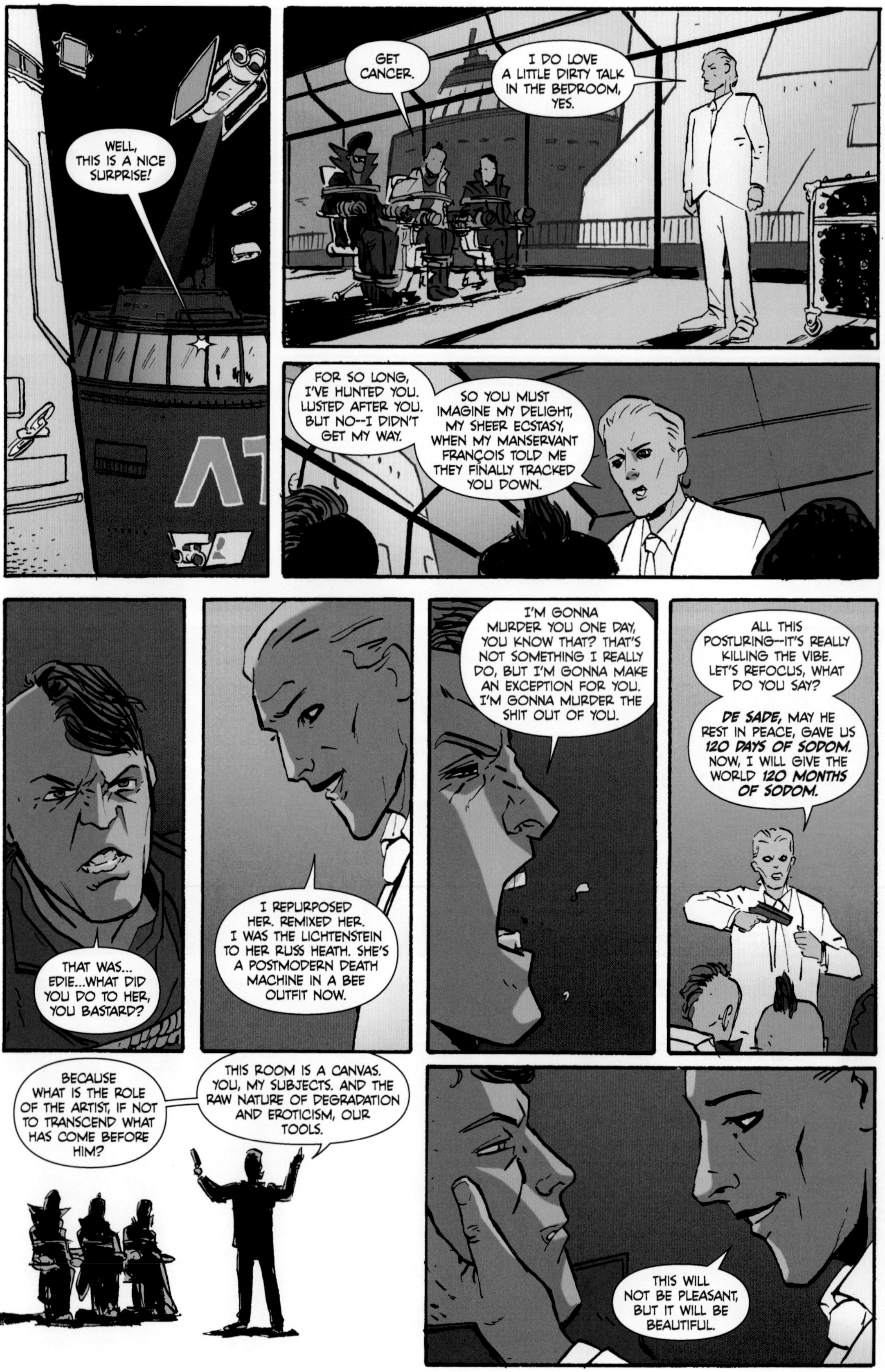
WELL, THIS IS A NICE SURPRISE!
GET CANCER.
I DO LOVE A LITTLE DIRTY TALK IN THE BEDROOM, YES.
FOR SO LONG, I'VE HUNTED YOU. LUSTED AFTER YOU. BUT NO--I DIDN'T GET MY WAY.
SO YOU MUST IMAGINE MY DELIGHT, MY SHEER ECSTASY, WHEN MY MANSERVANT FRANÇOIS TOLD ME THEY FINALLY TRACKED YOU DOWN.
THAT WAS... EDIE...WHAT DID YOU DO TO HER, YOU BASTARD?
I REPURPOSED HER. REMIXED HER. I WAS THE LICHTENSTEIN TO HER RUSS HEATH. SHE'S A POSTMODERN DEATH MACHINE IN A BEE OUTFIT NOW.
I'M GONNA MURDER YOU ONE DAY, YOU KNOW THAT? THAT'S NOT SOMETHING I REALLY DO, BUT I'M GONNA MAKE AN EXCEPTION FOR YOU. I'M GONNA MURDER THE SHIT OUT OF YOU.
ALL THIS POSTURING--IT'S REALLY KILLING THE VIBE. LET'S REFOCUS, WHAT DO YOU SAY?
DE SADE, MAY HE REST IN PEACE, GAVE US 120 DAYS OF SODOM. NOW, I WILL GIVE THE WORLD 120 MONTHS OF SODOM.
BECAUSE WHAT IS THE ROLE OF THE ARTIST, IF NOT TO TRANSCEND WHAT HAS COME BEFORE HIM?
THIS ROOM IS A CANVAS. YOU, MY SUBJECTS. AND THE RAW NATURE OF DEGRADATION AND EROTICISM, OUR TOOLS.
THIS WILL NOT BE PLEASANT, BUT IT WILL BE BEAUTIFUL.

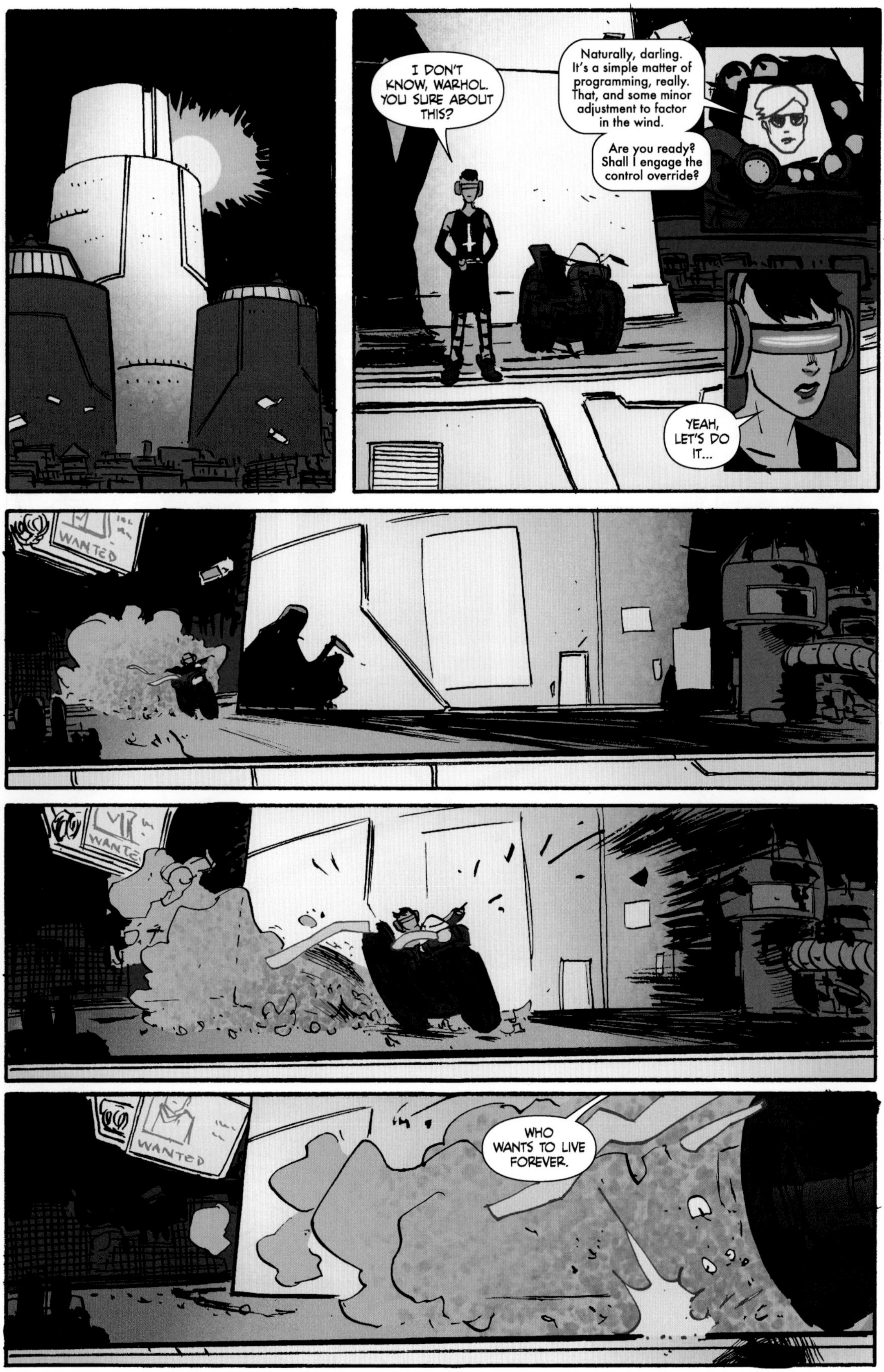
I DON'T KNOW, WARHOL. YOU SURE ABOUT THIS?
Naturally, darling. It's a simple matter of programming, really. That, and some minor adjustment to factor in the wind.
Are you ready? Shall I engage the control override?
YEAH, LET'S DO IT...
WANTED
WANTED
WANTED
WHO WANTS TO LIVE FOREVER.

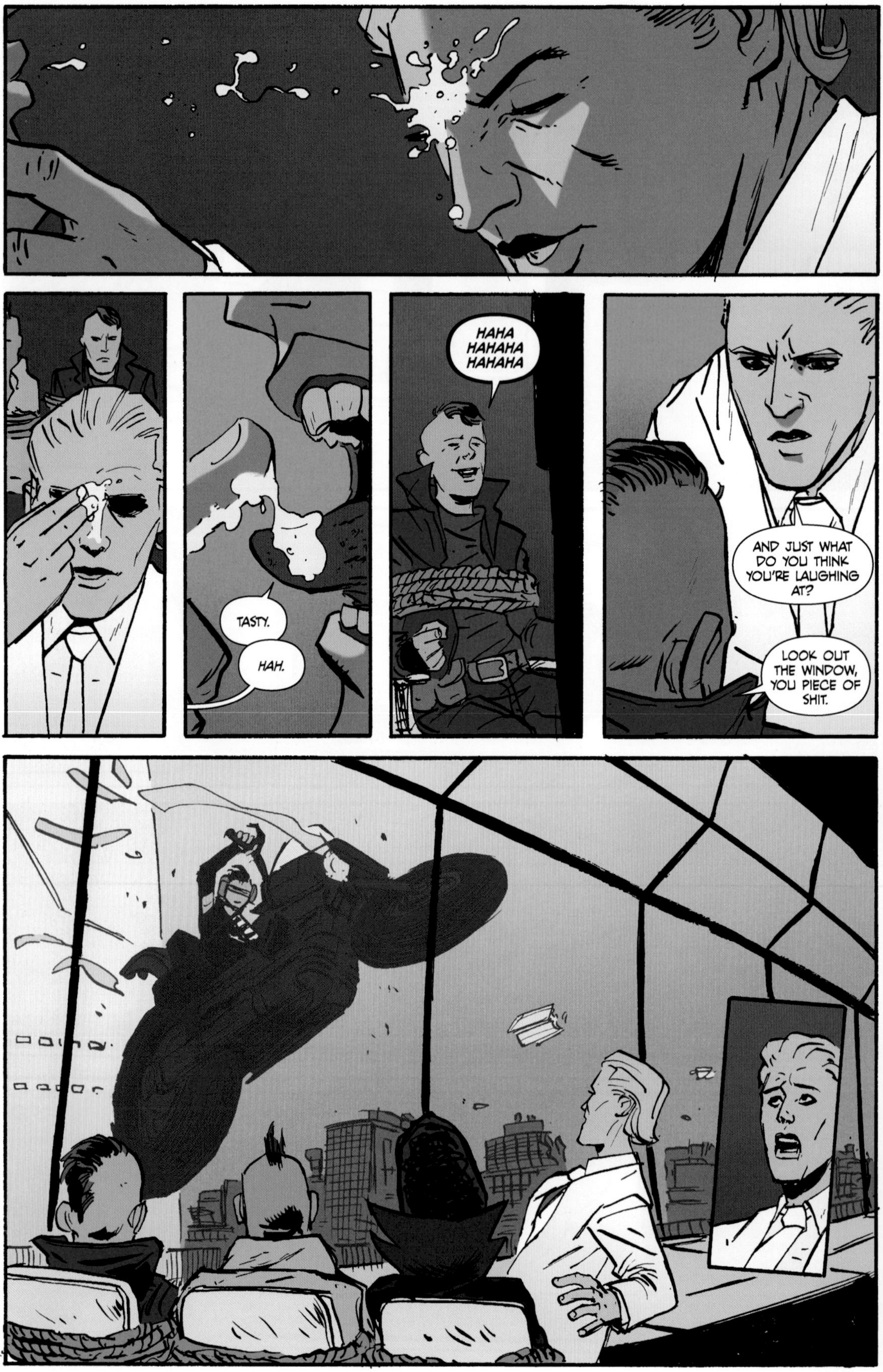
TASTY.
HAH.
HAHA HAHAHA HAHAHA
AND JUST WHAT DO YOU THINK YOU'RE LAUGHING AT?
LOOK OUT THE WINDOW, YOU PIECE OF SHIT.

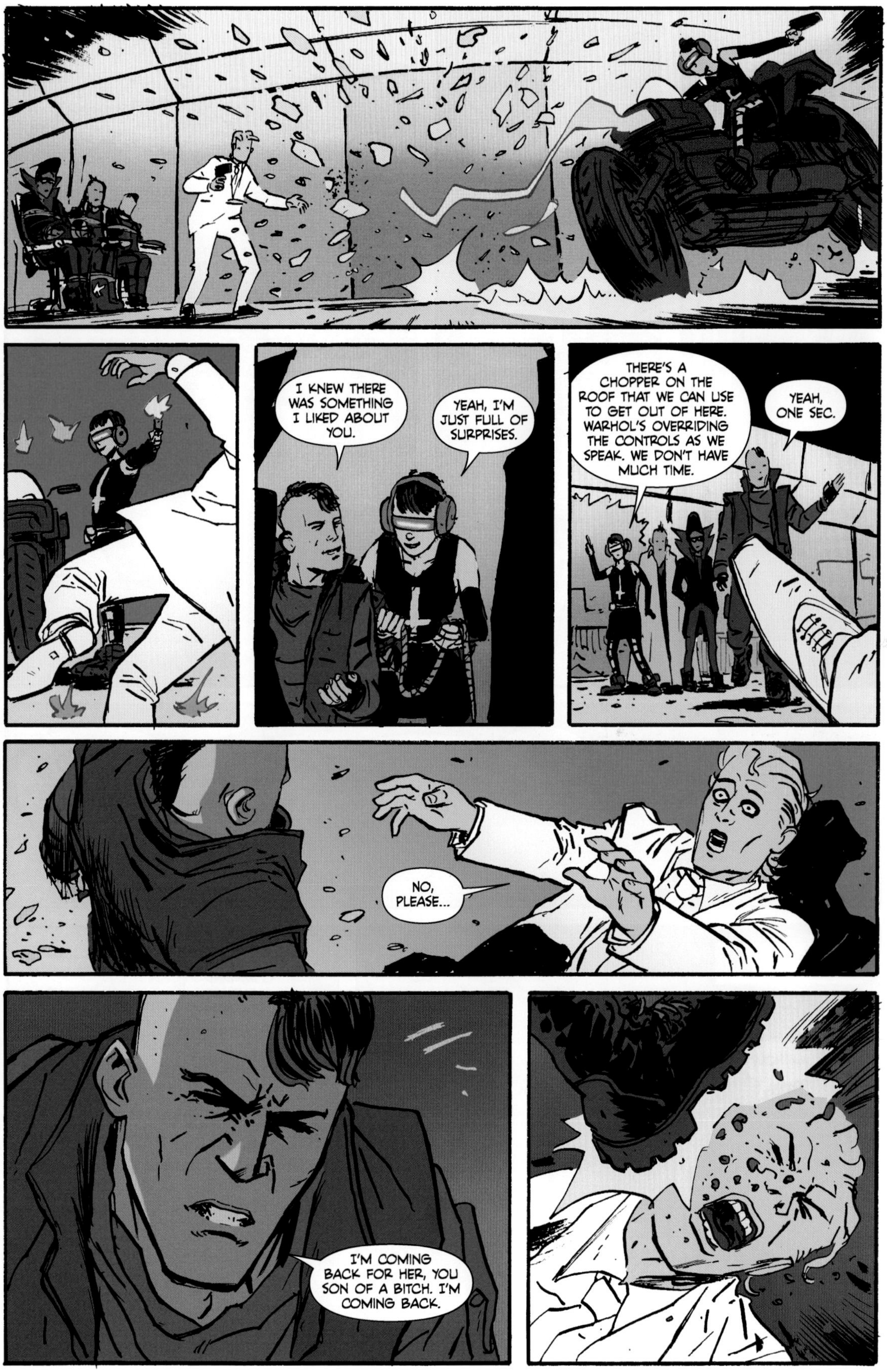
I KNEW THERE WAS SOMETHING I LIKED ABOUT YOU.
YEAH, I'M JUST FULL OF SURPRISES.
THERE'S A CHOPPER ON THE ROOF THAT WE CAN USE TO GET OUT OF HERE. WARHOL'S OVERRIDING THE CONTROLS AS WE SPEAK. WE DON'T HAVE MUCH TIME.
YEAH, ONE SEC.
NO, PLEASE...
I'M COMING BACK FOR HER, YOU SON OF A BITCH. I'M COMING BACK.

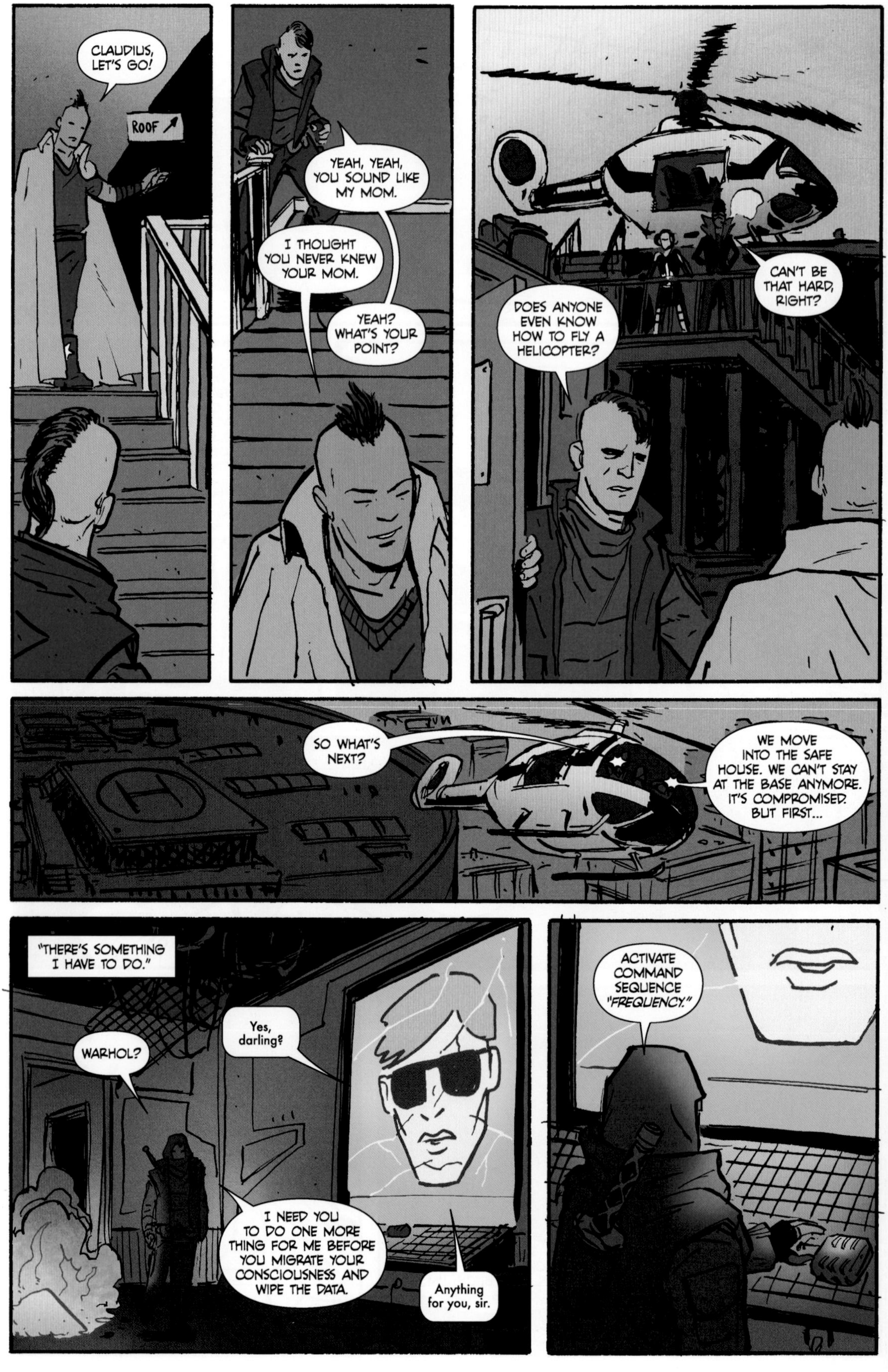
CLAUDIUS, LET'S GO!
ROOF
YEAH, YEAH, YOU SOUND LIKE MY MOM.
I THOUGHT YOU NEVER KNEW YOUR MOM.
YEAH? WHAT'S YOUR POINT?
DOES ANYONE EVEN KNOW HOW TO FLY A HELICOPTER?
CAN'T BE THAT HARD, RIGHT?
SO WHAT'S NEXT?
WE MOVE INTO THE SAFE HOUSE. WE CAN'T STAY AT THE BASE ANYMORE. IT'S COMPROMISED. BUT FIRST...
"THERE'S SOMETHING I HAVE TO DO."
WARHOL?
Yes, darling?
I NEED YOU TO DO ONE MORE THING FOR ME BEFORE YOU MIGRATE YOUR CONSCIOUSNESS AND WIPE THE DATA.
Anything for you, sir.
ACTIVATE COMMAND SEQUENCE "FREQUENCY."

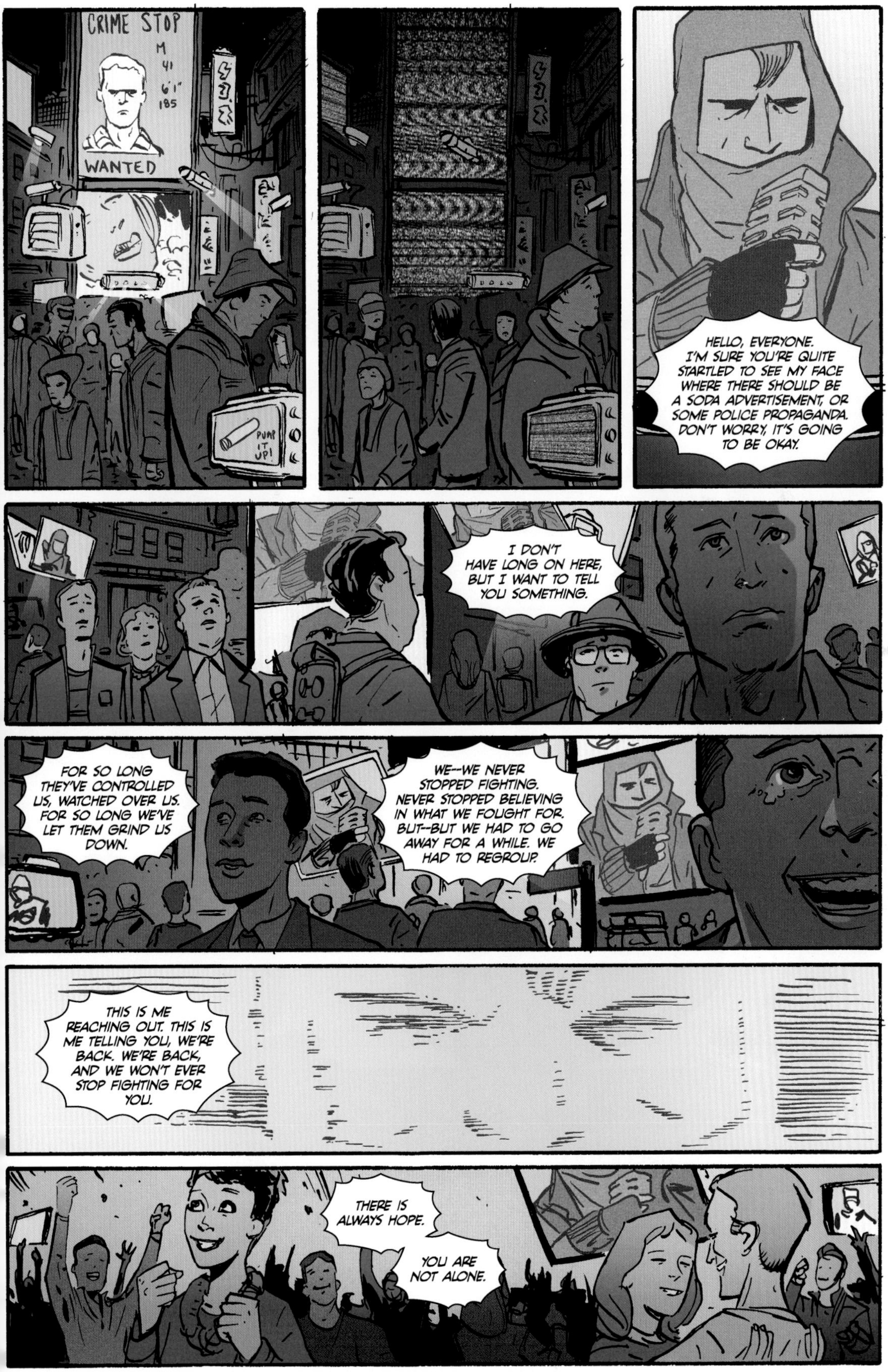
CRIME STOP
M 41 6'1" 185
WANTED
PUMP IT UP!
HELLO, EVERYONE. I'M SURE YOU'RE QUITE STARTLED TO SEE MY FACE WHERE THERE SHOULD BE A SODA ADVERTISEMENT, OR SOME POLICE PROPAGANDA. DON'T WORRY, IT'S GOING TO BE OKAY.
I DON'T HAVE LONG ON HERE, BUT I WANT TO TELL YOU SOMETHING.
FOR SO LONG THEY'VE CONTROLLED US, WATCHED OVER US. FOR SO LONG WE'VE LET THEM GRIND US DOWN.
WE--WE NEVER STOPPED FIGHTING. NEVER STOPPED BELIEVING IN WHAT WE FOUGHT FOR. BUT--BUT WE HAD TO GO AWAY FOR A WHILE. WE HAD TO REGROUP.
THIS IS ME REACHING OUT. THIS IS ME TELLING YOU, WE'RE BACK. WE'RE BACK, AND WE WON'T EVER STOP FIGHTING FOR YOU.
THERE IS ALWAYS HOPE.
YOU ARE NOT ALONE.

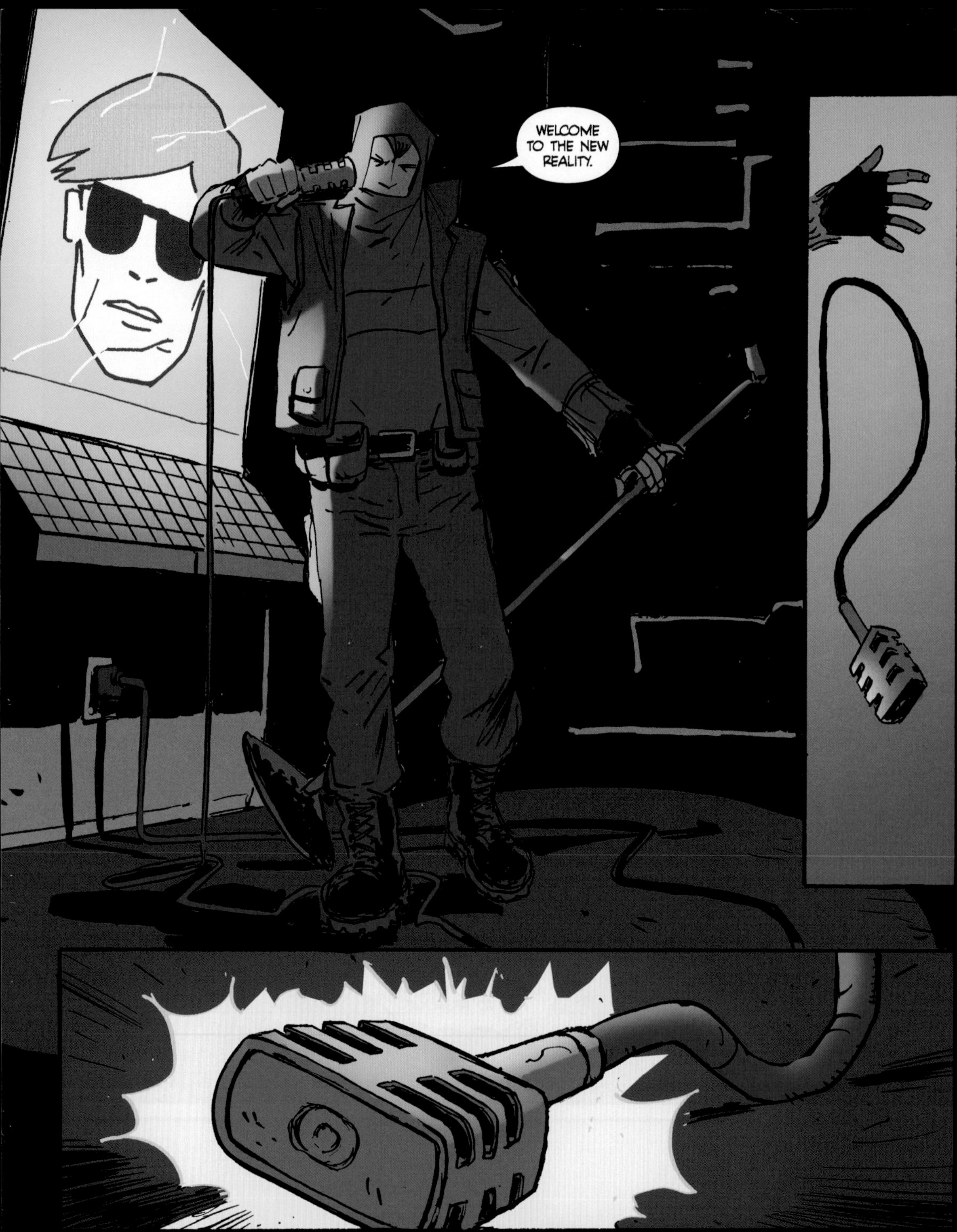
WELCOME TO THE NEW REALITY.

THE TRANSMISSION LASTED APPROXIMATELY FORTY-FIVE SECONDS.

FOLLOWING ITS CONCLUSION RIOTS ERUPTED
IN SEVERAL PARTS OF NEW YORK.

MINUTES LATER THE ONLY KNOWN BASE OF THE ENTITIES
WHO CALL THEMSELVES THE TOMORROWS SELF-DESTRUCTED.

# DIGITAL SHAMANISM

## (ART IS SCIENCE IS MAGIC)

THE LINE BETWEEN TECHNOLOGY AND MAGIC IS CONSTANTLY BLURRING.

We walk around like gods with little devices in our hands that connect us to the entire world, entire libraries, uncountable masses of information, without even thinking about it.

It's all magic. A sentiment that makes philistines increasingly uncomfortable when you bring it up.

It's all magic. Post-9/11 reality is afraid to indulge in magic, in pretend, in beautiful abstractions, because conditioning tells us that when confronted with the absolute horror of the events we witnessed, magic is something we should be ashamed of.

The lack of imagination (and fear of imagination) is toxic, and it's everywhere.

We live on a planet in a constant suicide pact with itself. We possess the means of producing clean energy yet allow the toxic control of capitalism to prevent us from utilizing it or bringing this technology to the masses.

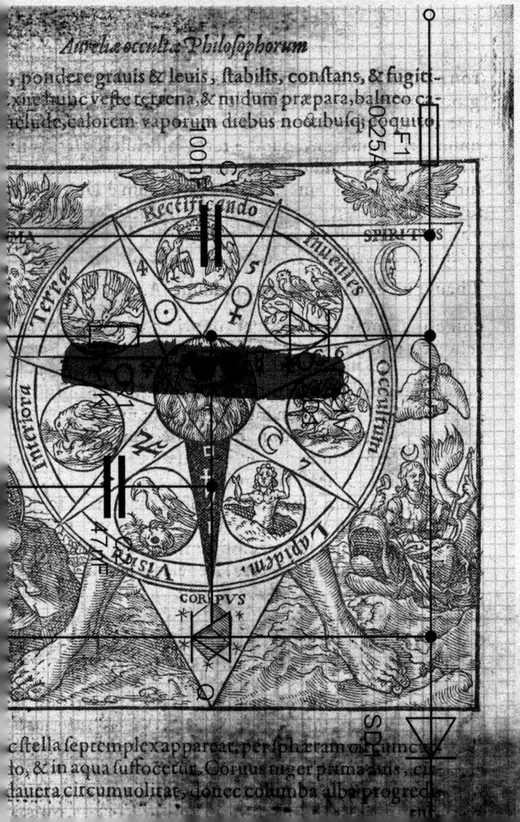
Aurelia occulta Philosophorum
Rectificando
Terrae
Interiora
Occultum
Lapidem
Inuenies
CORPVS
SPIRITVS
F1
0.25A
100n

If we were to travel back even forty, fifty years, conservatively, with the technology we possess now—with our iPhones, our Samsung Galaxys—we'd be met with stares of awe—of fear, even.

Travel back even further, and we'd likely be either revered or hunted for witchcraft. Magic and science are the same thing. A base set of commands that allows us to both quantify and redefine the parameters of our reality. Science is magic that we figured out how to see the coding—the framework—behind.

Magic is the indefinable, the things that slip past our perception, our understanding. What is magic in the moment may not always be "magic"; we may develop an understanding of the framework which governs the sequence. Alternatively, what is magic may always be magic, simply because it exists outside the realm of conventional coding, of conventional understanding.

**THE GREATEST TRICK THAT WAS EVER PULLED—BESIDES THE AFOREMENTIONED SHAMING OF MAGIC—WAS ALLOWING THOSE WHO SEEK TO OPPRESS AND RULE TO CONVINCE THE MASSES THAT SCIENCE AND ART WERE FUNDAMENTALLY DIFFERENT FORCES.**

Think about any piece of art you love—there's science, there's mechanics to the way it's constructed. There's beauty in the mechanics. Sometimes the only mechanics a work of art has is its inherent lack of mechanics. The nonlinear "dream" narratives of David Lynch (I hesitate to even say "dream" because I think on some level it does a disservice to the beauty of their construction). The stories within stories of a Kaufman screenplay. There's science behind the art.

Alternatively if we look at all science, we can see where it becomes art. The engineering, the sheer design marvel of the iPod. The sheer overwhelming fucking darkness of the moment atoms were split for the first time. There's beauty and art at the core of every scientific moment, whether we feel comfortable acknowledging it or not.

Science-fiction writers who predict new technologies, theoretical physicists postulating "many-worlds theory," comic writers talking about the "multiverse"—the line is blurring, and only if we embrace this blurring, observe the intersections, can we ever truly begin to paint an accurate picture of what reality truly is.

/// part two

# WHAT LIES BEYOND
# [OR] THE SPACES IN BETWEEN

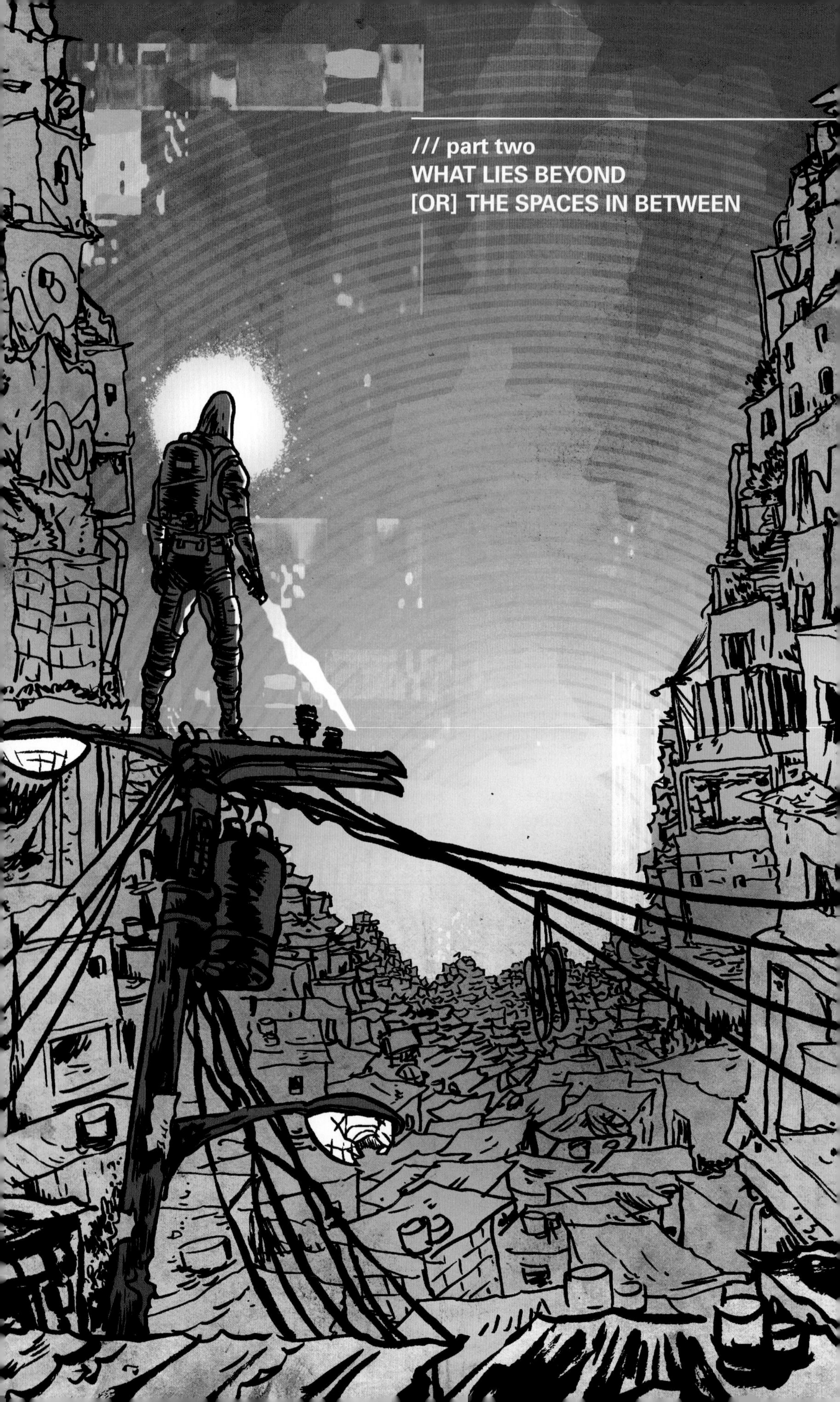

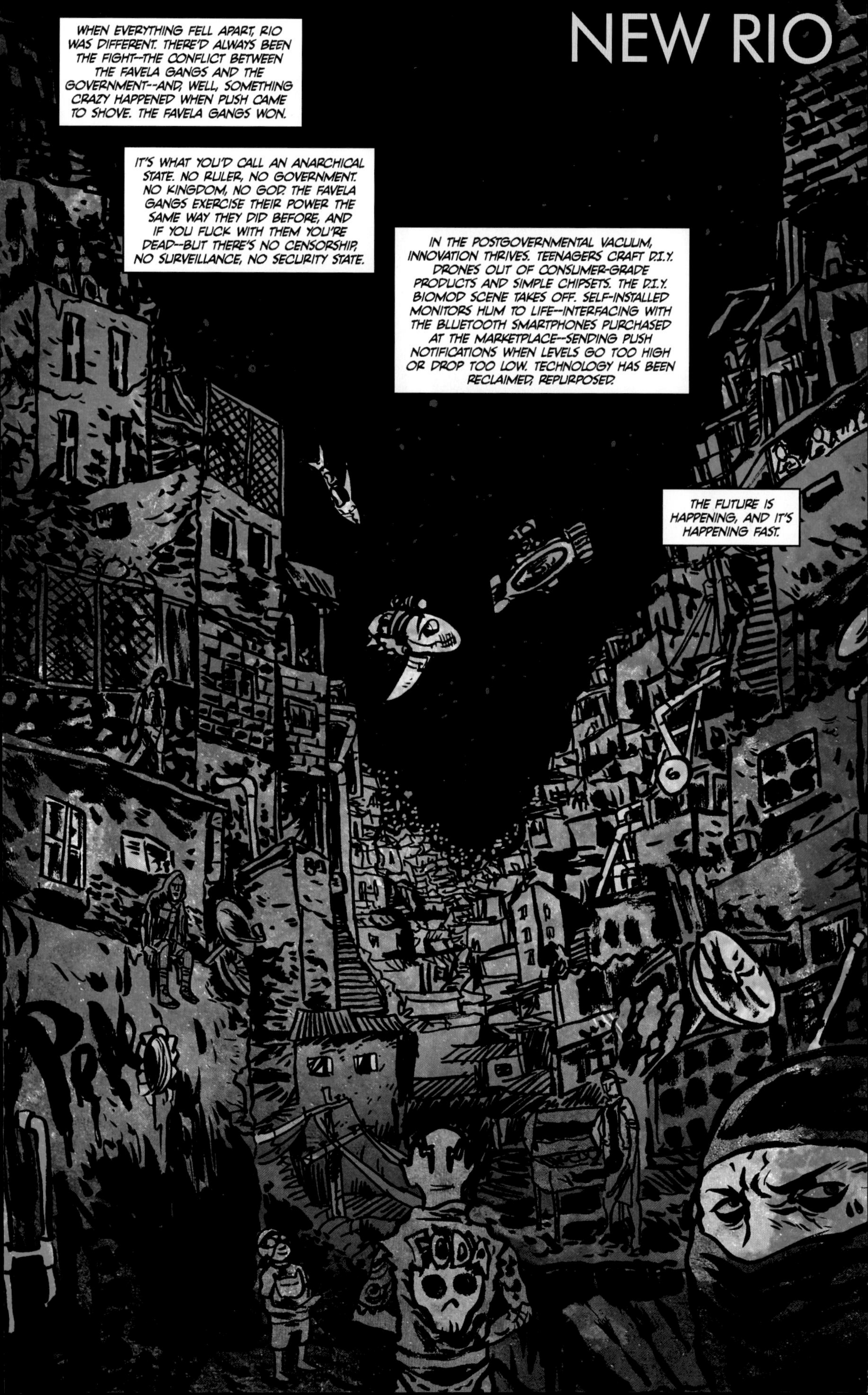
NEW RIO
WHEN EVERYTHING FELL APART, RIO WAS DIFFERENT. THERE'D ALWAYS BEEN THE FIGHT--THE CONFLICT BETWEEN THE FAVELA GANGS AND THE GOVERNMENT--AND, WELL, SOMETHING CRAZY HAPPENED WHEN PUSH CAME TO SHOVE. THE FAVELA GANGS WON.
IT'S WHAT YOU'D CALL AN ANARCHICAL STATE. NO RULER, NO GOVERNMENT. NO KINGDOM, NO GOD. THE FAVELA GANGS EXERCISE THEIR POWER THE SAME WAY THEY DID BEFORE, AND IF YOU FUCK WITH THEM YOU'RE DEAD--BUT THERE'S NO CENSORSHIP, NO SURVEILLANCE, NO SECURITY STATE.
IN THE POSTGOVERNMENTAL VACUUM, INNOVATION THRIVES. TEENAGERS CRAFT D.I.Y. DRONES OUT OF CONSUMER-GRADE PRODUCTS AND SIMPLE CHIPSETS. THE D.I.Y. BIOMOD SCENE TAKES OFF. SELF-INSTALLED MONITORS HUM TO LIFE--INTERFACING WITH THE BLUETOOTH SMARTPHONES PURCHASED AT THE MARKETPLACE--SENDING PUSH NOTIFICATIONS WHEN LEVELS GO TOO HIGH OR DROP TOO LOW. TECHNOLOGY HAS BEEN RECLAIMED, REPURPOSED.
THE FUTURE IS HAPPENING, AND IT'S HAPPENING FAST.

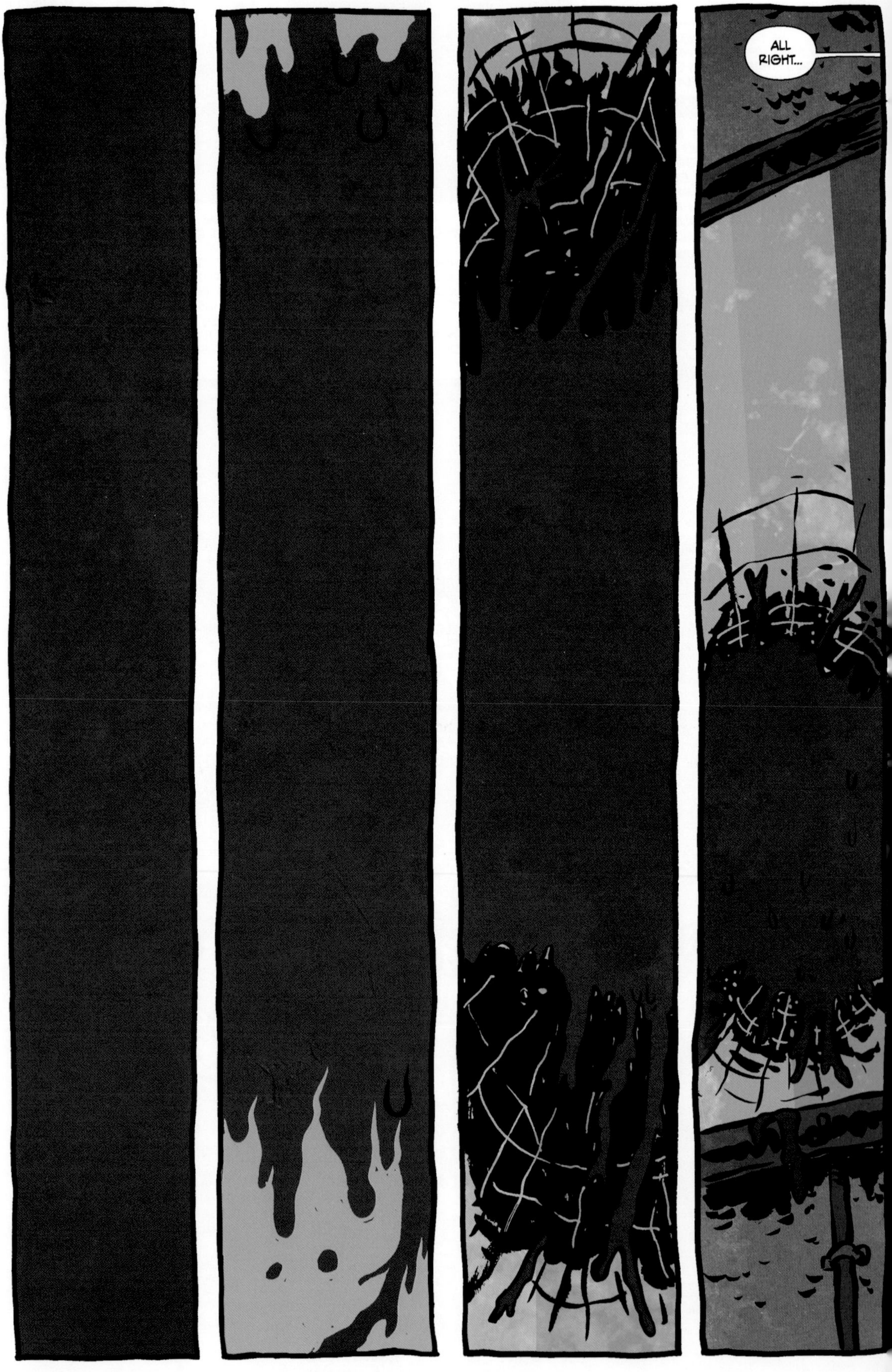
ALL RIGHT...

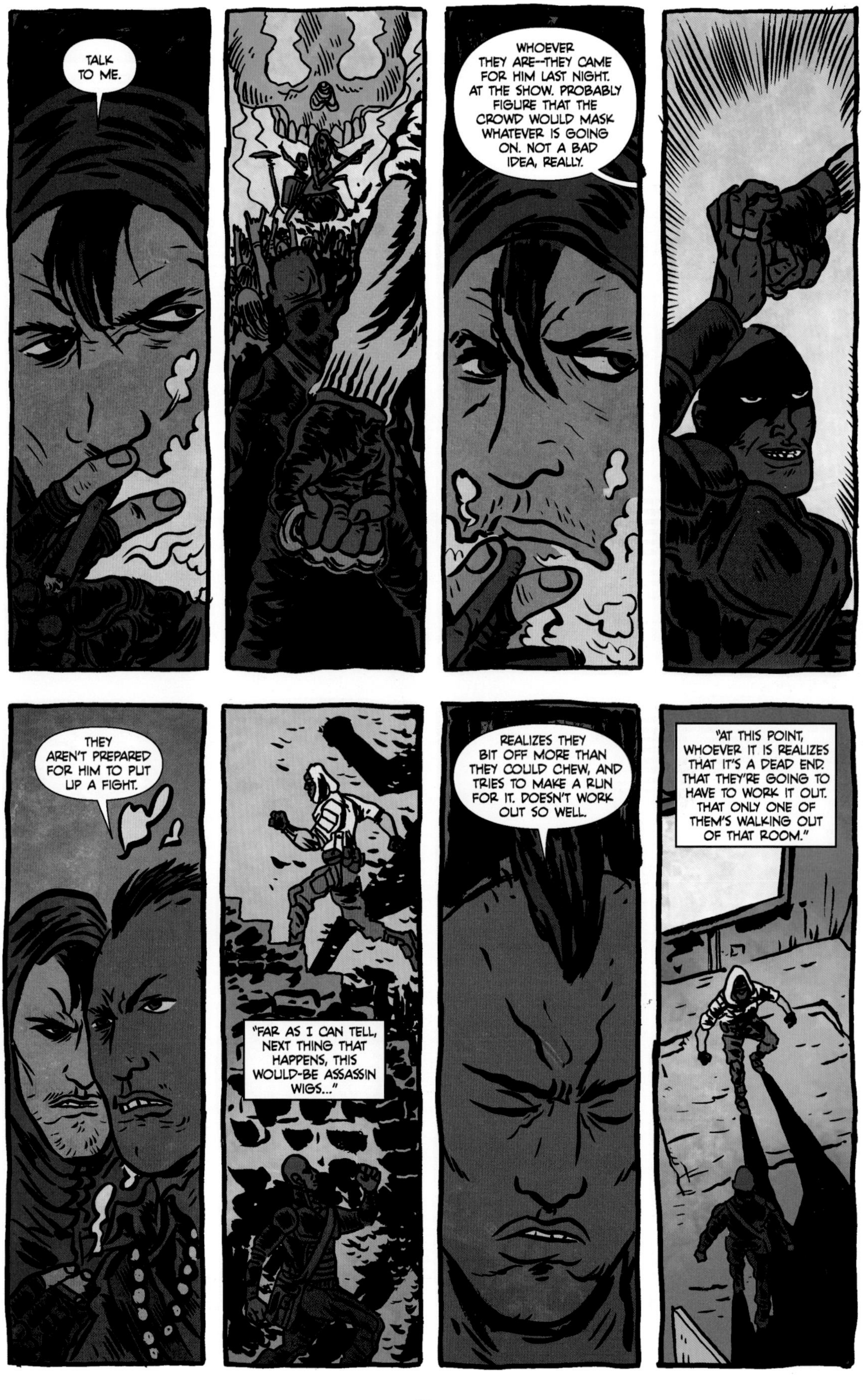

TALK TO ME.
WHOEVER THEY ARE--THEY CAME FOR HIM LAST NIGHT. AT THE SHOW. PROBABLY FIGURE THAT THE CROWD WOULD MASK WHATEVER IS GOING ON. NOT A BAD IDEA, REALLY.
THEY AREN'T PREPARED FOR HIM TO PUT UP A FIGHT.
"FAR AS I CAN TELL, NEXT THING THAT HAPPENS, THIS WOULD-BE ASSASSIN WIGS..."
REALIZES THEY BIT OFF MORE THAN THEY COULD CHEW, AND TRIES TO MAKE A RUN FOR IT. DOESN'T WORK OUT SO WELL.
"AT THIS POINT, WHOEVER IT IS REALIZES THAT IT'S A DEAD END. THAT THEY'RE GOING TO HAVE TO WORK IT OUT. THAT ONLY ONE OF THEM'S WALKING OUT OF THAT ROOM."

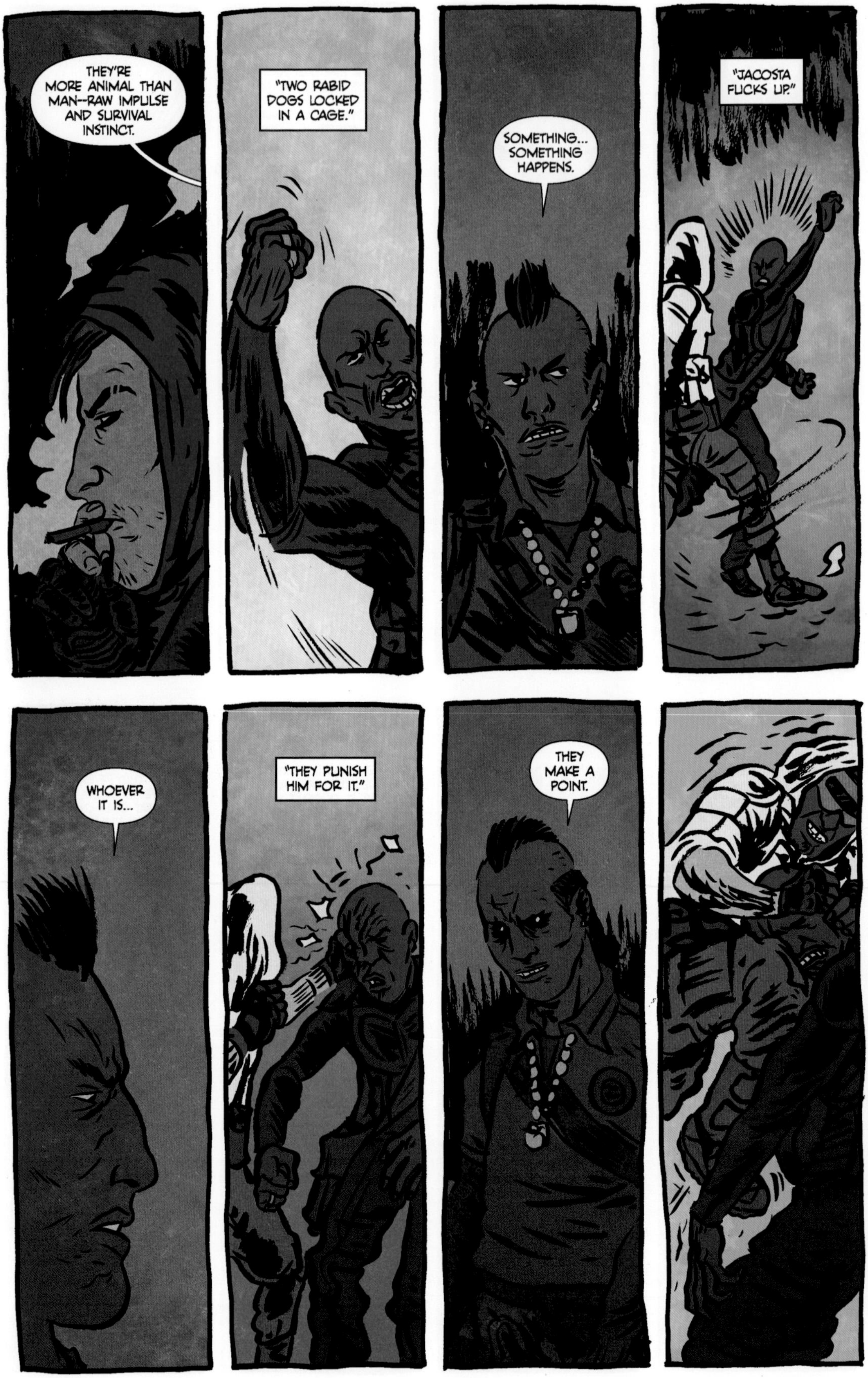
THEY'RE MORE ANIMAL THAN MAN--RAW IMPULSE AND SURVIVAL INSTINCT.
"TWO RABID DOGS LOCKED IN A CAGE."
SOMETHING... SOMETHING HAPPENS.
"JACOSTA FUCKS UP."
WHOEVER IT IS...
"THEY PUNISH HIM FOR IT."
THEY MAKE A POINT.

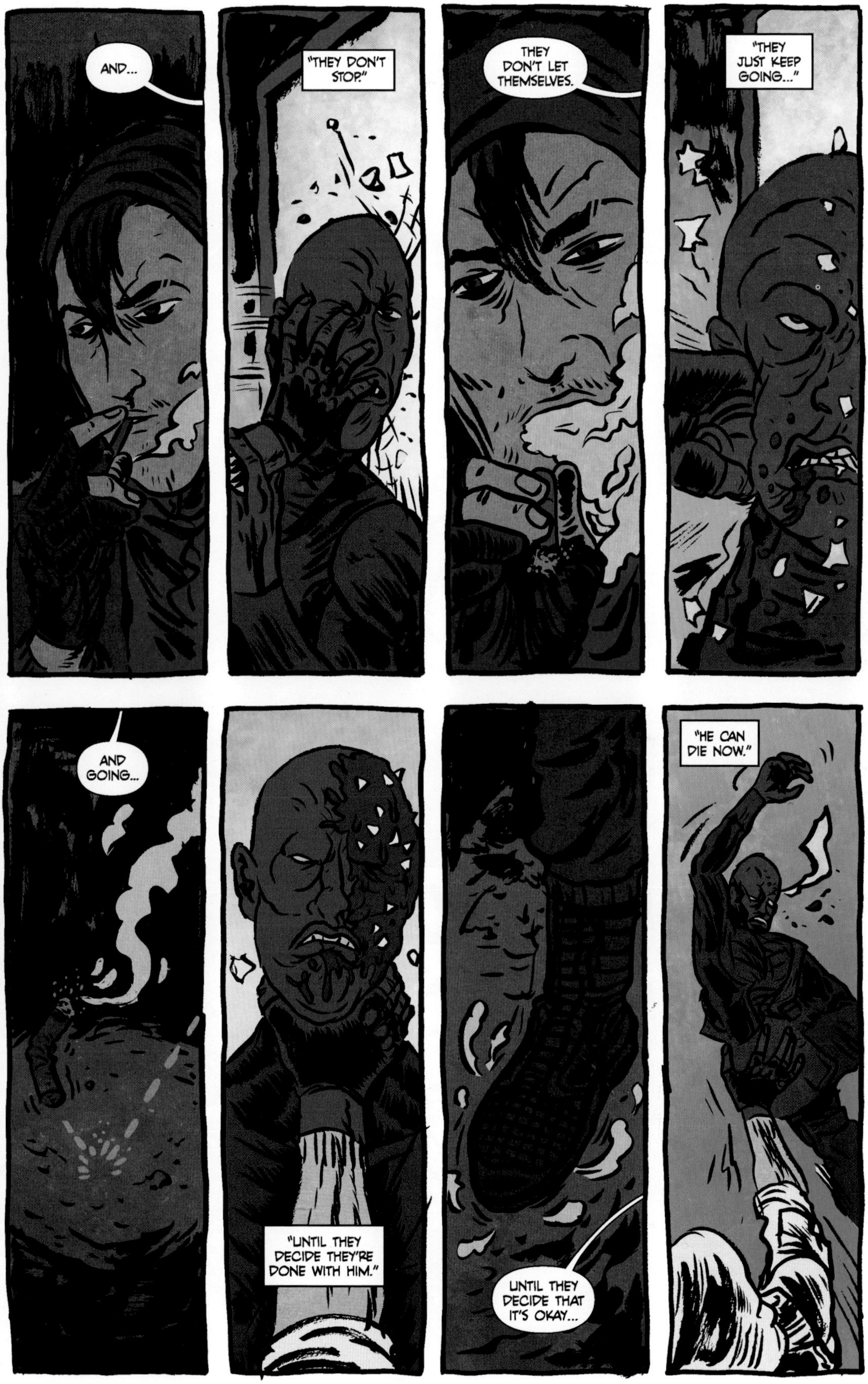
AND...
"THEY DON'T STOP."
THEY DON'T LET THEMSELVES.
"THEY JUST KEEP GOING..."
AND GOING...
"UNTIL THEY DECIDE THEY'RE DONE WITH HIM."
UNTIL THEY DECIDE THAT IT'S OKAY...
"HE CAN DIE NOW."

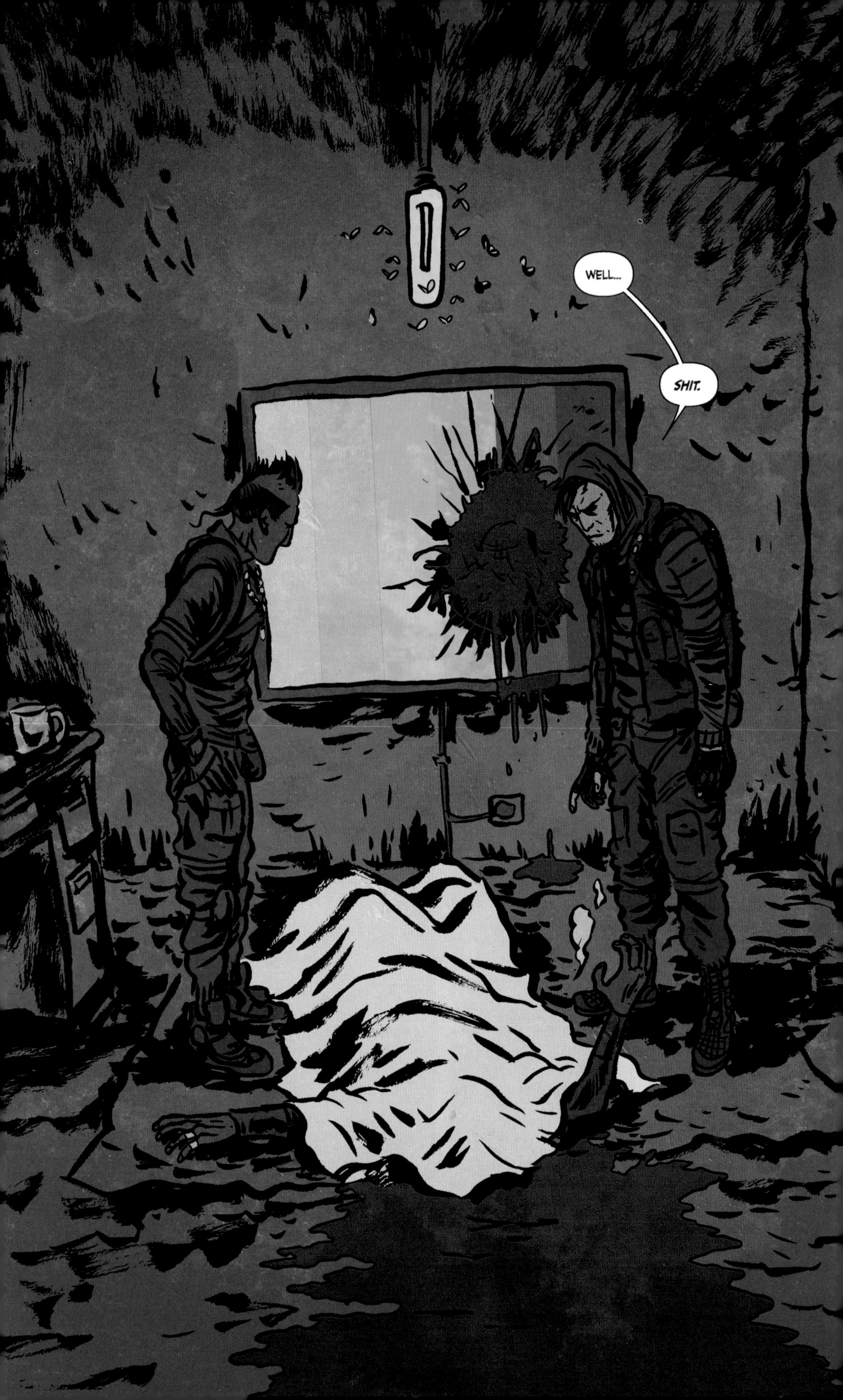
WELL...
SHIT.

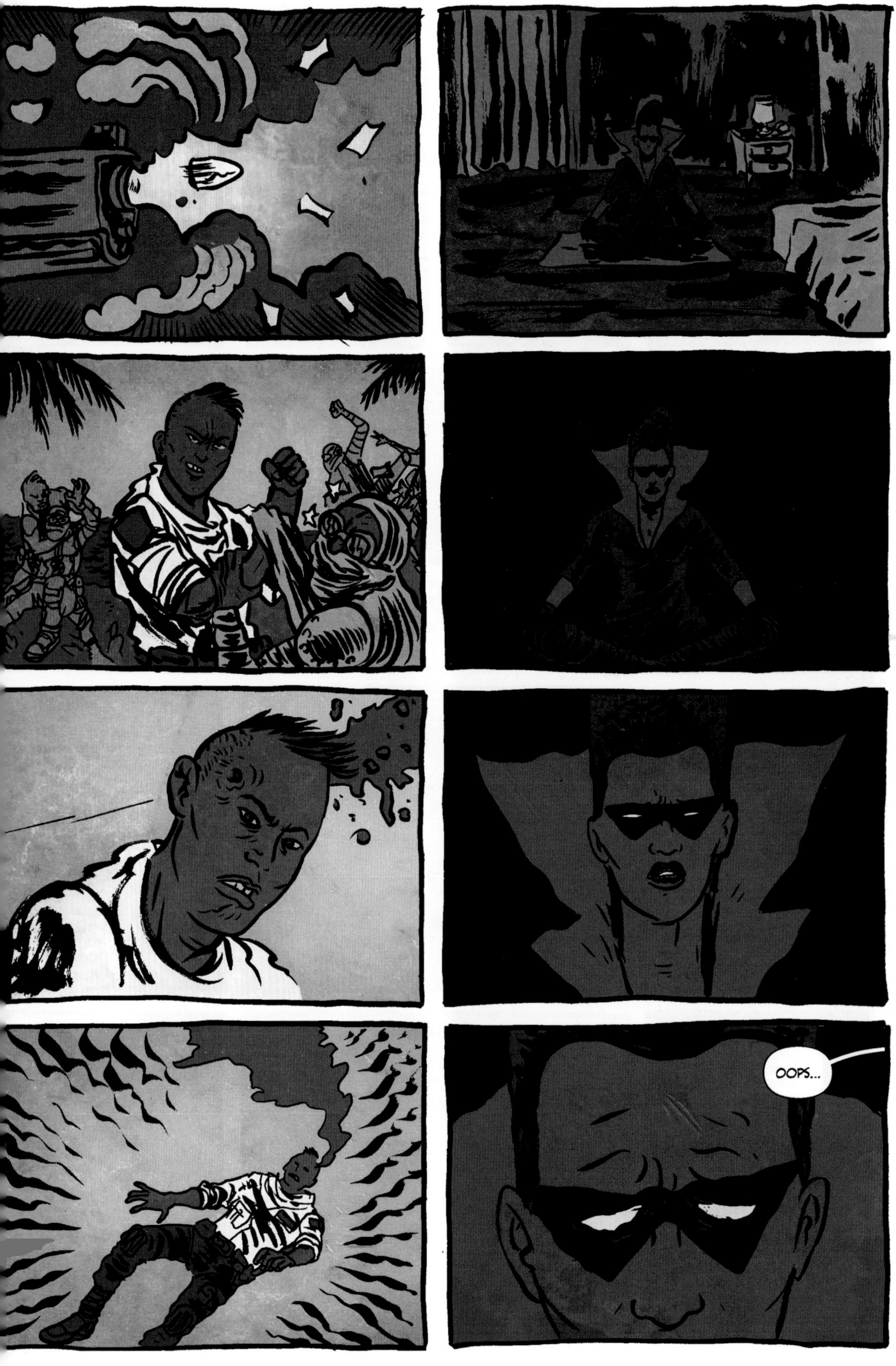
OOPS...

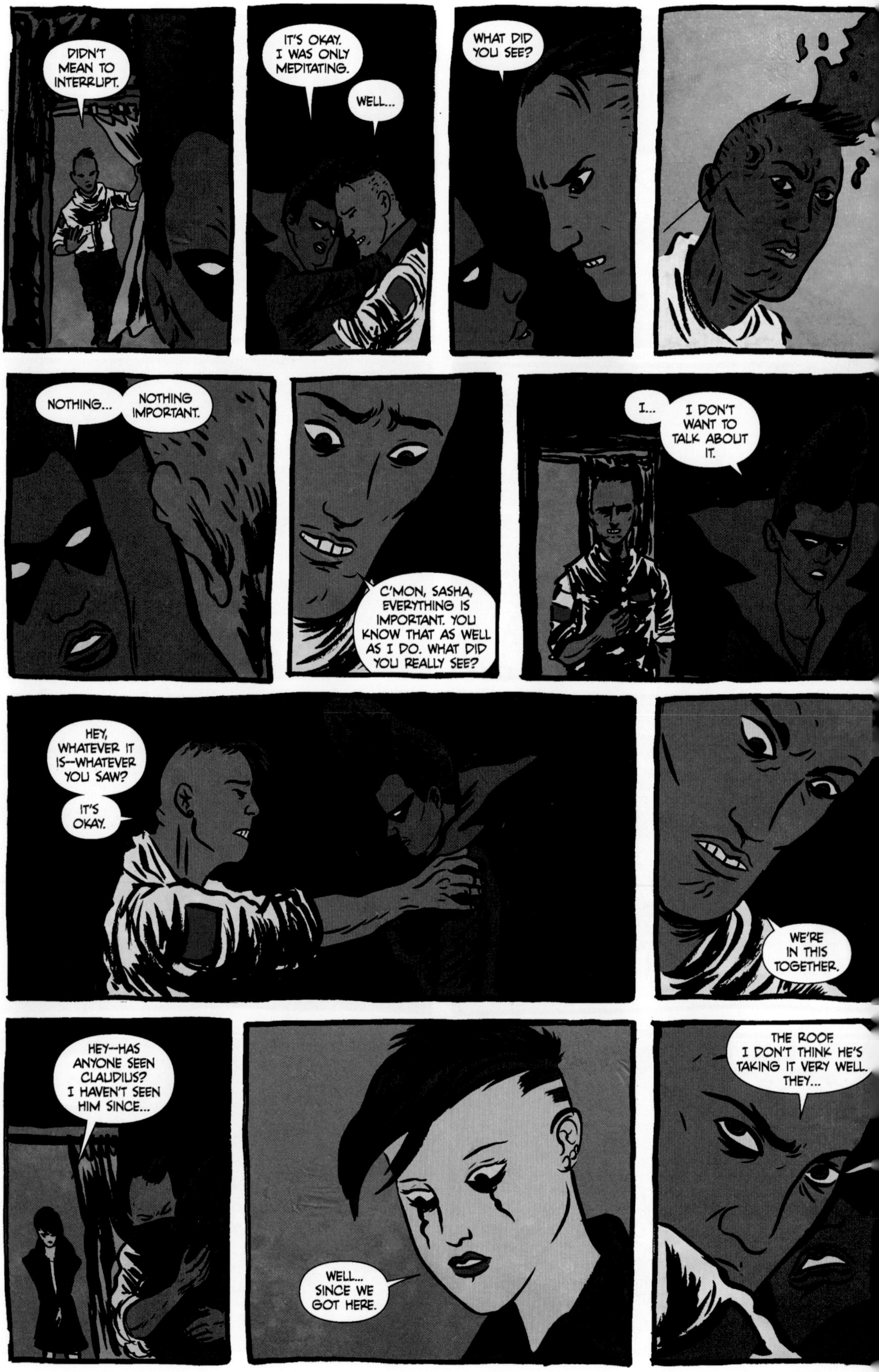
DIDN'T MEAN TO INTERRUPT.
IT'S OKAY. I WAS ONLY MEDITATING.
WELL...
WHAT DID YOU SEE?
NOTHING...
NOTHING IMPORTANT.
C'MON, SASHA, EVERYTHING IS IMPORTANT. YOU KNOW THAT AS WELL AS I DO. WHAT DID YOU REALLY SEE?
I...
I DON'T WANT TO TALK ABOUT IT.
HEY, WHATEVER IT IS--WHATEVER YOU SAW?
IT'S OKAY.
WE'RE IN THIS TOGETHER.
HEY--HAS ANYONE SEEN CLAUDIUS? I HAVEN'T SEEN HIM SINCE...
WELL... SINCE WE GOT HERE.
THE ROOF. I DON'T THINK HE'S TAKING IT VERY WELL. THEY...

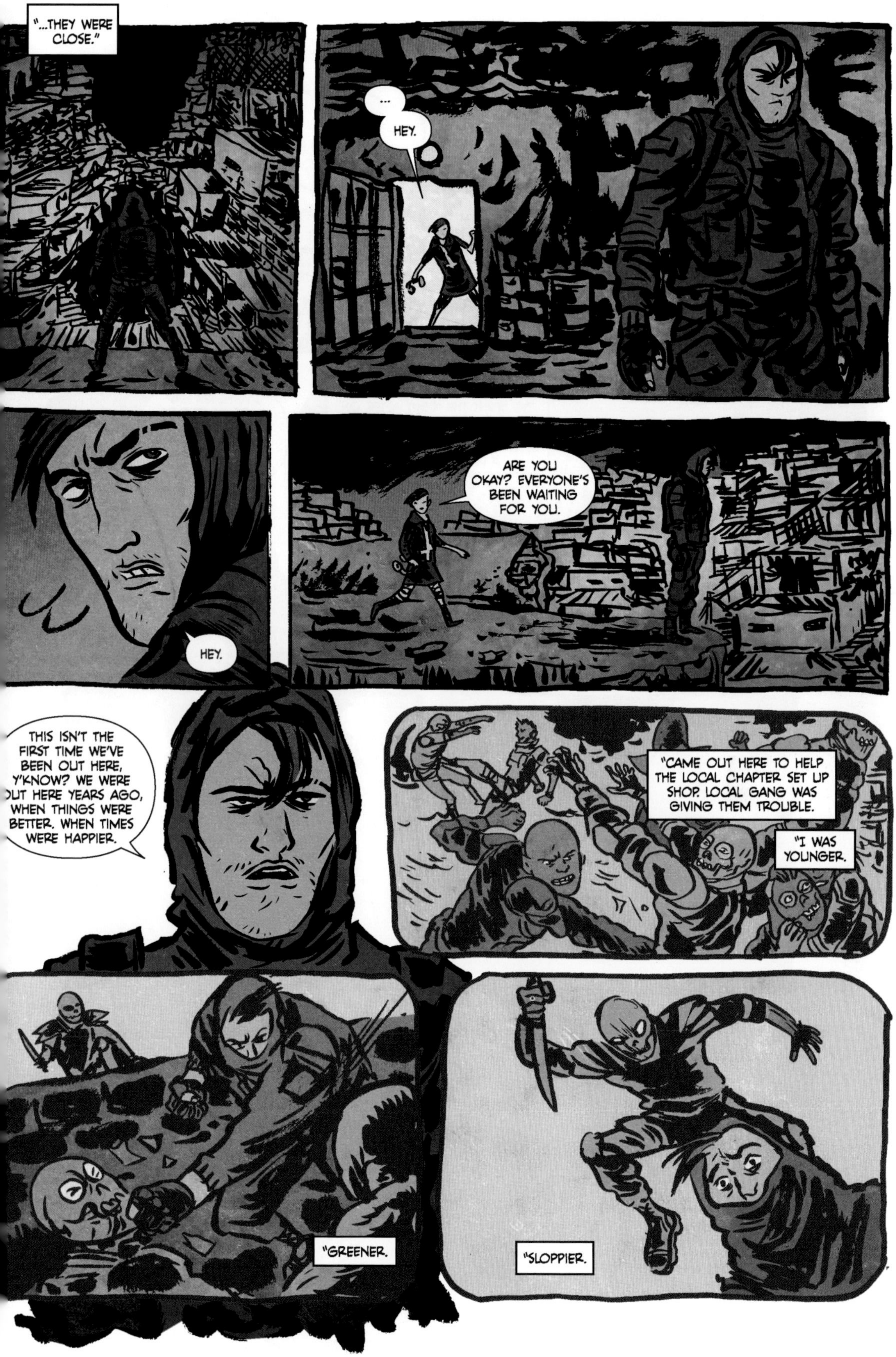

"...THEY WERE CLOSE."
...
HEY.
HEY.
ARE YOU OKAY? EVERYONE'S BEEN WAITING FOR YOU.
THIS ISN'T THE FIRST TIME WE'VE BEEN OUT HERE, Y'KNOW? WE WERE OUT HERE YEARS AGO, WHEN THINGS WERE BETTER. WHEN TIMES WERE HAPPIER.
"CAME OUT HERE TO HELP THE LOCAL CHAPTER SET UP SHOP. LOCAL GANG WAS GIVING THEM TROUBLE.
"I WAS YOUNGER.
"GREENER.
"SLOPPIER.

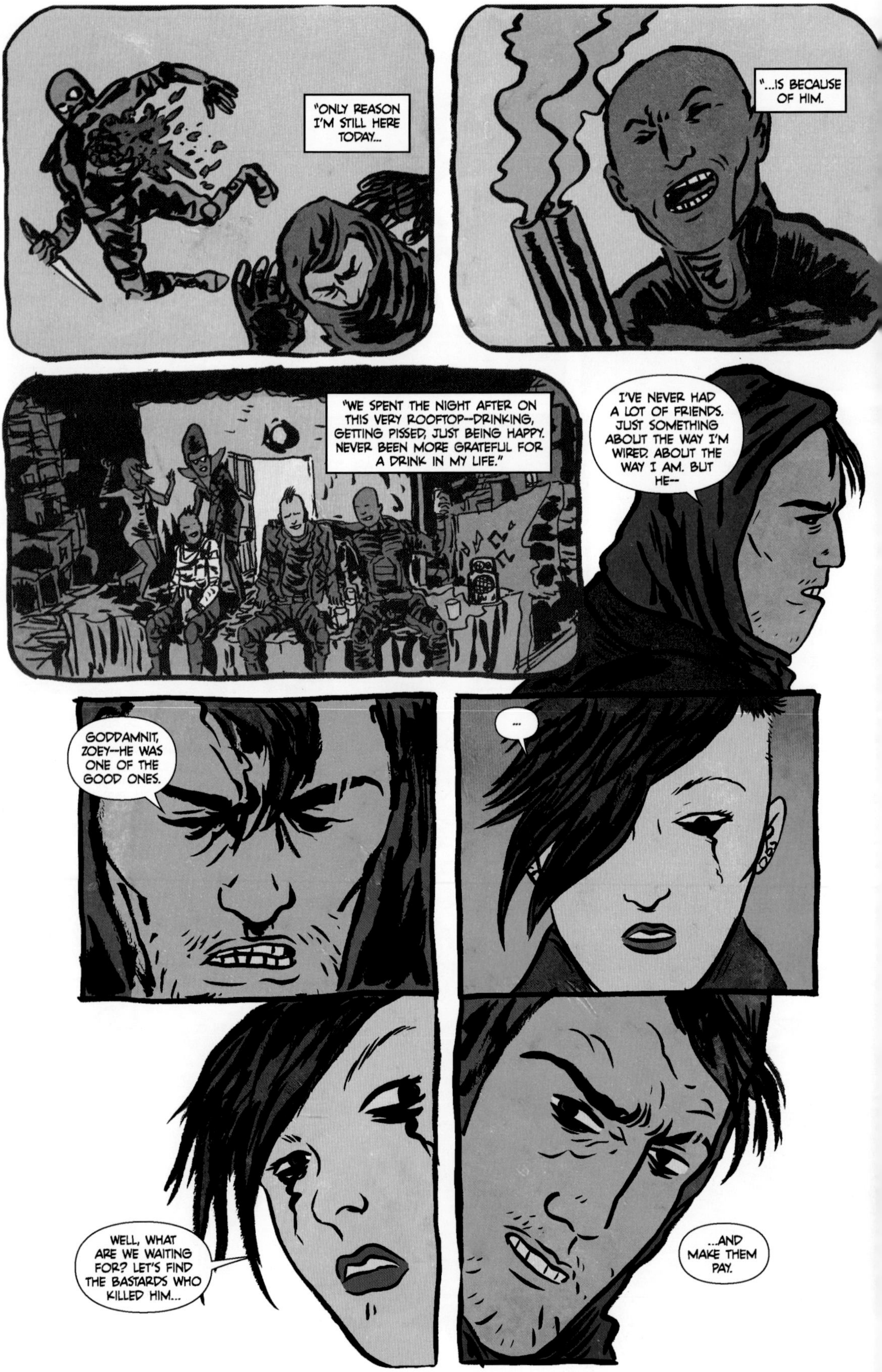
"ONLY REASON I'M STILL HERE TODAY...
"...IS BECAUSE OF HIM.
"WE SPENT THE NIGHT AFTER ON THIS VERY ROOFTOP--DRINKING, GETTING PISSED, JUST BEING HAPPY. NEVER BEEN MORE GRATEFUL FOR A DRINK IN MY LIFE."
I'VE NEVER HAD A LOT OF FRIENDS. JUST SOMETHING ABOUT THE WAY I'M WIRED. ABOUT THE WAY I AM. BUT HE--
GODDAMNIT, ZOEY--HE WAS ONE OF THE GOOD ONES.
...
WELL, WHAT ARE WE WAITING FOR? LET'S FIND THE BASTARDS WHO KILLED HIM...
...AND MAKE THEM PAY.

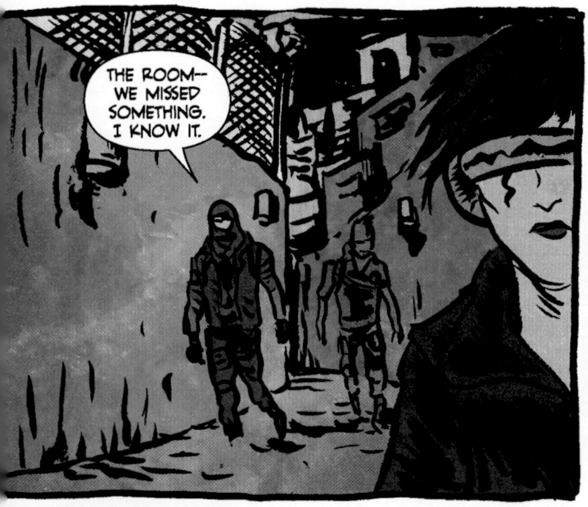
THE ROOM-- WE MISSED SOMETHING. I KNOW IT.

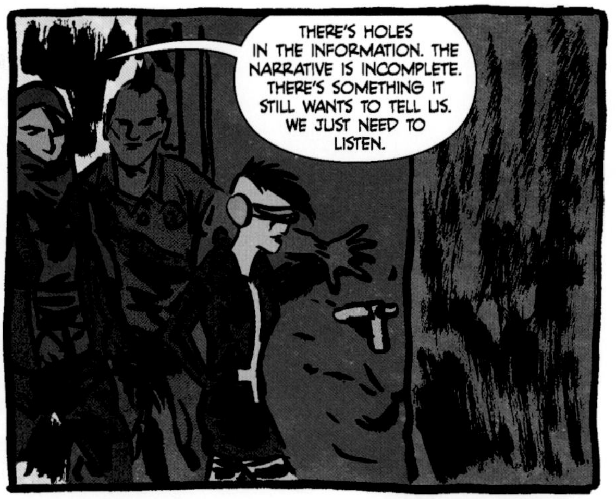
THERE'S HOLES IN THE INFORMATION. THE NARRATIVE IS INCOMPLETE. THERE'S SOMETHING IT STILL WANTS TO TELL US. WE JUST NEED TO LISTEN.

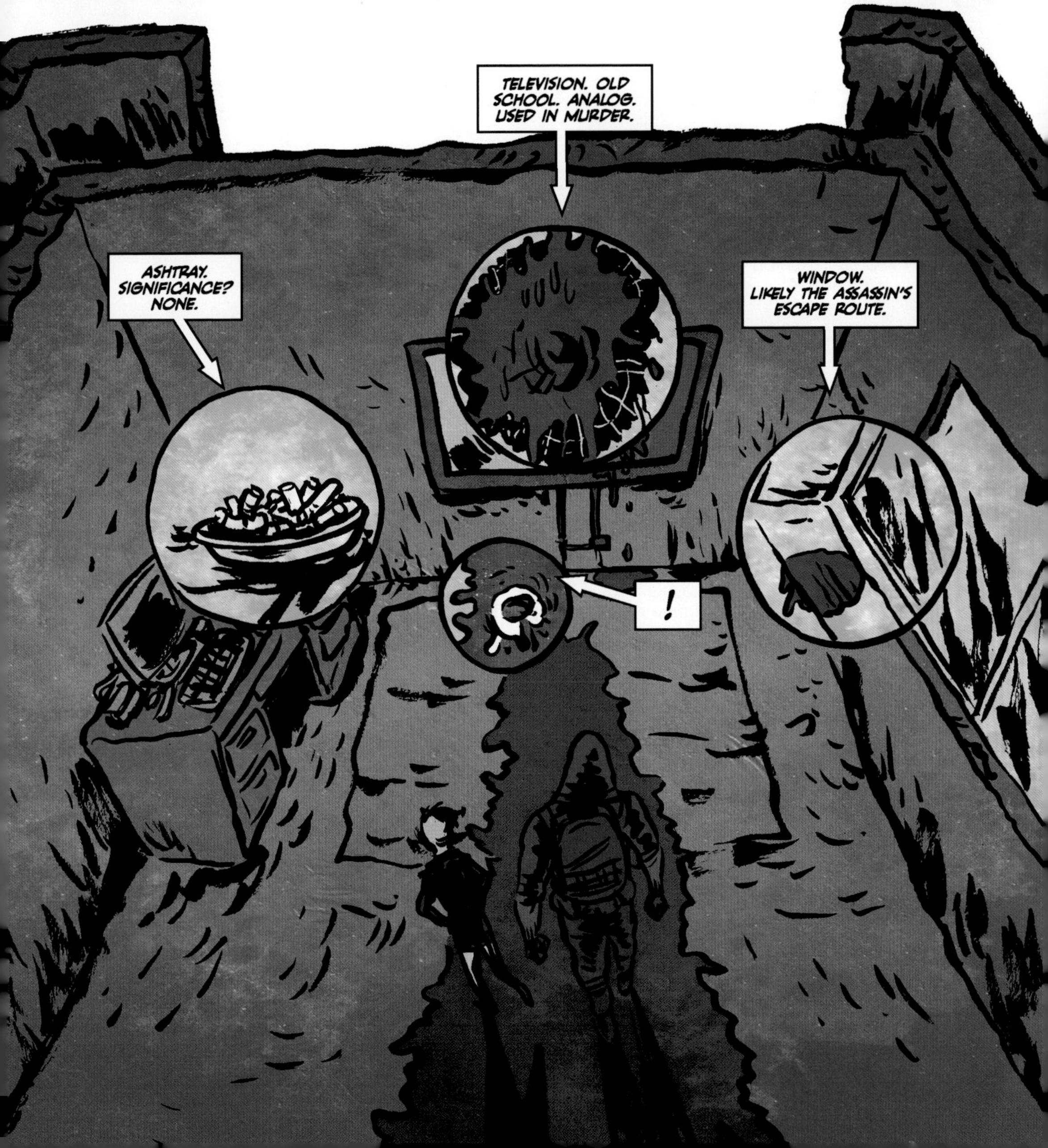
TELEVISION. OLD SCHOOL. ANALOG. USED IN MURDER.
ASHTRAY. SIGNIFICANCE? NONE.
WINDOW. LIKELY THE ASSASSIN'S ESCAPE ROUTE.
!

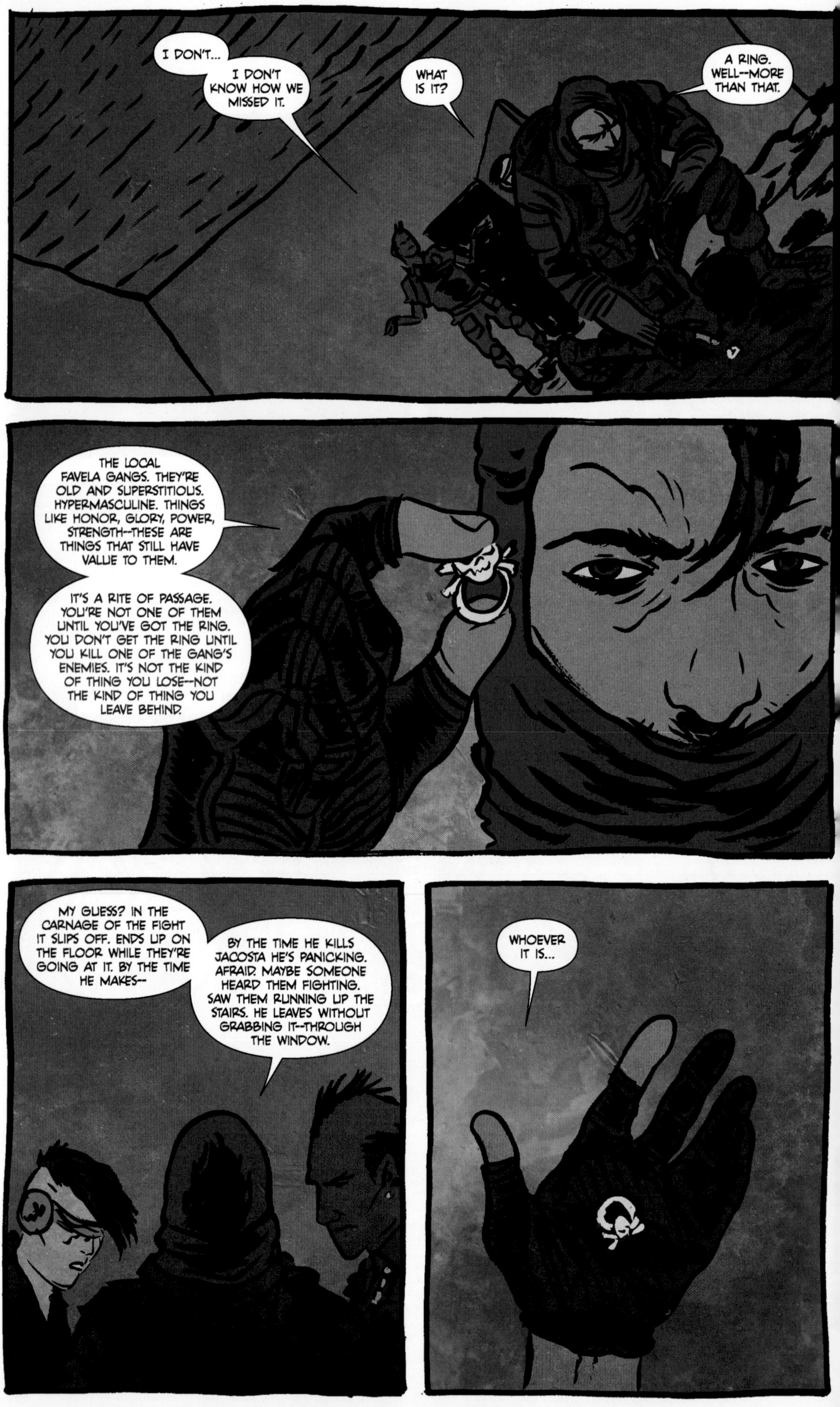
I DON'T...
I DON'T KNOW HOW WE MISSED IT.
WHAT IS IT?
A RING. WELL--MORE THAN THAT.
THE LOCAL FAVELA GANGS. THEY'RE OLD AND SUPERSTITIOUS. HYPERMASCULINE. THINGS LIKE HONOR, GLORY, POWER, STRENGTH--THESE ARE THINGS THAT STILL HAVE VALUE TO THEM.
IT'S A RITE OF PASSAGE. YOU'RE NOT ONE OF THEM UNTIL YOU'VE GOT THE RING. YOU DON'T GET THE RING UNTIL YOU KILL ONE OF THE GANG'S ENEMIES. IT'S NOT THE KIND OF THING YOU LOSE--NOT THE KIND OF THING YOU LEAVE BEHIND.
MY GUESS? IN THE CARNAGE OF THE FIGHT IT SLIPS OFF. ENDS UP ON THE FLOOR WHILE THEY'RE GOING AT IT. BY THE TIME HE MAKES--
BY THE TIME HE KILLS JACOSTA HE'S PANICKING. AFRAID. MAYBE SOMEONE HEARD THEM FIGHTING. SAW THEM RUNNING UP THE STAIRS. HE LEAVES WITHOUT GRABBING IT--THROUGH THE WINDOW.
WHOEVER IT IS...

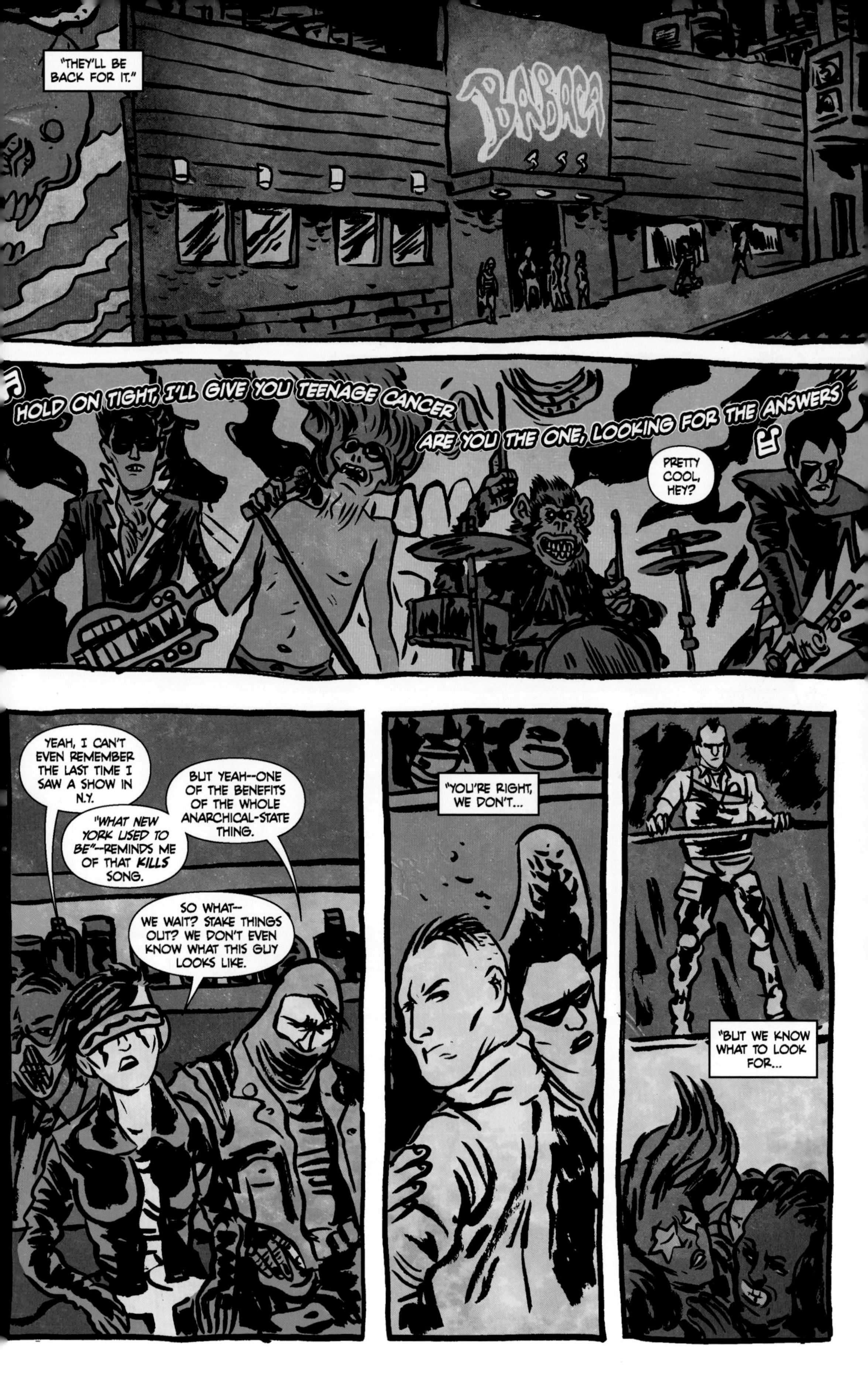
"THEY'LL BE BACK FOR IT."
HOLD ON TIGHT, I'LL GIVE YOU TEENAGE CANCER
ARE YOU THE ONE, LOOKING FOR THE ANSWERS
PRETTY COOL, HEY?
YEAH, I CAN'T EVEN REMEMBER THE LAST TIME I SAW A SHOW IN N.Y.
"WHAT NEW YORK USED TO BE"--REMINDS ME OF THAT KILLS SONG.
BUT YEAH--ONE OF THE BENEFITS OF THE WHOLE ANARCHICAL-STATE THING.
SO WHAT-- WE WAIT? STAKE THINGS OUT? WE DON'T EVEN KNOW WHAT THIS GUY LOOKS LIKE.
"YOU'RE RIGHT, WE DON'T...
"BUT WE KNOW WHAT TO LOOK FOR...

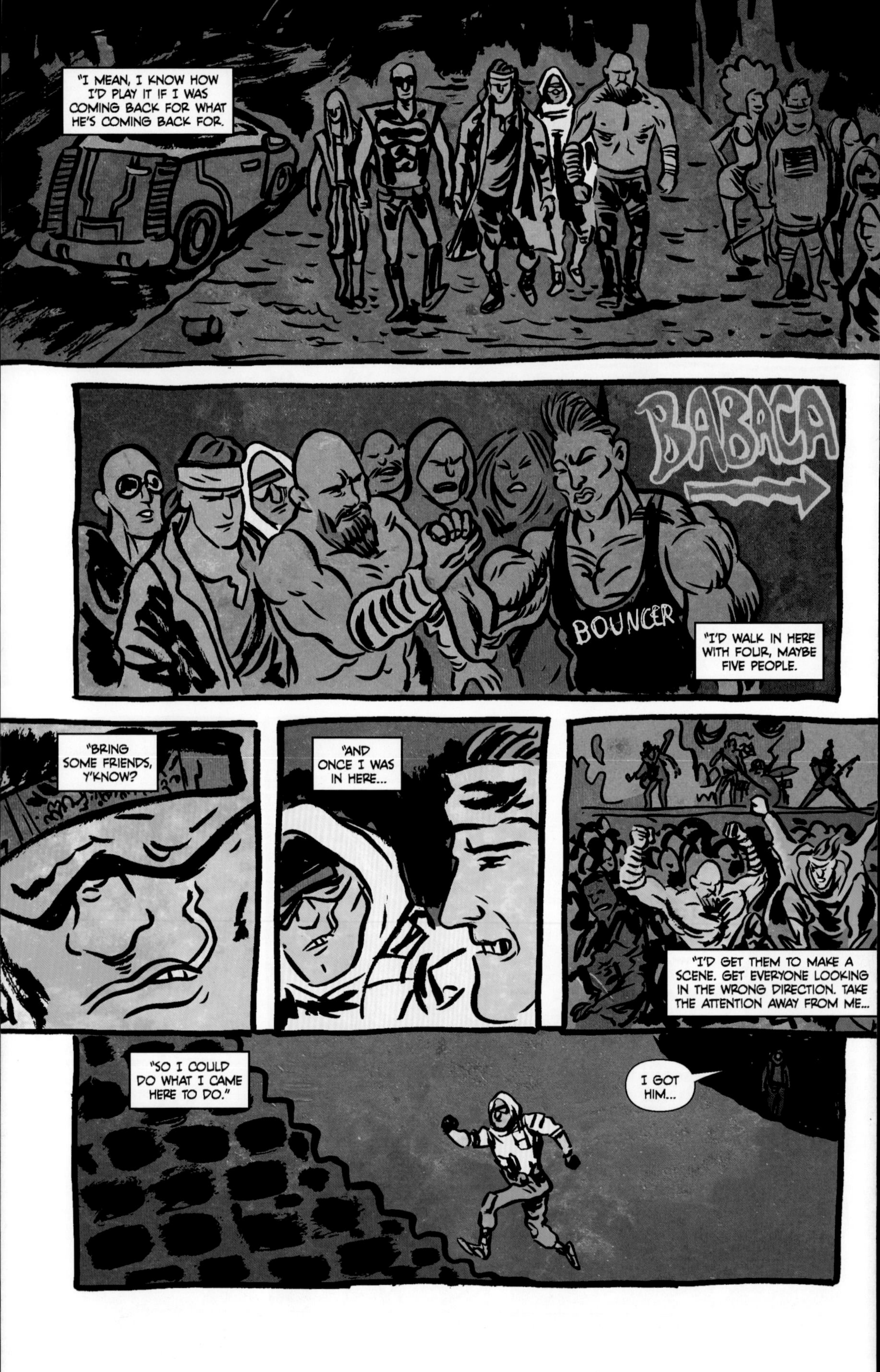
"I MEAN, I KNOW HOW I'D PLAY IT IF I WAS COMING BACK FOR WHAT HE'S COMING BACK FOR.
BABACA
BOUNCER
"I'D WALK IN HERE WITH FOUR, MAYBE FIVE PEOPLE.
"BRING SOME FRIENDS, Y'KNOW?
"AND ONCE I WAS IN HERE...
"I'D GET THEM TO MAKE A SCENE. GET EVERYONE LOOKING IN THE WRONG DIRECTION. TAKE THE ATTENTION AWAY FROM ME...
"SO I COULD DO WHAT I CAME HERE TO DO."
I GOT HIM...

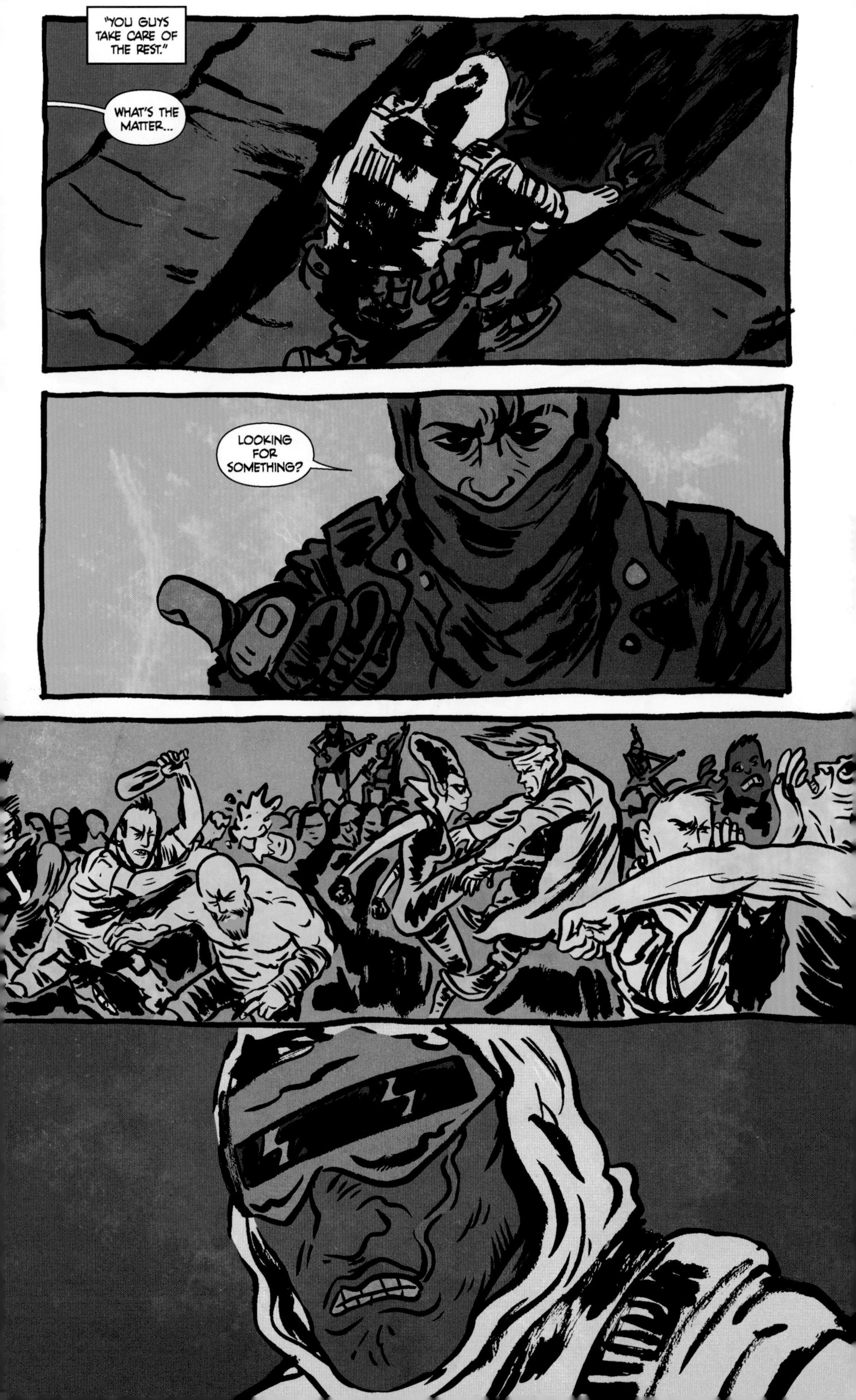
"YOU GUYS TAKE CARE OF THE REST."
WHAT'S THE MATTER...
LOOKING FOR SOMETHING?

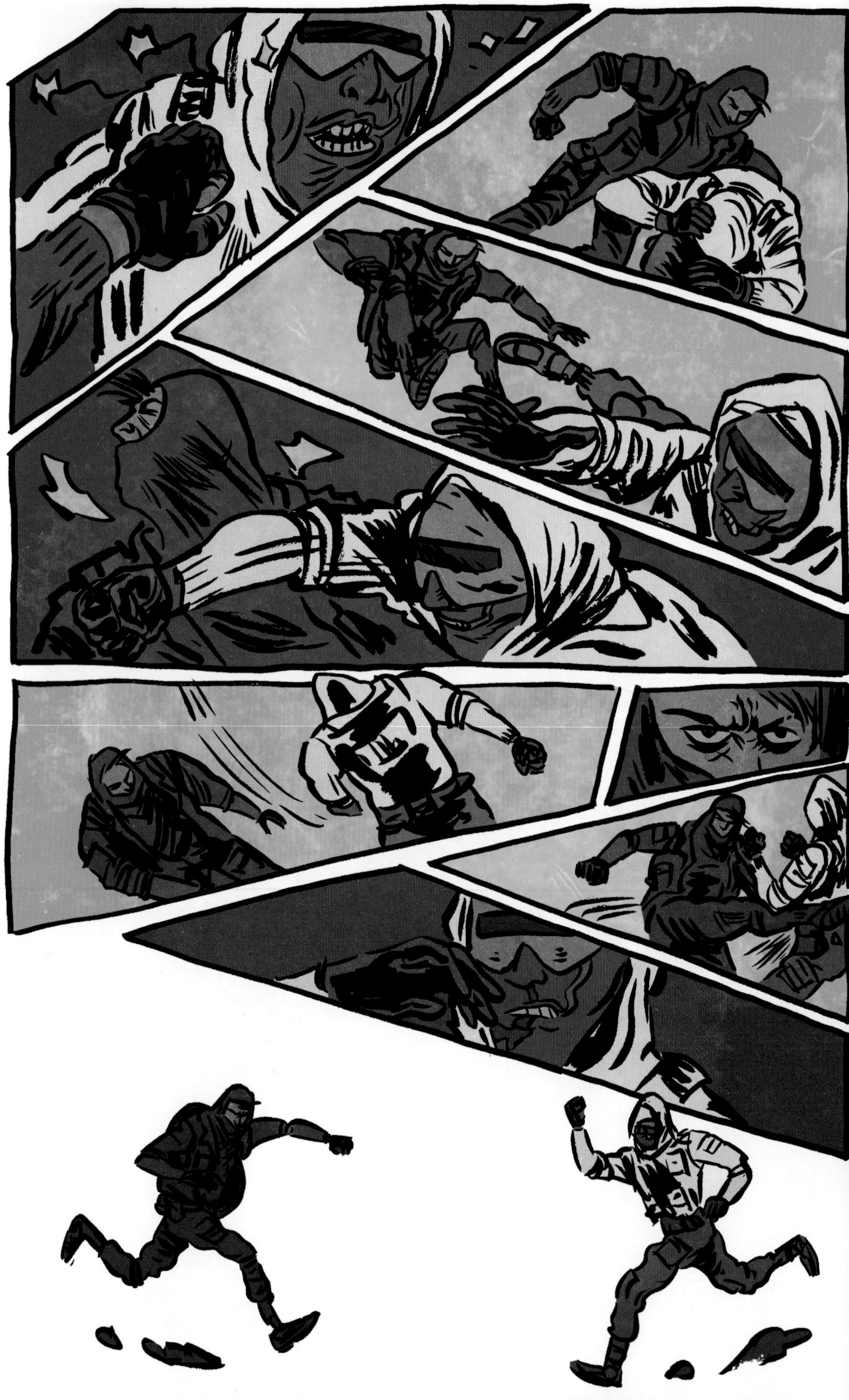

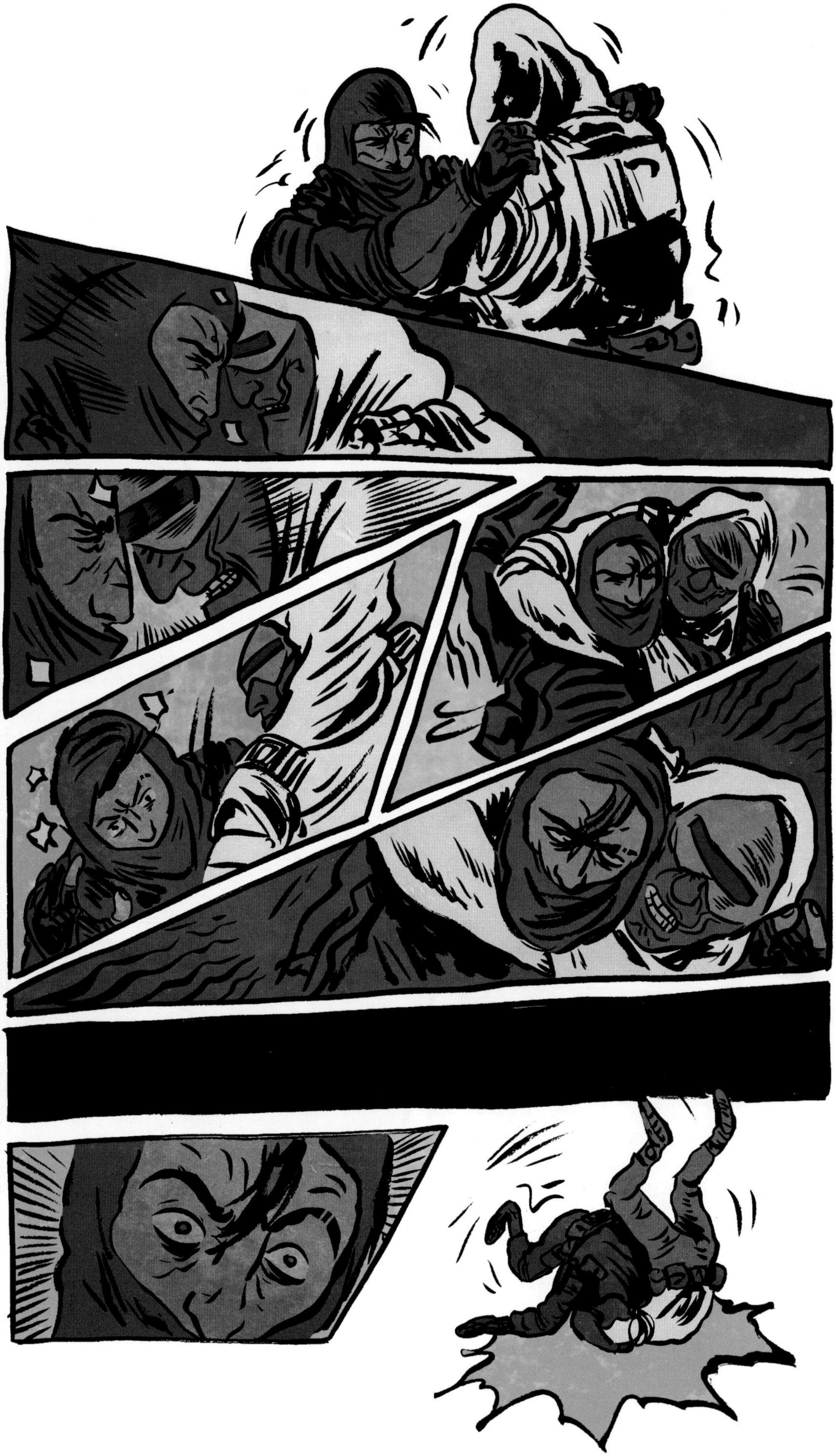

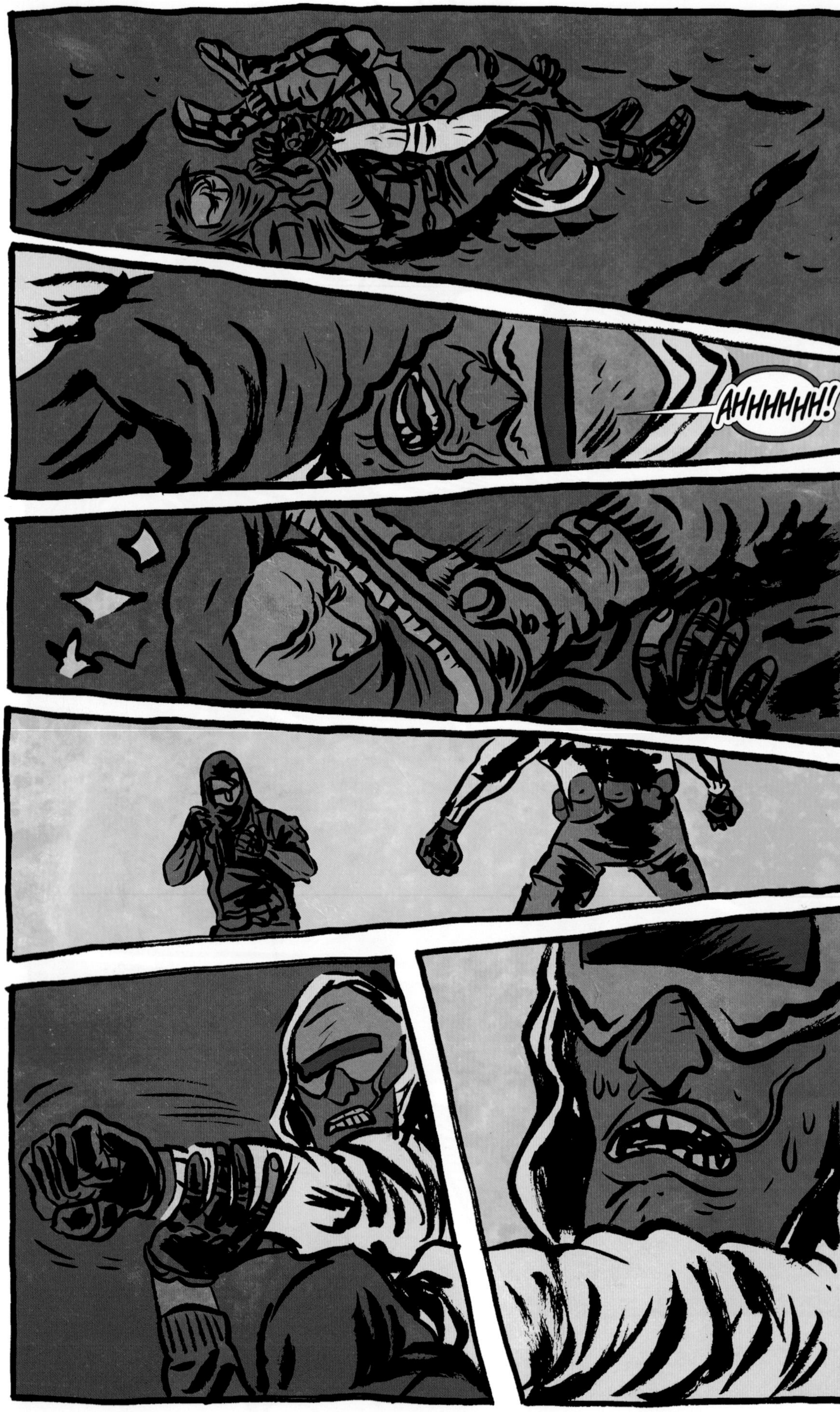
AHHHHHH!

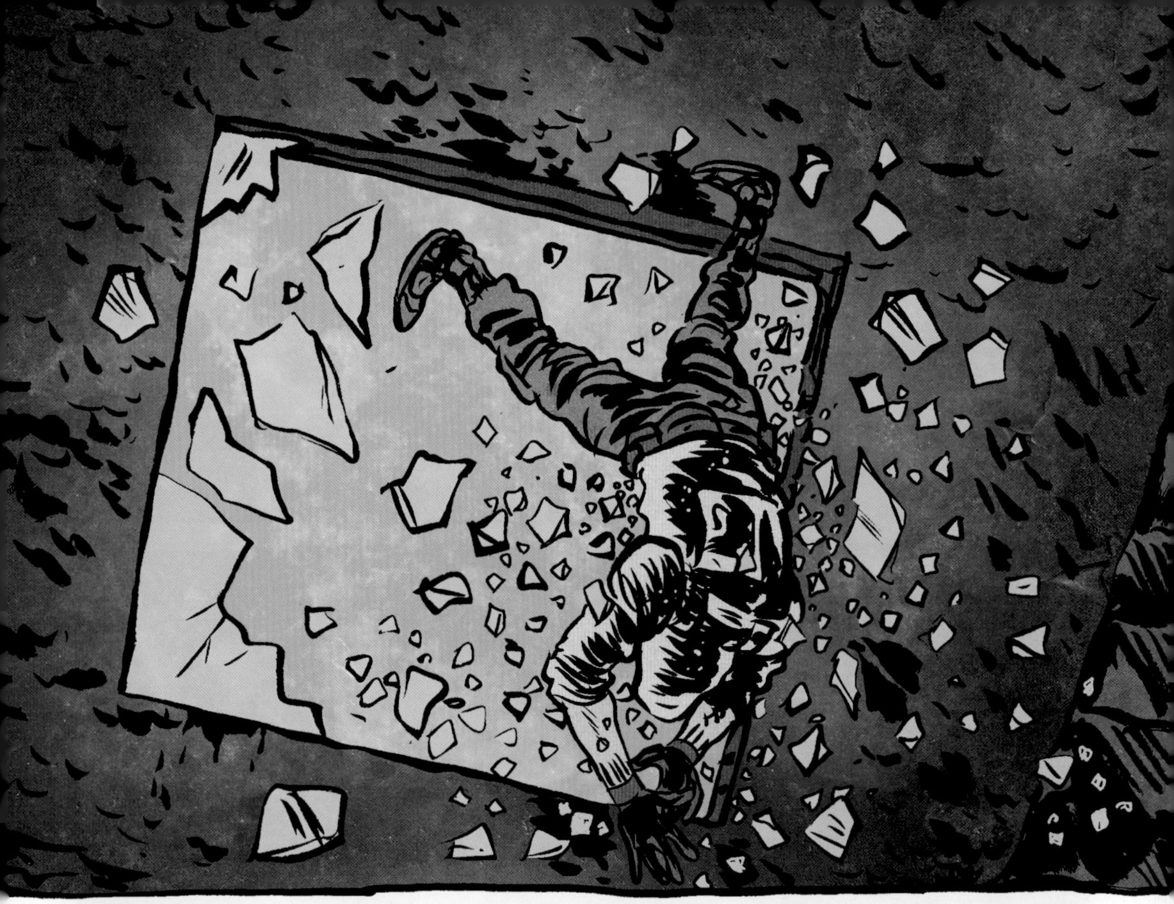

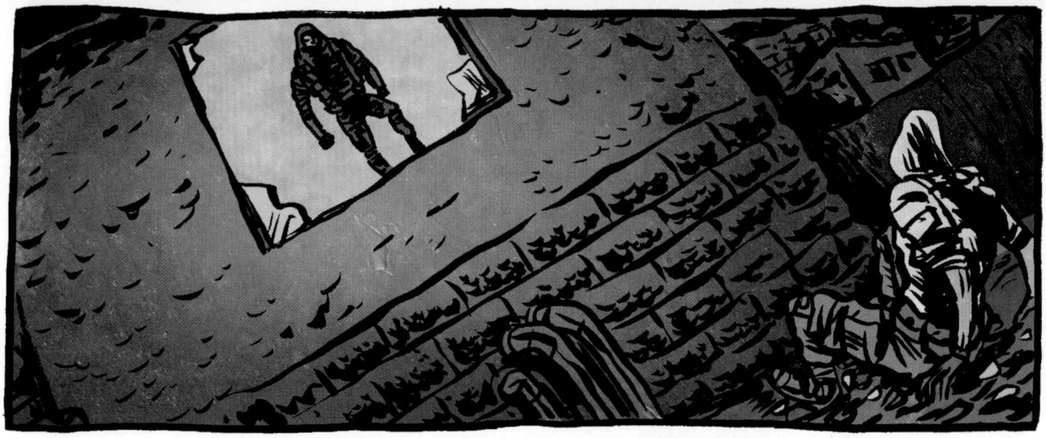

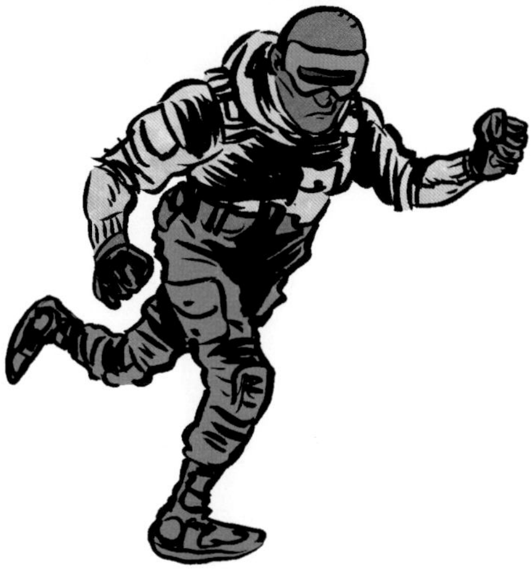

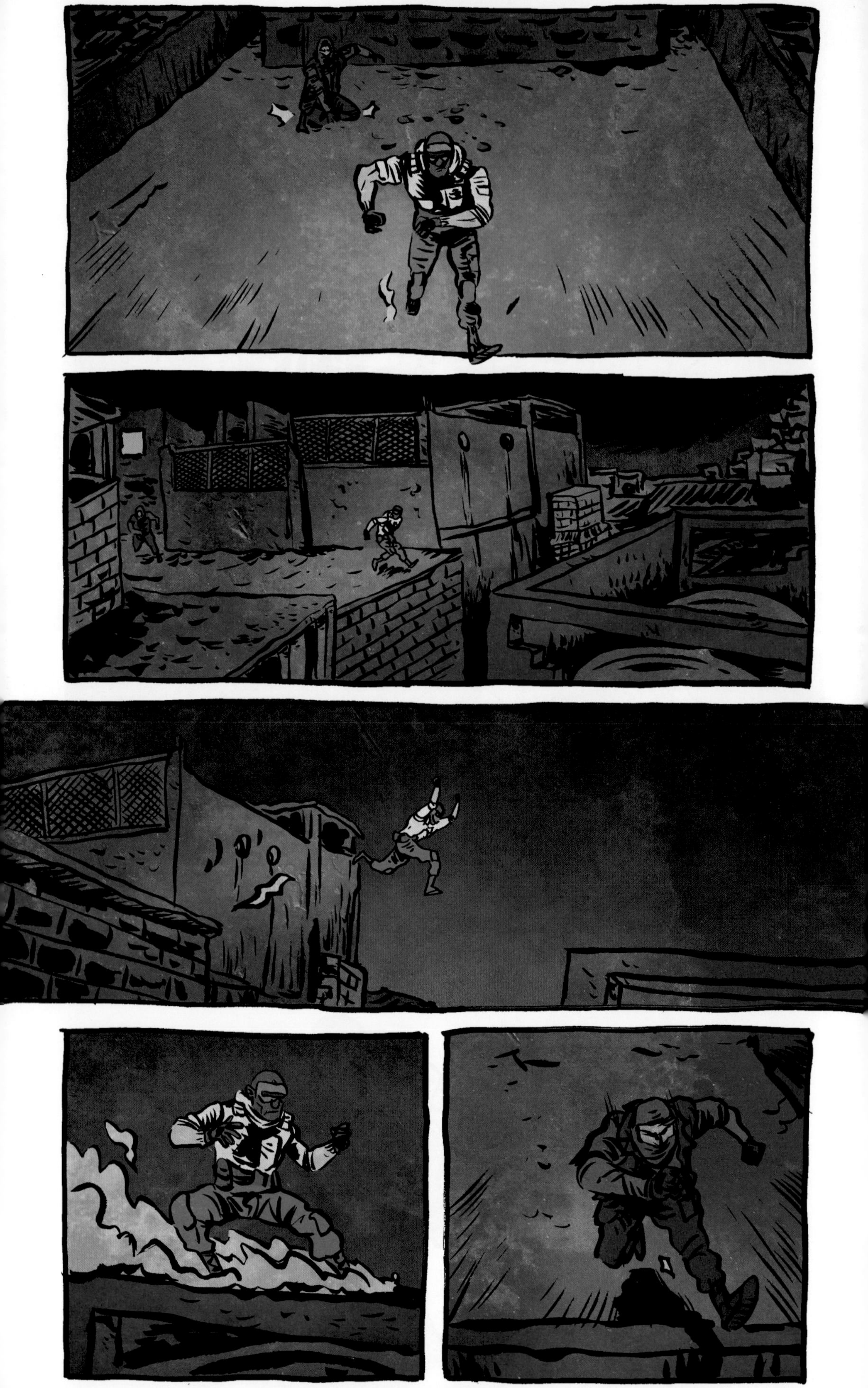

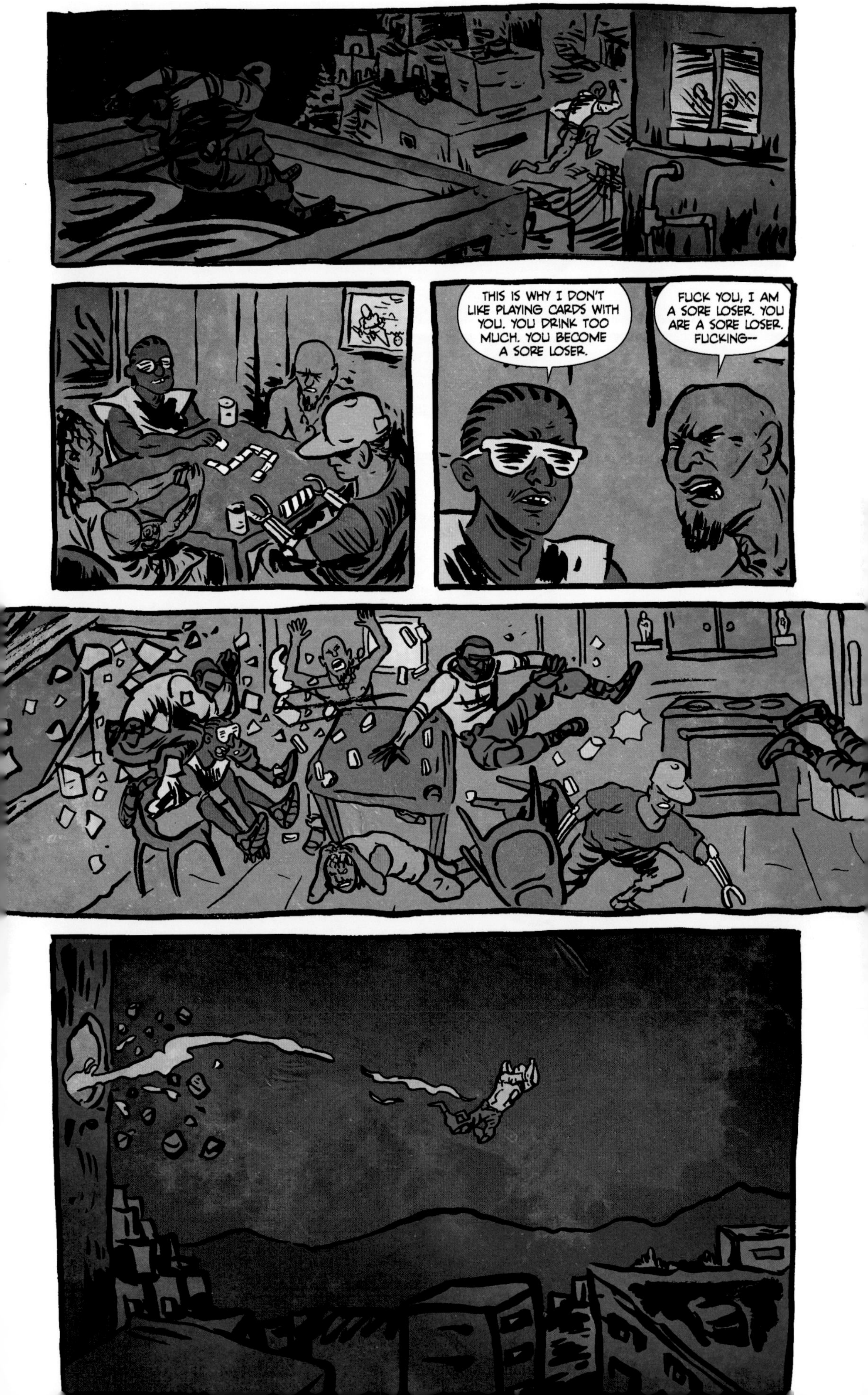
THIS IS WHY I DON'T LIKE PLAYING CARDS WITH YOU. YOU DRINK TOO MUCH. YOU BECOME A SORE LOSER.
FUCK YOU, I AM A SORE LOSER. YOU ARE A SORE LOSER. FUCKING--

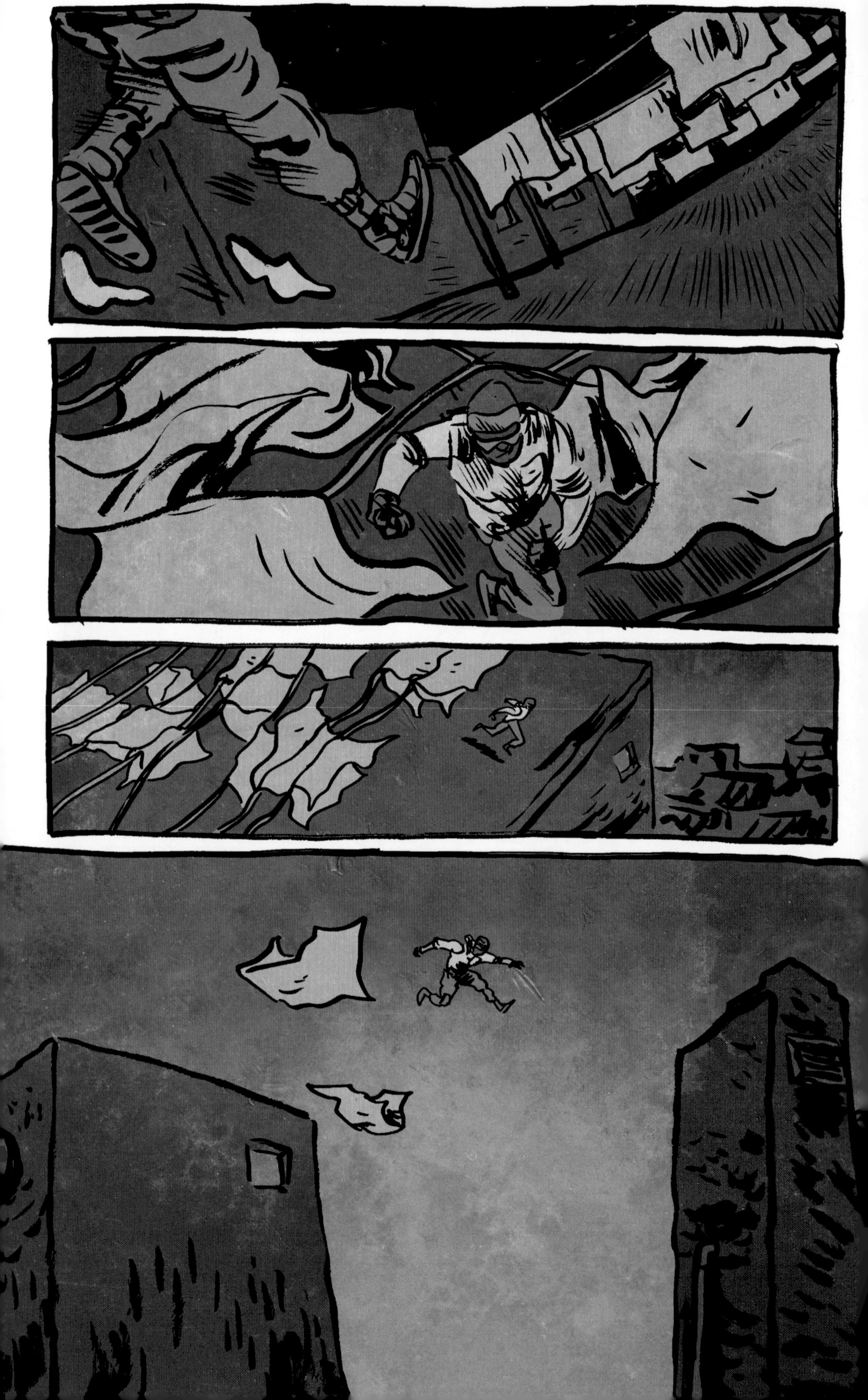

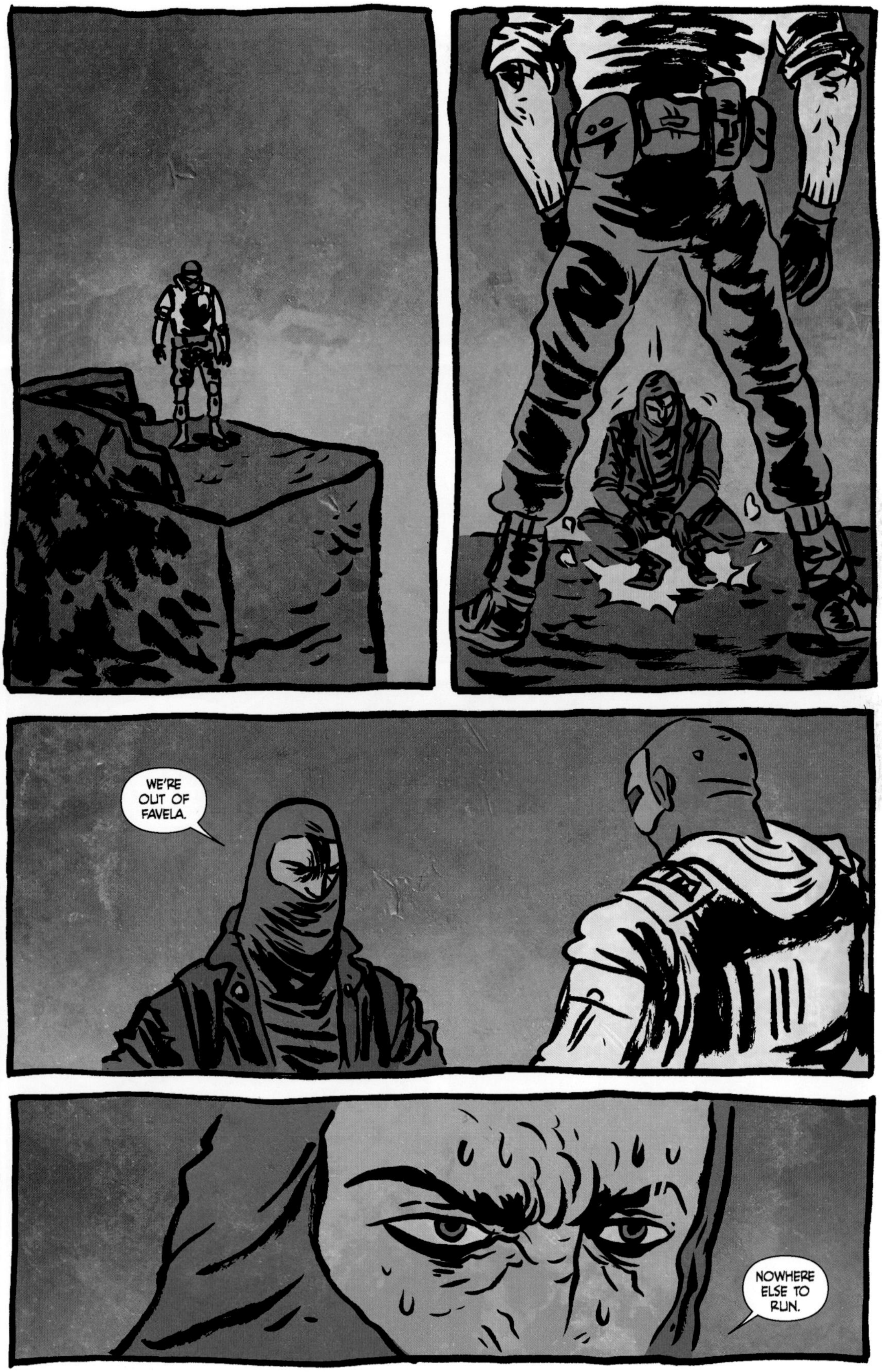
WE'RE OUT OF FAVELA.
NOWHERE ELSE TO RUN.

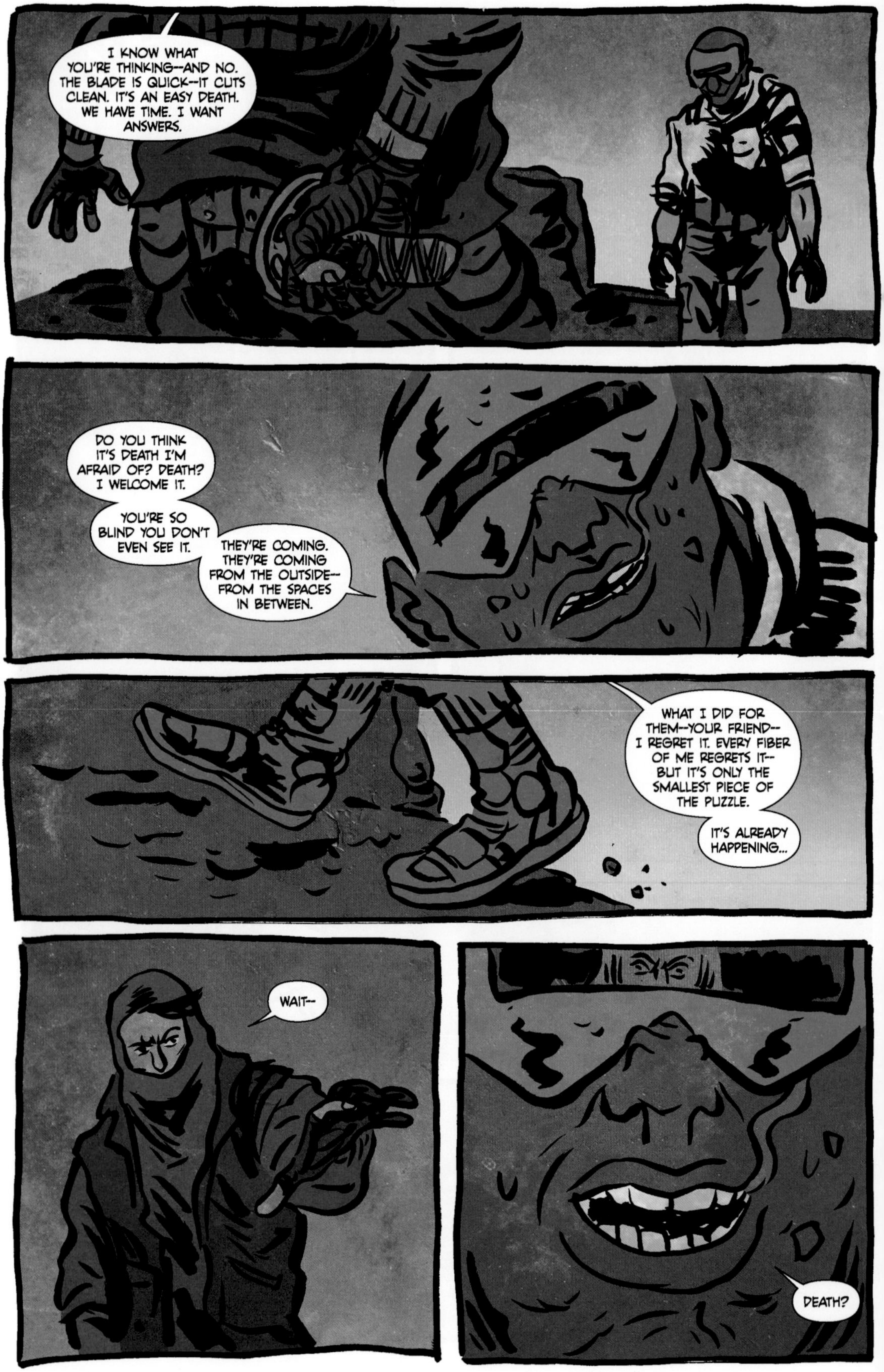
I KNOW WHAT YOU'RE THINKING--AND NO. THE BLADE IS QUICK--IT CUTS CLEAN. IT'S AN EASY DEATH. WE HAVE TIME. I WANT ANSWERS.
DO YOU THINK IT'S DEATH I'M AFRAID OF? DEATH? I WELCOME IT.
YOU'RE SO BLIND YOU DON'T EVEN SEE IT.
THEY'RE COMING. THEY'RE COMING FROM THE OUTSIDE-- FROM THE SPACES IN BETWEEN.
WHAT I DID FOR THEM--YOUR FRIEND-- I REGRET IT. EVERY FIBER OF ME REGRETS IT-- BUT IT'S ONLY THE SMALLEST PIECE OF THE PUZZLE.
IT'S ALREADY HAPPENING...
WAIT--
DEATH?

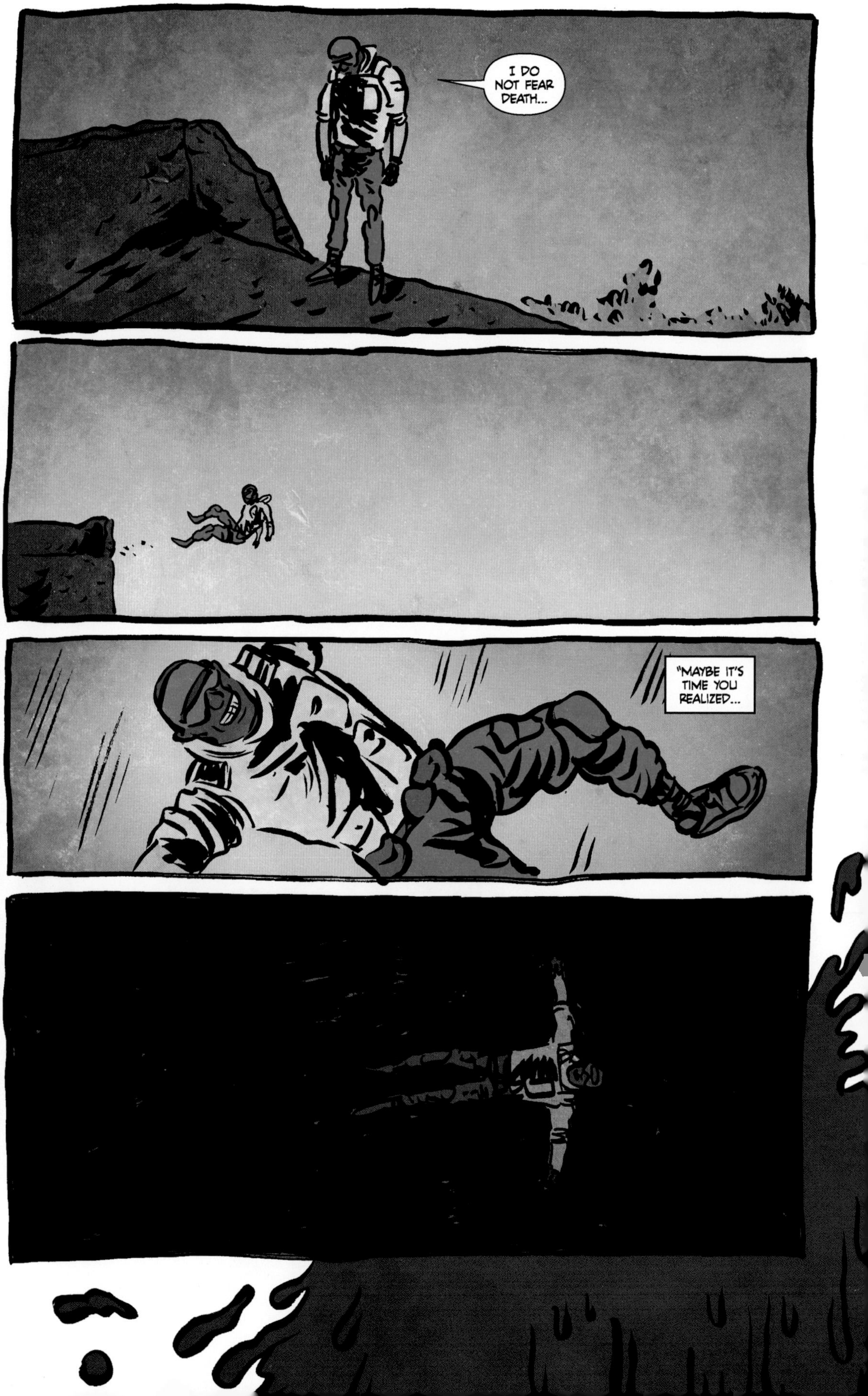
I DO NOT FEAR DEATH...
"MAYBE IT'S TIME YOU REALIZED...

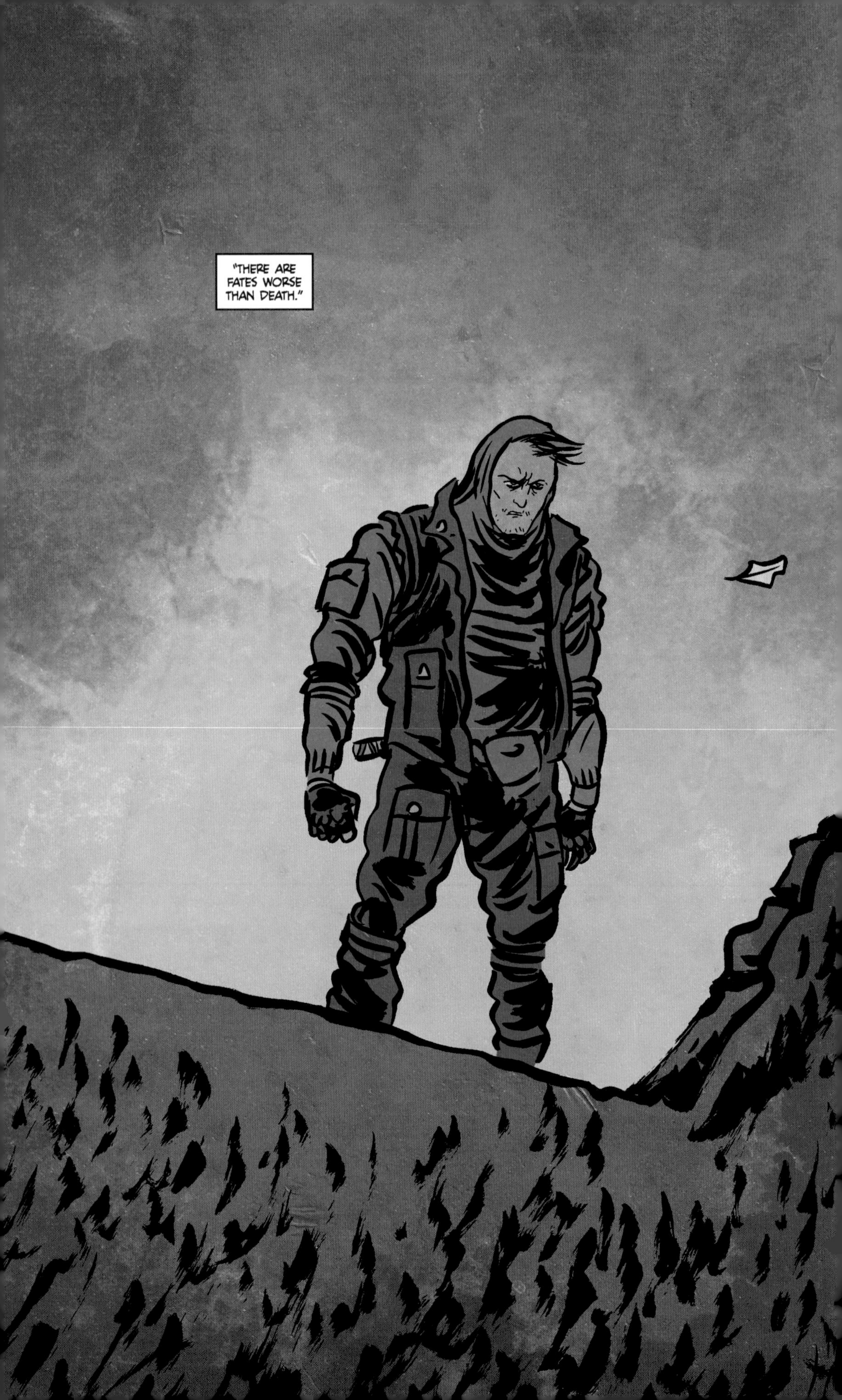
"THERE ARE FATES WORSE THAN DEATH."

**UEDA:** >> I DON'T UNDERSTAND.

**???:** >> IT'S NOT ABOUT UNDERSTANDING. IT'S ABOUT OBEDIENCE—SUBSERVIENCE, DOING WHAT IS NEEDED FOR THE REALIZATION OF A VISION.

>> THE APP—IS IT READY?

**UEDA:** >> IT'S READY. WE SLOW ROLLED IT OUT, TESTING THE STRENGTH OF THE PROGRAMMING TO ENSURE EFFECTIVENESS. IT'LL WORK.

>> I STILL—I STILL DON'T UNDERSTAND...THIS. THE ASSASSINATION IN RIO. HOW DOES THIS FIT INTO THE ENDGAME?

**???:** >> YOU DON'T REALLY FIT INTO THE ENDGAME AT ALL. YOU'RE A DISRUPTIVE FORCE—A DISTRACTION TO KEEP THEM FROM LOOKING AT THE HORIZON AND SEEING WHAT'S REALLY COMING.

>> GOODBYE.

/// END Transmission. >>

/// part three

# RAINDROPS OVER TOKYO

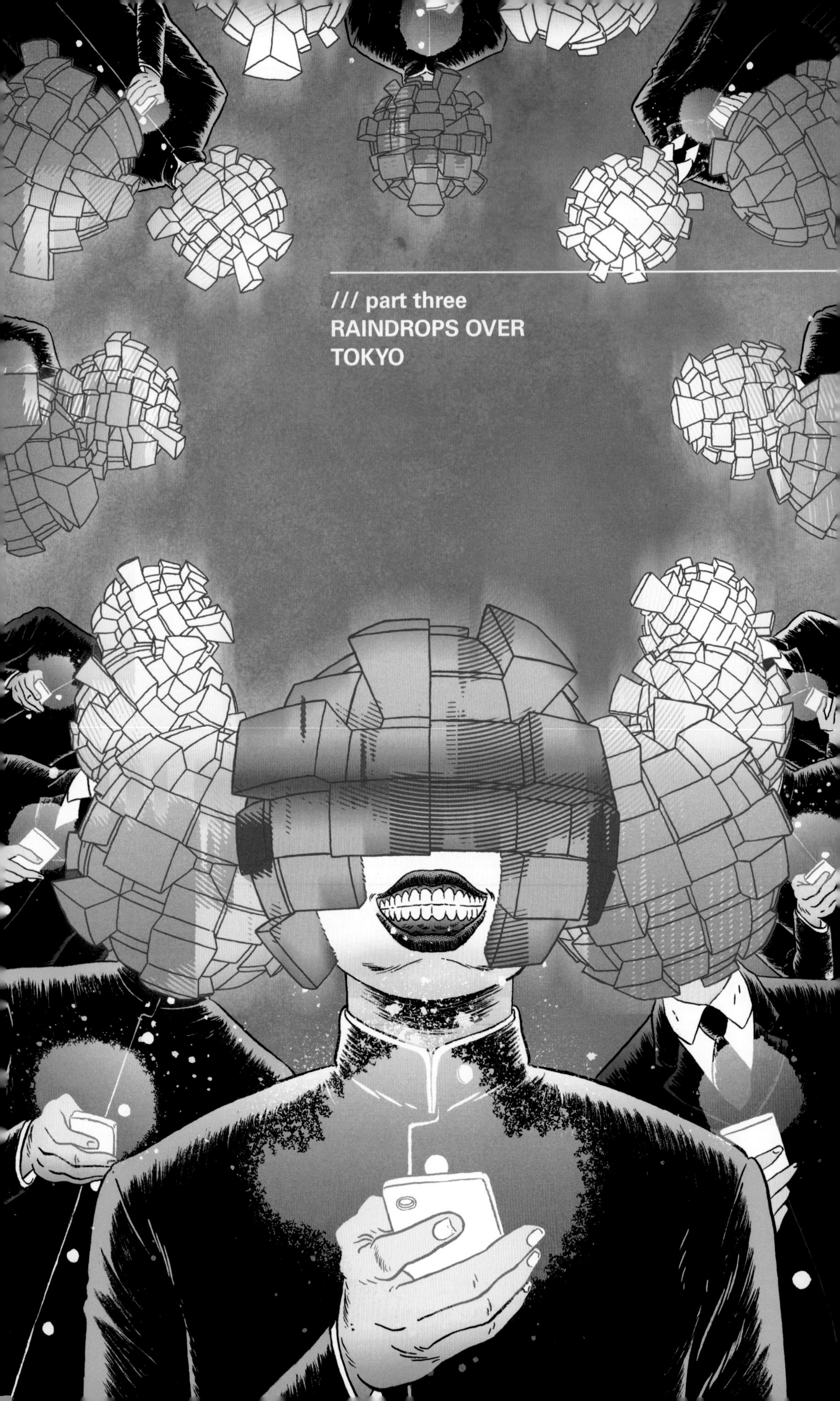

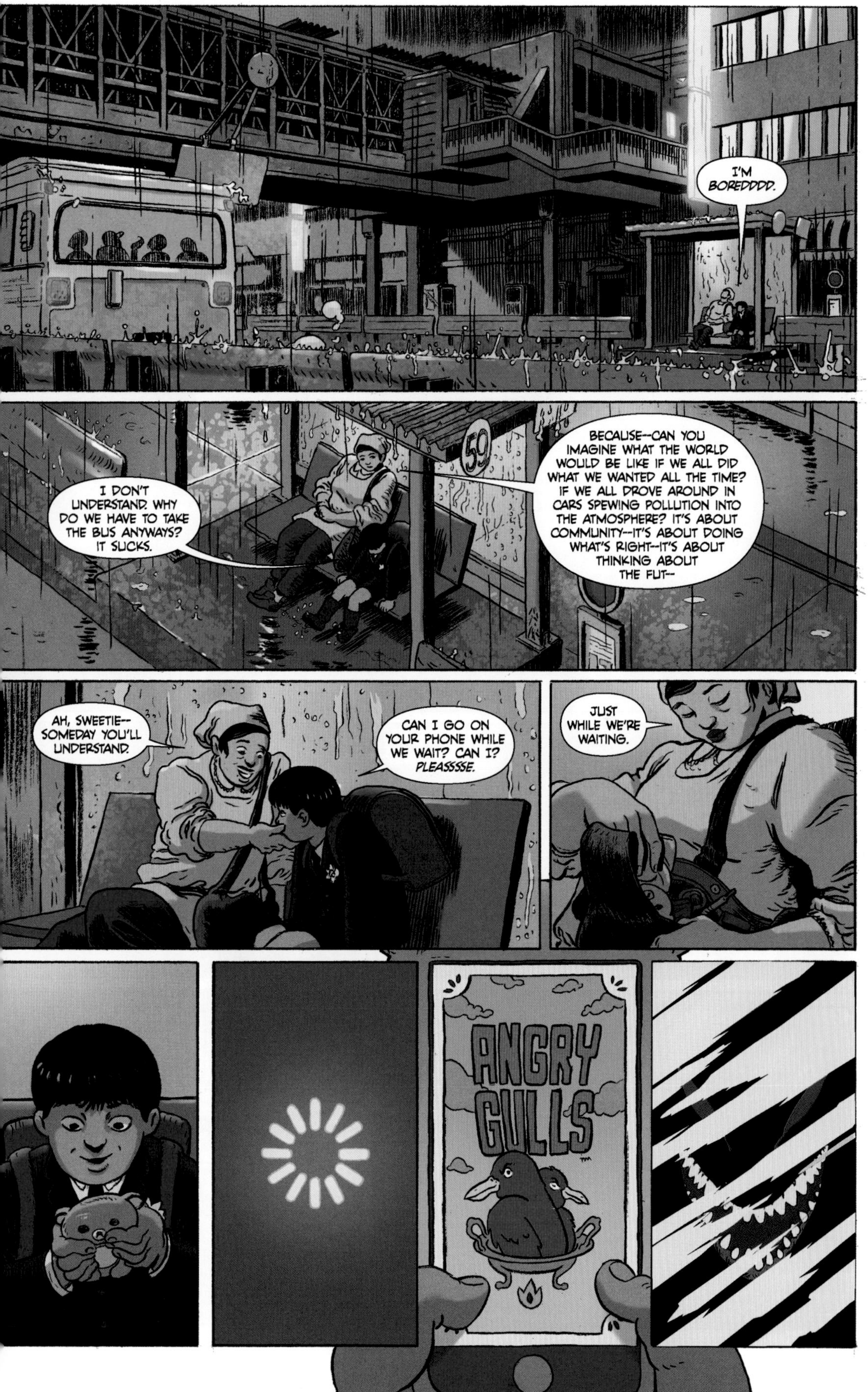
I'M BOREDDDD.
I DON'T UNDERSTAND. WHY DO WE HAVE TO TAKE THE BUS ANYWAYS? IT SUCKS.
BECAUSE--CAN YOU IMAGINE WHAT THE WORLD WOULD BE LIKE IF WE ALL DID WHAT WE WANTED ALL THE TIME? IF WE ALL DROVE AROUND IN CARS SPEWING POLLUTION INTO THE ATMOSPHERE? IT'S ABOUT COMMUNITY--IT'S ABOUT DOING WHAT'S RIGHT--IT'S ABOUT THINKING ABOUT THE FUT--
AH, SWEETIE-- SOMEDAY YOU'LL UNDERSTAND.
CAN I GO ON YOUR PHONE WHILE WE WAIT? CAN I? *PLEASSSSE.*
JUST WHILE WE'RE WAITING.
ANGRY GULLS

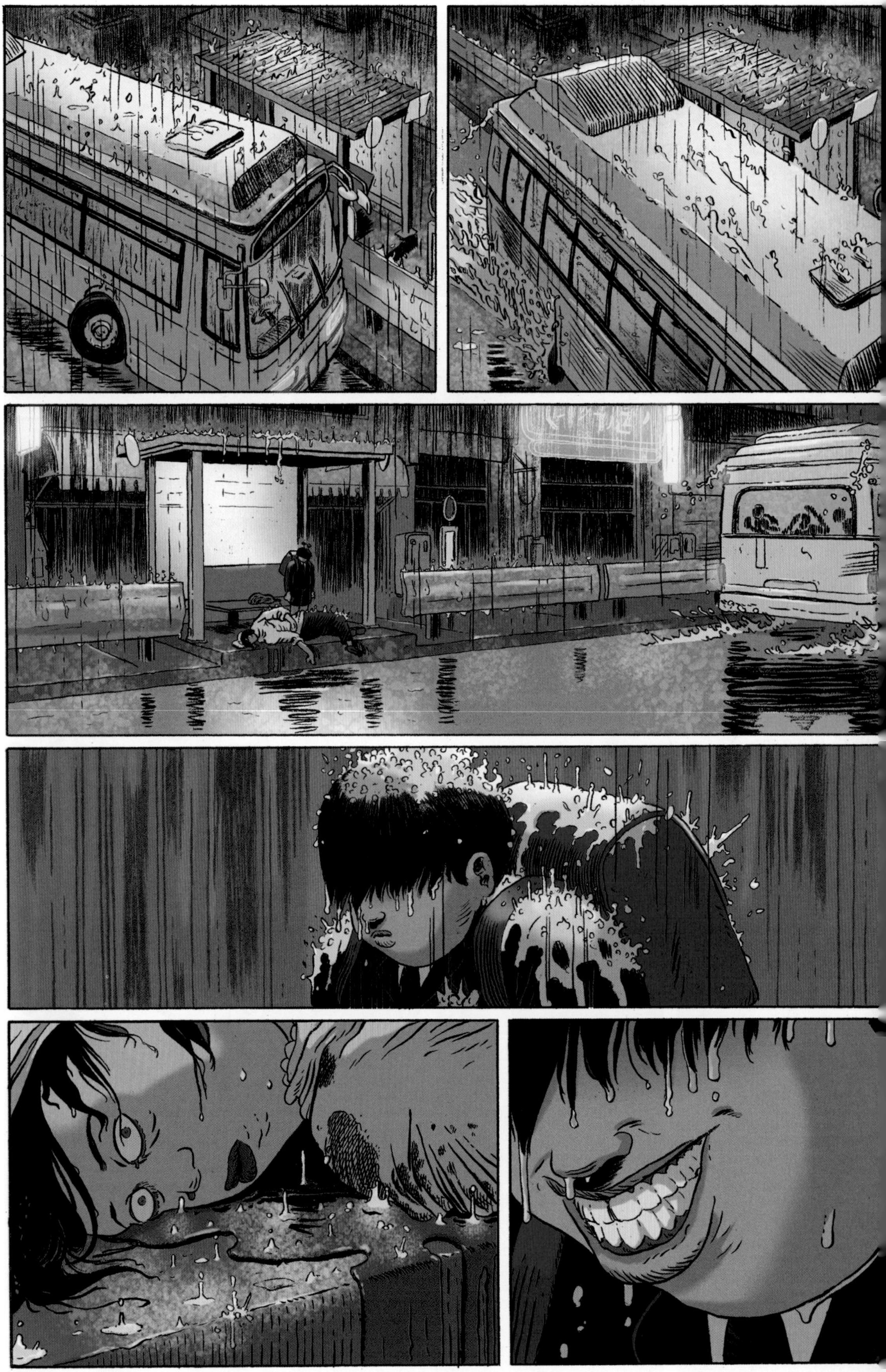

YOU'RE EARLY.

I'M NOT STAYING--JUST NEEDED TO TALK.

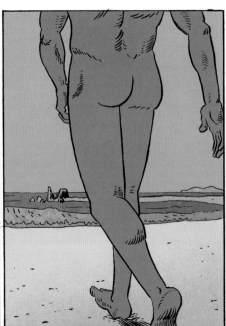

HERE, SIT. I JUST BREWED SOME TEA.

THE TEA IS GOOD. IT--IT'S THE SAME STUFF WE USED TO BREW. FROM THE MARKET. BAI HAO WHITE TIP.

GUILTY AS CHARGED...

NOW WHY DON'T YOU TELL ME...

WHY ARE YOU HERE?

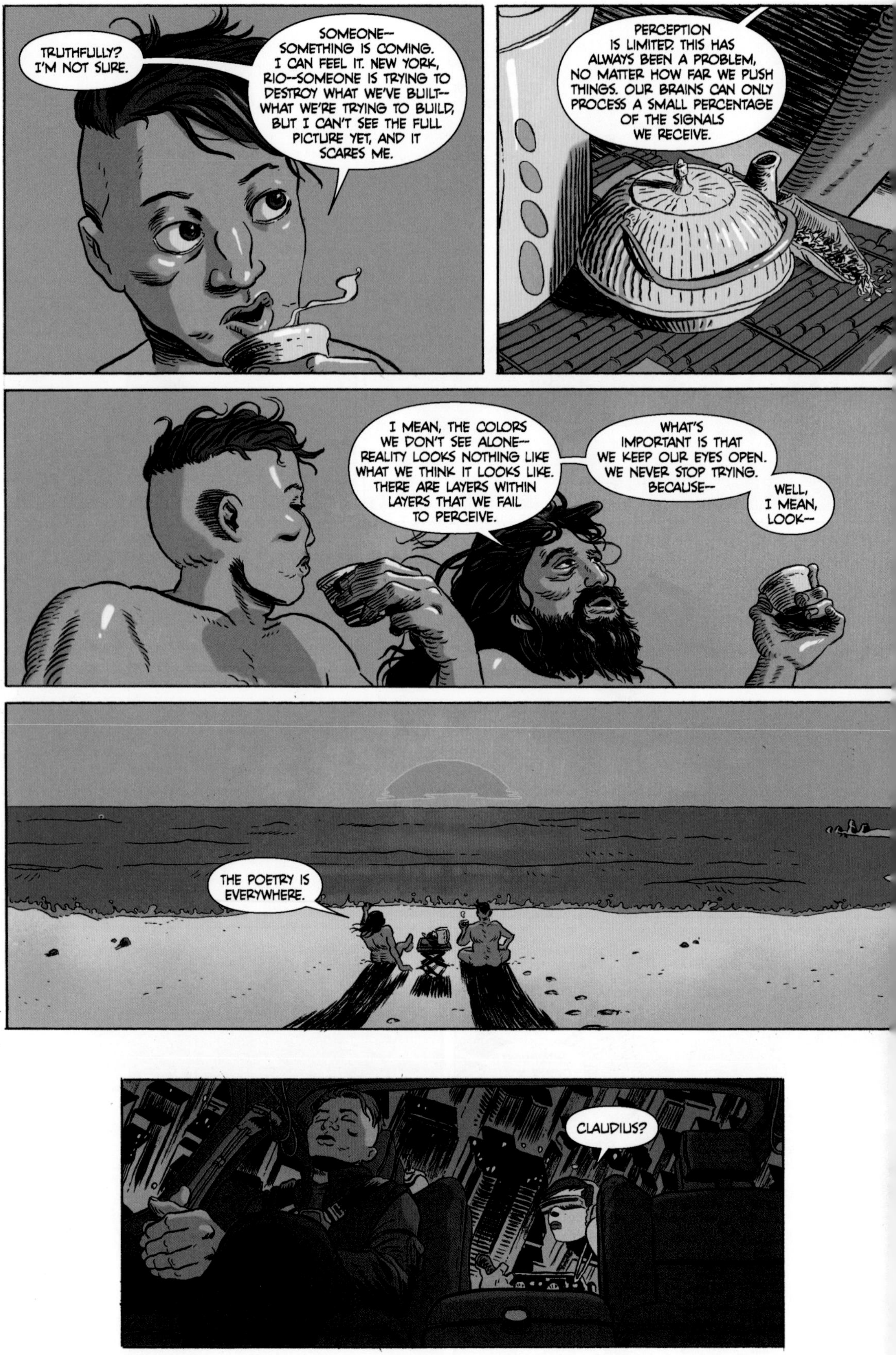
TRUTHFULLY? I'M NOT SURE.
SOMEONE-- SOMETHING IS COMING. I CAN FEEL IT. NEW YORK, RIO--SOMEONE IS TRYING TO DESTROY WHAT WE'VE BUILT-- WHAT WE'RE TRYING TO BUILD, BUT I CAN'T SEE THE FULL PICTURE YET, AND IT SCARES ME.
PERCEPTION IS LIMITED. THIS HAS ALWAYS BEEN A PROBLEM, NO MATTER HOW FAR WE PUSH THINGS. OUR BRAINS CAN ONLY PROCESS A SMALL PERCENTAGE OF THE SIGNALS WE RECEIVE.
I MEAN, THE COLORS WE DON'T SEE ALONE-- REALITY LOOKS NOTHING LIKE WHAT WE THINK IT LOOKS LIKE. THERE ARE LAYERS WITHIN LAYERS THAT WE FAIL TO PERCEIVE.
WHAT'S IMPORTANT IS THAT WE KEEP OUR EYES OPEN. WE NEVER STOP TRYING. BECAUSE--
WELL, I MEAN, LOOK--
THE POETRY IS EVERYWHERE.
CLAUDIUS?

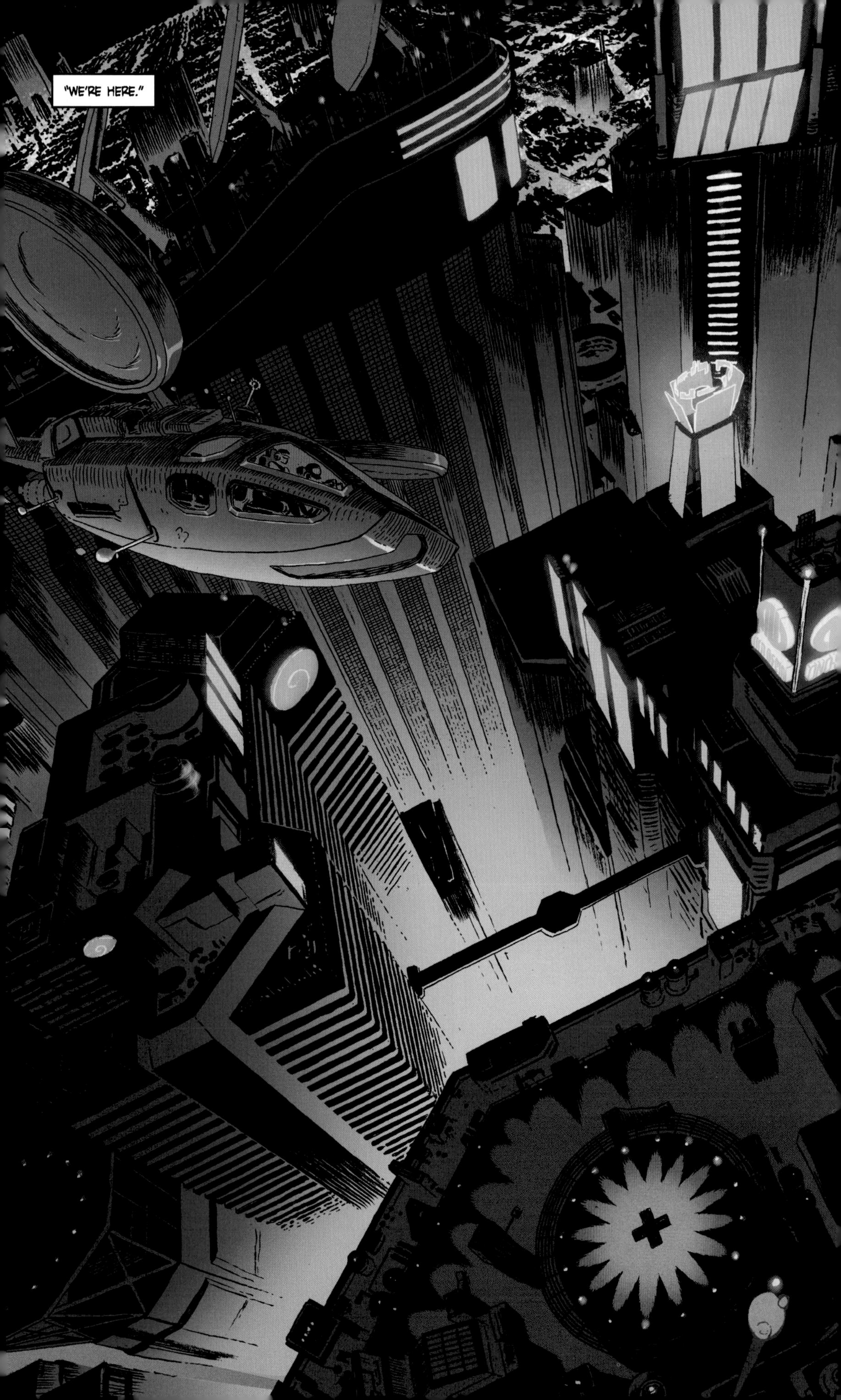
"WE'RE HERE."

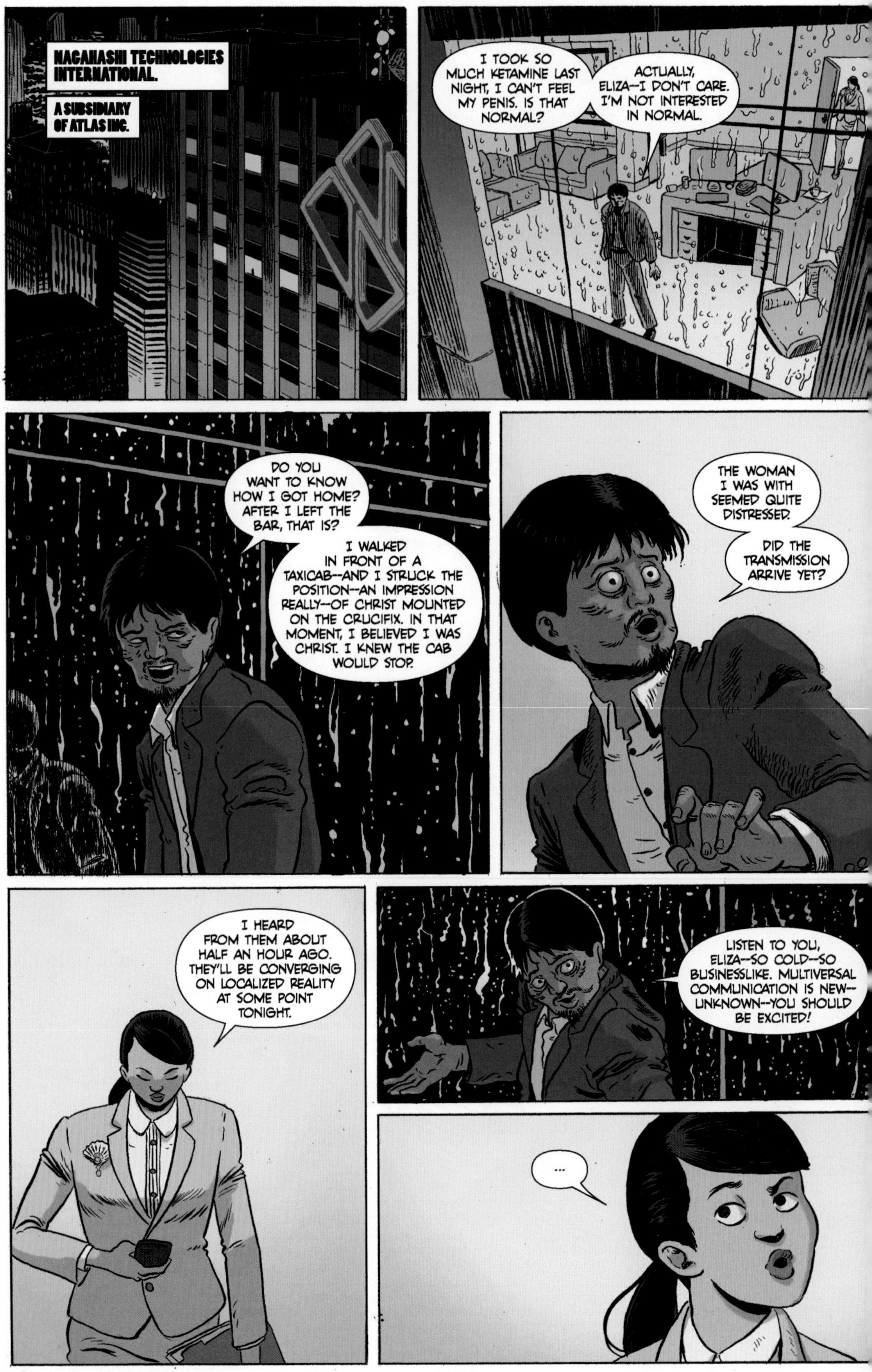
NAGAHASHI TECHNOLOGIES INTERNATIONAL.
A SUBSIDIARY OF ATLAS INC.
I TOOK SO MUCH KETAMINE LAST NIGHT, I CAN'T FEEL MY PENIS. IS THAT NORMAL?
ACTUALLY, ELIZA--I DON'T CARE. I'M NOT INTERESTED IN NORMAL.
DO YOU WANT TO KNOW HOW I GOT HOME? AFTER I LEFT THE BAR, THAT IS?
I WALKED IN FRONT OF A TAXICAB--AND I STRUCK THE POSITION--AN IMPRESSION REALLY--OF CHRIST MOUNTED ON THE CRUCIFIX. IN THAT MOMENT, I BELIEVED I WAS CHRIST. I KNEW THE CAB WOULD STOP.
THE WOMAN I WAS WITH SEEMED QUITE DISTRESSED.
DID THE TRANSMISSION ARRIVE YET?
I HEARD FROM THEM ABOUT HALF AN HOUR AGO. THEY'LL BE CONVERGING ON LOCALIZED REALITY AT SOME POINT TONIGHT.
LISTEN TO YOU, ELIZA--SO COLD--SO BUSINESSLIKE. MULTIVERSAL COMMUNICATION IS NEW--UNKNOWN--YOU SHOULD BE EXCITED!
...

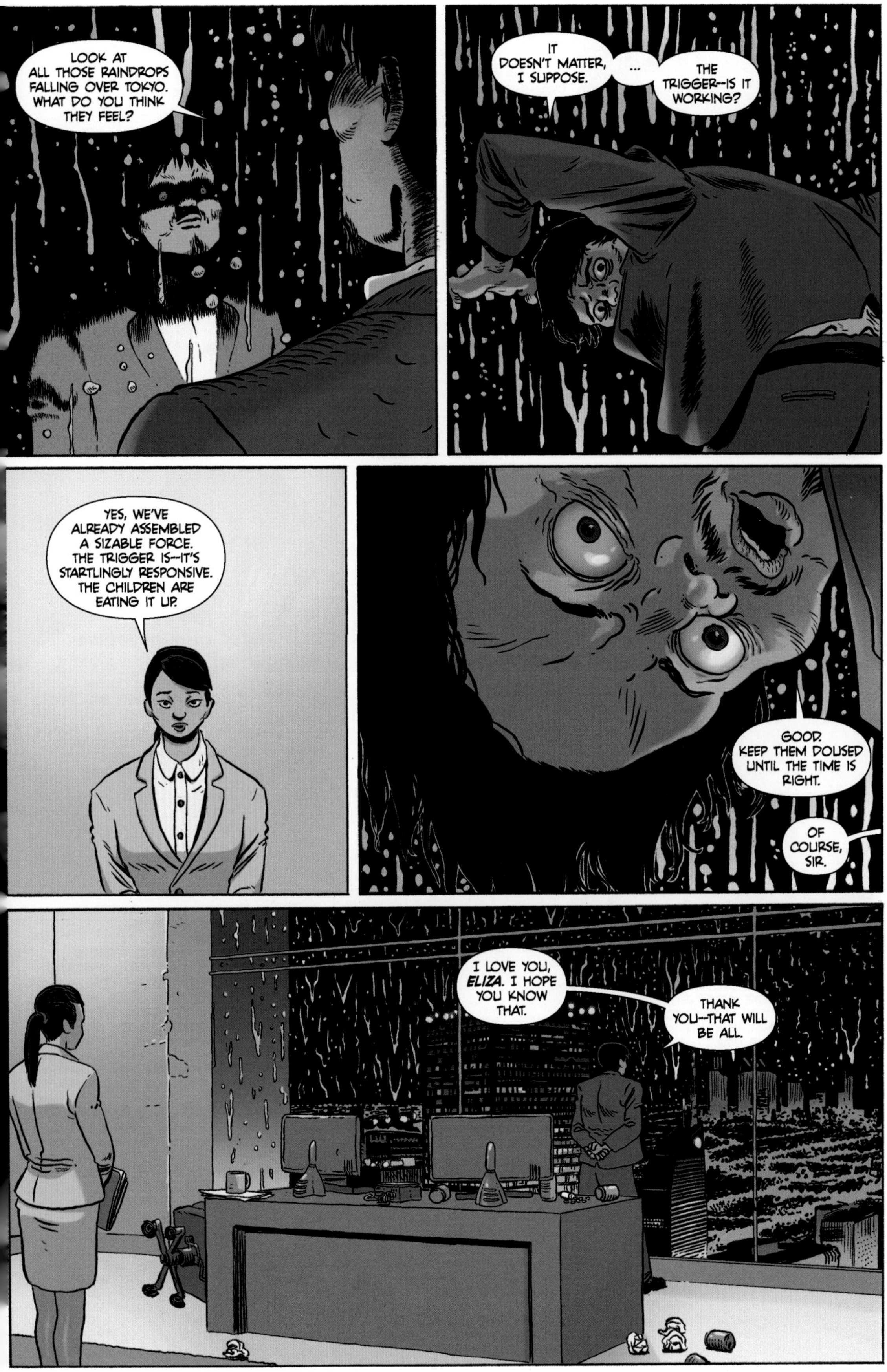
LOOK AT ALL THOSE RAINDROPS FALLING OVER TOKYO. WHAT DO YOU THINK THEY FEEL?
IT DOESN'T MATTER, I SUPPOSE.
...
THE TRIGGER--IS IT WORKING?
YES, WE'VE ALREADY ASSEMBLED A SIZABLE FORCE. THE TRIGGER IS--IT'S STARTLINGLY RESPONSIVE. THE CHILDREN ARE EATING IT UP.
GOOD. KEEP THEM DOUSED UNTIL THE TIME IS RIGHT.
OF COURSE, SIR.
I LOVE YOU, ELIZA. I HOPE YOU KNOW THAT.
THANK YOU--THAT WILL BE ALL.

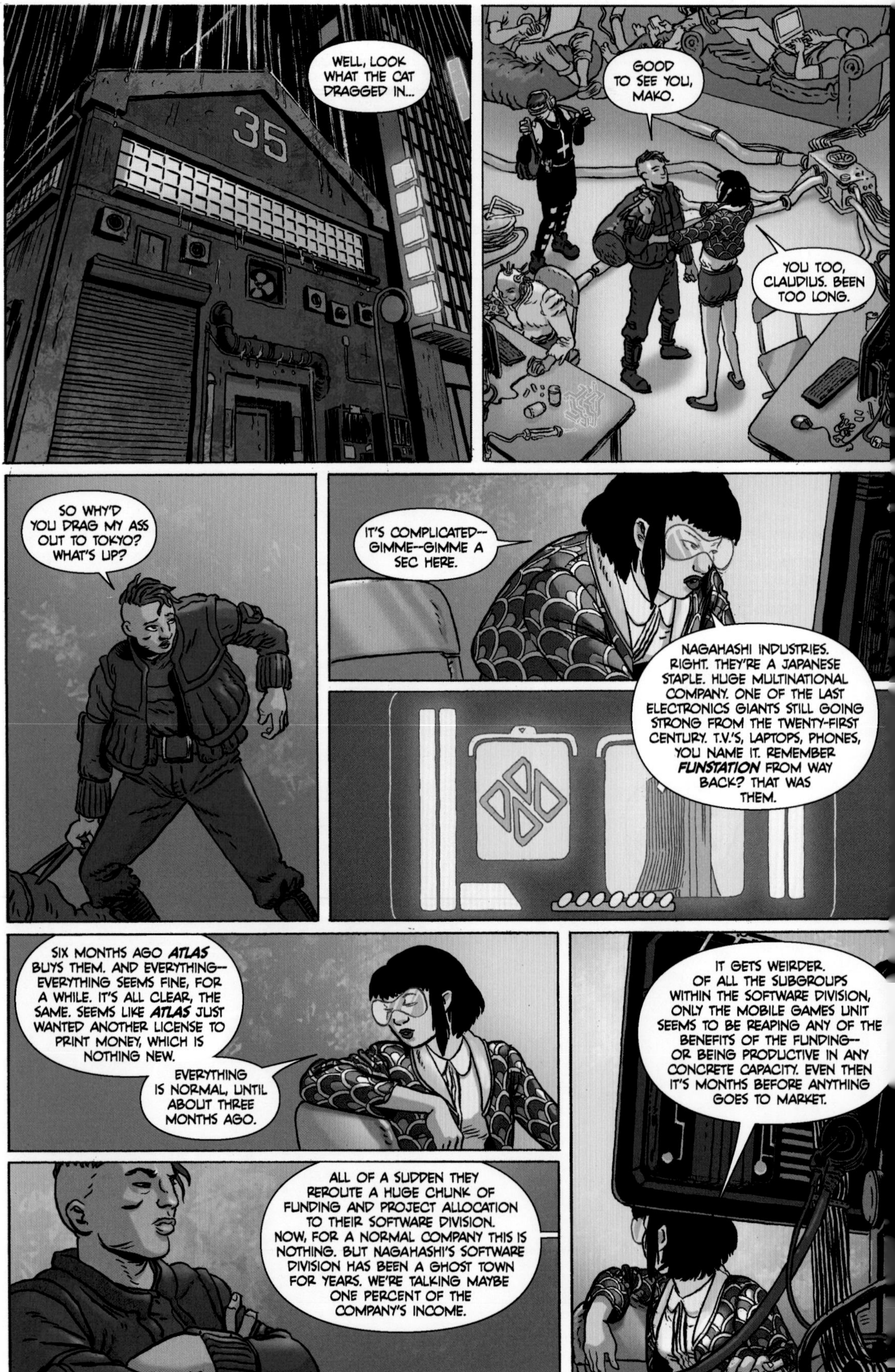
WELL, LOOK WHAT THE CAT DRAGGED IN...
35
GOOD TO SEE YOU, MAKO.
YOU TOO, CLAUDIUS. BEEN TOO LONG.
SO WHY'D YOU DRAG MY ASS OUT TO TOKYO? WHAT'S UP?
IT'S COMPLICATED-- GIMME--GIMME A SEC HERE.
NAGAHASHI INDUSTRIES. RIGHT. THEY'RE A JAPANESE STAPLE. HUGE MULTINATIONAL COMPANY. ONE OF THE LAST ELECTRONICS GIANTS STILL GOING STRONG FROM THE TWENTY-FIRST CENTURY. T.V.'S, LAPTOPS, PHONES, YOU NAME IT. REMEMBER ***FUNSTATION*** FROM WAY BACK? THAT WAS THEM.
SIX MONTHS AGO ***ATLAS*** BUYS THEM. AND EVERYTHING-- EVERYTHING SEEMS FINE, FOR A WHILE. IT'S ALL CLEAR, THE SAME. SEEMS LIKE ***ATLAS*** JUST WANTED ANOTHER LICENSE TO PRINT MONEY, WHICH IS NOTHING NEW.
EVERYTHING IS NORMAL, UNTIL ABOUT THREE MONTHS AGO.
IT GETS WEIRDER. OF ALL THE SUBGROUPS WITHIN THE SOFTWARE DIVISION, ONLY THE MOBILE GAMES UNIT SEEMS TO BE REAPING ANY OF THE BENEFITS OF THE FUNDING-- OR BEING PRODUCTIVE IN ANY CONCRETE CAPACITY. EVEN THEN IT'S MONTHS BEFORE ANYTHING GOES TO MARKET.
ALL OF A SUDDEN THEY REROUTE A HUGE CHUNK OF FUNDING AND PROJECT ALLOCATION TO THEIR SOFTWARE DIVISION. NOW, FOR A NORMAL COMPANY THIS IS NOTHING. BUT NAGAHASHI'S SOFTWARE DIVISION HAS BEEN A GHOST TOWN FOR YEARS. WE'RE TALKING MAYBE ONE PERCENT OF THE COMPANY'S INCOME.

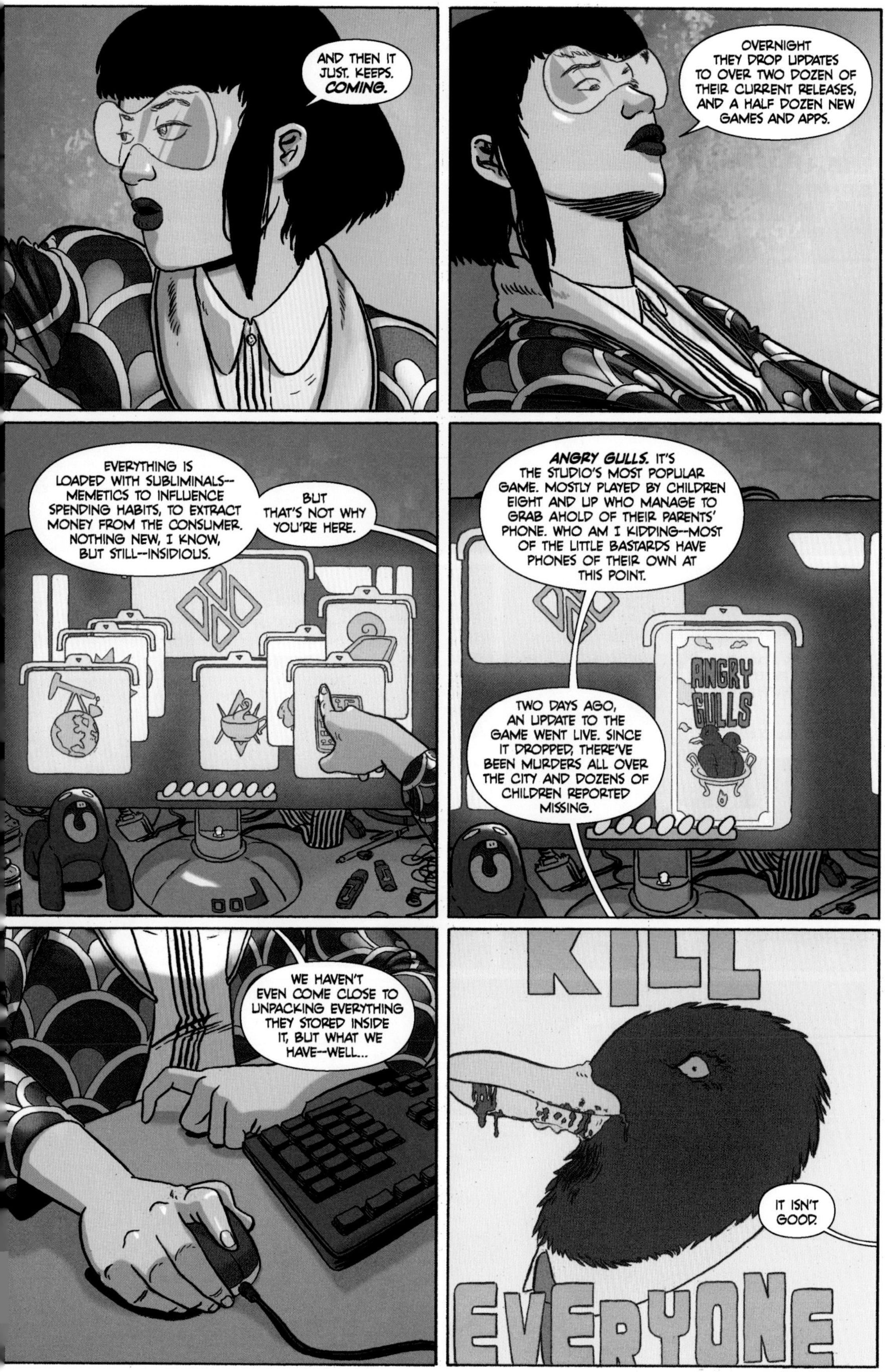
AND THEN IT JUST. KEEPS. *COMING.*
OVERNIGHT THEY DROP UPDATES TO OVER TWO DOZEN OF THEIR CURRENT RELEASES, AND A HALF DOZEN NEW GAMES AND APPS.
EVERYTHING IS LOADED WITH SUBLIMINALS--MEMETICS TO INFLUENCE SPENDING HABITS, TO EXTRACT MONEY FROM THE CONSUMER. NOTHING NEW, I KNOW, BUT STILL--INSIDIOUS.
BUT THAT'S NOT WHY YOU'RE HERE.
*ANGRY GULLS.* IT'S THE STUDIO'S MOST POPULAR GAME. MOSTLY PLAYED BY CHILDREN EIGHT AND UP WHO MANAGE TO GRAB AHOLD OF THEIR PARENTS' PHONE. WHO AM I KIDDING--MOST OF THE LITTLE BASTARDS HAVE PHONES OF THEIR OWN AT THIS POINT.
ANGRY GULLS
TWO DAYS AGO, AN UPDATE TO THE GAME WENT LIVE. SINCE IT DROPPED, THERE'VE BEEN MURDERS ALL OVER THE CITY AND DOZENS OF CHILDREN REPORTED MISSING.
WE HAVEN'T EVEN COME CLOSE TO UNPACKING EVERYTHING THEY STORED INSIDE IT, BUT WHAT WE HAVE--WELL...
KILL
IT ISN'T GOOD.
EVERYONE

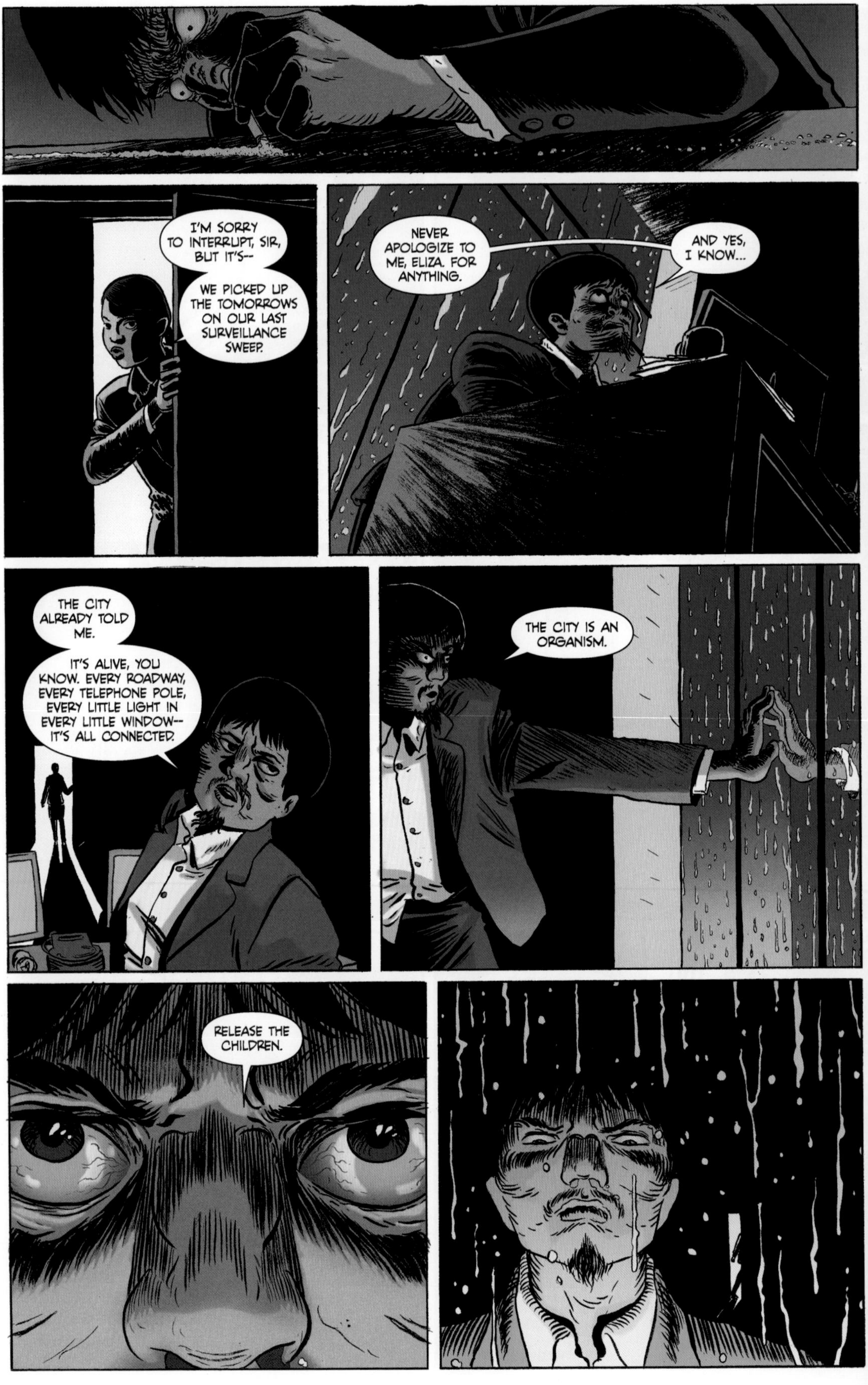
I'M SORRY TO INTERRUPT, SIR, BUT IT'S--
WE PICKED UP THE TOMORROWS ON OUR LAST SURVEILLANCE SWEEP.
NEVER APOLOGIZE TO ME, ELIZA. FOR ANYTHING.
AND YES, I KNOW...
THE CITY ALREADY TOLD ME.
IT'S ALIVE, YOU KNOW. EVERY ROADWAY, EVERY TELEPHONE POLE, EVERY LITTLE LIGHT IN EVERY LITTLE WINDOW-- IT'S ALL CONNECTED.
THE CITY IS AN ORGANISM.
RELEASE THE CHILDREN.

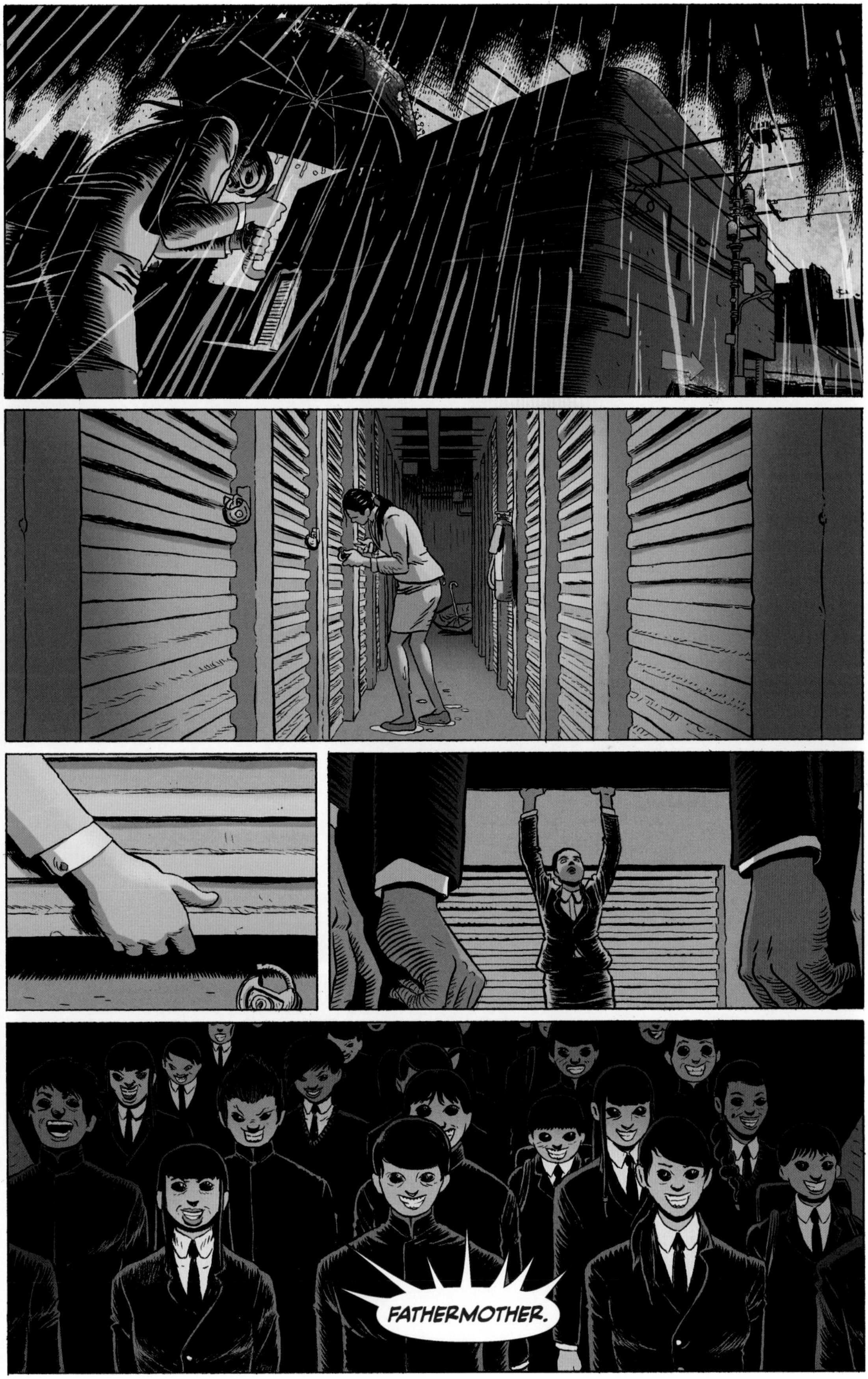
FATHERMOTHER.

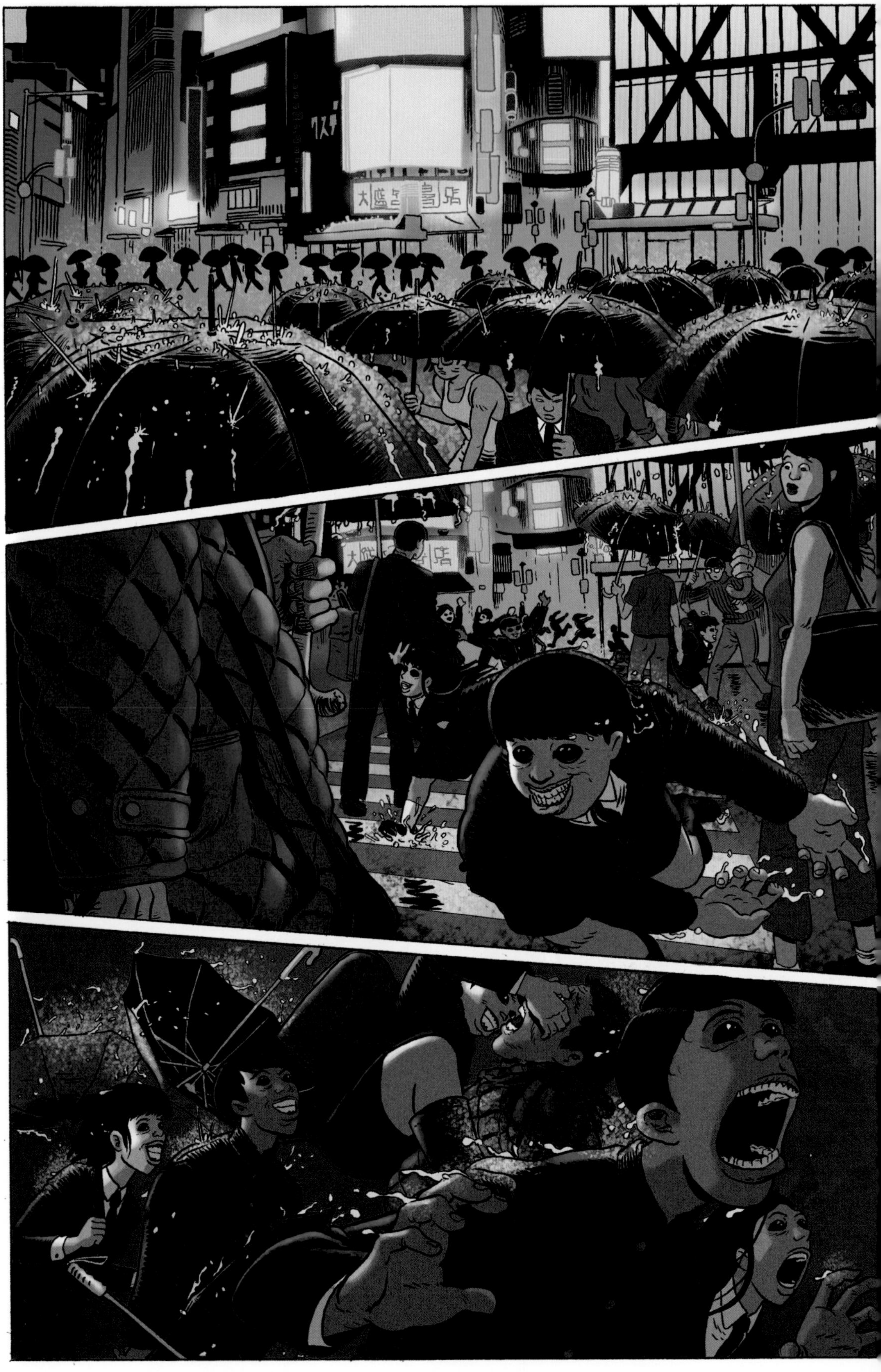

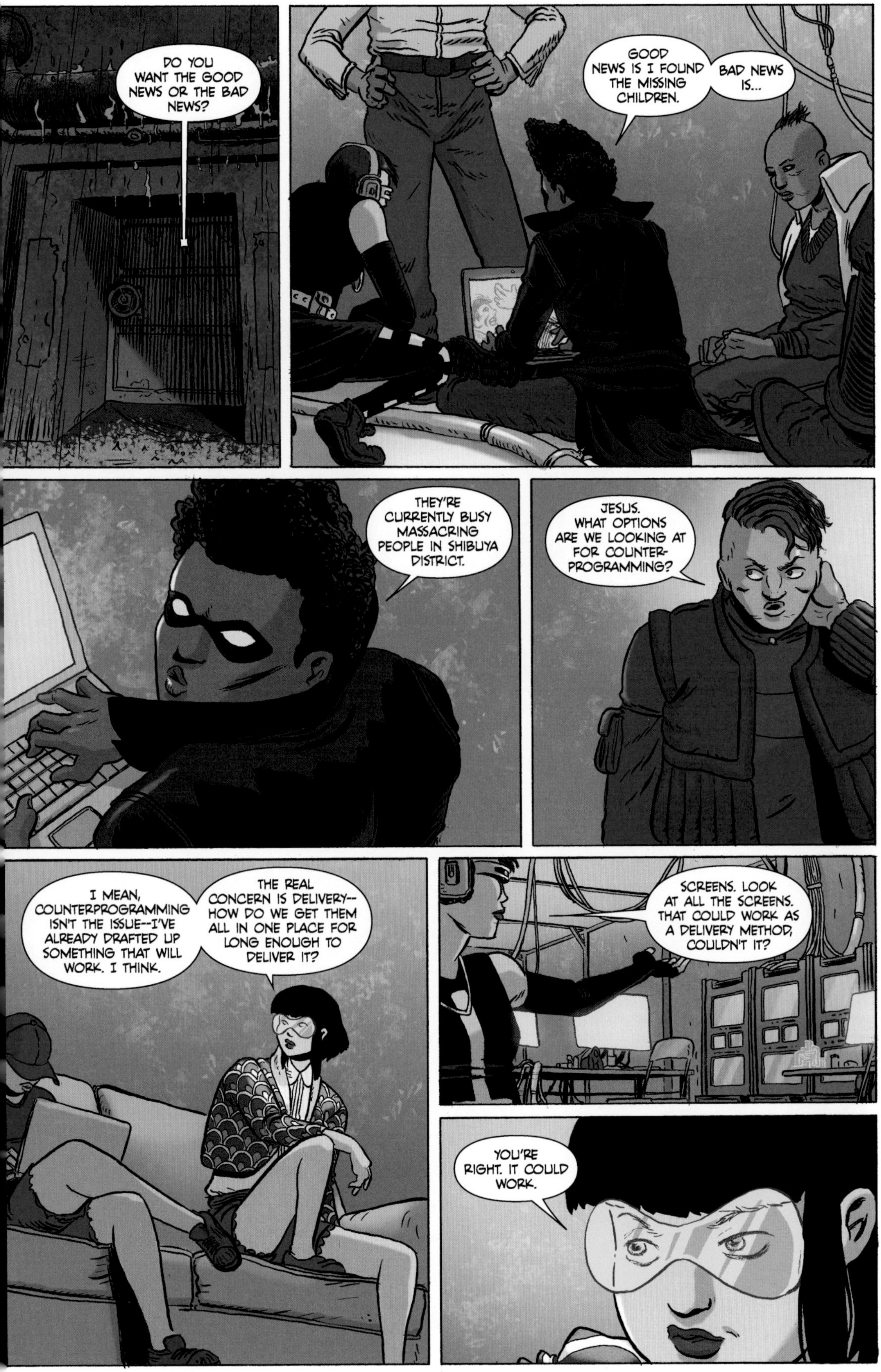
DO YOU WANT THE GOOD NEWS OR THE BAD NEWS?
GOOD NEWS IS I FOUND THE MISSING CHILDREN.
BAD NEWS IS...
THEY'RE CURRENTLY BUSY MASSACRING PEOPLE IN SHIBUYA DISTRICT.
JESUS. WHAT OPTIONS ARE WE LOOKING AT FOR COUNTER-PROGRAMMING?
I MEAN, COUNTERPROGRAMMING ISN'T THE ISSUE--I'VE ALREADY DRAFTED UP SOMETHING THAT WILL WORK. I THINK.
THE REAL CONCERN IS DELIVERY--HOW DO WE GET THEM ALL IN ONE PLACE FOR LONG ENOUGH TO DELIVER IT?
SCREENS. LOOK AT ALL THE SCREENS. THAT COULD WORK AS A DELIVERY METHOD, COULDN'T IT?
YOU'RE RIGHT. IT COULD WORK.

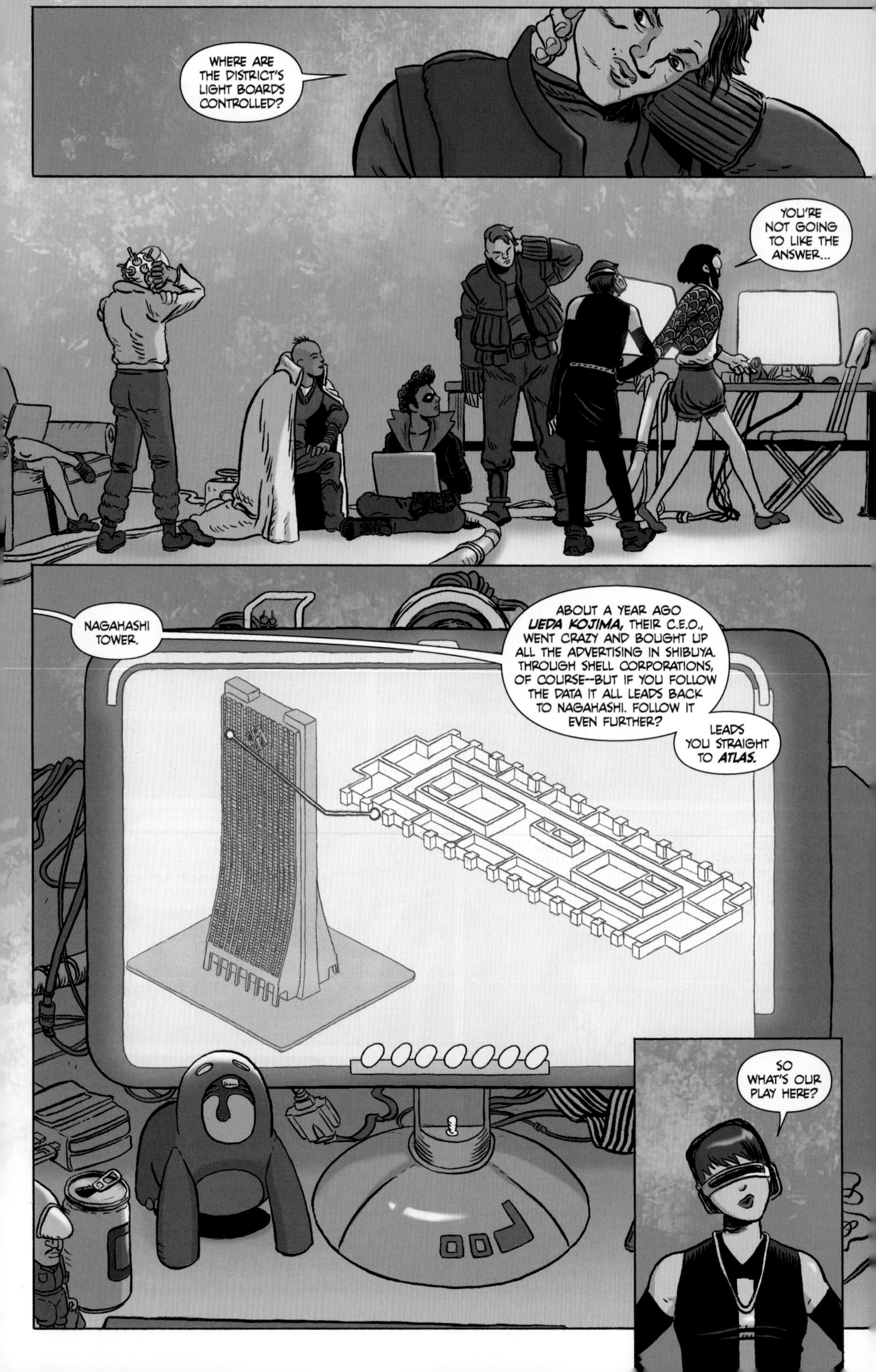
WHERE ARE THE DISTRICT'S LIGHT BOARDS CONTROLLED?
YOU'RE NOT GOING TO LIKE THE ANSWER...
NAGAHASHI TOWER.
ABOUT A YEAR AGO UEDA KOJIMA, THEIR C.E.O., WENT CRAZY AND BOUGHT UP ALL THE ADVERTISING IN SHIBUYA. THROUGH SHELL CORPORATIONS, OF COURSE--BUT IF YOU FOLLOW THE DATA IT ALL LEADS BACK TO NAGAHASHI. FOLLOW IT EVEN FURTHER?
LEADS YOU STRAIGHT TO ATLAS.
SO WHAT'S OUR PLAY HERE?

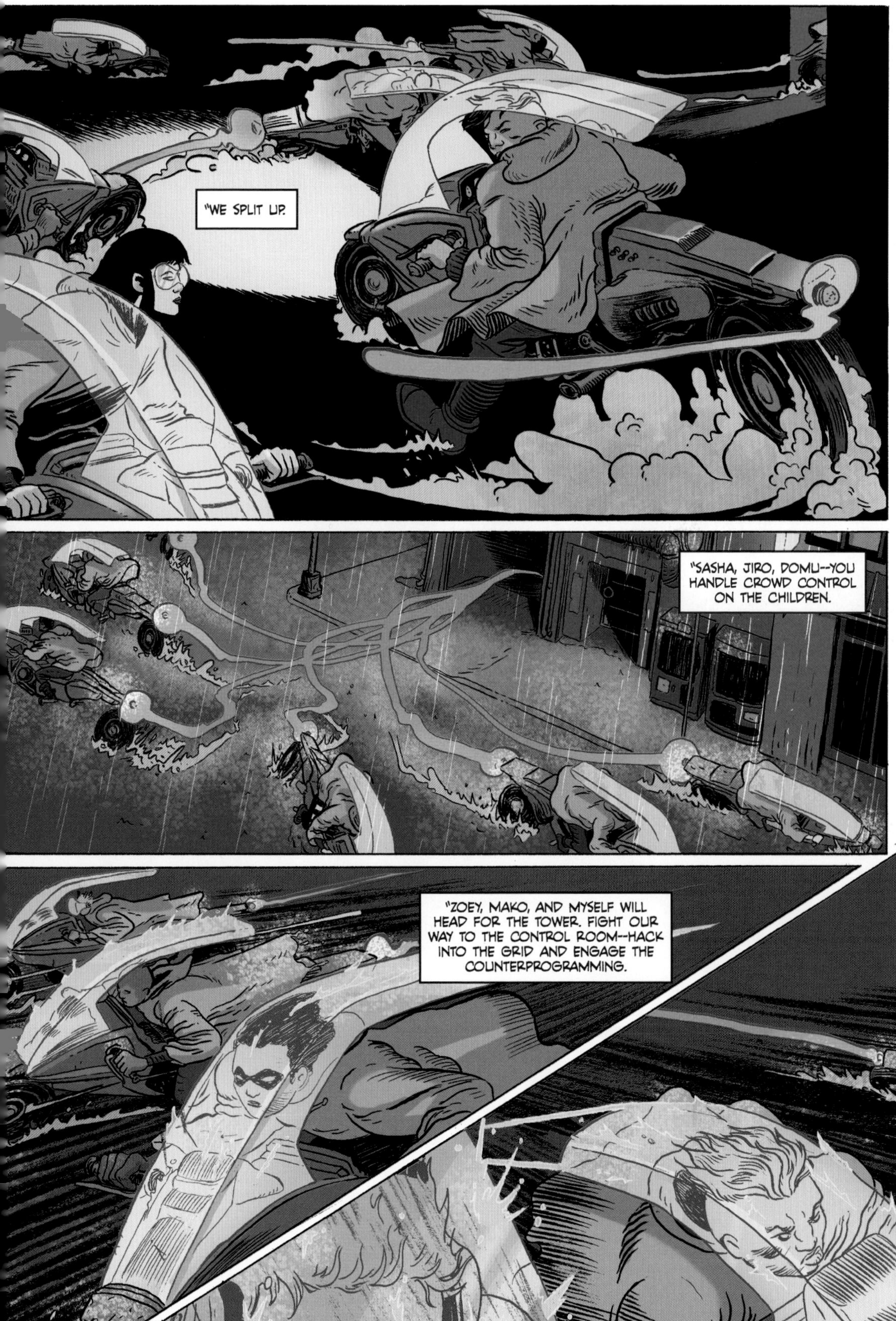
"WE SPLIT UP.
"SASHA, JIRO, DOMU--YOU HANDLE CROWD CONTROL ON THE CHILDREN.
"ZOEY, MAKO, AND MYSELF WILL HEAD FOR THE TOWER. FIGHT OUR WAY TO THE CONTROL ROOM--HACK INTO THE GRID AND ENGAGE THE COUNTERPROGRAMMING.

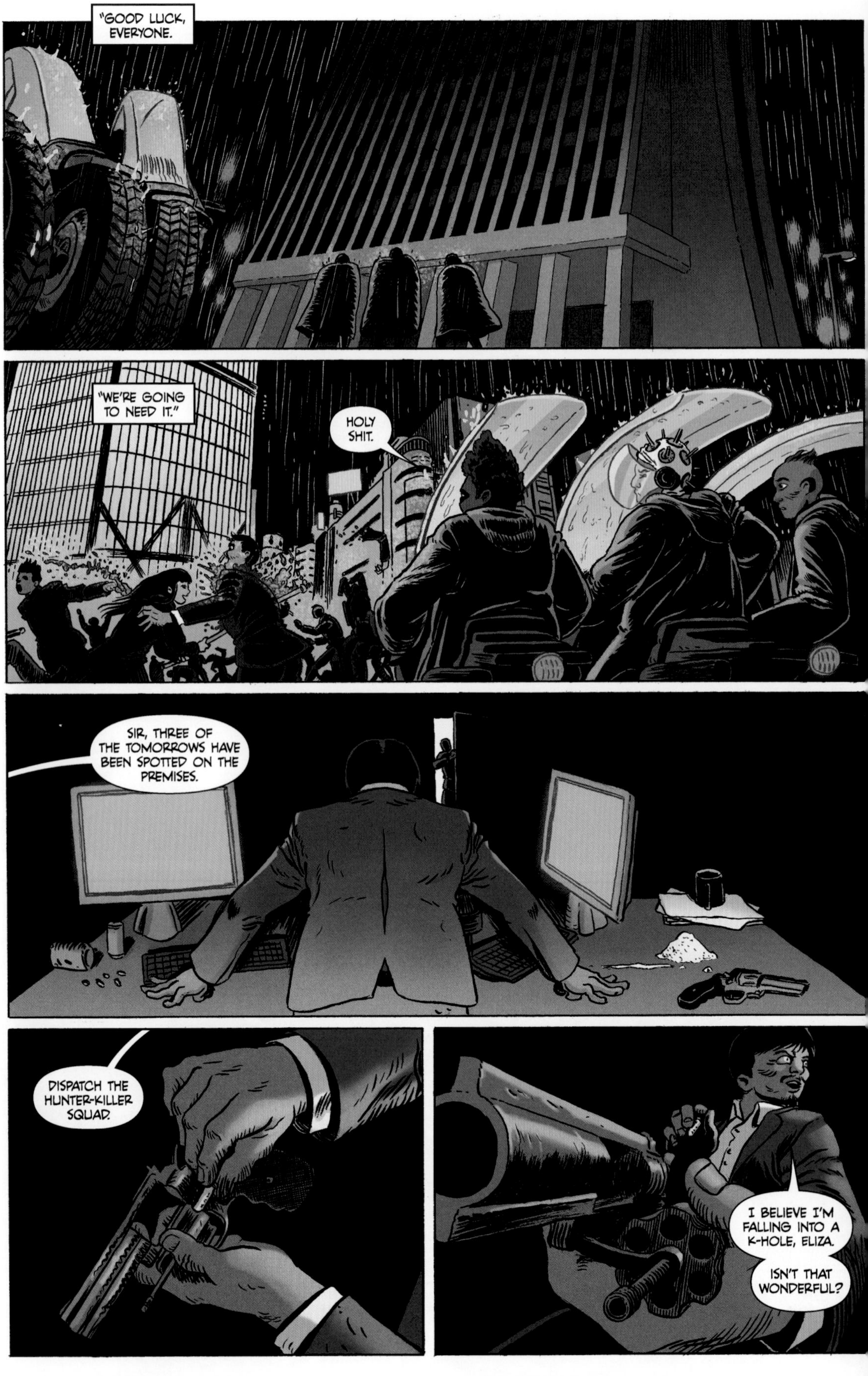
"GOOD LUCK, EVERYONE.
"WE'RE GOING TO NEED IT."
HOLY SHIT.
SIR, THREE OF THE TOMORROWS HAVE BEEN SPOTTED ON THE PREMISES.
DISPATCH THE HUNTER-KILLER SQUAD.
I BELIEVE I'M FALLING INTO A K-HOLE, ELIZA.
ISN'T THAT WONDERFUL?

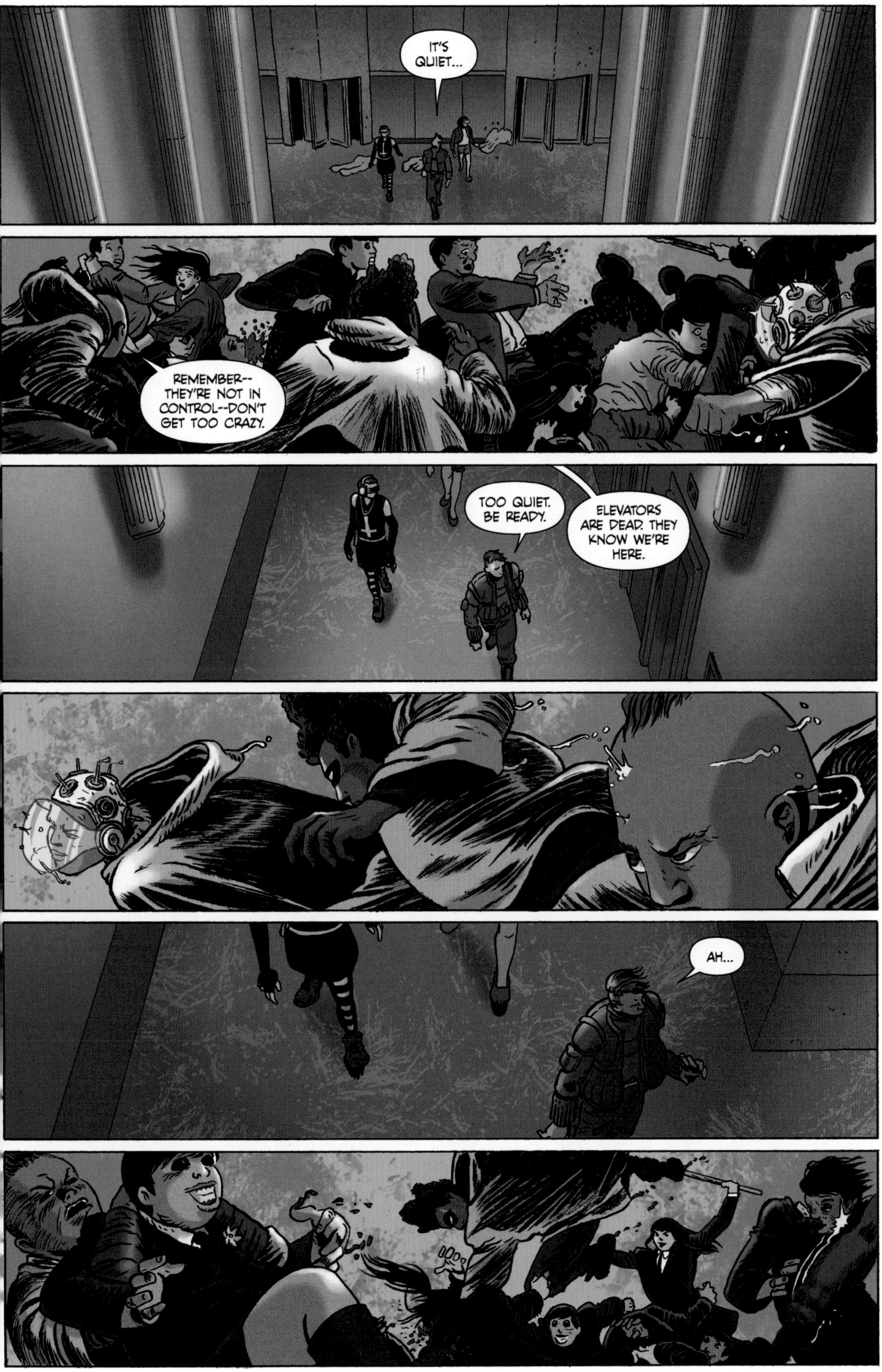
IT'S QUIET...
REMEMBER-- THEY'RE NOT IN CONTROL--DON'T GET TOO CRAZY.
TOO QUIET. BE READY.
ELEVATORS ARE DEAD. THEY KNOW WE'RE HERE.
AH...

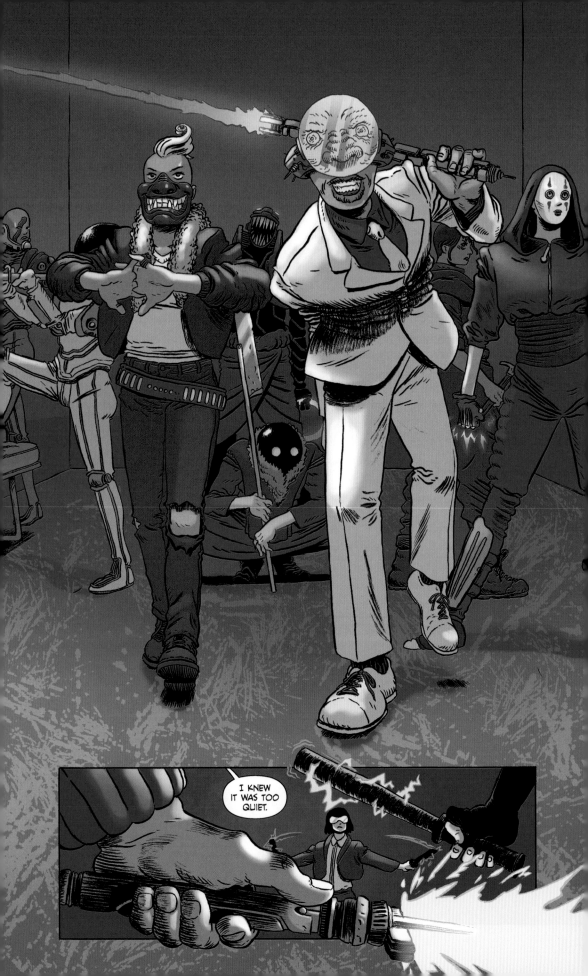

I KNEW IT WAS TOO QUIET.

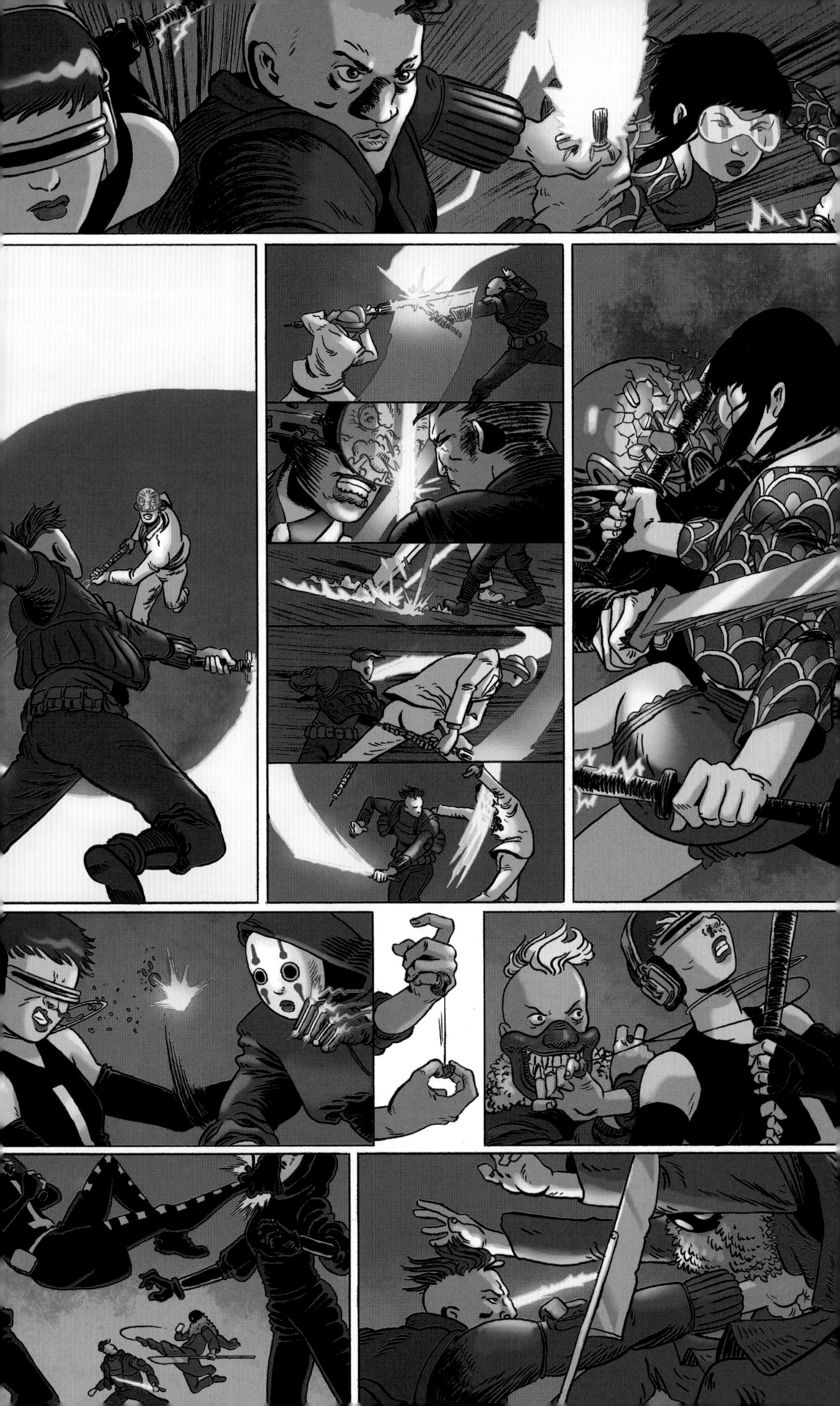

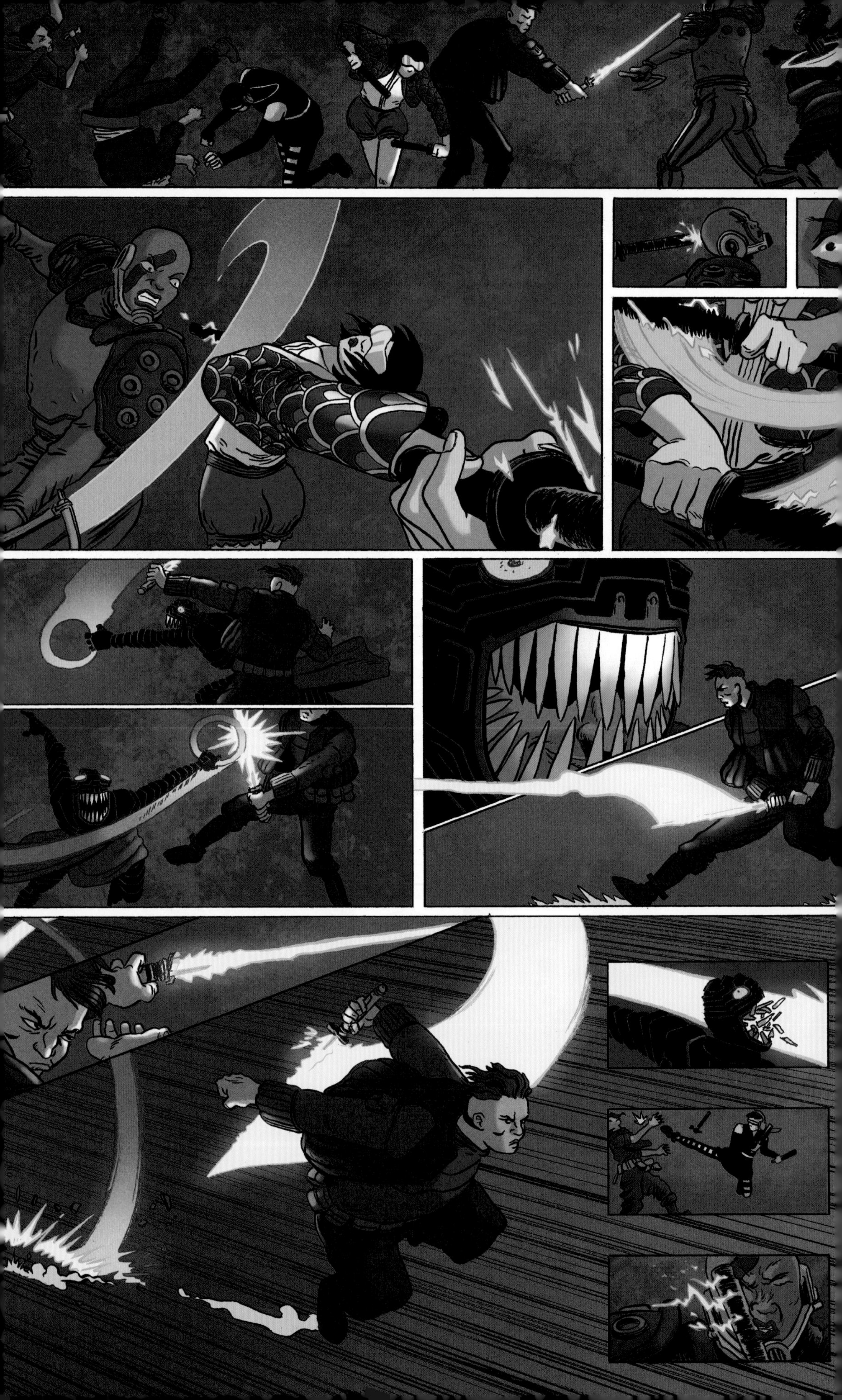

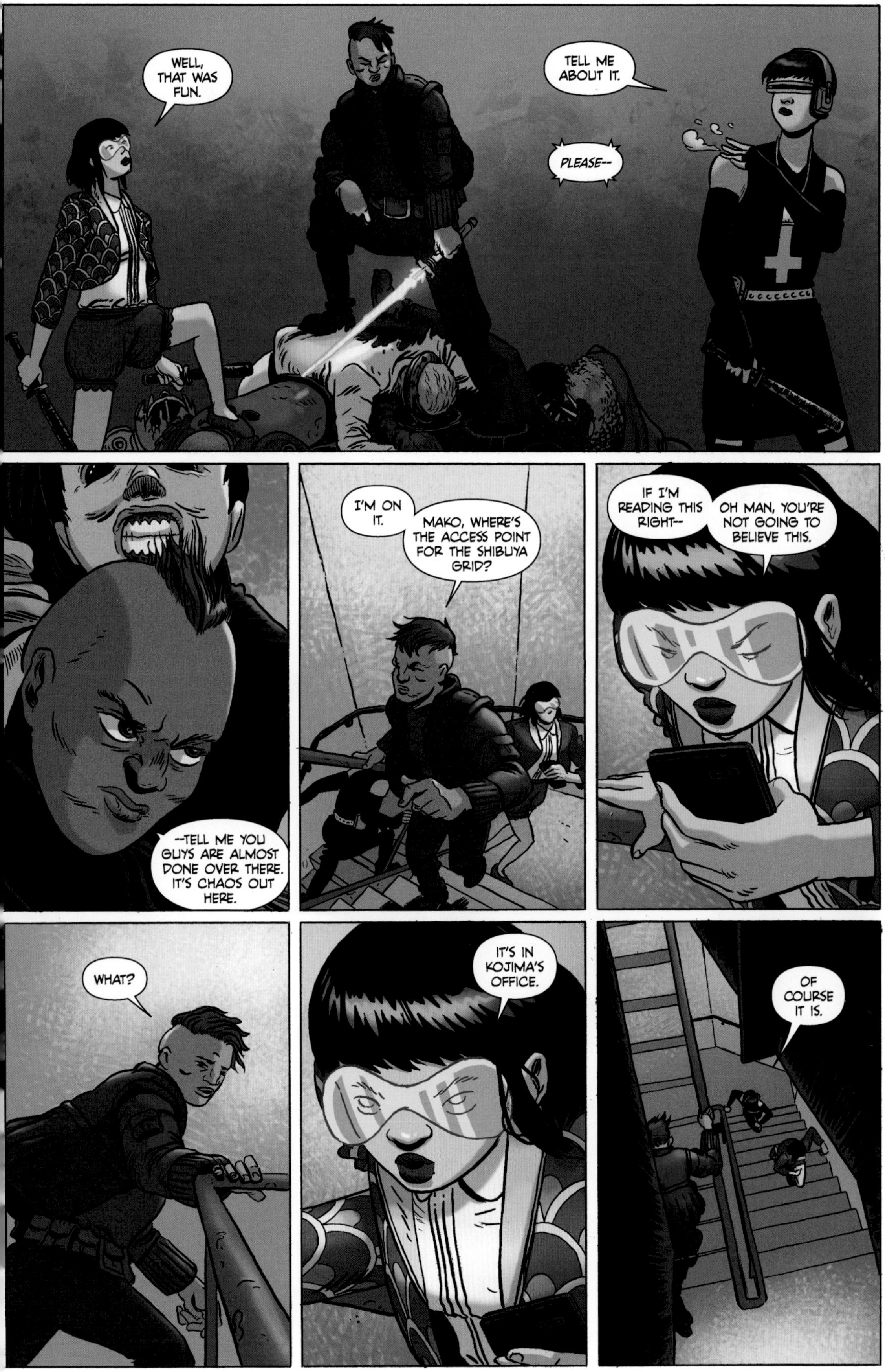

WELL, THAT WAS FUN.
TELL ME ABOUT IT.
PLEASE--
--TELL ME YOU GUYS ARE ALMOST DONE OVER THERE. IT'S CHAOS OUT HERE.
I'M ON IT.
MAKO, WHERE'S THE ACCESS POINT FOR THE SHIBUYA GRID?
IF I'M READING THIS RIGHT--
OH MAN, YOU'RE NOT GOING TO BELIEVE THIS.
WHAT?
IT'S IN KOJIMA'S OFFICE.
OF COURSE IT IS.

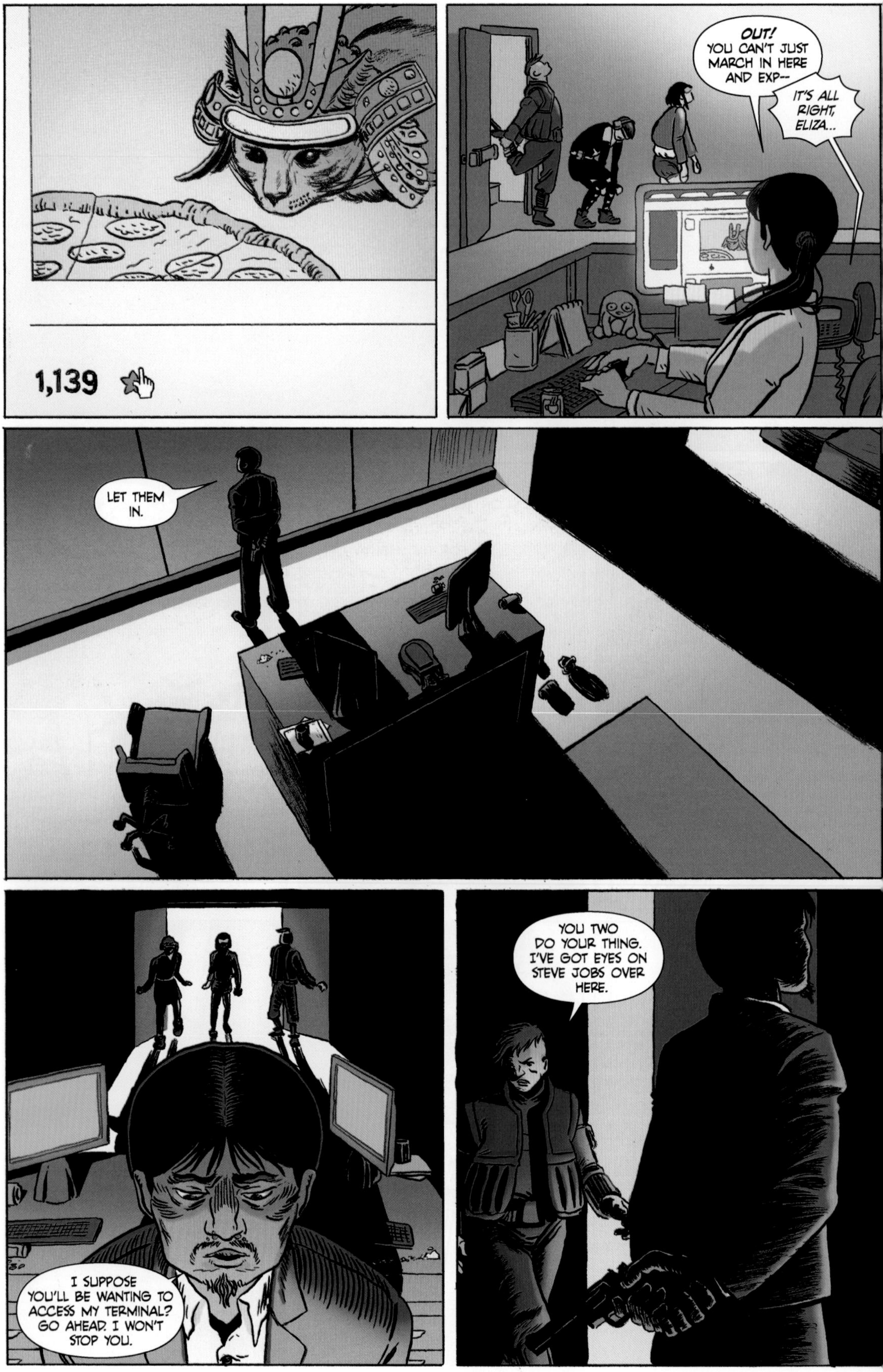
1,139
OUT!
YOU CAN'T JUST MARCH IN HERE AND EXP--
IT'S ALL RIGHT, ELIZA...
LET THEM IN.
I SUPPOSE YOU'LL BE WANTING TO ACCESS MY TERMINAL? GO AHEAD. I WON'T STOP YOU.
YOU TWO DO YOUR THING. I'VE GOT EYES ON STEVE JOBS OVER HERE.

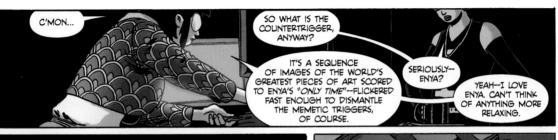

C'MON...

SO WHAT IS THE COUNTERTRIGGER, ANYWAY?

IT'S A SEQUENCE OF IMAGES OF THE WORLD'S GREATEST PIECES OF ART SCORED TO ENYA'S *ONLY TIME*--FLICKERED FAST ENOUGH TO DISMANTLE THE MEMETIC TRIGGERS, OF COURSE.

SERIOUSLY-- ENYA?

YEAH--I LOVE ENYA. CAN'T THINK OF ANYTHING MORE RELAXING.

ALL RIGHT, WE ARE...

GO.

SWEET JESUS, WHAT IS TAKING YOU--

♫ WHO CAN SAYYYY-- ♫

LISTEN: ENYA, "ONLY TIME" (3:38)

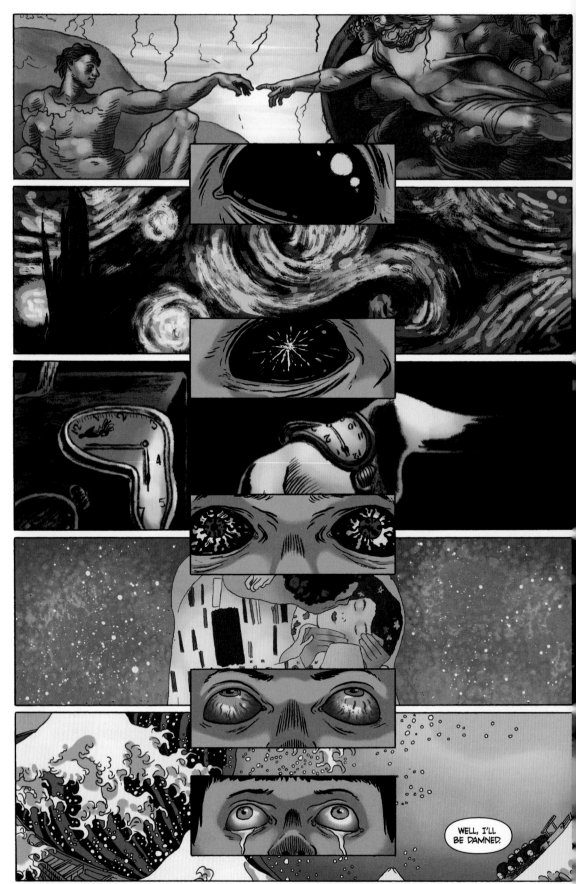

KEYWORDS: MICHELANGELO, VAN GOGH, DALÍ, KLIMT, HOKUSAI.

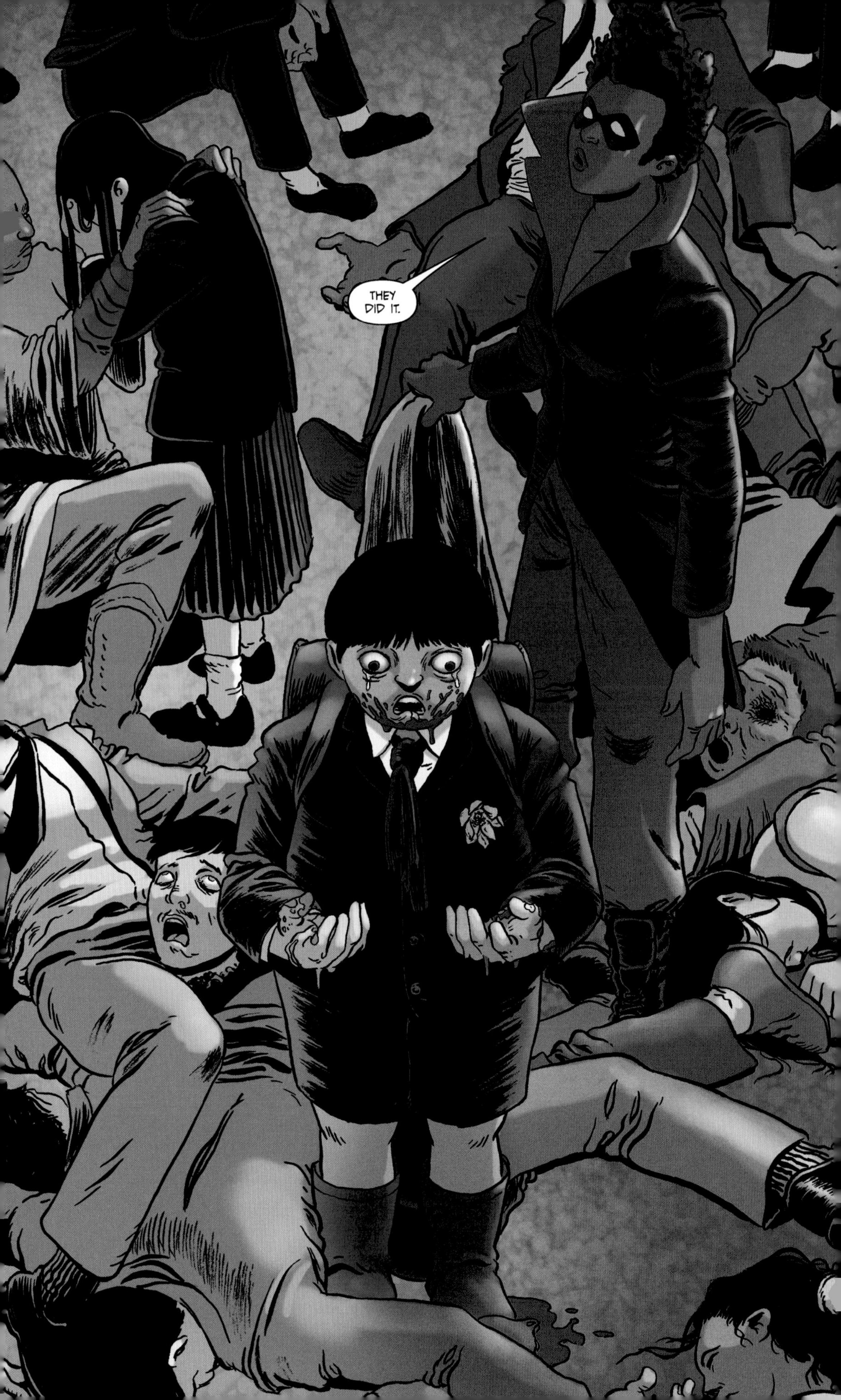
THEY DID IT.

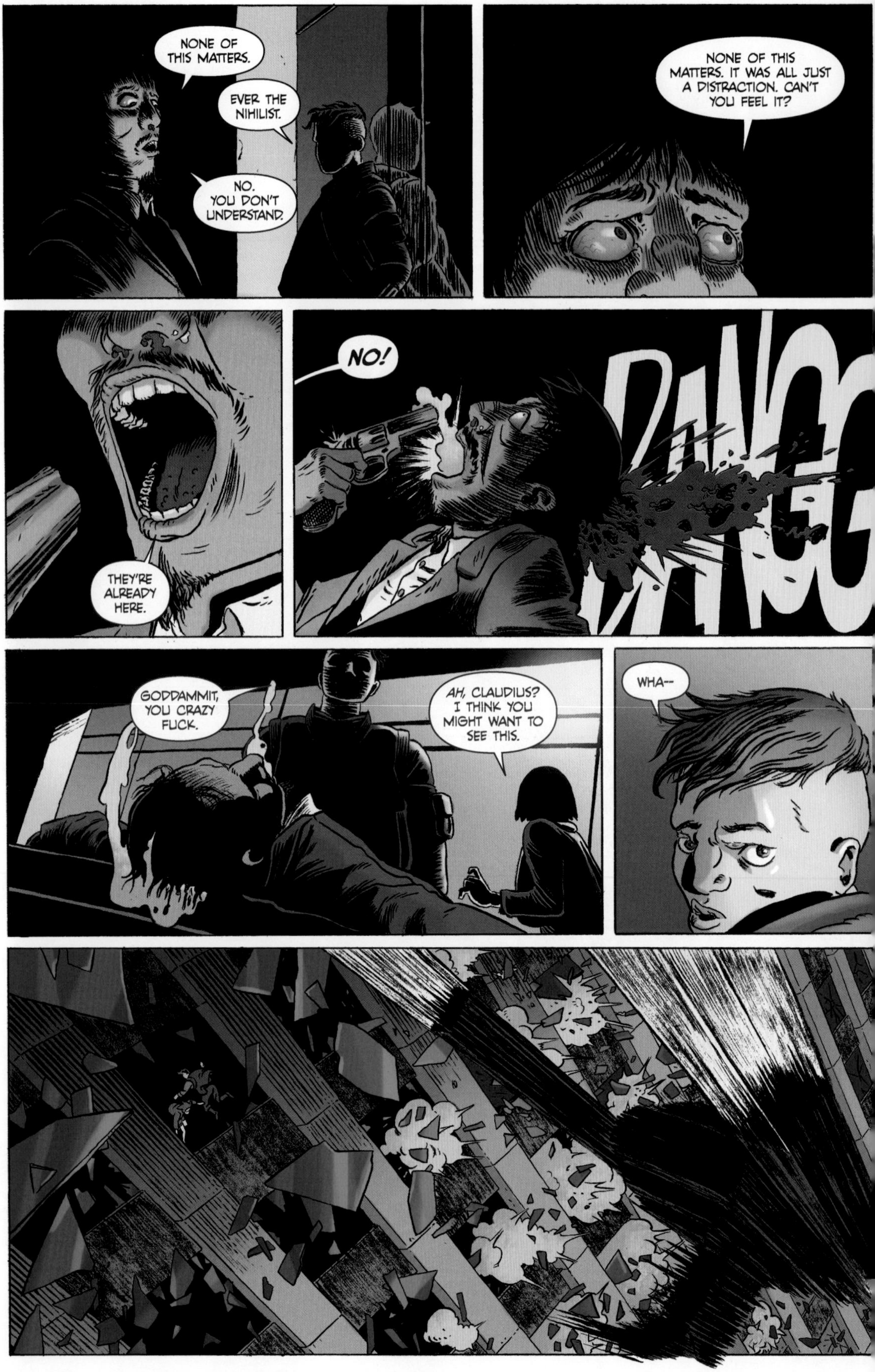
NONE OF THIS MATTERS.
EVER THE NIHILIST.
NO. YOU DON'T UNDERSTAND.
NONE OF THIS MATTERS. IT WAS ALL JUST A DISTRACTION. CAN'T YOU FEEL IT?
THEY'RE ALREADY HERE.
NO!
BANG
GODDAMMIT, YOU CRAZY FUCK.
AH, CLAUDIUS? I THINK YOU MIGHT WANT TO SEE THIS.
WHA--

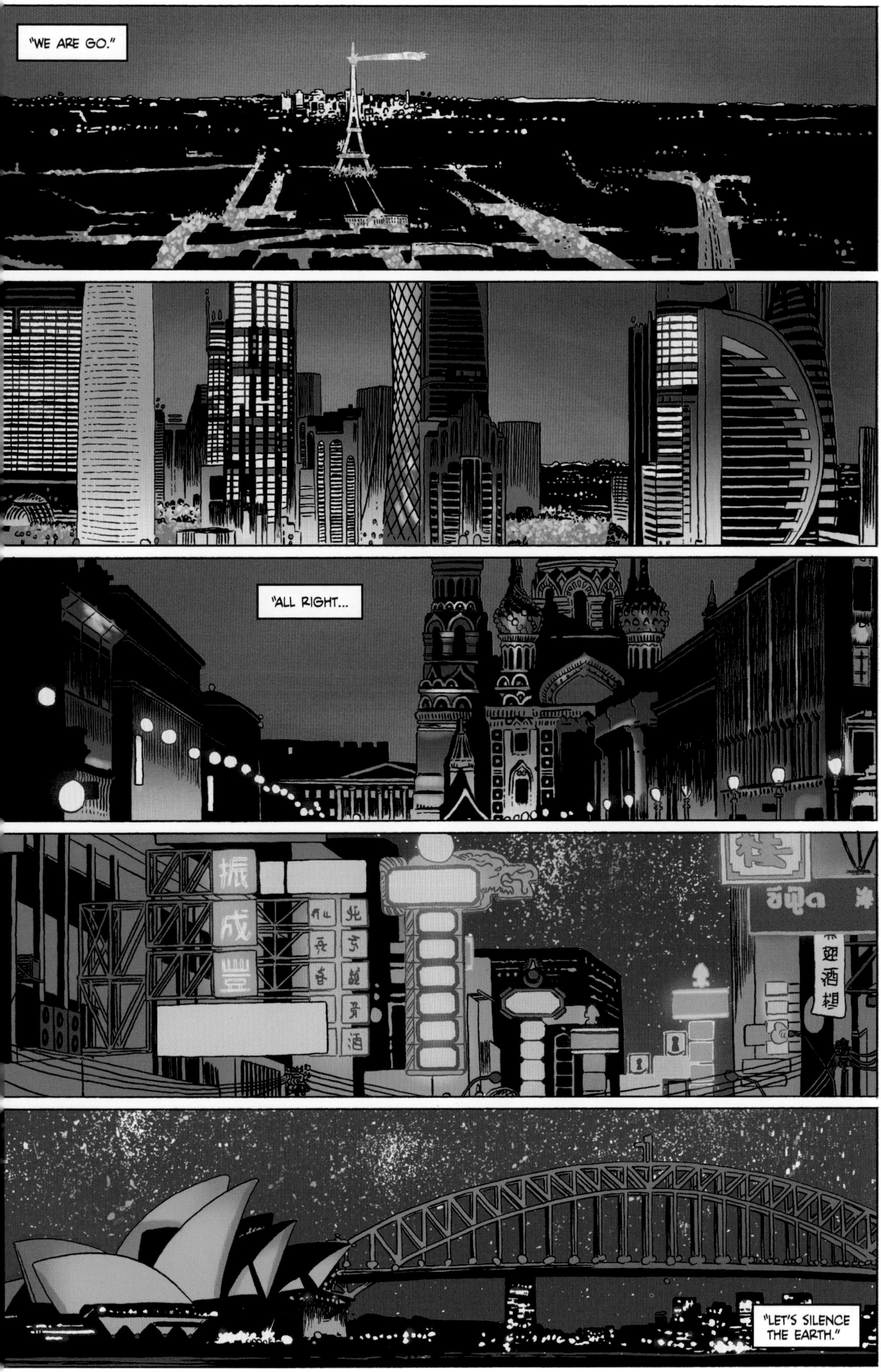
"WE ARE GO."
"ALL RIGHT...
"LET'S SILENCE THE EARTH."

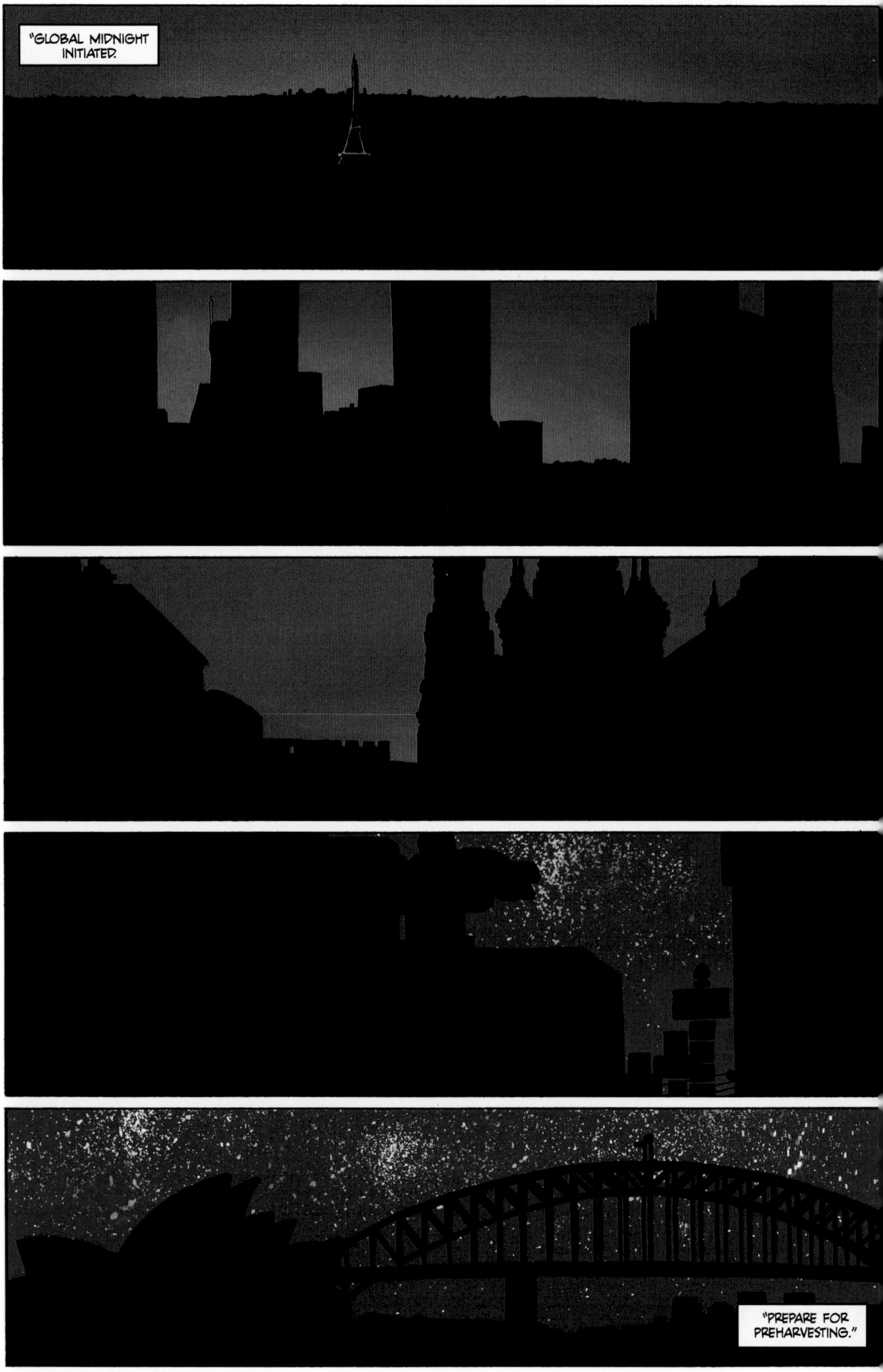
"GLOBAL MIDNIGHT INITIATED.
"PREPARE FOR PREHARVESTING."

>> DEDICATED TO

HIDEO KOJIMA

AND

FUMITO UEDA

/// END Transmission. >>

/// part four

# CONSTELLATIONS

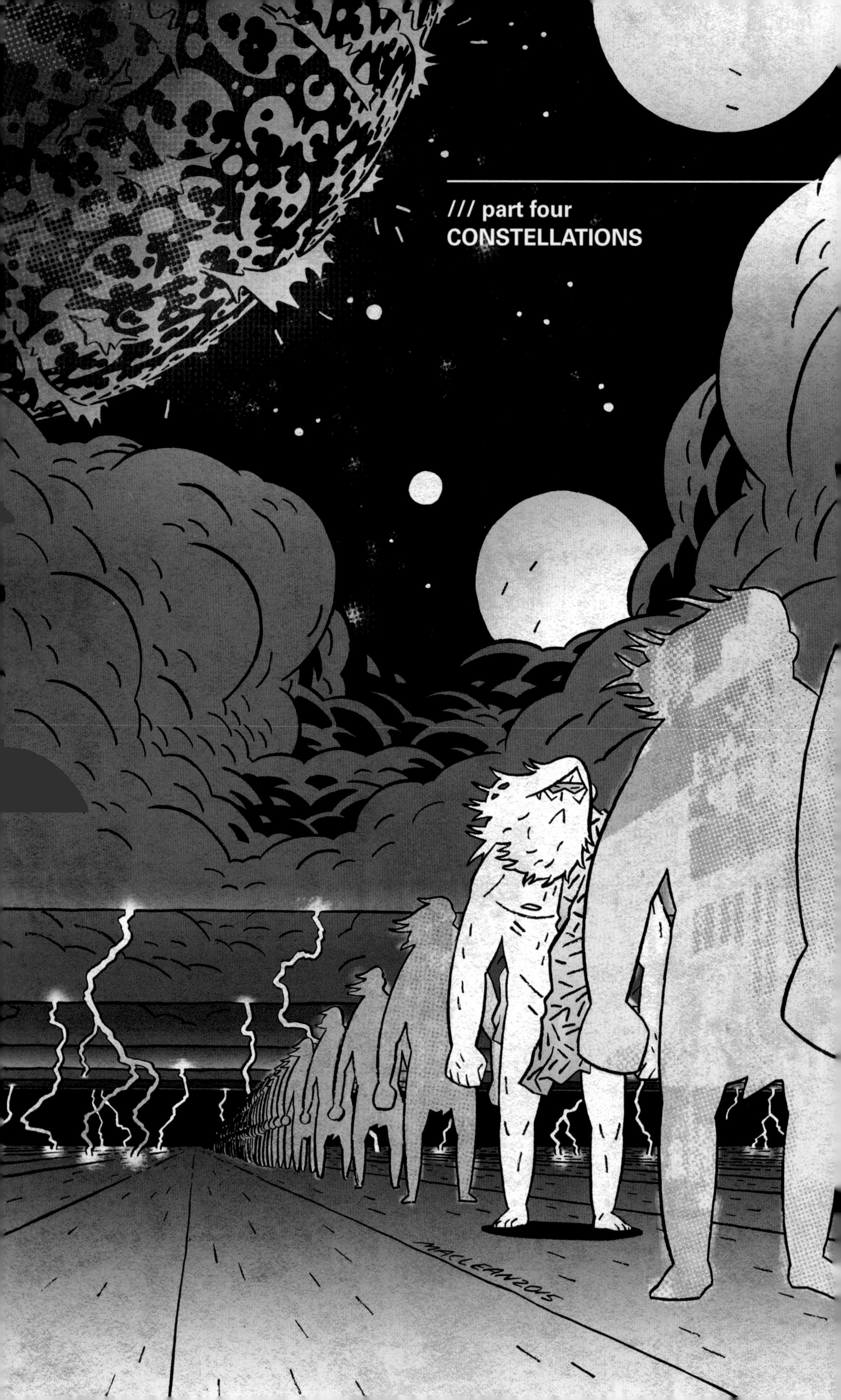
MACLEAN2015

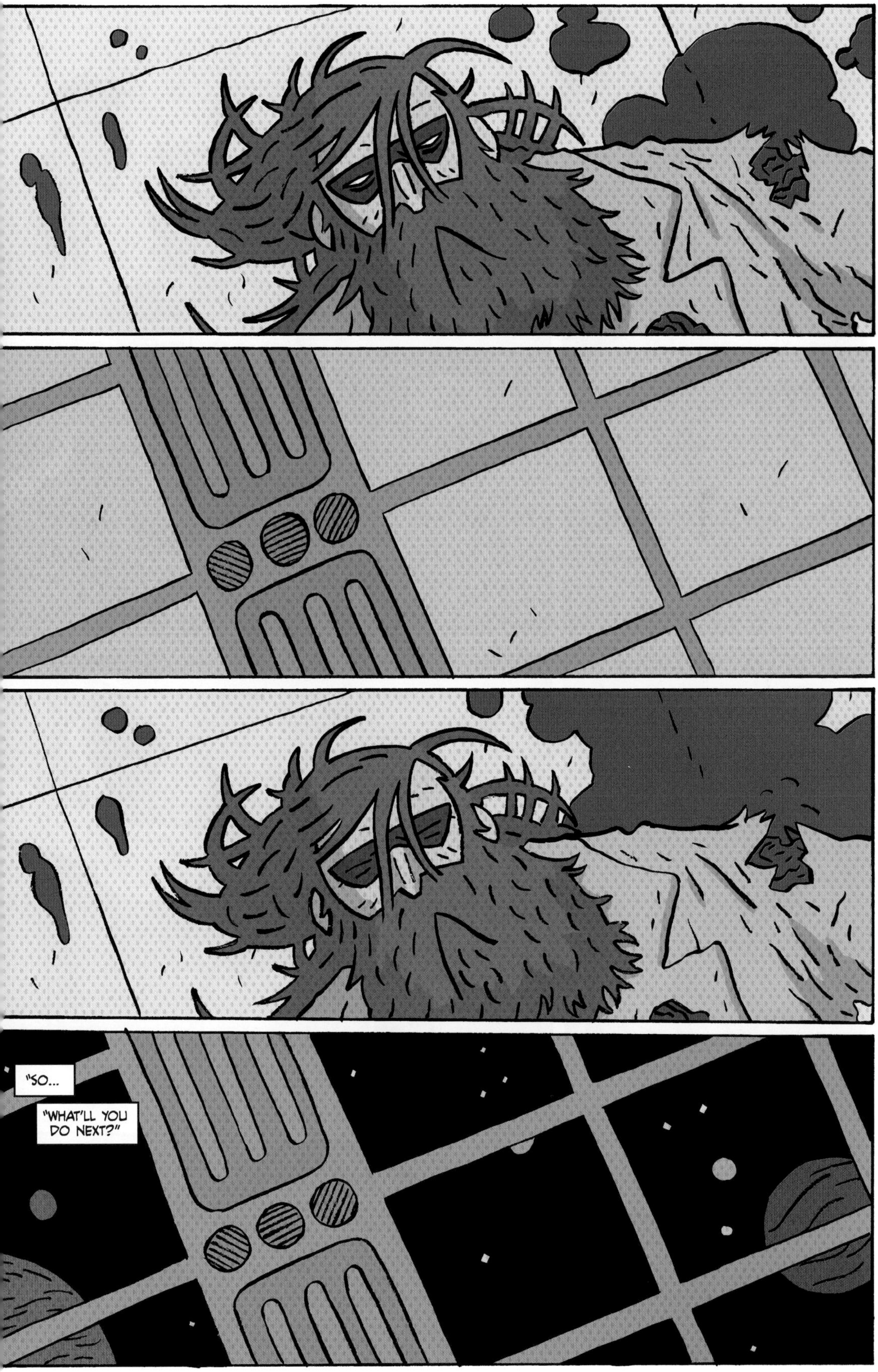
"SO...
"WHAT'LL YOU DO NEXT?"

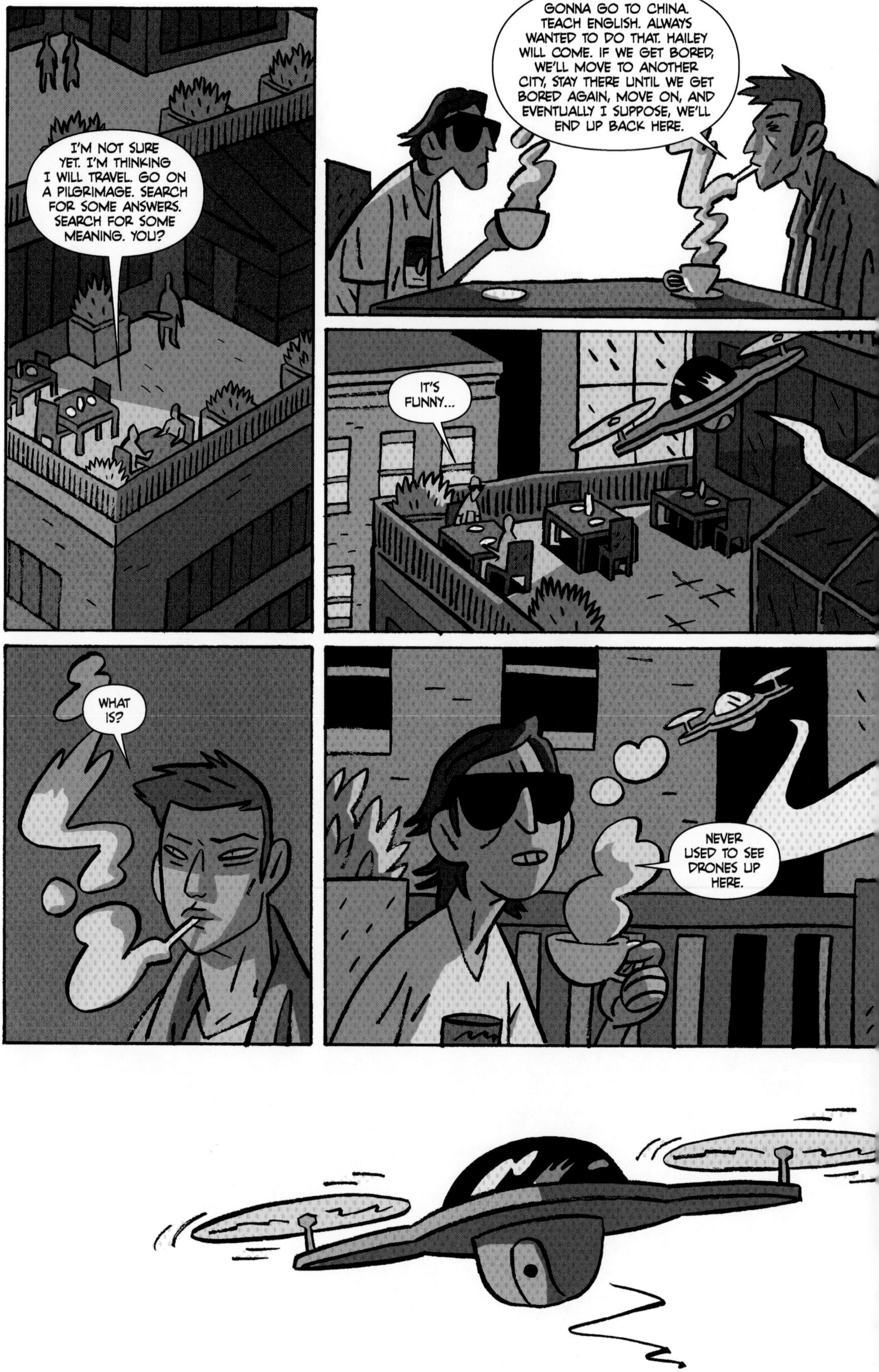

I'M NOT SURE YET. I'M THINKING I WILL TRAVEL. GO ON A PILGRIMAGE. SEARCH FOR SOME ANSWERS. SEARCH FOR SOME MEANING. YOU?
GONNA GO TO CHINA. TEACH ENGLISH. ALWAYS WANTED TO DO THAT. HAILEY WILL COME. IF WE GET BORED, WE'LL MOVE TO ANOTHER CITY, STAY THERE UNTIL WE GET BORED AGAIN, MOVE ON, AND EVENTUALLY I SUPPOSE, WE'LL END UP BACK HERE.
IT'S FUNNY...
WHAT IS?
NEVER USED TO SEE DRONES UP HERE.

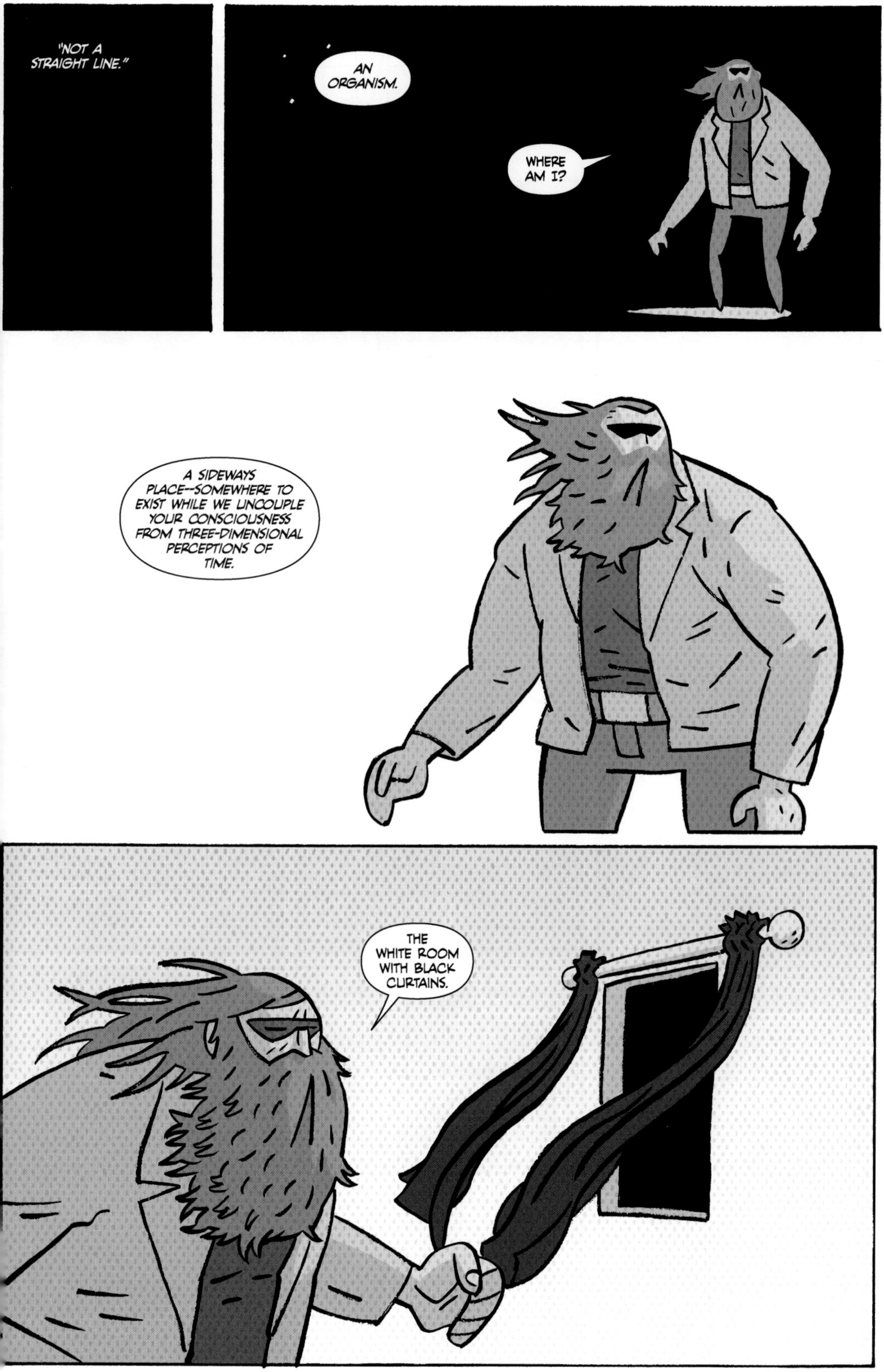
"NOT A STRAIGHT LINE."
AN ORGANISM.
WHERE AM I?
A SIDEWAYS PLACE--SOMEWHERE TO EXIST WHILE WE UNCOUPLE YOUR CONSCIOUSNESS FROM THREE-DIMENSIONAL PERCEPTIONS OF TIME.
THE WHITE ROOM WITH BLACK CURTAINS.

SIX.

WHEN I WAS SIX...

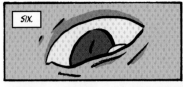

WHEN I WAS SIX I GOT MY FIRST SPLINTER.

FROM A RAILING AT MY GRANDPARENTS' HOUSE. THE PAINT WAS FADED AND THE WOOD WAS PEELING.

MY MOM WARNED ME NOT TO TOUCH IT.

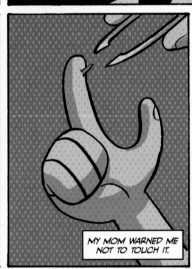

BUT I TOUCHED IT ANYWAY.

OWWWWW OWWWWWW!

HOLD STILL...

THAT WAS THE FIRST TIME I REALIZED...

THERE WE GO.

...THAT EVERY ACTION...

I LOVE YOU, MOMMY.

...HAD A CONSEQUENCE.

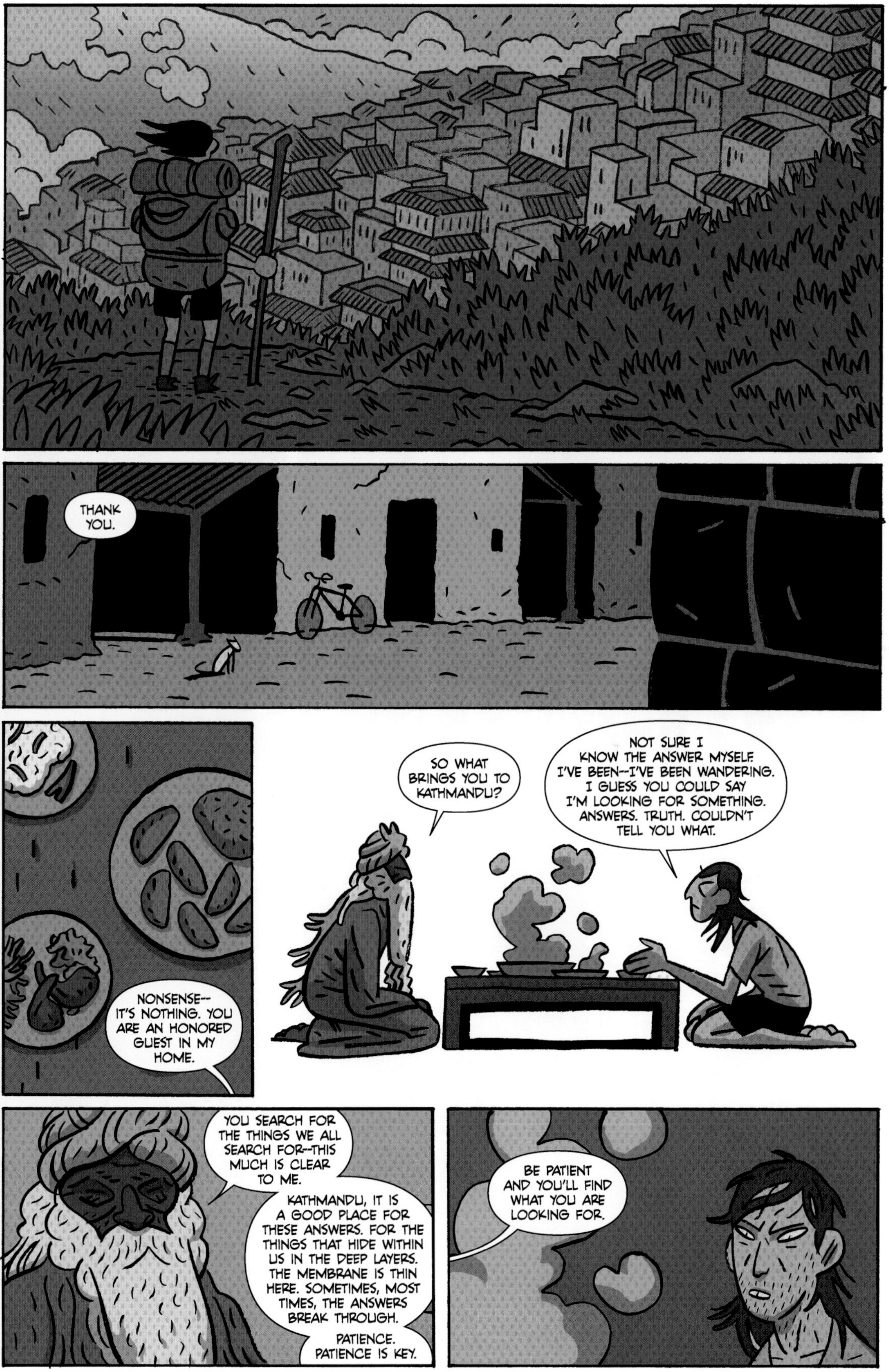
THANK YOU.
SO WHAT BRINGS YOU TO KATHMANDU?
NOT SURE I KNOW THE ANSWER MYSELF. I'VE BEEN--I'VE BEEN WANDERING. I GUESS YOU COULD SAY I'M LOOKING FOR SOMETHING. ANSWERS. TRUTH. COULDN'T TELL YOU WHAT.
NONSENSE-- IT'S NOTHING. YOU ARE AN HONORED GUEST IN MY HOME.
YOU SEARCH FOR THE THINGS WE ALL SEARCH FOR--THIS MUCH IS CLEAR TO ME.
KATHMANDU, IT IS A GOOD PLACE FOR THESE ANSWERS. FOR THE THINGS THAT HIDE WITHIN US IN THE DEEP LAYERS. THE MEMBRANE IS THIN HERE. SOMETIMES, MOST TIMES, THE ANSWERS BREAK THROUGH.
PATIENCE. PATIENCE IS KEY.
BE PATIENT AND YOU'LL FIND WHAT YOU ARE LOOKING FOR.

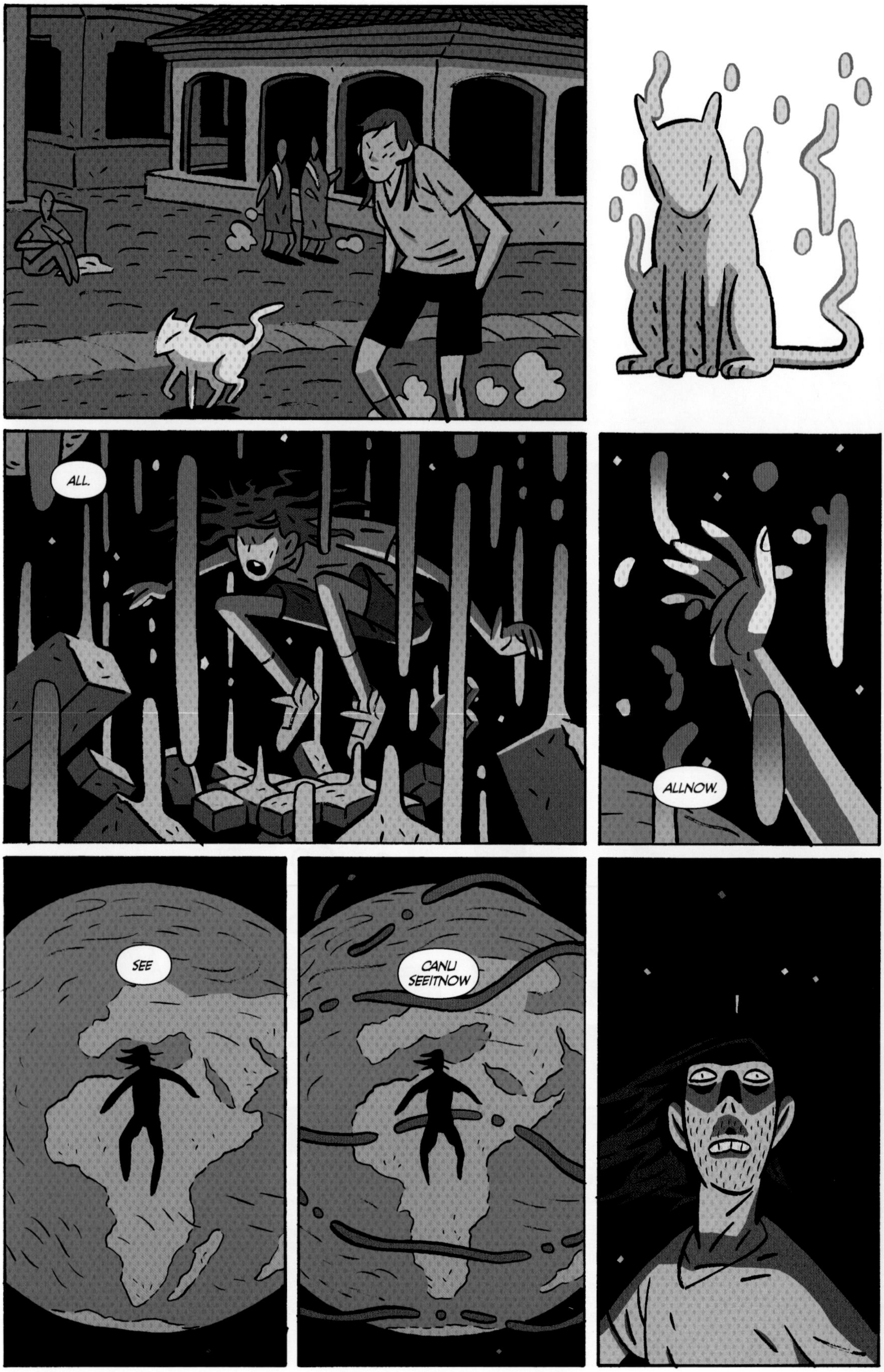
ALL.
ALLNOW.
SEE
CANU
SEEITNOW

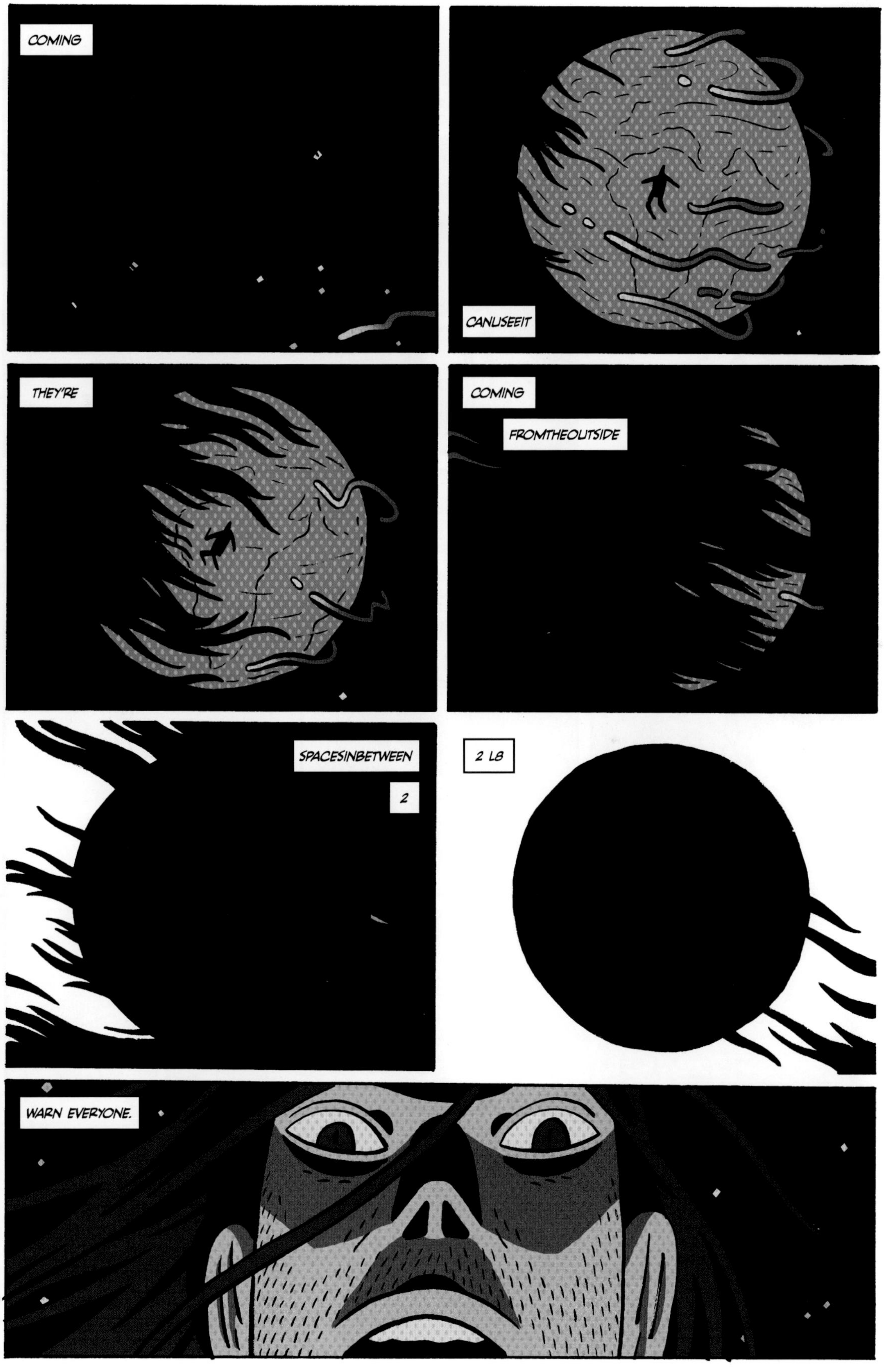
COMING
CANUSEEIT
THEY'RE
COMING
FROMTHEOUTSIDE
SPACESINBETWEEN
2
2 LB
WARN EVERYONE.

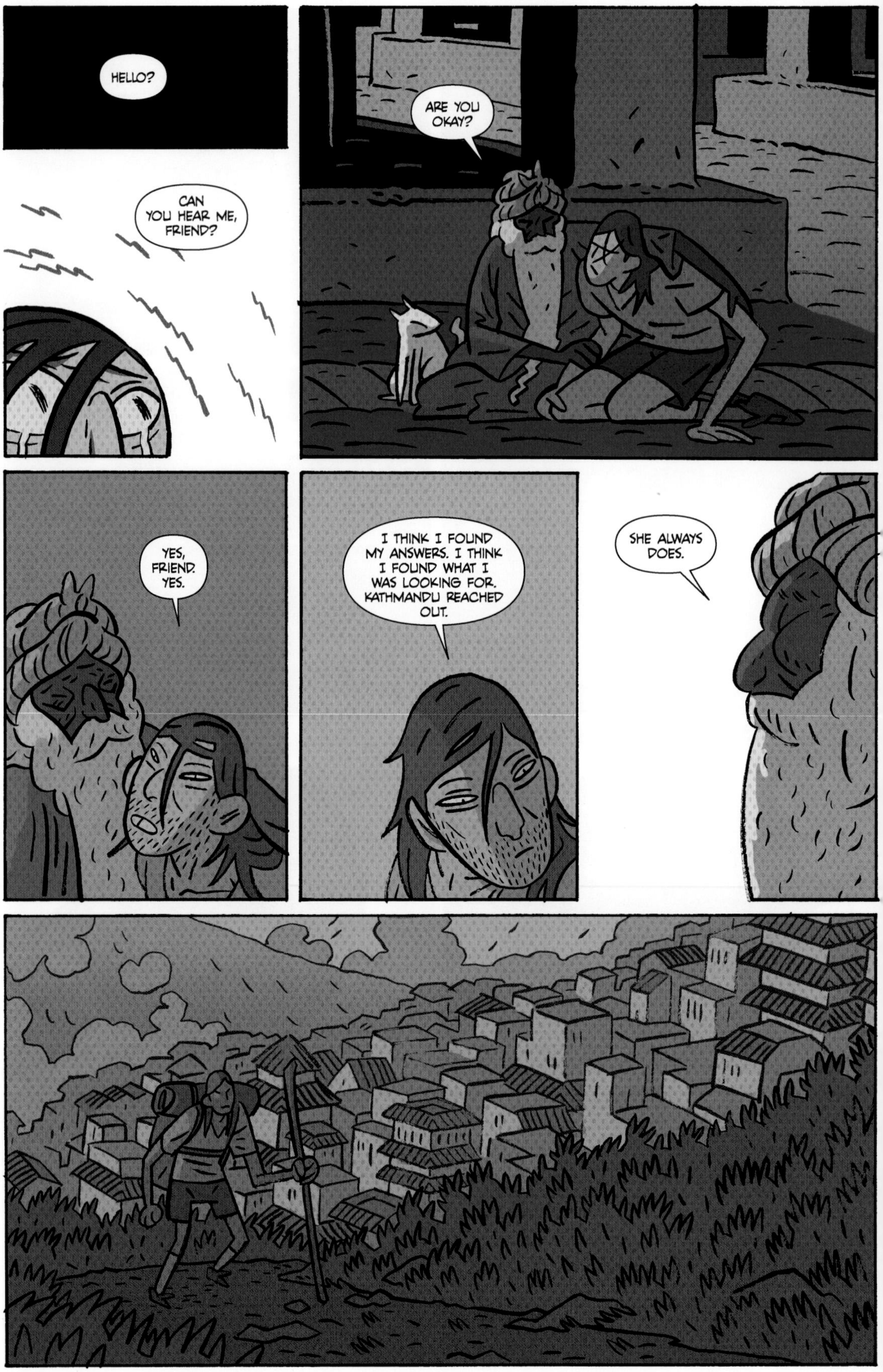
HELLO?
ARE YOU OKAY?
CAN YOU HEAR ME, FRIEND?
YES, FRIEND. YES.
I THINK I FOUND MY ANSWERS. I THINK I FOUND WHAT I WAS LOOKING FOR. KATHMANDU REACHED OUT.
SHE ALWAYS DOES.

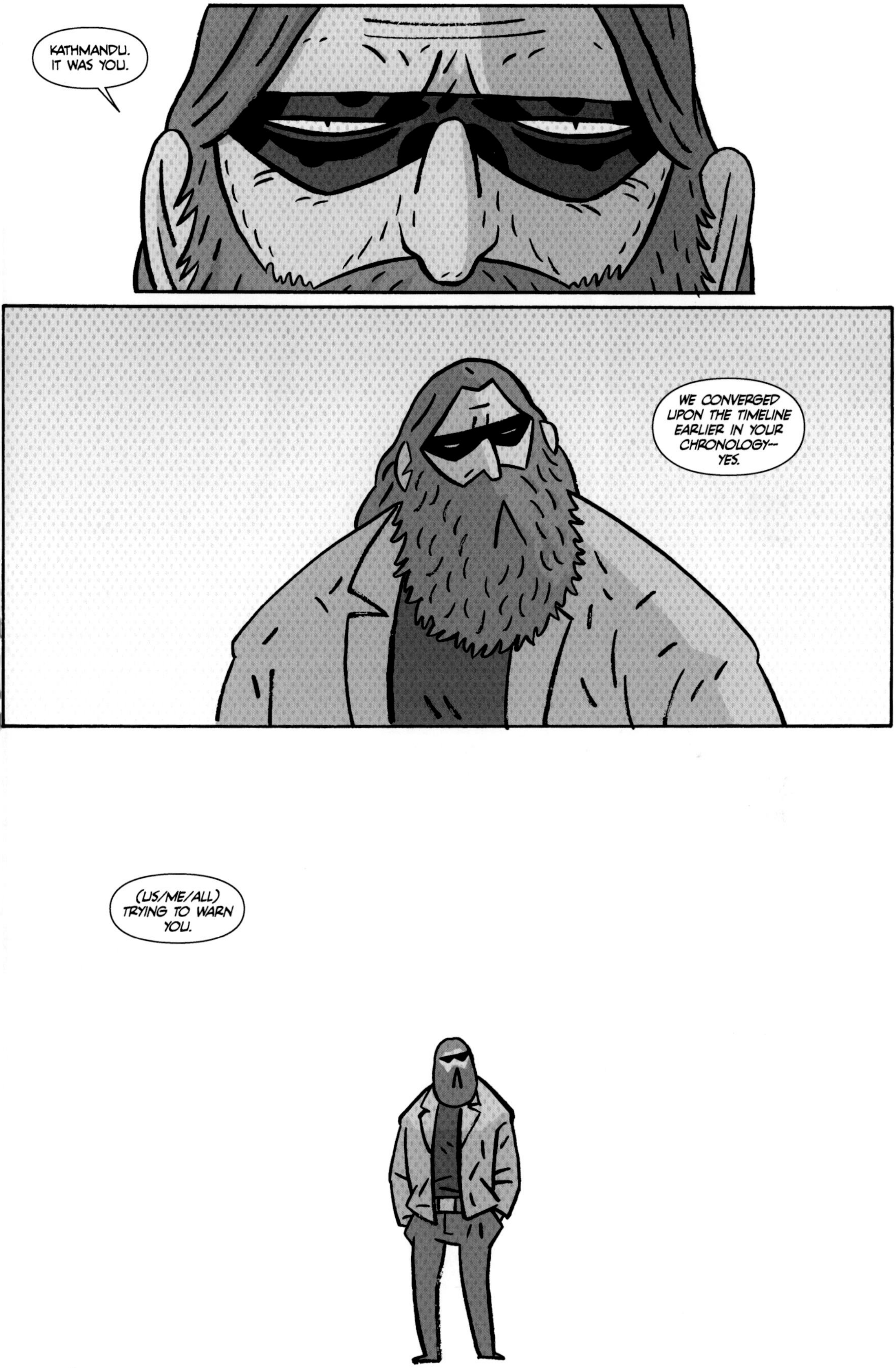
KATHMANDU. IT WAS YOU.
WE CONVERGED UPON THE TIMELINE EARLIER IN YOUR CHRONOLOGY-- YES.
(US/ME/ALL) TRYING TO WARN YOU.

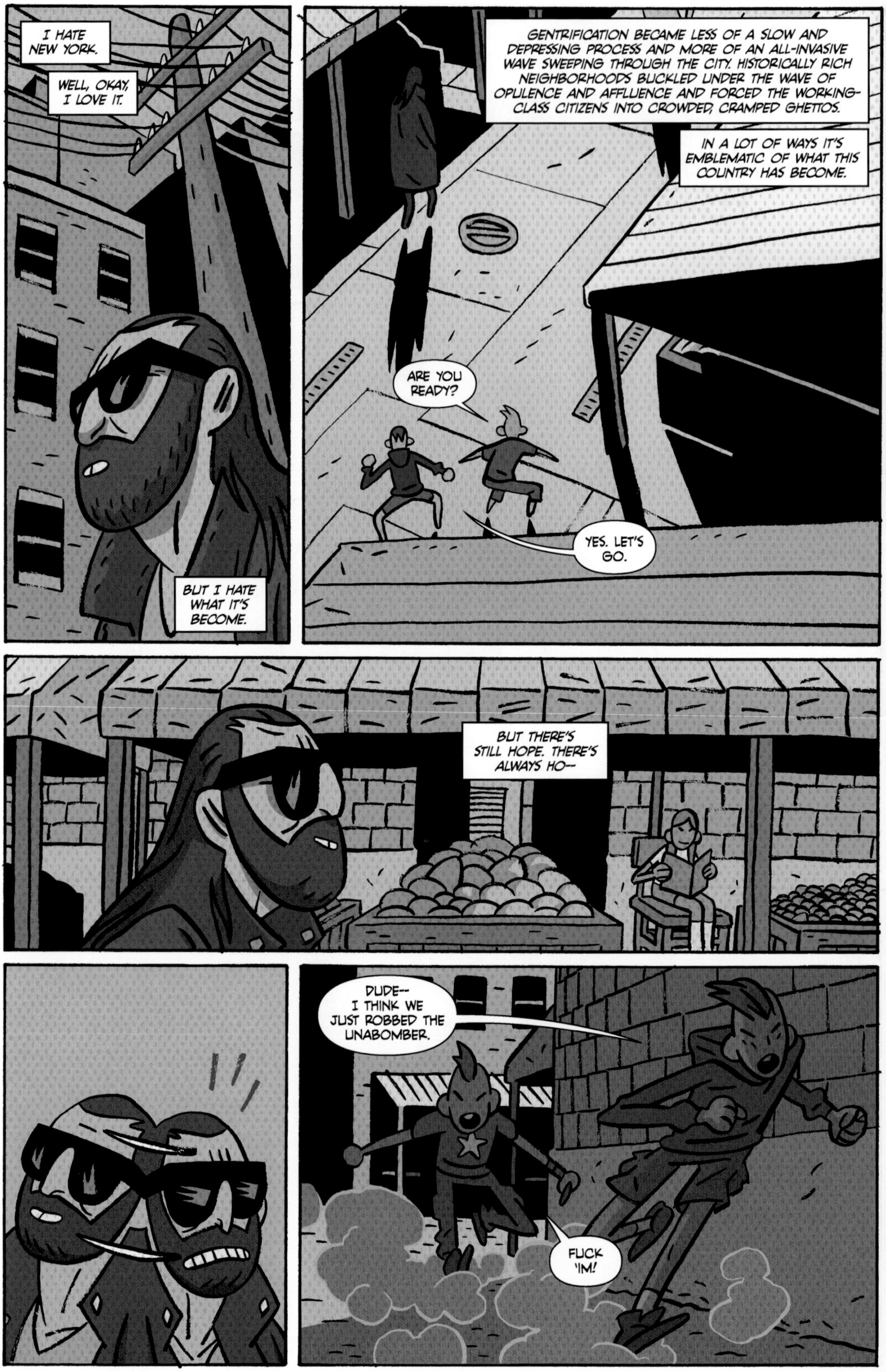
I HATE NEW YORK.
WELL, OKAY, I LOVE IT.
BUT I HATE WHAT IT'S BECOME.
GENTRIFICATION BECAME LESS OF A SLOW AND DEPRESSING PROCESS AND MORE OF AN ALL-INVASIVE WAVE SWEEPING THROUGH THE CITY. HISTORICALLY RICH NEIGHBORHOODS BUCKLED UNDER THE WAVE OF OPULENCE AND AFFLUENCE AND FORCED THE WORKING-CLASS CITIZENS INTO CROWDED, CRAMPED GHETTOS.
IN A LOT OF WAYS IT'S EMBLEMATIC OF WHAT THIS COUNTRY HAS BECOME.
ARE YOU READY?
YES. LET'S GO.
BUT THERE'S STILL HOPE. THERE'S ALWAYS HO--
DUDE-- I THINK WE JUST ROBBED THE UNABOMBER.
FUCK 'IM!

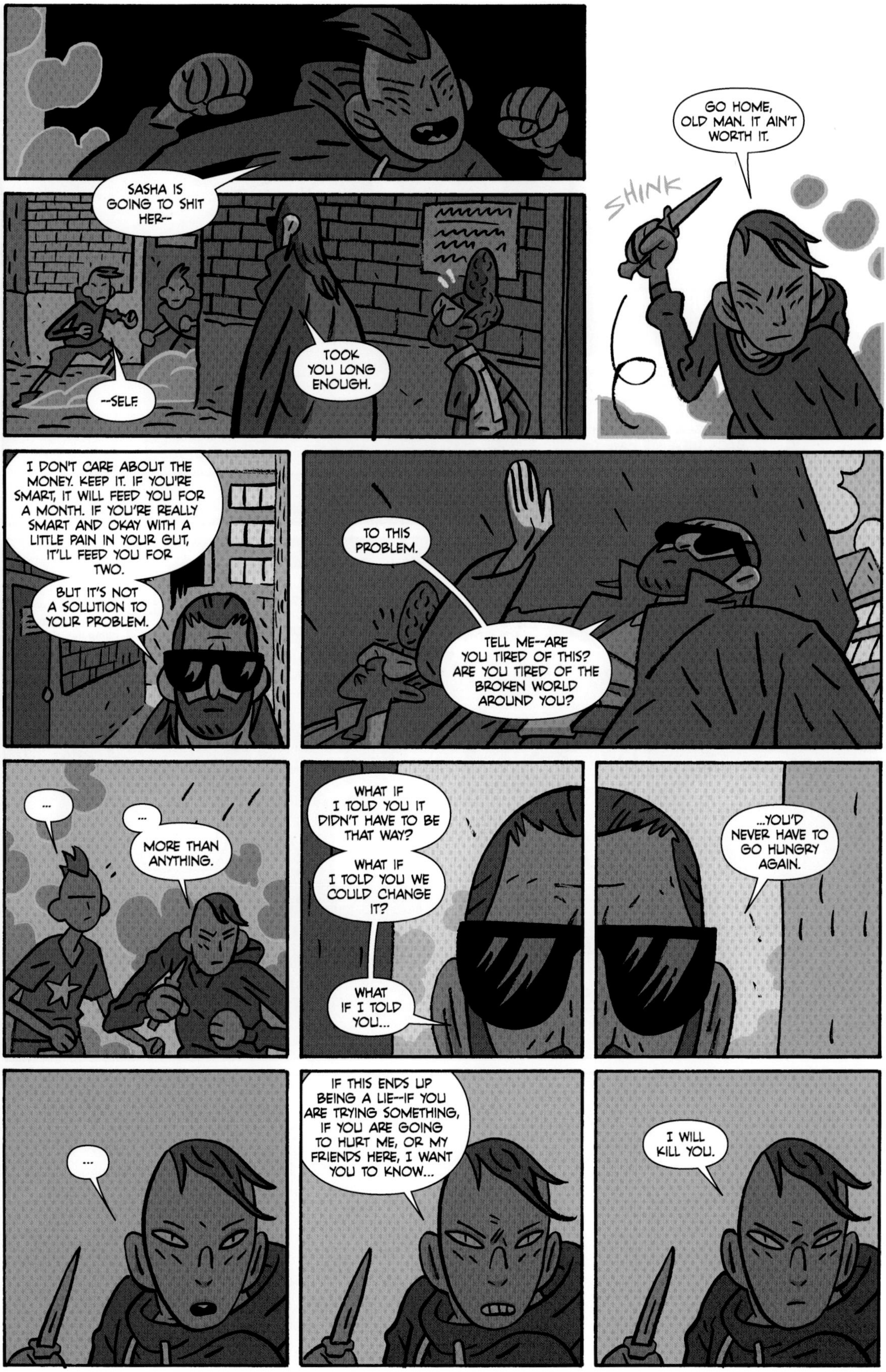
GO HOME, OLD MAN. IT AIN'T WORTH IT.
SHINK
SASHA IS GOING TO SHIT HER--
--SELF.
TOOK YOU LONG ENOUGH.
I DON'T CARE ABOUT THE MONEY. KEEP IT. IF YOU'RE SMART, IT WILL FEED YOU FOR A MONTH. IF YOU'RE REALLY SMART AND OKAY WITH A LITTLE PAIN IN YOUR GUT, IT'LL FEED YOU FOR TWO.
BUT IT'S NOT A SOLUTION TO YOUR PROBLEM.
TO THIS PROBLEM.
TELL ME--ARE YOU TIRED OF THIS? ARE YOU TIRED OF THE BROKEN WORLD AROUND YOU?
...
...
MORE THAN ANYTHING.
WHAT IF I TOLD YOU IT DIDN'T HAVE TO BE THAT WAY?
WHAT IF I TOLD YOU WE COULD CHANGE IT?
WHAT IF I TOLD YOU...
...YOU'D NEVER HAVE TO GO HUNGRY AGAIN.
...
IF THIS ENDS UP BEING A LIE--IF YOU ARE TRYING SOMETHING, IF YOU ARE GOING TO HURT ME, OR MY FRIENDS HERE, I WANT YOU TO KNOW...
I WILL KILL YOU.

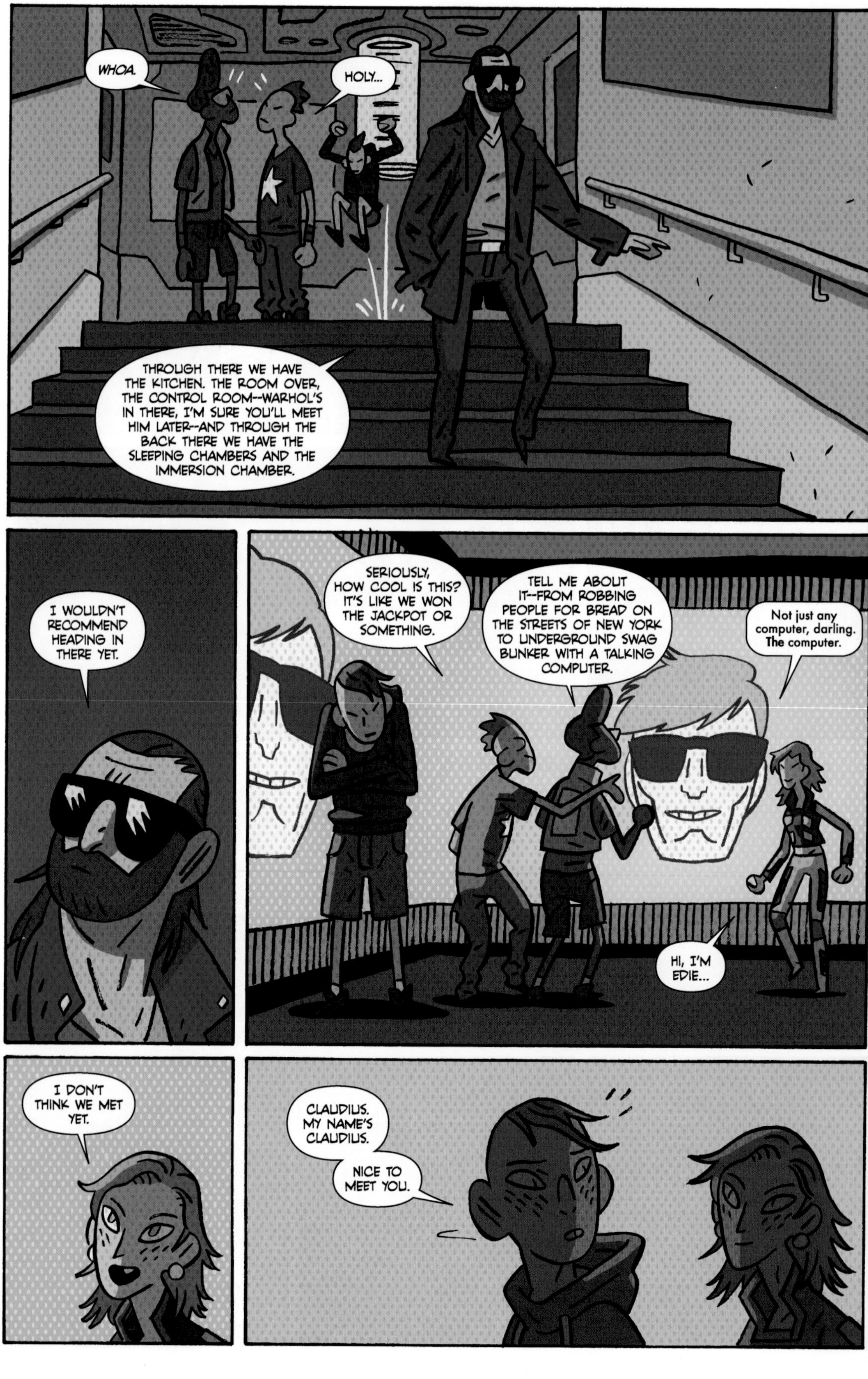
WHOA.
HOLY...
THROUGH THERE WE HAVE THE KITCHEN. THE ROOM OVER, THE CONTROL ROOM--WARHOL'S IN THERE, I'M SURE YOU'LL MEET HIM LATER--AND THROUGH THE BACK THERE WE HAVE THE SLEEPING CHAMBERS AND THE IMMERSION CHAMBER.
I WOULDN'T RECOMMEND HEADING IN THERE YET.
SERIOUSLY, HOW COOL IS THIS? IT'S LIKE WE WON THE JACKPOT OR SOMETHING.
TELL ME ABOUT IT--FROM ROBBING PEOPLE FOR BREAD ON THE STREETS OF NEW YORK TO UNDERGROUND SWAG BUNKER WITH A TALKING COMPUTER.
Not just any computer, darling. The computer.
HI, I'M EDIE...
I DON'T THINK WE MET YET.
CLAUDIUS. MY NAME'S CLAUDIUS.
NICE TO MEET YOU.

ROOM SWEATING IDEA LIKE A VIRUS CAN'T FORGET KATHMANDU

KATHMANDU IDEAS IN YOUR VEINS LIKE A VIRUS YOU CAN'T SWEAT OUT NO MATTER HOW HARD YOU TRY

TOO LATE WARN THEM ALL DO SOMETHING DO ANYTHING

LAPTOP LIKE A WEAPON USE IT WARN EVERYONE

LAPTOP LIKE A WEAPON WRITE YOUR WAY OUT WRITE YOUR WAY OUT WRITE YOUR WAY OUT OF THE DEAD FUTURE

NOT TOO LATE NEVER TOO LATE

THE TOMORROW M
BY ALDOUS ELLIS

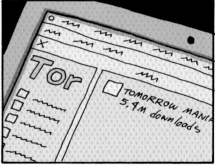

Tor

TOMORROW MANI
5.4m downloads

THE TOMORROW MANIFESTO BY ALDOUS ELLIS

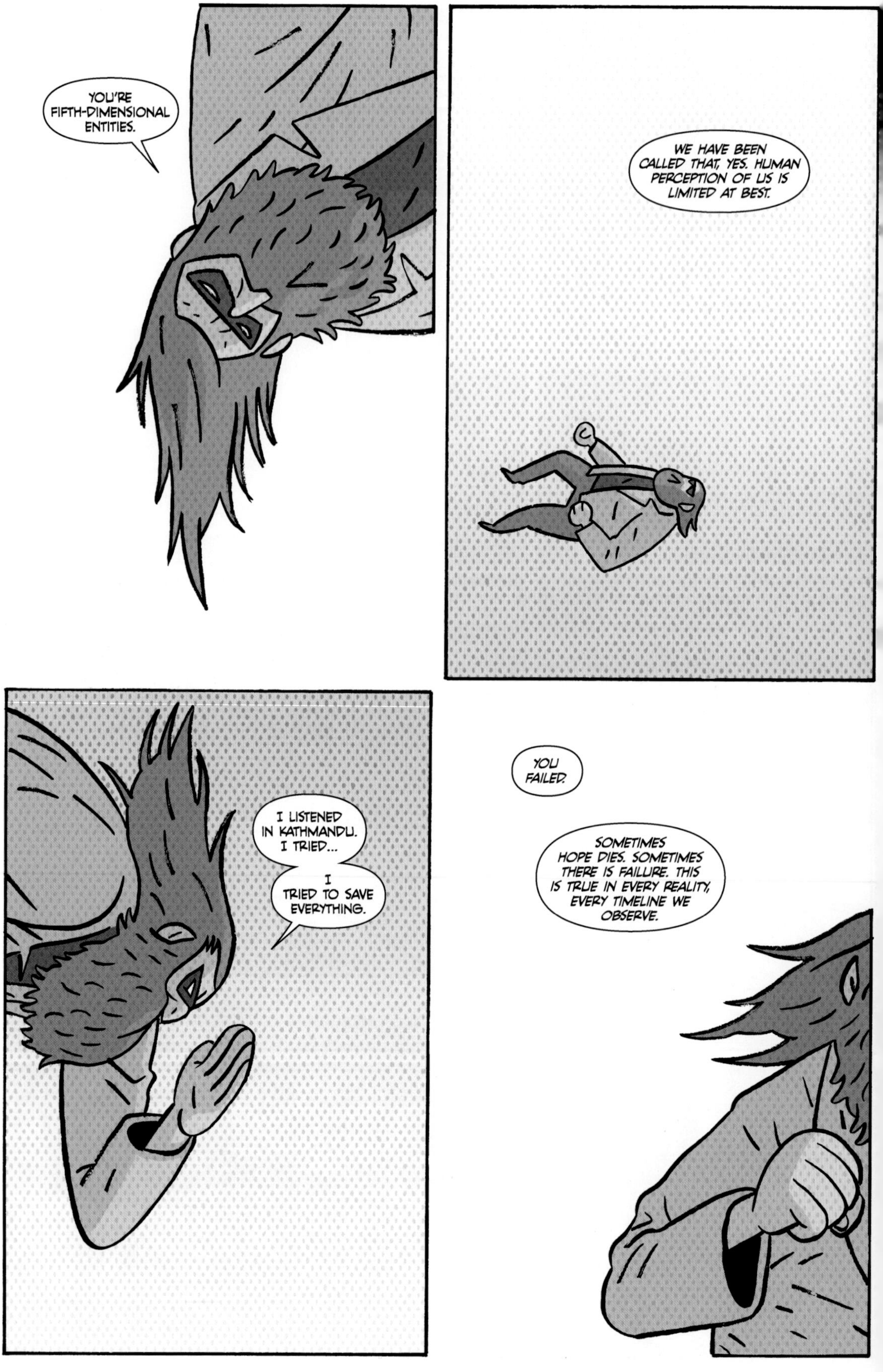
YOU'RE FIFTH-DIMENSIONAL ENTITIES.
WE HAVE BEEN CALLED THAT, YES. HUMAN PERCEPTION OF US IS LIMITED AT BEST.
I LISTENED IN KATHMANDU. I TRIED...
I TRIED TO SAVE EVERYTHING.
YOU FAILED.
SOMETIMES HOPE DIES. SOMETIMES THERE IS FAILURE. THIS IS TRUE IN EVERY REALITY, EVERY TIMELINE WE OBSERVE.

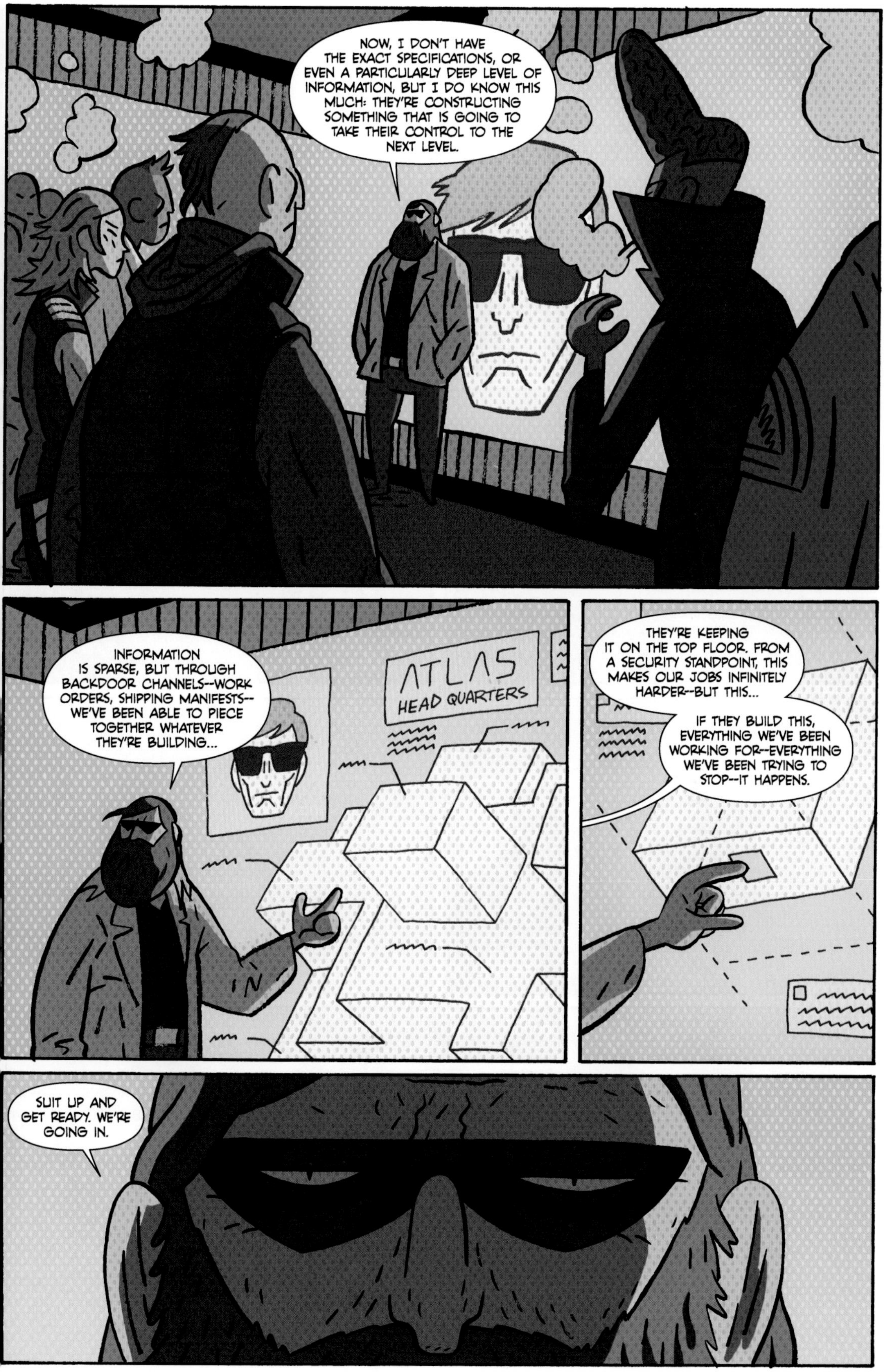
NOW, I DON'T HAVE THE EXACT SPECIFICATIONS, OR EVEN A PARTICULARLY DEEP LEVEL OF INFORMATION, BUT I DO KNOW THIS MUCH: THEY'RE CONSTRUCTING SOMETHING THAT IS GOING TO TAKE THEIR CONTROL TO THE NEXT LEVEL.
INFORMATION IS SPARSE, BUT THROUGH BACKDOOR CHANNELS--WORK ORDERS, SHIPPING MANIFESTS--WE'VE BEEN ABLE TO PIECE TOGETHER WHATEVER THEY'RE BUILDING...
ATLAS
HEAD QUARTERS
THEY'RE KEEPING IT ON THE TOP FLOOR. FROM A SECURITY STANDPOINT, THIS MAKES OUR JOBS INFINITELY HARDER--BUT THIS...
IF THEY BUILD THIS, EVERYTHING WE'VE BEEN WORKING FOR--EVERYTHING WE'VE BEEN TRYING TO STOP--IT HAPPENS.
SUIT UP AND GET READY. WE'RE GOING IN.

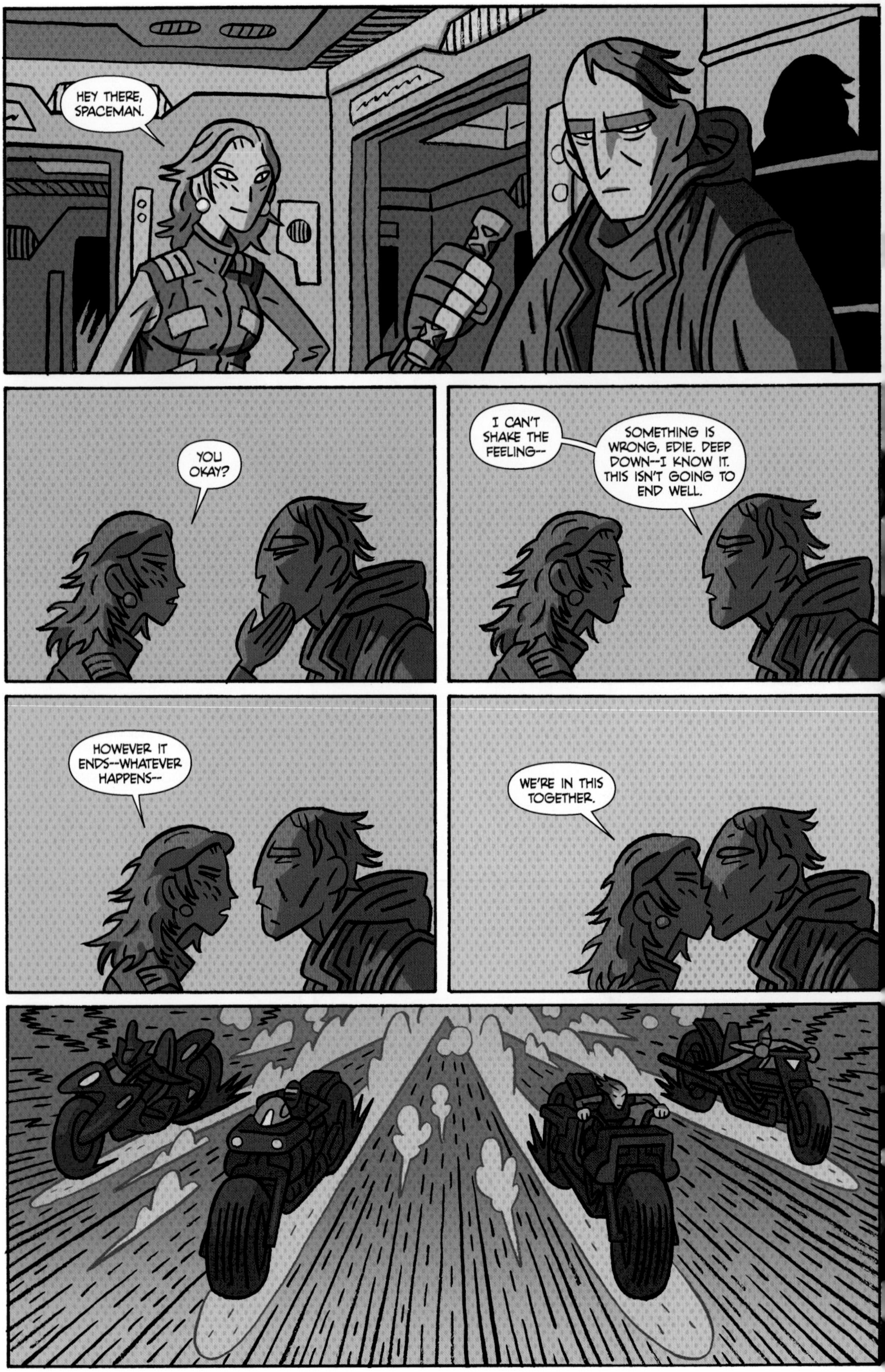
HEY THERE, SPACEMAN.
YOU OKAY?
I CAN'T SHAKE THE FEELING--
SOMETHING IS WRONG, EDIE. DEEP DOWN--I KNOW IT. THIS ISN'T GOING TO END WELL.
HOWEVER IT ENDS--WHATEVER HAPPENS--
WE'RE IN THIS TOGETHER.

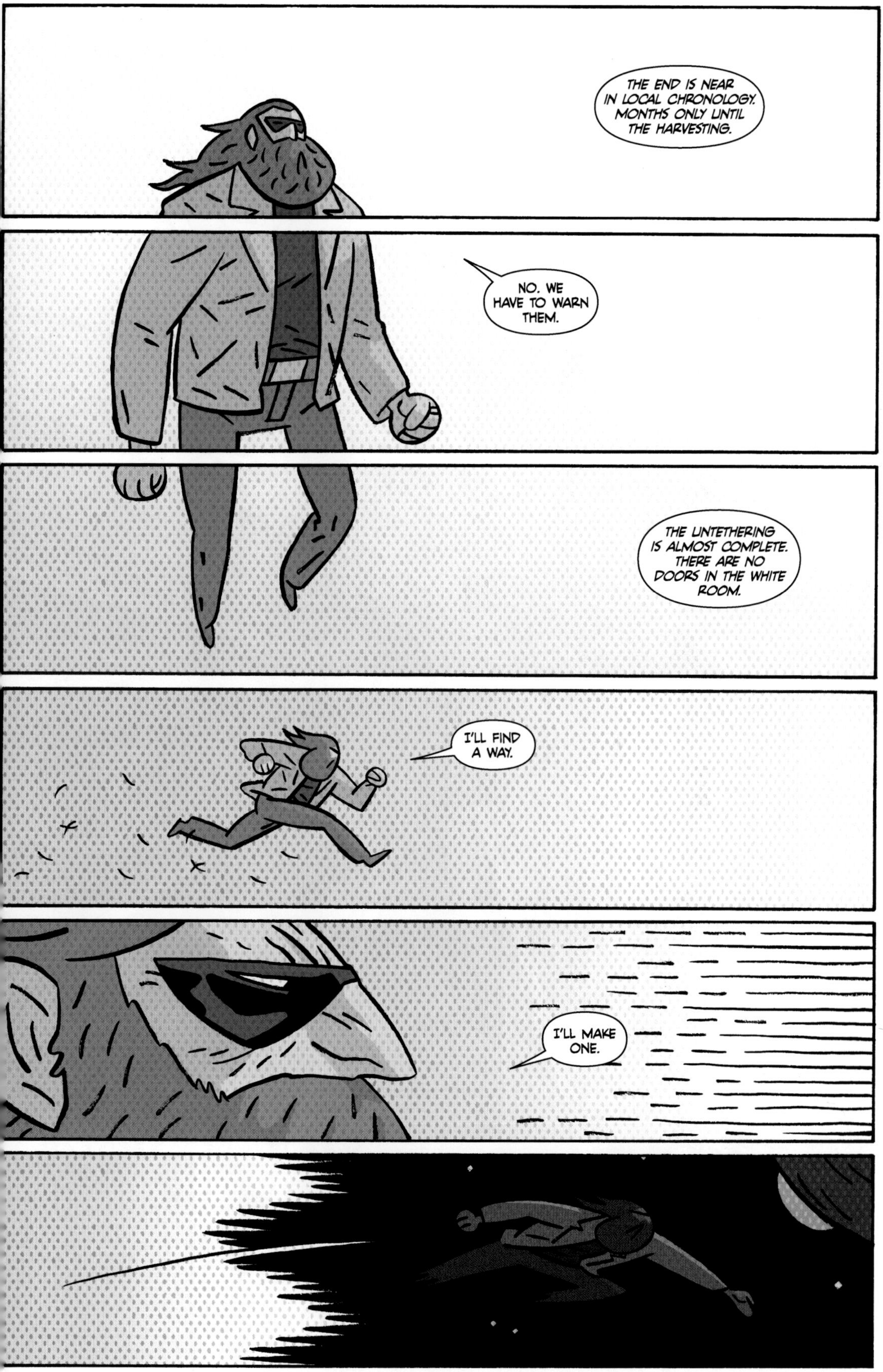
THE END IS NEAR IN LOCAL CHRONOLOGY. MONTHS ONLY UNTIL THE HARVESTING.
NO. WE HAVE TO WARN THEM.
THE UNTETHERING IS ALMOST COMPLETE. THERE ARE NO DOORS IN THE WHITE ROOM.
I'LL FIND A WAY.
I'LL MAKE ONE.

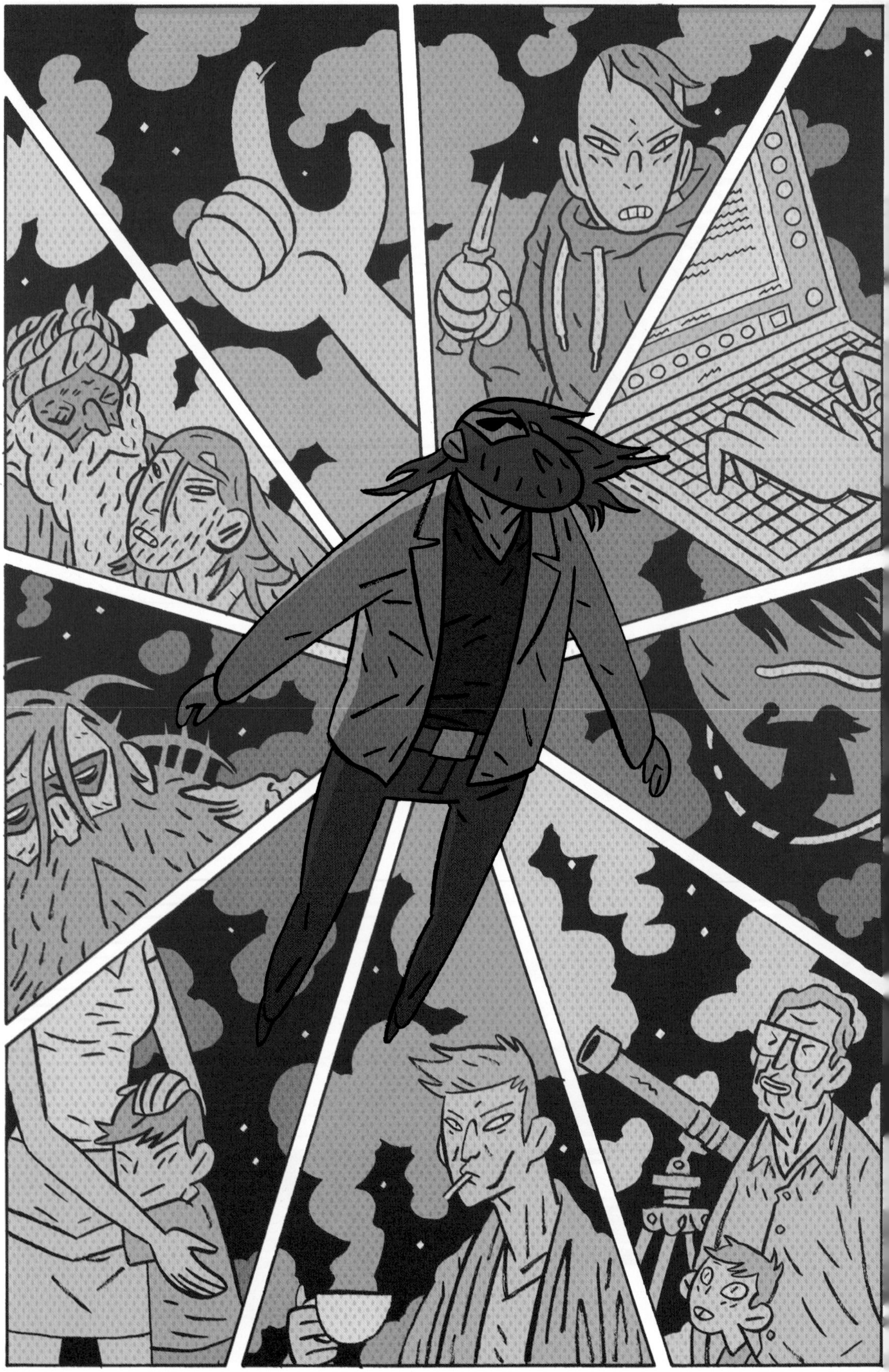

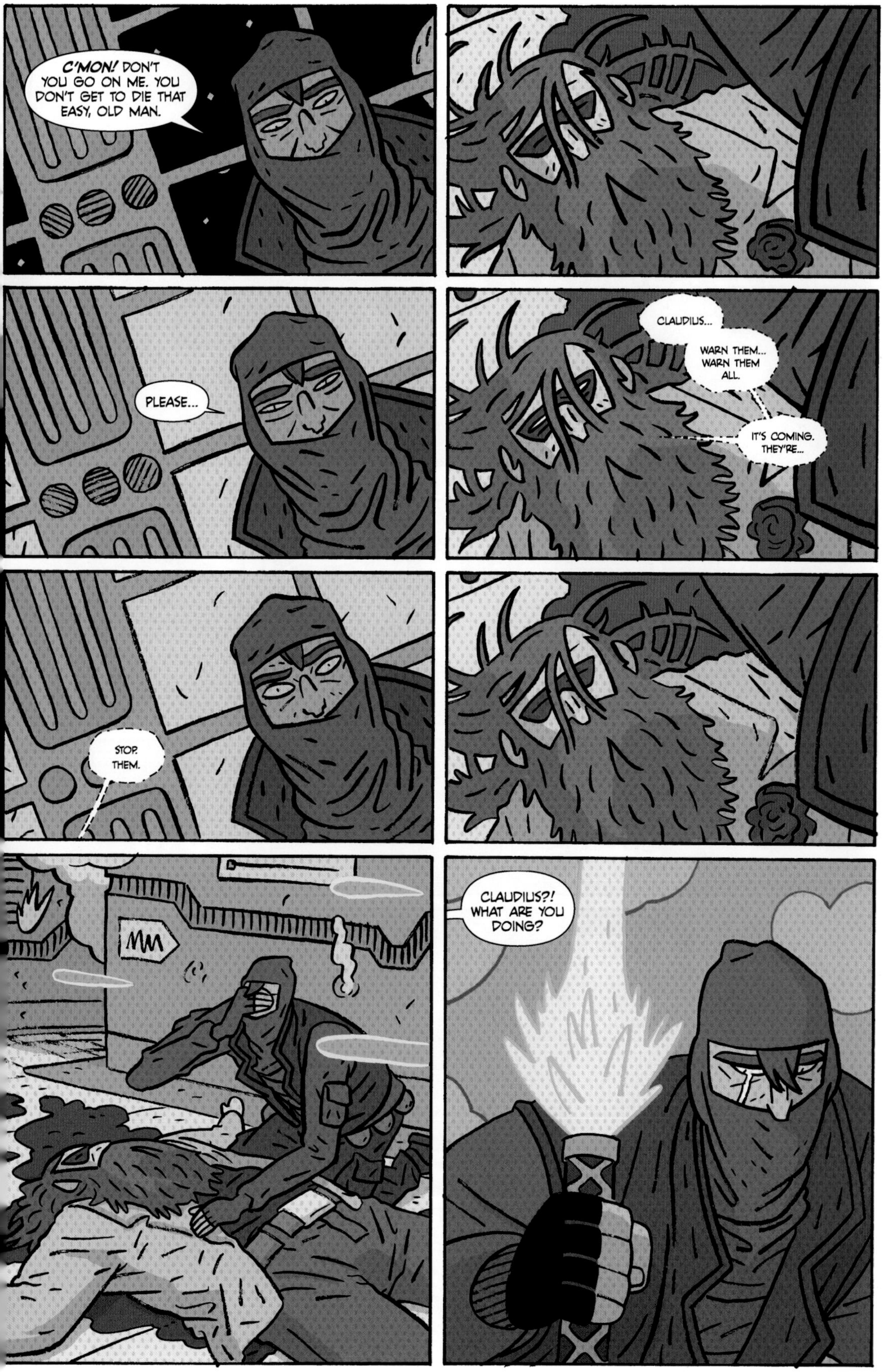
C'MON! DON'T YOU GO ON ME. YOU DON'T GET TO DIE THAT EASY, OLD MAN.
PLEASE...
CLAUDIUS...
WARN THEM... WARN THEM ALL.
IT'S COMING. THEY'RE...
STOP. THEM.
CLAUDIUS?! WHAT ARE YOU DOING?

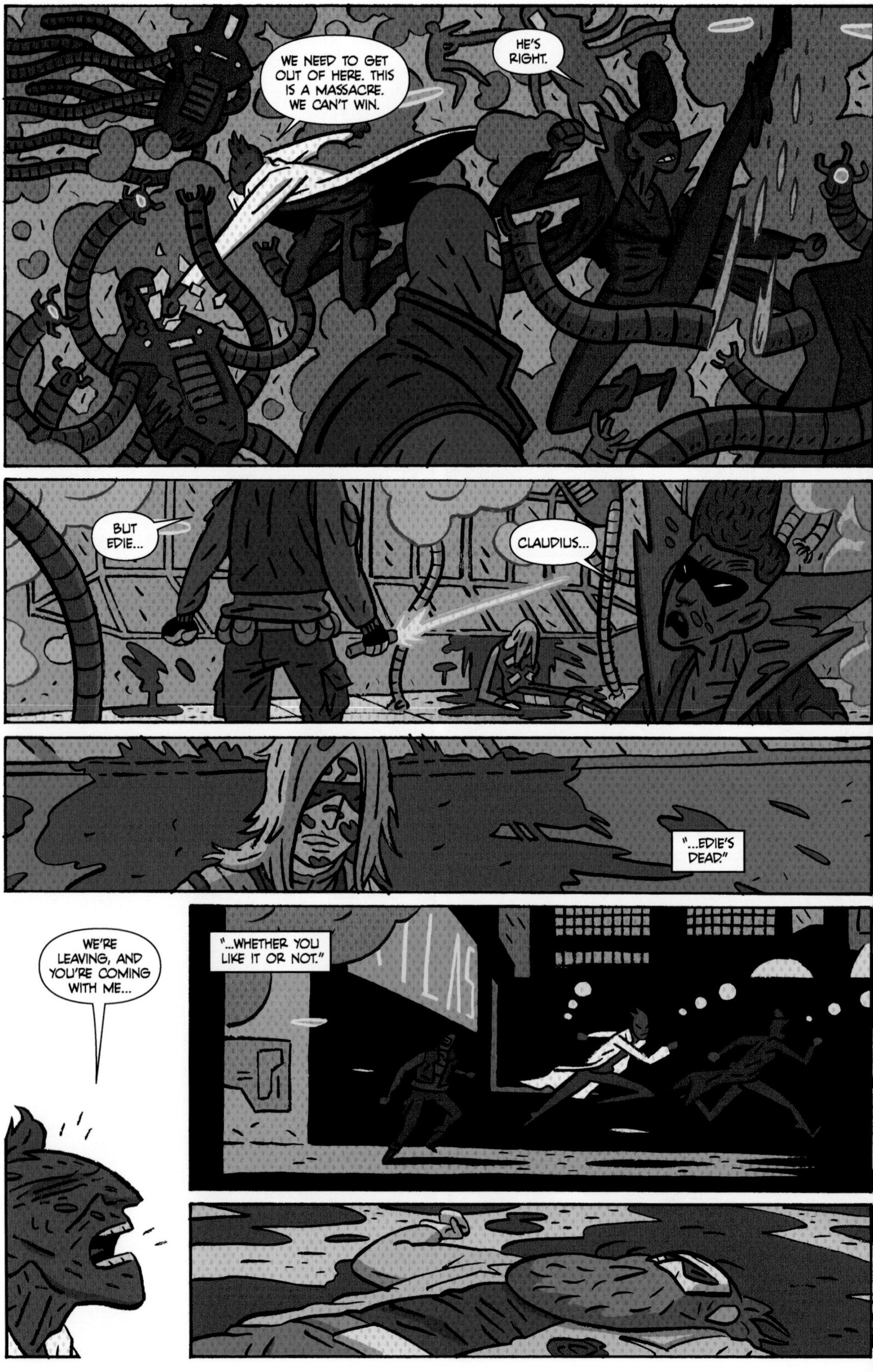
WE NEED TO GET OUT OF HERE. THIS IS A MASSACRE. WE CAN'T WIN.
HE'S RIGHT.
BUT EDIE...
CLAUDIUS...
"...EDIE'S DEAD."
WE'RE LEAVING, AND YOU'RE COMING WITH ME...
"...WHETHER YOU LIKE IT OR NOT."

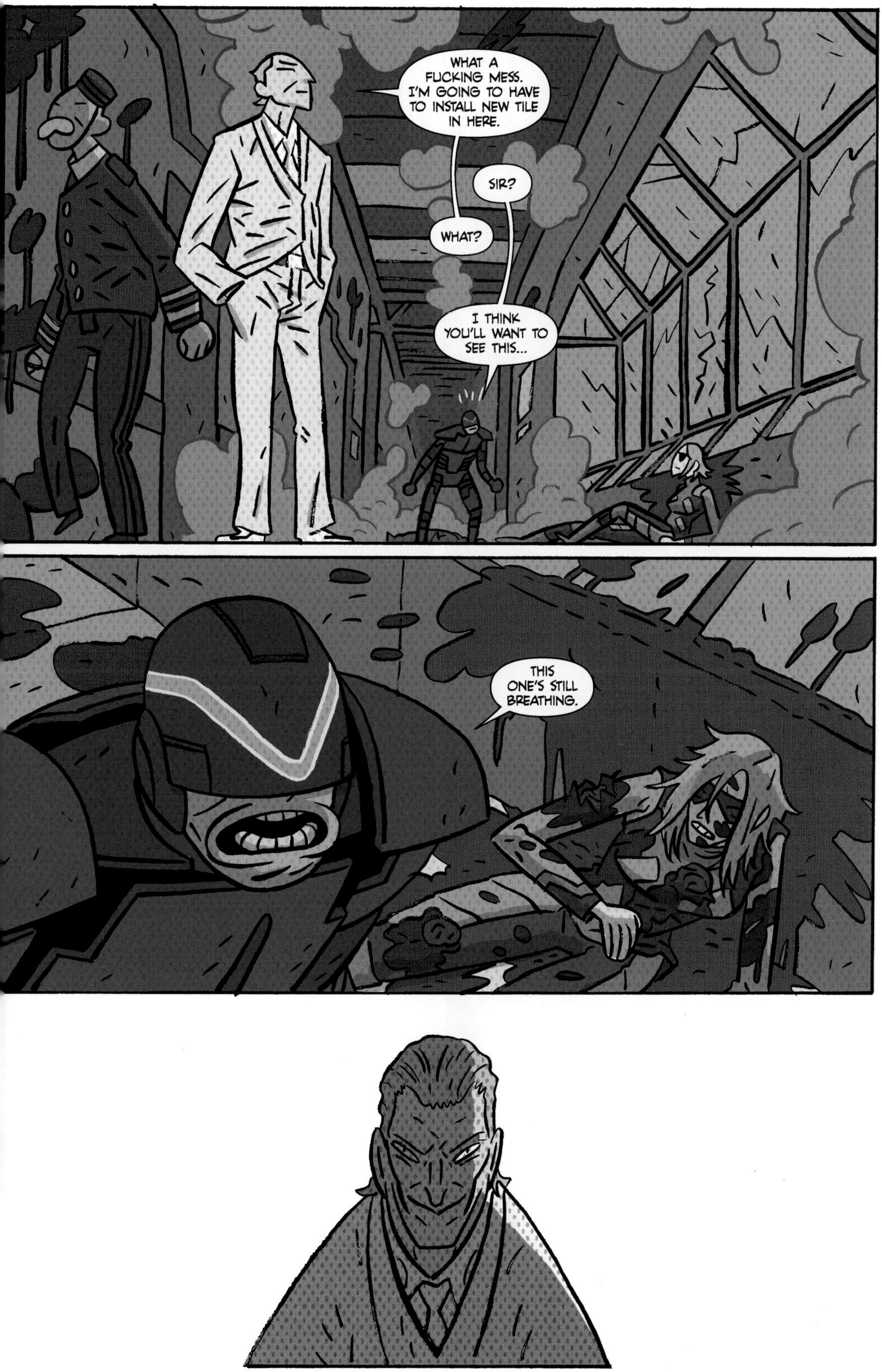
WHAT A FUCKING MESS. I'M GOING TO HAVE TO INSTALL NEW TILE IN HERE.
SIR?
WHAT?
I THINK YOU'LL WANT TO SEE THIS...
THIS ONE'S STILL BREATHING.

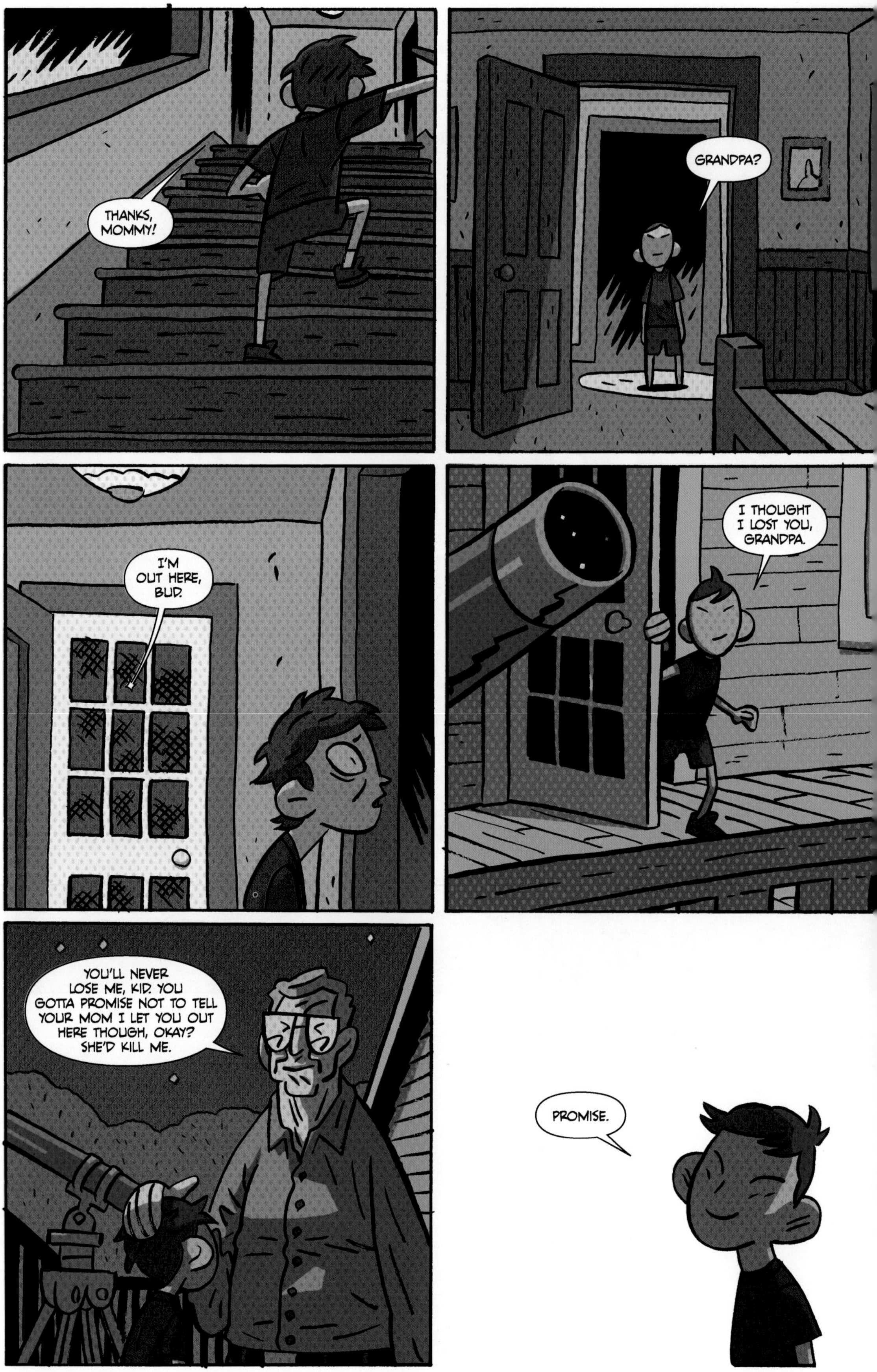
THANKS, MOMMY!
GRANDPA?
I'M OUT HERE, BUD.
I THOUGHT I LOST YOU, GRANDPA.
YOU'LL NEVER LOSE ME, KID. YOU GOTTA PROMISE NOT TO TELL YOUR MOM I LET YOU OUT HERE THOUGH, OKAY? SHE'D KILL ME.
PROMISE.

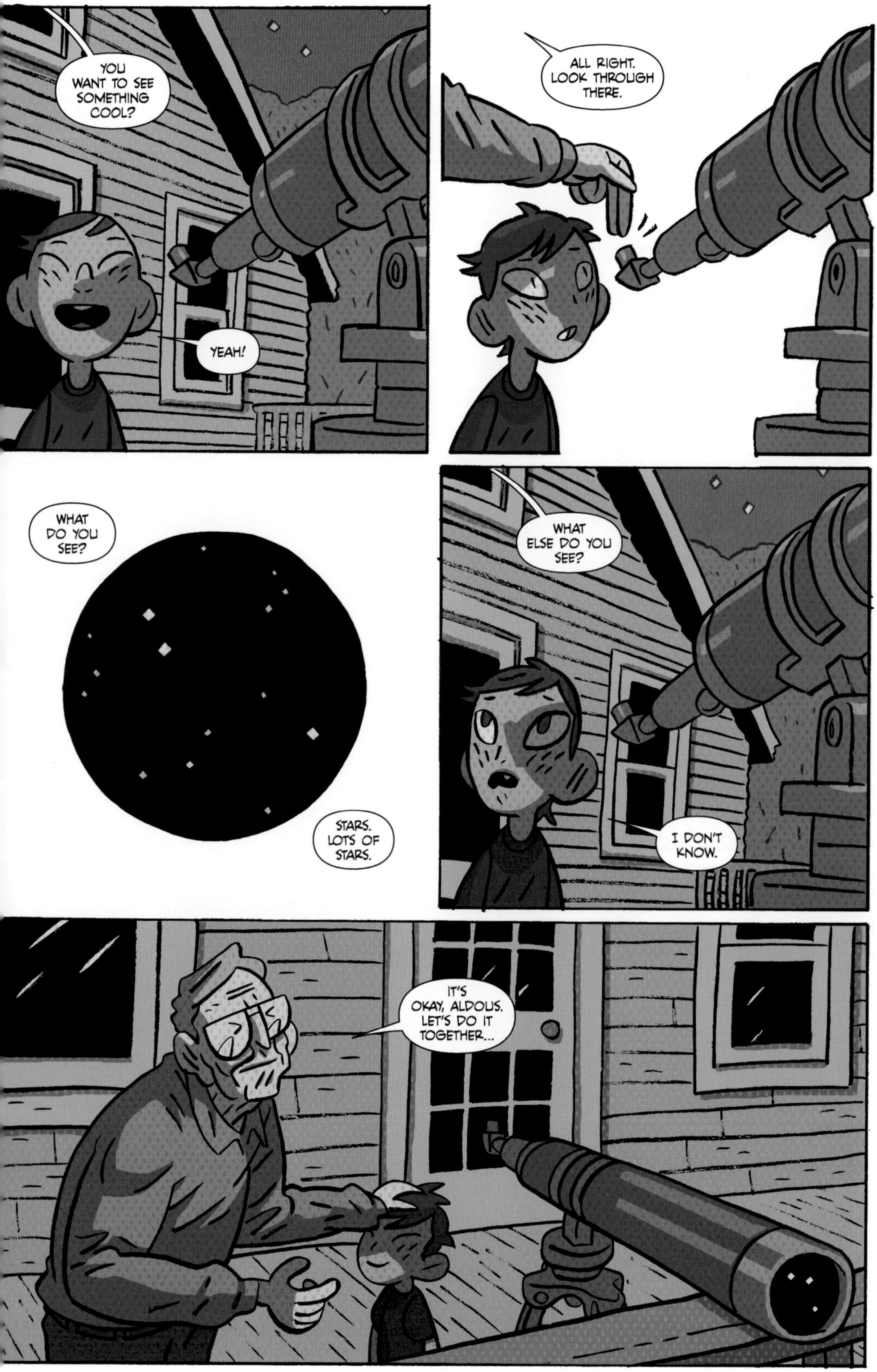
YOU WANT TO SEE SOMETHING COOL?
YEAH!
ALL RIGHT. LOOK THROUGH THERE.
WHAT DO YOU SEE?
STARS. LOTS OF STARS.
WHAT ELSE DO YOU SEE?
I DON'T KNOW.
IT'S OKAY, ALDOUS. LET'S DO IT TOGETHER...

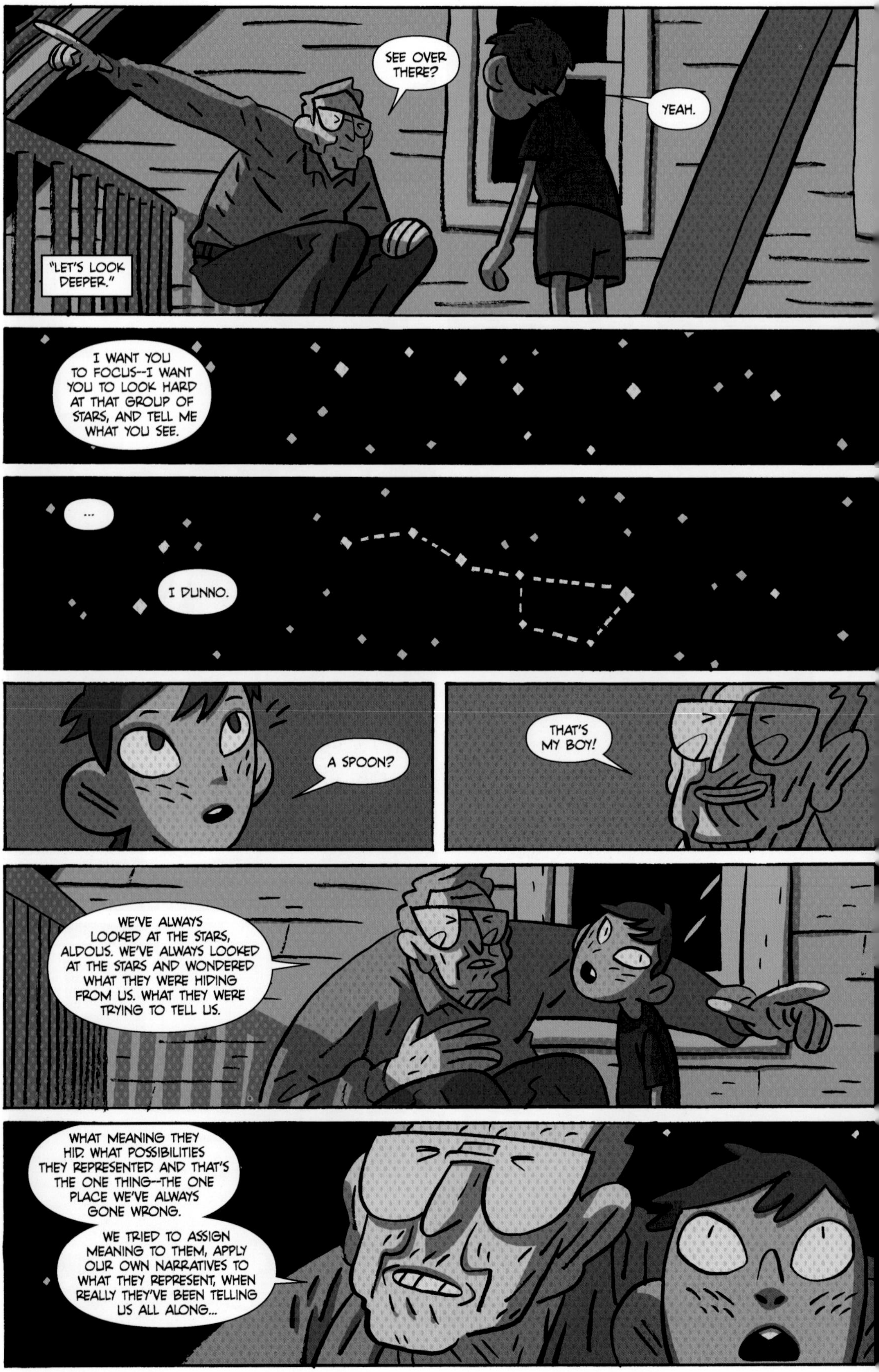

SEE OVER THERE?
YEAH.
"LET'S LOOK DEEPER."
I WANT YOU TO FOCUS--I WANT YOU TO LOOK HARD AT THAT GROUP OF STARS, AND TELL ME WHAT YOU SEE.
...
I DUNNO.
A SPOON?
THAT'S MY BOY!
WE'VE ALWAYS LOOKED AT THE STARS, ALDOUS. WE'VE ALWAYS LOOKED AT THE STARS AND WONDERED WHAT THEY WERE HIDING FROM US. WHAT THEY WERE TRYING TO TELL US.
WHAT MEANING THEY HID. WHAT POSSIBILITIES THEY REPRESENTED. AND THAT'S THE ONE THING--THE ONE PLACE WE'VE ALWAYS GONE WRONG.
WE TRIED TO ASSIGN MEANING TO THEM, APPLY OUR OWN NARRATIVES TO WHAT THEY REPRESENT, WHEN REALLY THEY'VE BEEN TELLING US ALL ALONG...

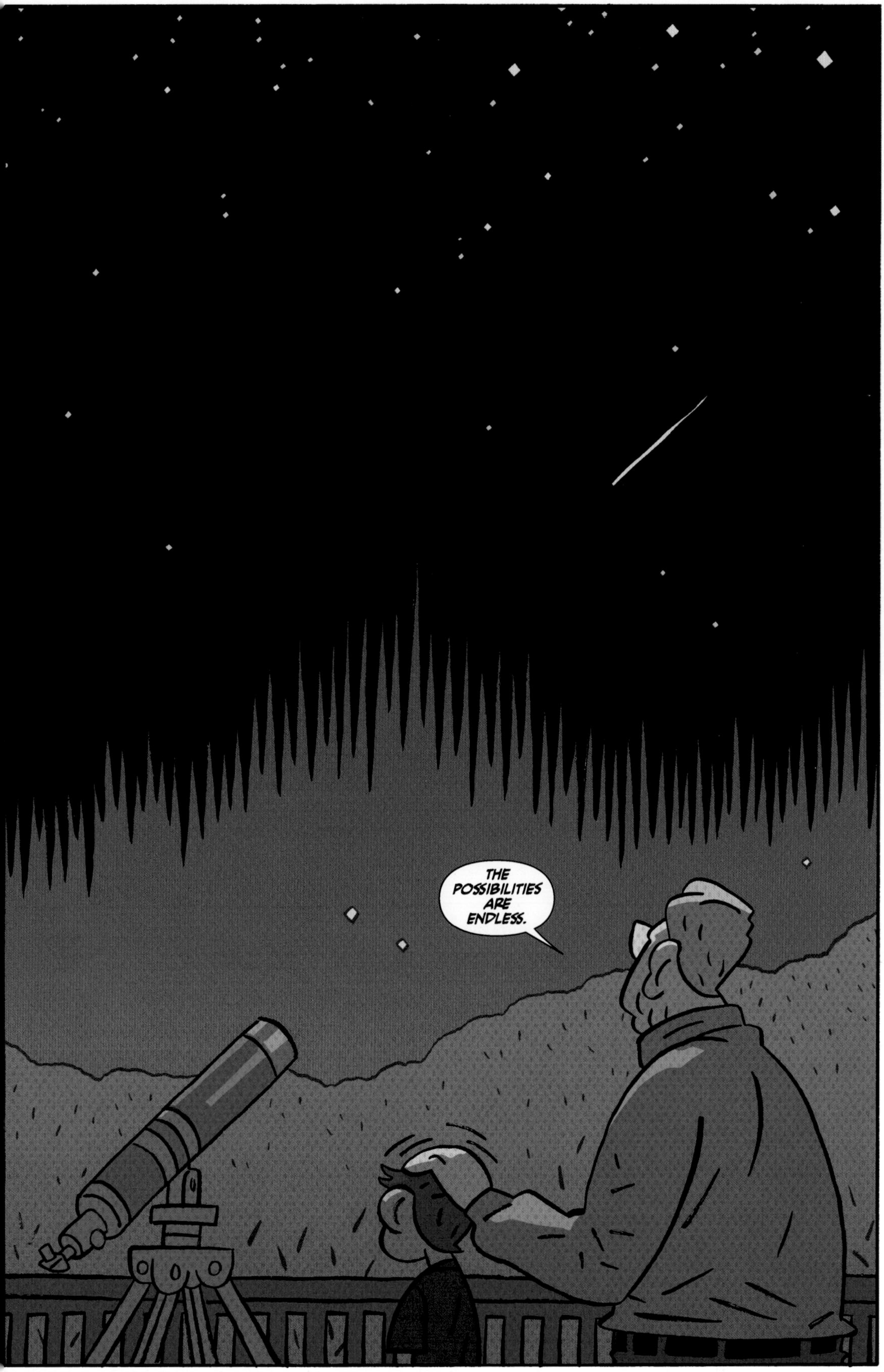
THE POSSIBILITIES ARE ENDLESS.

# ALL TOMOR-ROWS PARTIES

GAVIN SHANE

**ALDOUS ELLIS IS AN ENIGMA.** His work, known across the globe, is stirring up political waves and helping ignite a global movement that follows the views presented in his manifesto, yet some see worrying parallels between the manifesto's call to arms and the dangerous, cult-like teachings of entities such as Scientology.

Although averse to traditional press interactions, Aldous agreed to sit with *Virtue* founder Gavin Shane for a rare interview.

**GAVIN SHANE:** Thanks for taking the time to sit down with me today, Aldous.

**ALDOUS ELLIS:** No problem, Gavin. Thanks for having me.

**GS:** Let's start with the question on everyone's lips: what are the Tomorrows?

**AE:** Cutting right to the chase, hey? I like that. Well, sorry to disappoint, Gavin, but I don't have a concrete answer for you. Part of what we're trying to do here is erode traditional structures. Reject binary classifications—dualist worldviews—us vs. them mentalities. In that regard, we're unclassifiable. If I personally, as a member of the group you're referring to, had to describe some similarity between our actions, I would say that we behave in a way that we believe will contribute to or create a better future—one we feel we're not presently on a course to arrive at.

**GS:** Can you see why an answer like that would make people uncomfortable?

**AE:** I mean, sure. I can easily see how it'd make people uncomfortable. I never

signed on to be a provider of comfort, though. Do you think innovation is bred of comfort? How many times in the course of our history can the emergence of an advancement be ascribed to a place of comfort? None. That's not how it works.

**GS:** You've spoken out against the current administration. Can you elaborate on that?

**AE:** I mean, I can—but that's not really the point.

**GS:** Oh?

**AE:** It's a symptom of a country that operates and has operated for a very long time under the confines of a very broken political system. One that has allowed the blurring of corporate interest and government policy to a degree where the two are virtually indistinguishable. Partisanship has also eroded the country. Gun violence—mass shootings from gun violence—has been an issue since the 2010s, and all this time later, we haven't seen gun-control legislation. This is a self-perpetuating cycle, and ouroboros,

our political system (much like our economy), exists perpetually within a suicide pact with itself.

**GS:** You touched on violence—gun violence in particular—but how would you respond, how would you defend the violence that the followers of your manifesto—of your "teachings," if you will—have perpetrated?

**AE:** Violence is—it's wrong. I can never reconcile it. In my heart of hearts I know that nothing emerges from violence. But it's the world we're living in. The parameters we're operating within—they force violence upon us, and in the interest of protecting ourselves, enacting the changes we need to course-correct our reality, unfortunately they (myself included) have been forced to inflict violence. It's not something we're proud of—it's not something we celebrate—but we hope and pray that from this self-defense—this unavoidable violence—beauty and nonviolence can emerge. It's one of many great paradoxes we face when navigating reality.

# THE REBIRTH of TERRANCE GATTICA

CONTINUED FROM PAGE 89

Gattica takes a long draw on his cigarette—one he admits he shouldn't be smoking—and then takes a sip of his green tea. "I don't know. It's a lot like learning to live again, if that makes sense. You sort of have to realign everything you knew—this entire mode of existence you were operating within. Only once you've been away from it for a while do you realize what a dark fucking place it was. I mean—I think I realized it at the time, but I needed the push, I needed help to get out of it." When pressed on what his next projects are, Gattica remains tight lipped. "Let's see, there's the TV pilot I'm working on, there's the last issue of the book I'm doing at Dark Horse, and beyond that, we'll see. Hopefully we'll get around to making a second volume of that one. I really love writing it, and it would be nice to wrap the story up. Beyond that, I'm not quitting writing or anything. I'm just only interested in putting things into the universe that are meaningful to me, that have something to say, that make me feel something. There's too much art—too much content these days that's

||||||||||||||||||||||||||||||||||||||||||||||||||||||

> ## "I'm not quitting writing or anything. I'm just only interested in putting things into the universe that are meaningful to me."

meaningless. People don't think about what they make anymore. This industry, more than anything, seems to celebrate that—that vanilla, single-serve, easily delivered narrative. I don't know. I don't begrudge anyone that—I've enjoyed those stories myself—but I think maybe the right move for me at this point is to just step back until I figure out what it is I want to say. That make sense? Truth be told, I'll probably change my mind tomorrow."

When our conversation is over, Gattica shakes my hand and thanks me for the interview before leaving. Through the window I watch him light another cigarette, which he makes quick work of before stomping it out to catch a cab. As he enters the cab, the clouds part and the sun peeks out, momentarily blinding me. As the cab disappears into the crowded street, I find myself thinking: Terrance Gattica is going to be okay. ◄◄◄◄

CONTINUED FROM PAGE 56

GS: You just opened chapters in Rio—and in Tokyo, correct? How's that going?

AE: It's exciting. It's so fucking exciting. Rio in particular. I think the things that are happening there right now—ten-year-old kids building fucking drones—these sort of garage scientists that are carving out the future, innovating and inventing new technologies—it's so brilliant. That's where the future is coming from. It's the perfect place for us. New York—America

> # "ALL SYSTEMS ARE FLUID, REALITY IS HACKABLE, AND IF YOU WISH TO SEE CHANGE, YOU ONLY NEED TO ACT IN ORDER TO CREATE IT."

is such a fucking mess right now. Canada's not much better either. Harper has been in power too long. We're seeing a lot of scary policy and behaviors from that government. It's—really historically we saw the same behavior from his father when he was in power in the early 2000s, so I don't know why I'm surprised. That said, I'm hoping we can do some good by opening up our chapters in Calgary and Vancouver. Those will be up and running in the next month or two here. I'm really excited to see where it goes.

GS: In your manifesto you talk at length about something you refer to as "digital shamanism"—can you elaborate on this concept for our readers?

AE: Sure. Well, simply put, digital shamanism is, at its core, the belief that all systems, reality included, are governed by coding, and that this coding itself is hackable. The larger implication of this is that all systems are fluid, reality is hackable, and if you wish to see change, you only need to act in order to create it. Beyond that, within the manifesto I spend time exploring in much greater depth the line, or lack thereof, between science and magic. And who benefits from the creation of a distinction between the two.

GS: That's interesting, to say the least. Do you think commenting on issues like magic, like technology, will scare away parties primarily interested in your political views?

AE: It's not all or nothing. Like I said before, this isn't some sort of cult of personality. I welcome discourse, discussion. Part of gaining intelligence, gaining any sort of real knowledge, is being open to the concept of being wrong. There's nothing wrong about being wrong. It's how we learn. Mistakes are a training tool for our future discussions. The Tomorrows—if we're anything, we're an open dialogue about reality, always challenging each other and exploring new ways of thinking. Whether it's my closest confidant or a ten-year-old recruit, I'm open to being challenged.

GS: All right, I don't want to keep you too long here, Aldous, so let's just ask the question that everybody wants to hear the answer to: what is the future?

AE: Whatever we want it to be. ◄◄◄◄

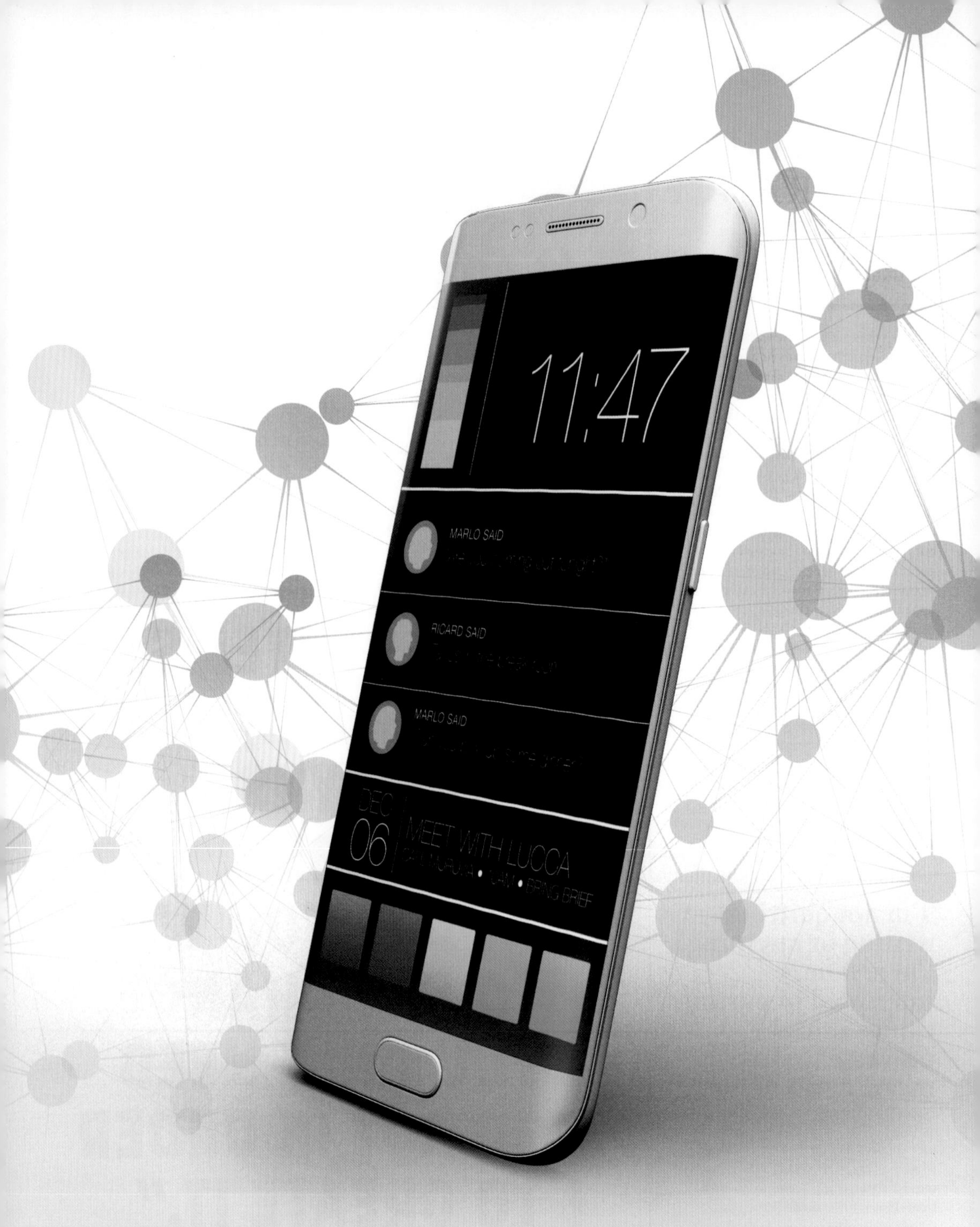
11:47
MARLO SAID
RICARD SAID
MARLO SAID
DEC
06
MEET WITH LUCCA
BRING BRIEF

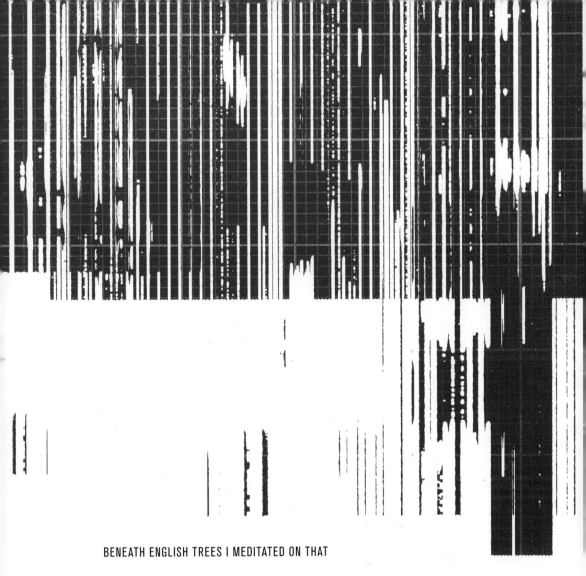

BENEATH ENGLISH TREES I MEDITATED ON THAT

LOST MAZE: I IMAGINED IT INVIOLATE AND PERFECT AT THE SECRET CREST OF A MOUNTAIN;

I IMAGINED IT ERASED BY RICE FIELDS OR BENEATH THE WATER; I IMAGINED IT INFINITE,

NO LONGER COMPOSED OF OCTAGONAL KIOSKS AND RETURNING PATHS, BUT OF RIVERS

AND PROVINCES AND KINGDOMS . . . I THOUGHT OF A LABYRINTH OF LABYRINTHS, OF ONE

SINUOUS SPREADING LABYRINTH THAT WOULD ENCOMPASS THE PAST AND THE FUTURE

AND IN SOME WAY INVOLVE THE STARS.

**–JORGE LUIS BORGES**
"THE GARDEN OF FORKING PATHS"

# part five

# A BEGINNER'S GUIDE TO DESTROYING THE MULTIVERSE

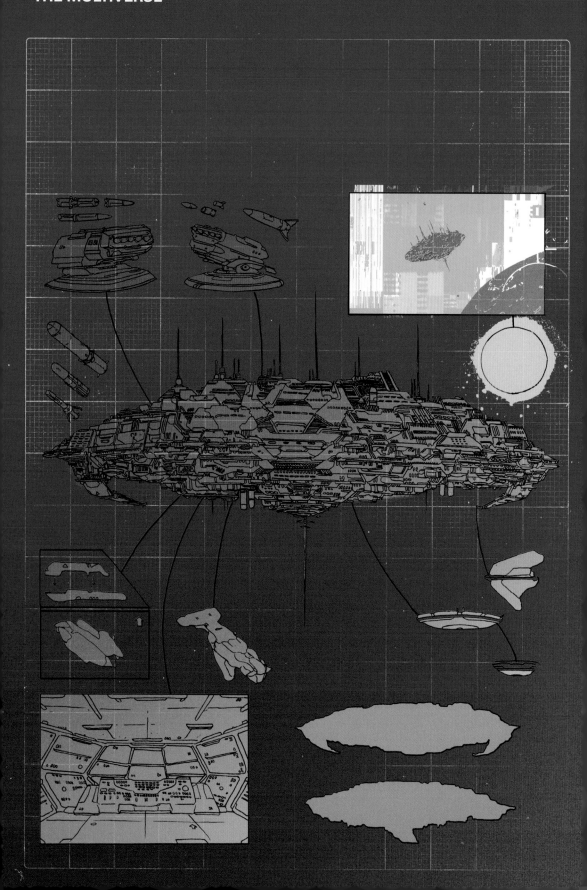

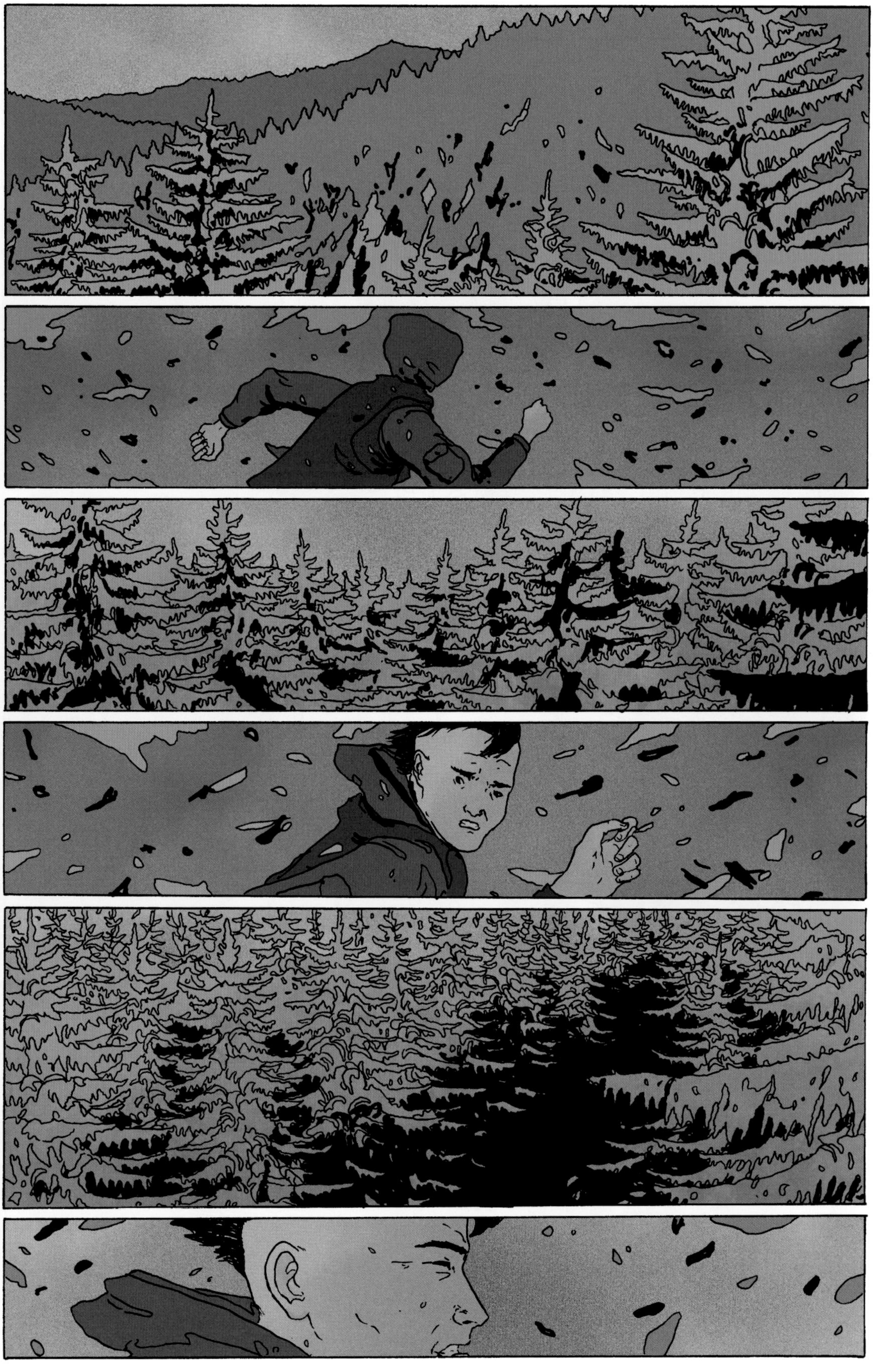

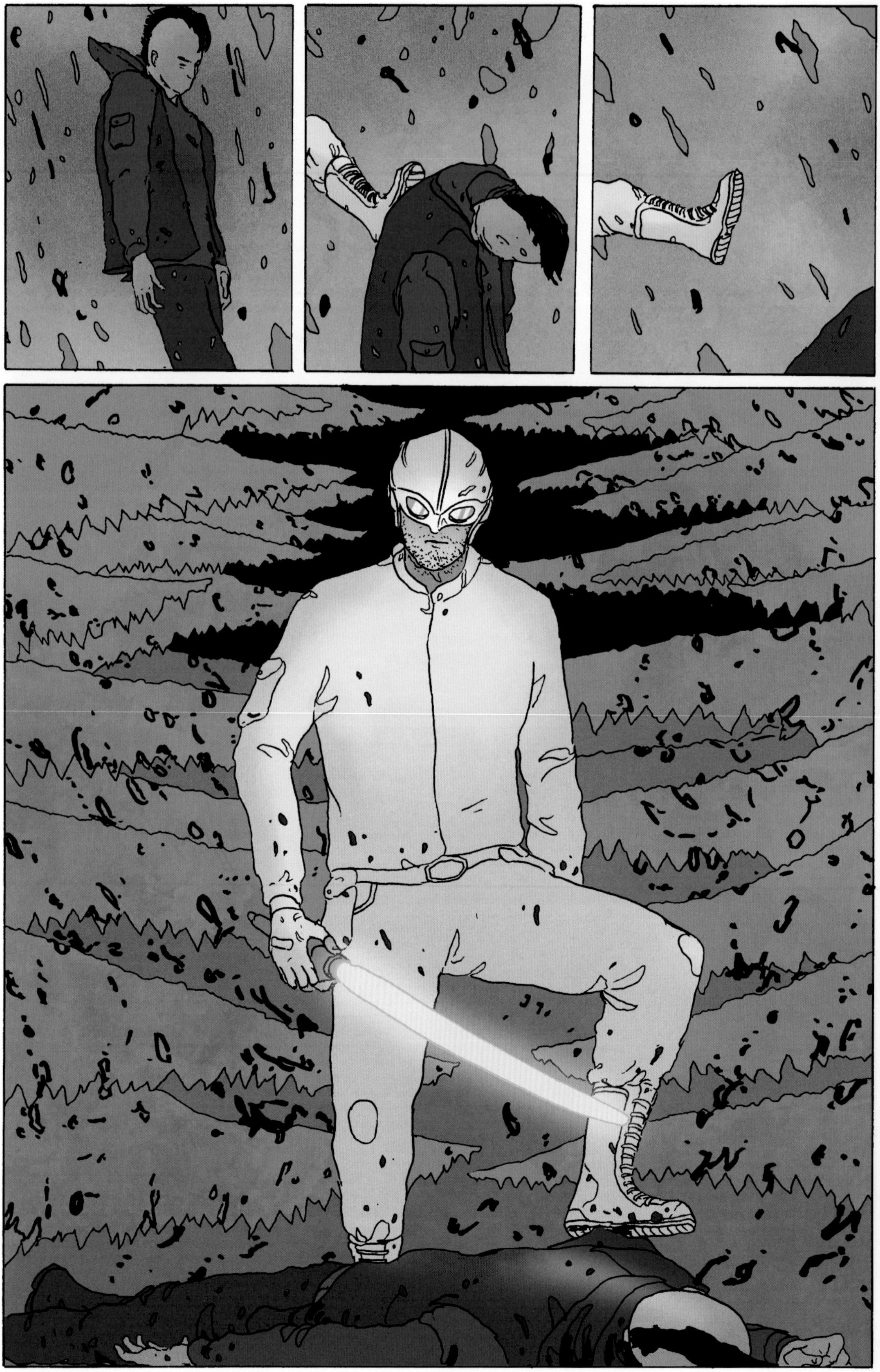

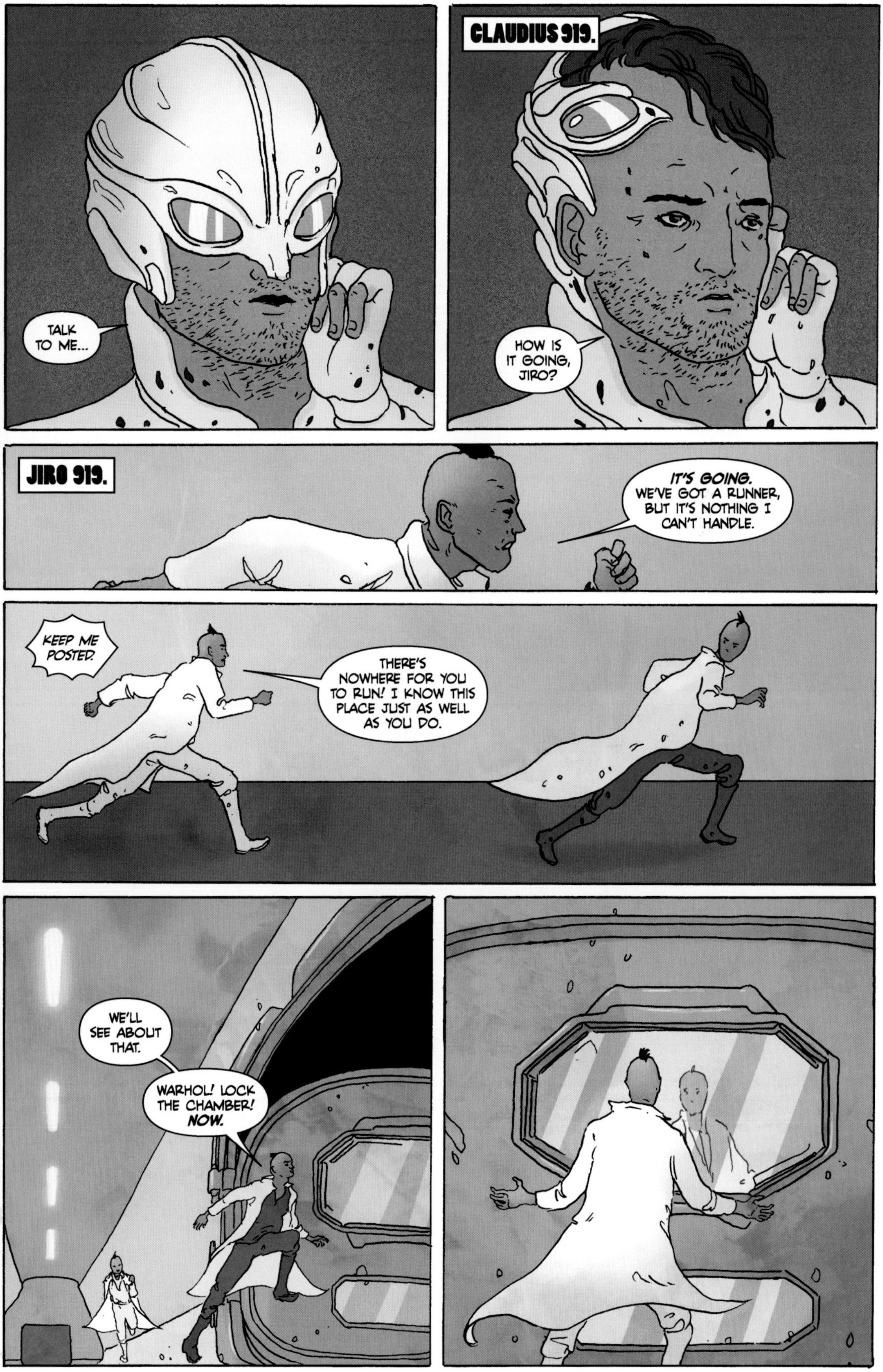
TALK TO ME...
CLAUDIUS 919.
HOW IS IT GOING, JIRO?
JIRO 919.
IT'S GOING. WE'VE GOT A RUNNER, BUT IT'S NOTHING I CAN'T HANDLE.
KEEP ME POSTED.
THERE'S NOWHERE FOR YOU TO RUN! I KNOW THIS PLACE JUST AS WELL AS YOU DO.
WE'LL SEE ABOUT THAT.
WARHOL! LOCK THE CHAMBER! NOW.

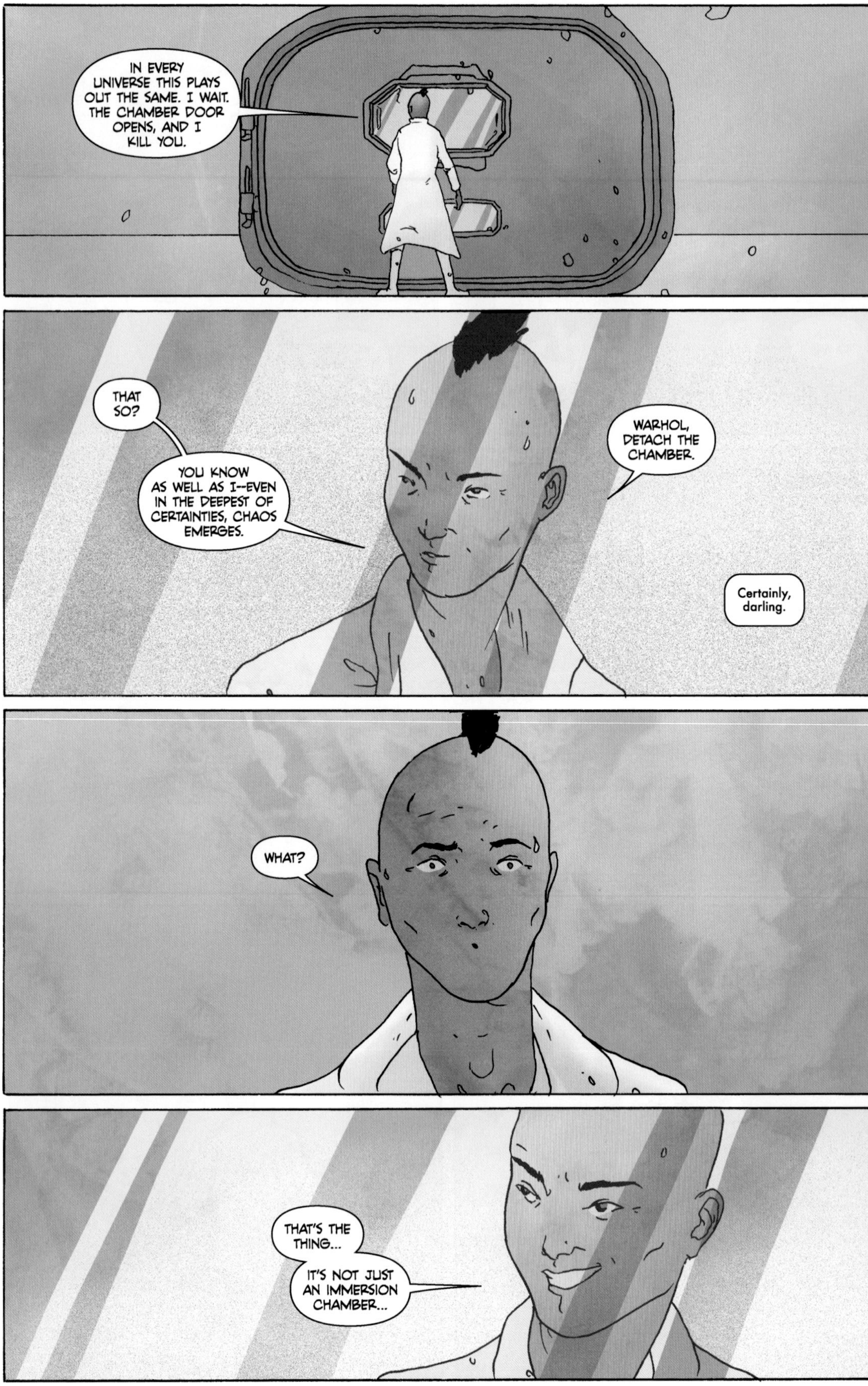
IN EVERY UNIVERSE THIS PLAYS OUT THE SAME. I WAIT. THE CHAMBER DOOR OPENS, AND I KILL YOU.
THAT SO?
YOU KNOW AS WELL AS I--EVEN IN THE DEEPEST OF CERTAINTIES, CHAOS EMERGES.
WARHOL, DETACH THE CHAMBER.
Certainly, darling.
WHAT?
THAT'S THE THING...
IT'S NOT JUST AN IMMERSION CHAMBER...

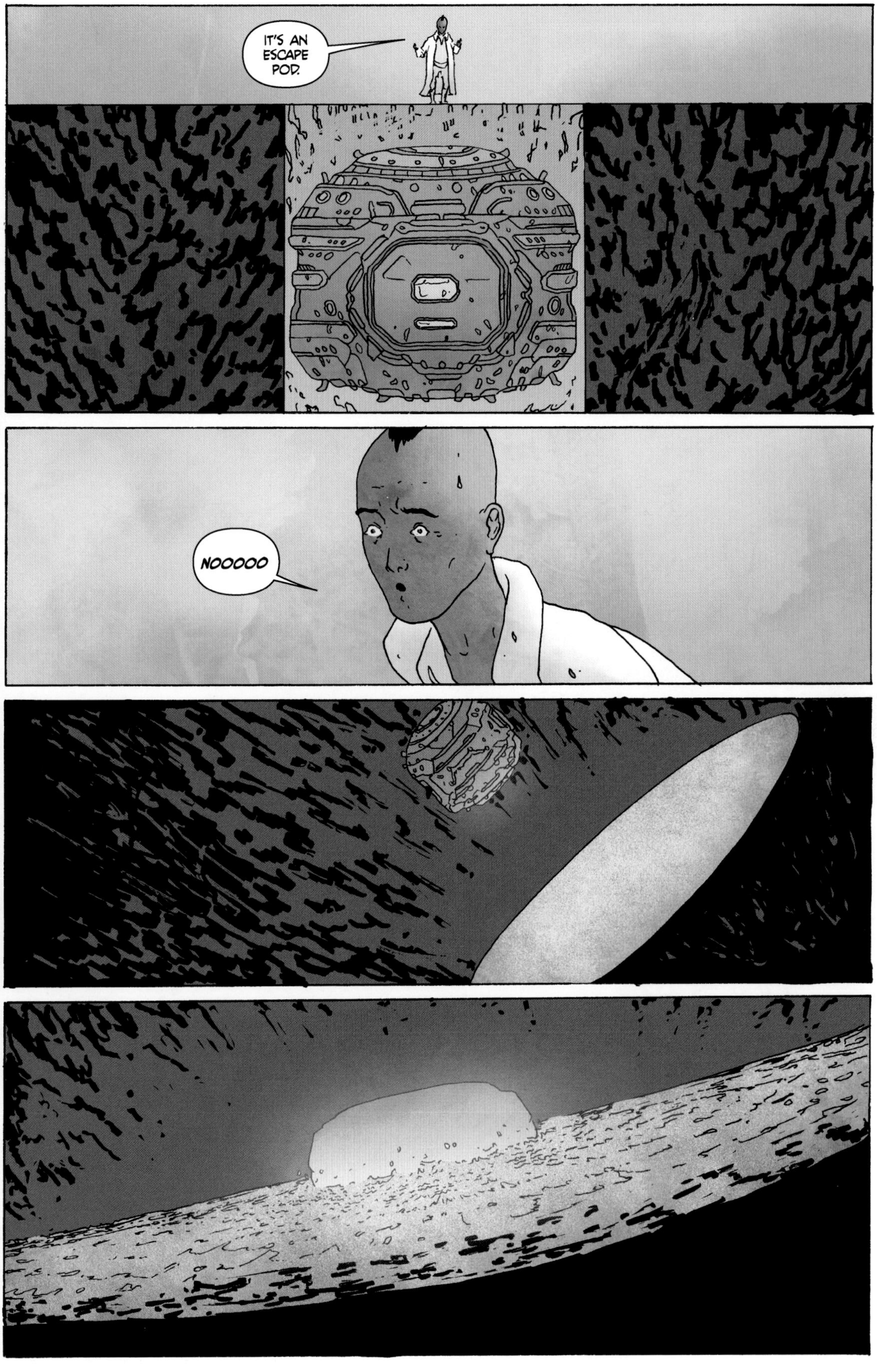
IT'S AN ESCAPE POD.
NOOOOO

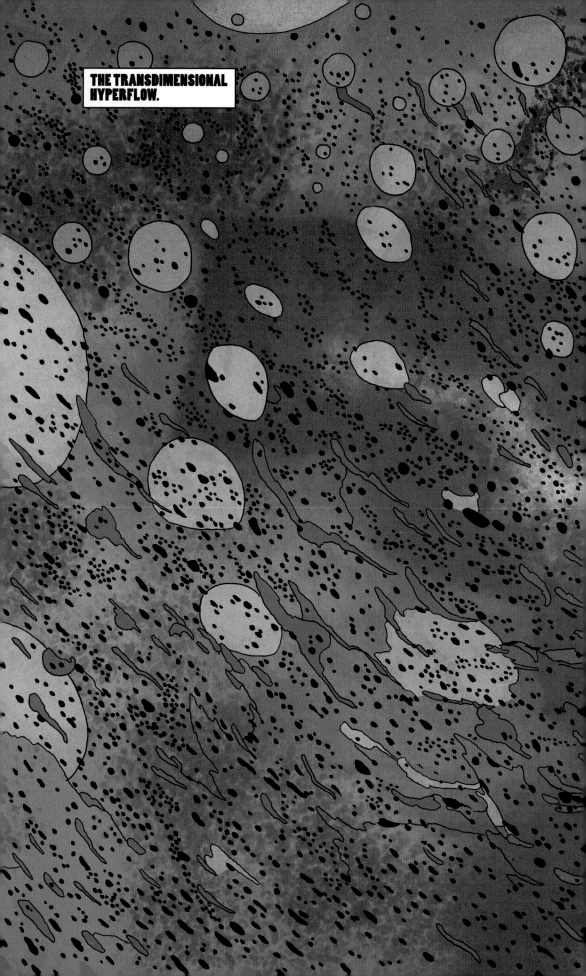

THE TRANSDIMENSIONAL
HYPERFLOW.

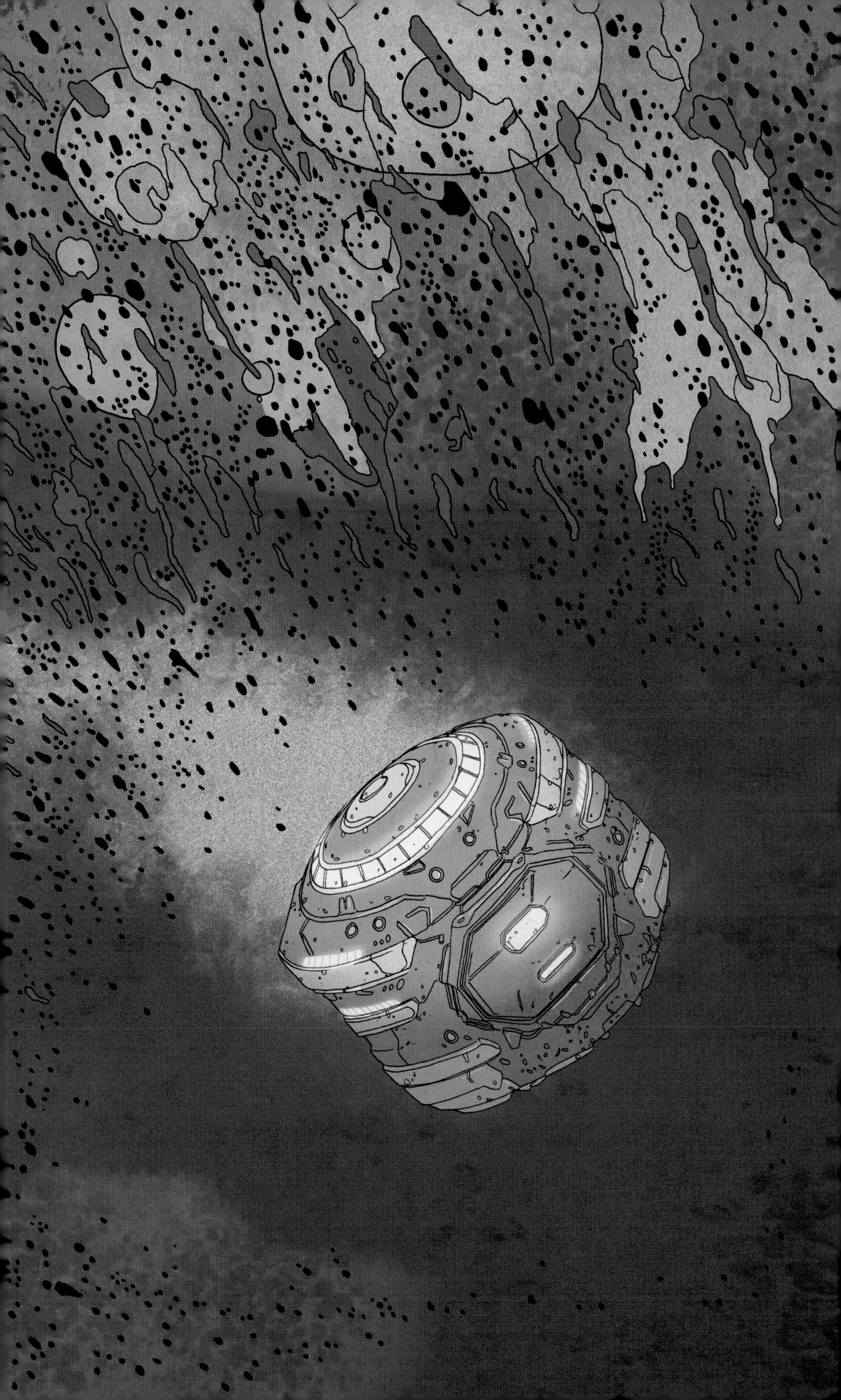

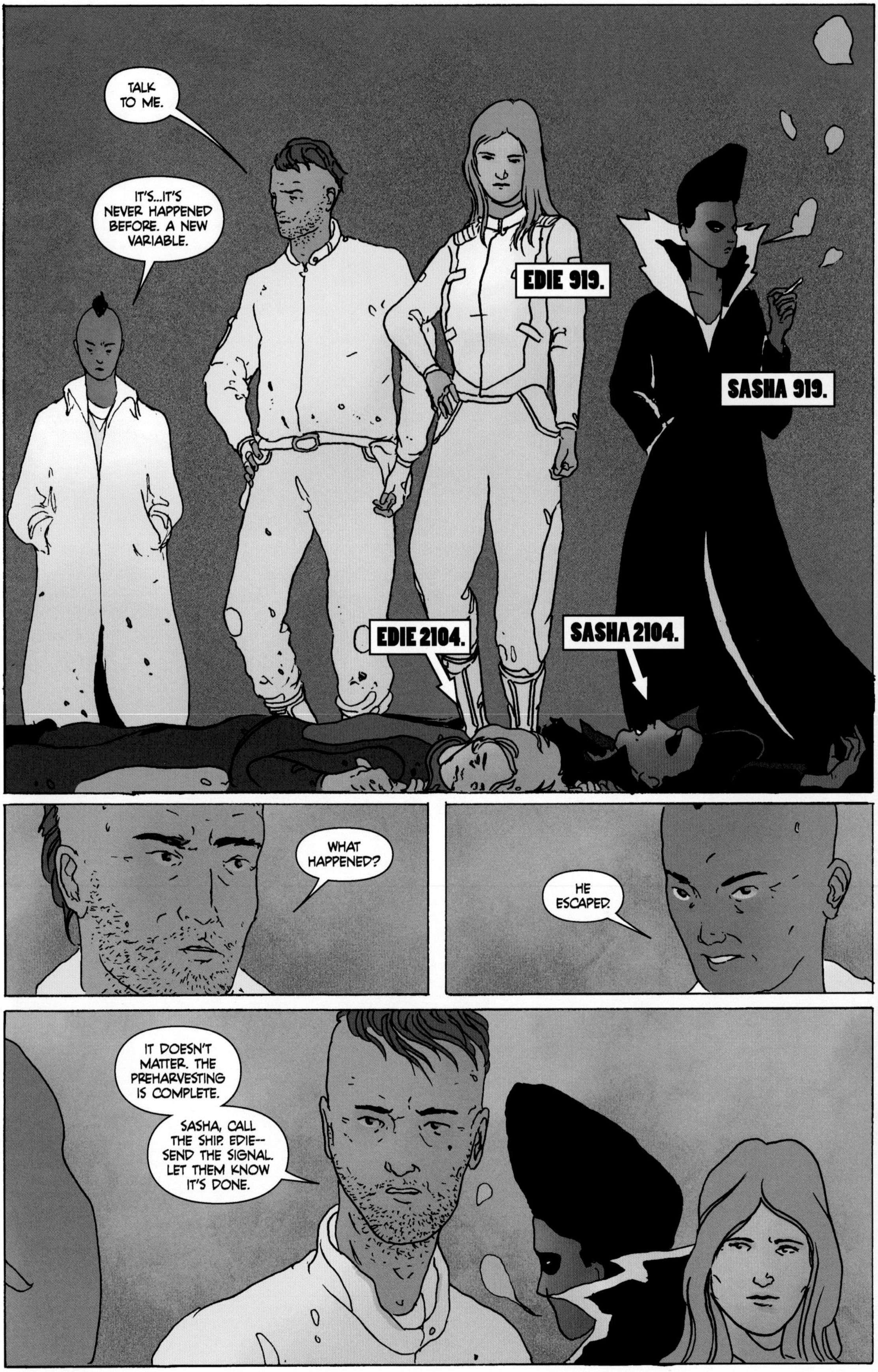
TALK TO ME.
IT'S...IT'S NEVER HAPPENED BEFORE. A NEW VARIABLE.
EDIE 919.
SASHA 919.
EDIE 2104.
SASHA 2104.
WHAT HAPPENED?
HE ESCAPED.
IT DOESN'T MATTER. THE PREHARVESTING IS COMPLETE.
SASHA, CALL THE SHIP. EDIE-- SEND THE SIGNAL. LET THEM KNOW IT'S DONE.

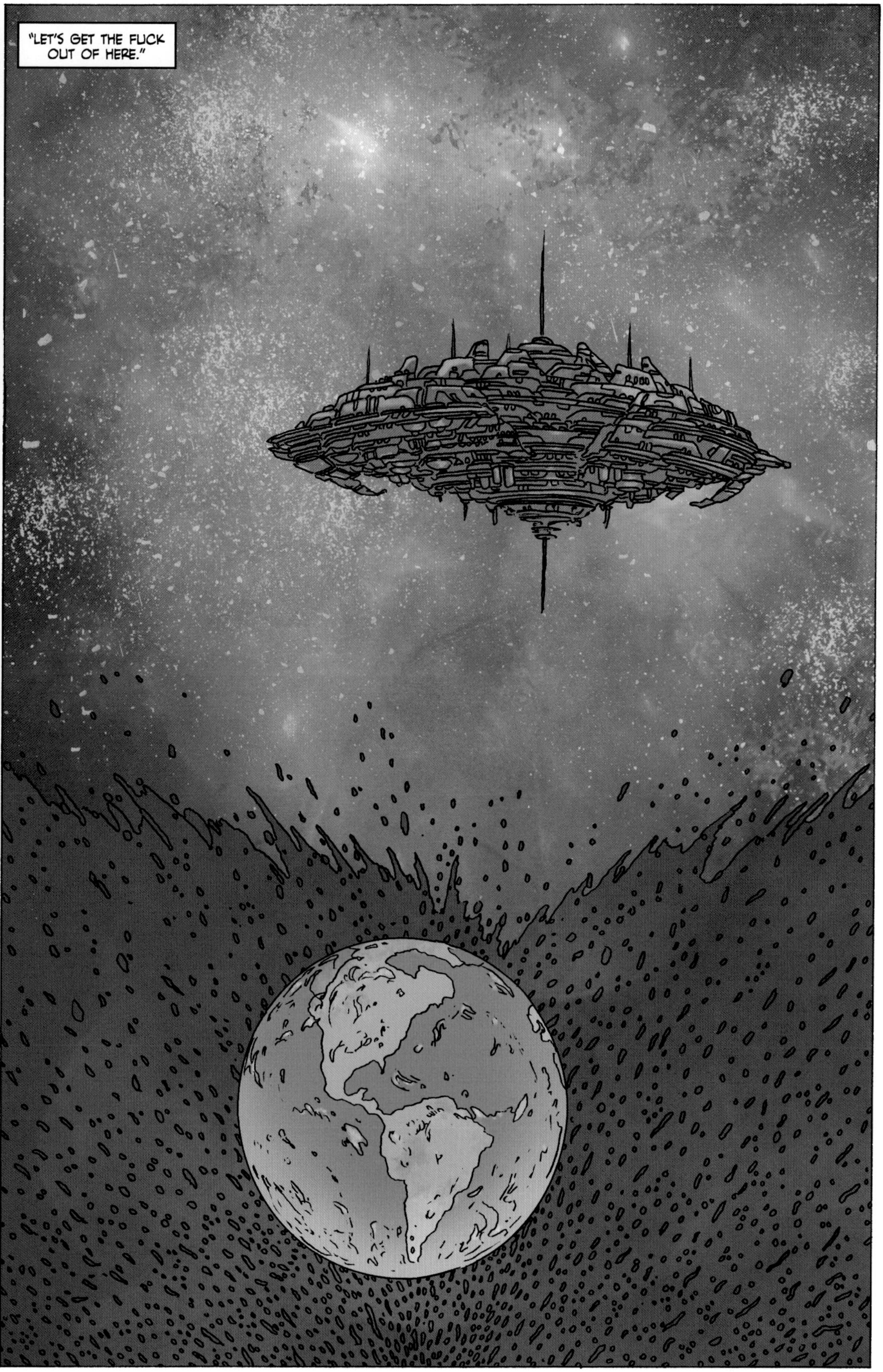
"LET'S GET THE FUCK OUT OF HERE."

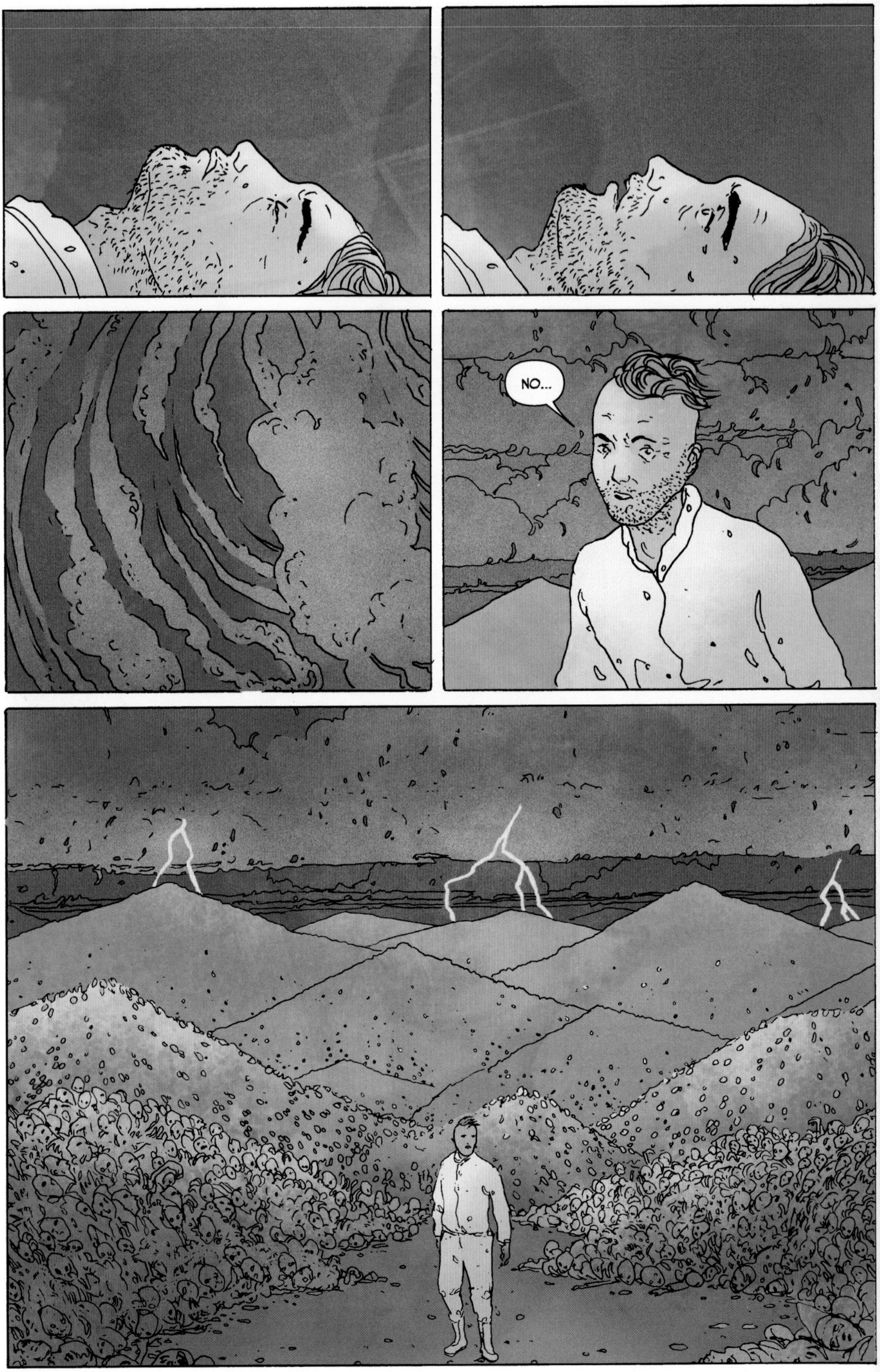
NO...

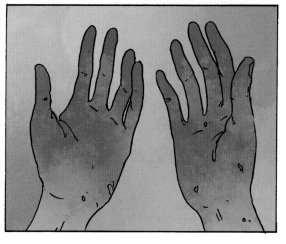

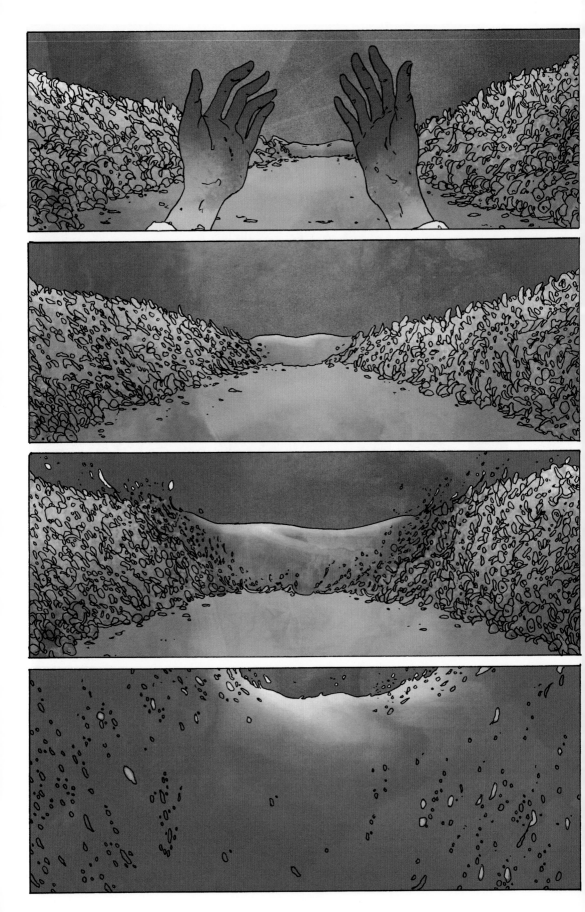

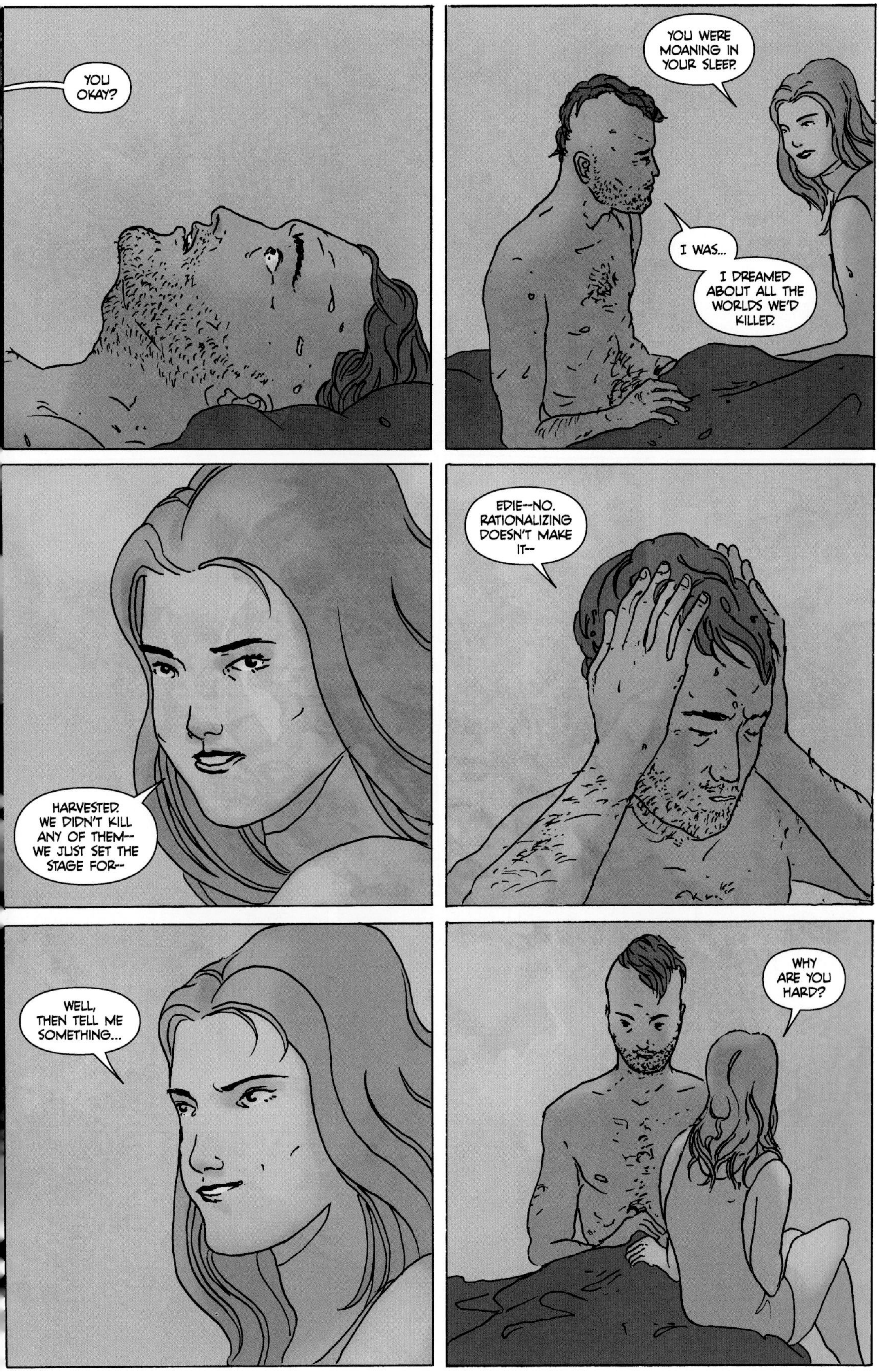
YOU OKAY?
YOU WERE MOANING IN YOUR SLEEP.
I WAS...
I DREAMED ABOUT ALL THE WORLDS WE'D KILLED.
HARVESTED. WE DIDN'T KILL ANY OF THEM-- WE JUST SET THE STAGE FOR--
EDIE--NO. RATIONALIZING DOESN'T MAKE IT--
WELL, THEN TELL ME SOMETHING...
WHY ARE YOU HARD?

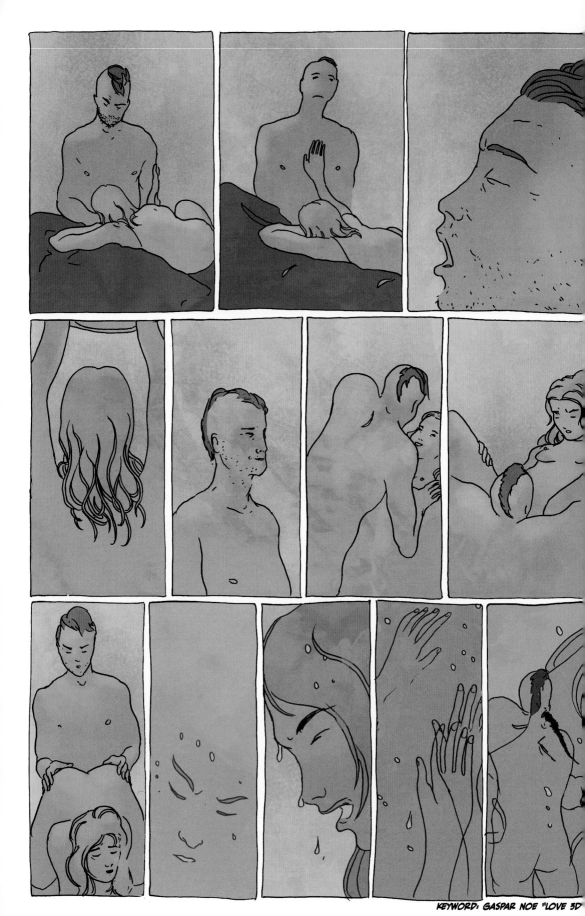

KEYWORD: GASPAR NOE "LOVE 3D"

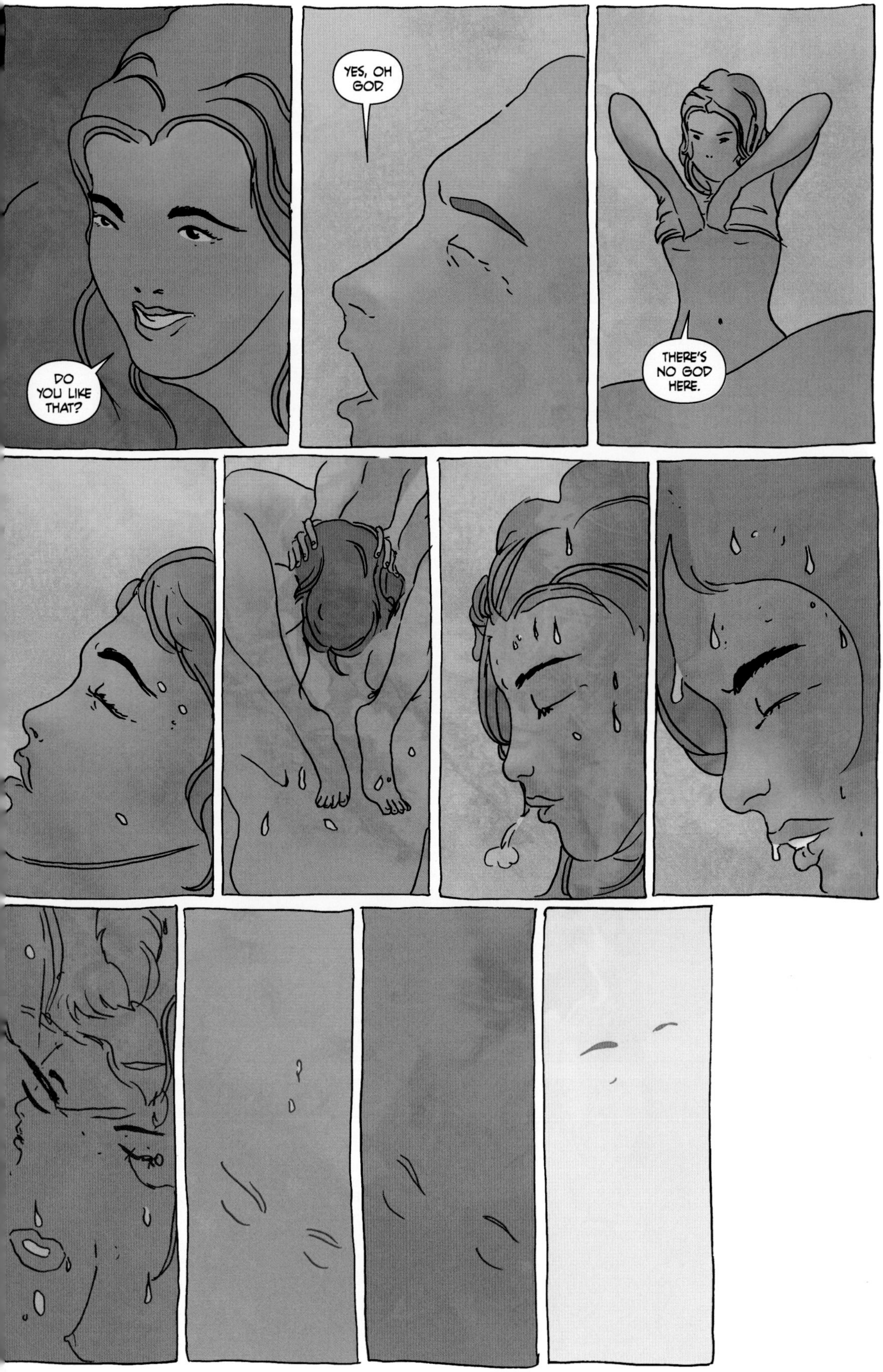
DO YOU LIKE THAT?
YES, OH GOD.
THERE'S NO GOD HERE.

EARTH 919.

SO...

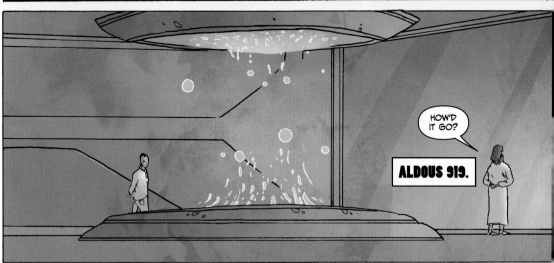

HOW'D IT GO?

ALDOUS 919.

IT WAS...

MESSY. TO SAY THE LEAST. BUT THE HARVEST WENT THROUGH AS PLANNED. THEY GOT WHAT THEY WANTED.

I DON'T KNOW WHY I BOTHER ASKING--I SAW IT ALL ON THE EVERFLOW. BUT STILL--IT'S GOOD TO HEAR IT FROM YOU.

...

CLAUDIUS? WHAT IS IT, SON? SPEAK UP.

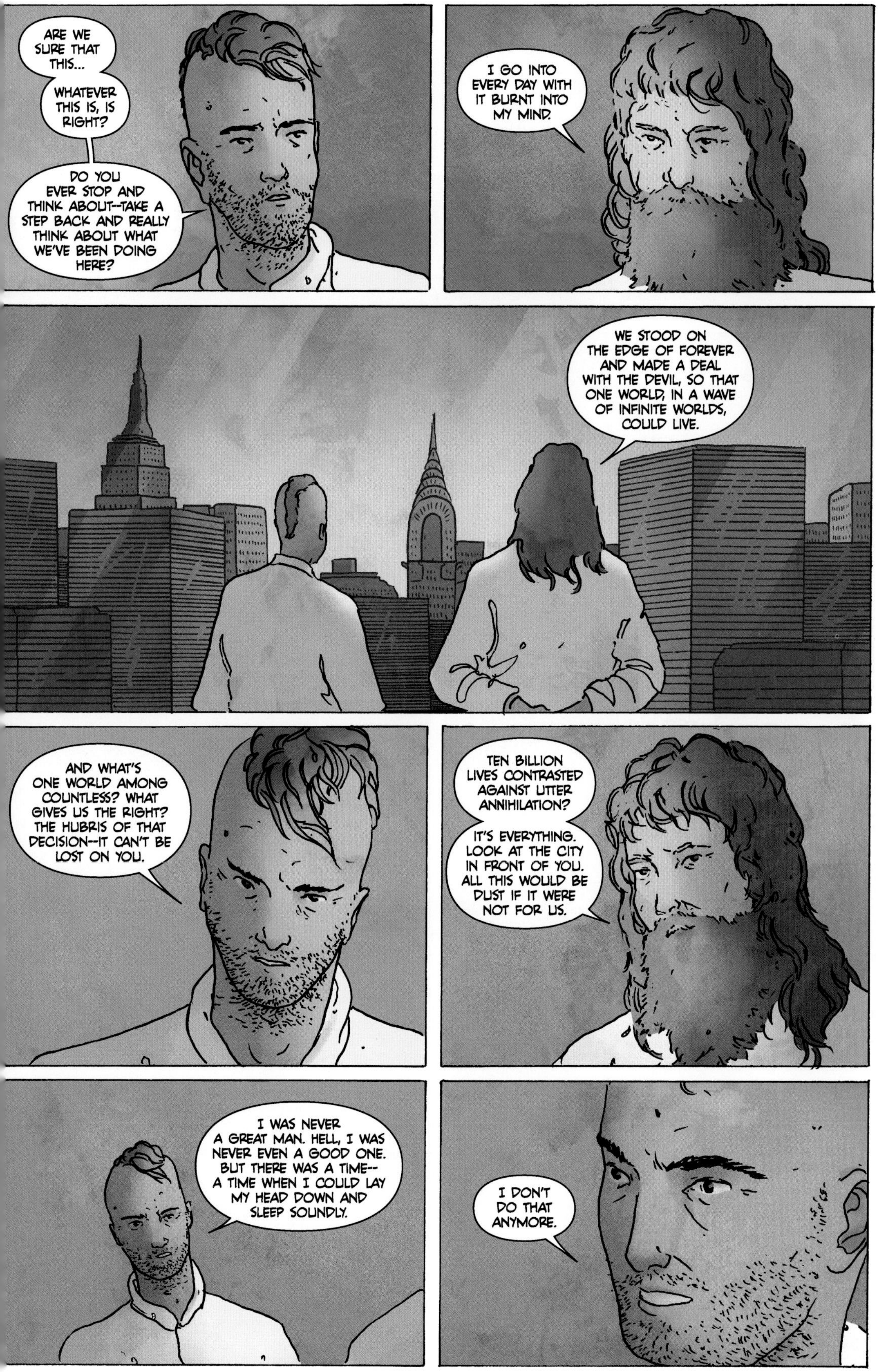
ARE WE SURE THAT THIS...
WHATEVER THIS IS, IS RIGHT?
DO YOU EVER STOP AND THINK ABOUT--TAKE A STEP BACK AND REALLY THINK ABOUT WHAT WE'VE BEEN DOING HERE?
I GO INTO EVERY DAY WITH IT BURNT INTO MY MIND.
WE STOOD ON THE EDGE OF FOREVER AND MADE A DEAL WITH THE DEVIL, SO THAT ONE WORLD, IN A WAVE OF INFINITE WORLDS, COULD LIVE.
AND WHAT'S ONE WORLD AMONG COUNTLESS? WHAT GIVES US THE RIGHT? THE HUBRIS OF THAT DECISION--IT CAN'T BE LOST ON YOU.
TEN BILLION LIVES CONTRASTED AGAINST UTTER ANNIHILATION?
IT'S EVERYTHING. LOOK AT THE CITY IN FRONT OF YOU. ALL THIS WOULD BE DUST IF IT WERE NOT FOR US.
I WAS NEVER A GREAT MAN. HELL, I WAS NEVER EVEN A GOOD ONE. BUT THERE WAS A TIME-- A TIME WHEN I COULD LAY MY HEAD DOWN AND SLEEP SOUNDLY.
I DON'T DO THAT ANYMORE.

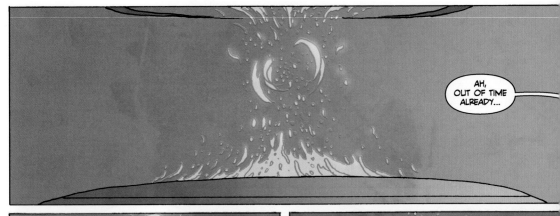

AH, OUT OF TIME ALREADY...

LET'S SEE...

WHERE ARE WE HEADED NOW?

CLAUDIUS... I'M--I...

NO, IT'S OKAY. I'M--I'M SORRY, OLD FRIEND. WHATEVER LINES WE'VE CROSSED...WHATEVER DEALS WE'VE MADE, WE DID IT TOGETHER. IT WAS SILLY OF ME TO FORGET THAT.

WE JUST--WE JUST NEED TO REALIZE THAT WHEN THIS IS ALL OVER, AT THE END OF EVERYTHING...

WE WILL BE JUDGED. WE'LL HAVE TO ANSWER FOR WHAT WE'VE DONE--AND...

IT WON'T BE PRETTY.

GOODBYE, MY FRIEND.

WARHOL--SPOOL UP THE EPIPHANY ENGINES.

Consider the engines spooled, darling.

LOOK, CLAUDIUS-- ABOUT EARLIER...

WE'RE GOOD, BROTHER. WE'RE GOOD.

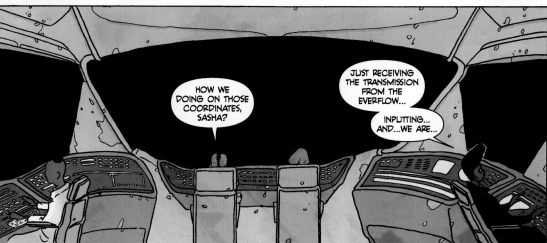

HOW WE DOING ON THOSE COORDINATES, SASHA?

JUST RECEIVING THE TRANSMISSION FROM THE EVERFLOW...

INPUTING... AND...WE ARE...

...GOOD.

JIRO-- READOUT ON THE KIRBY CORES?

CORES ARE AT 100%. WE ARE SET FOR LAUNCH.

WELL, IN THAT CASE...

"PUNCH IT."

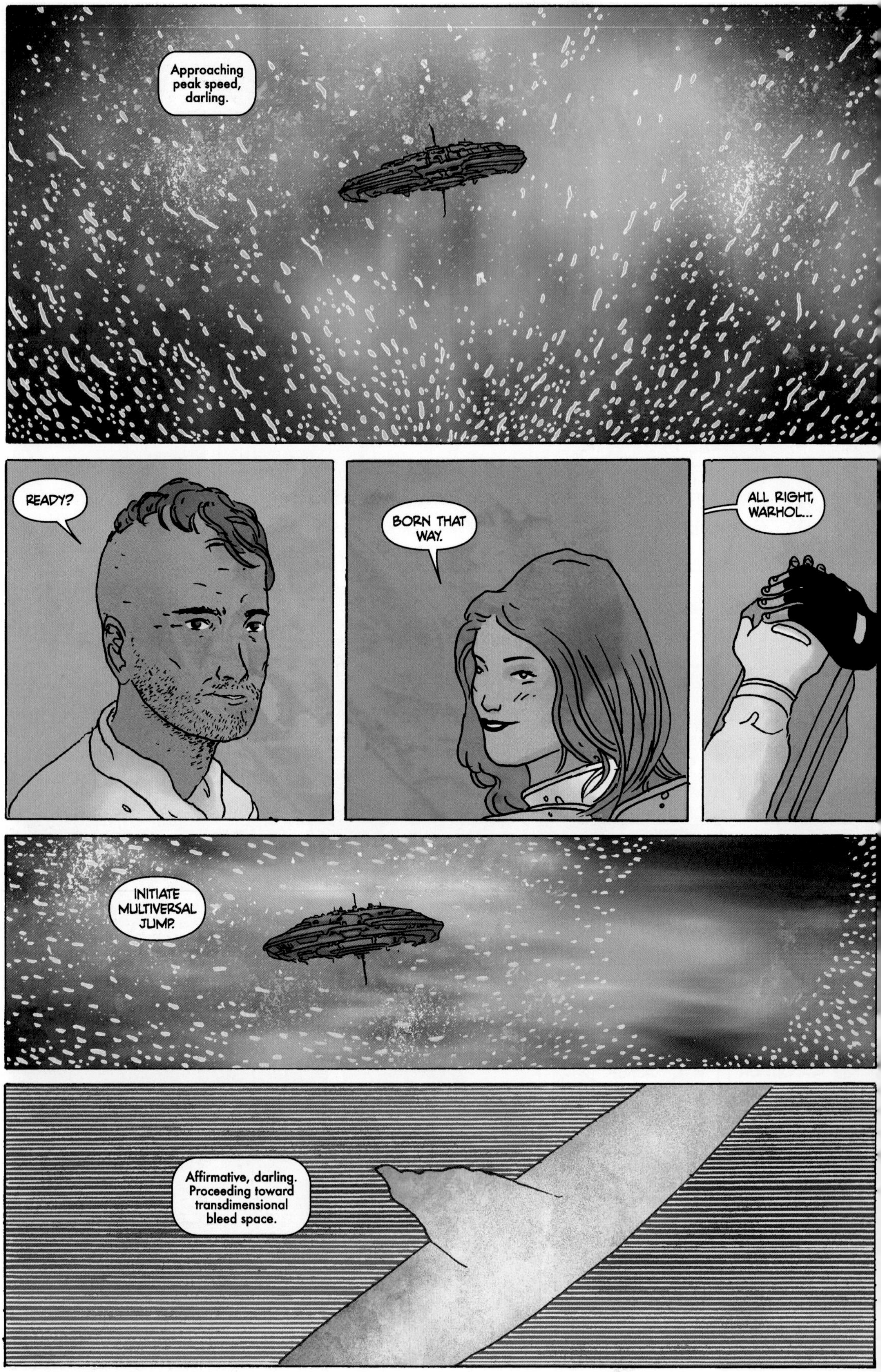

Approaching peak speed, darling.
READY?
BORN THAT WAY.
ALL RIGHT, WARHOL...
INITIATE MULTIVERSAL JUMP.
Affirmative, darling. Proceeding toward transdimensional bleed space.

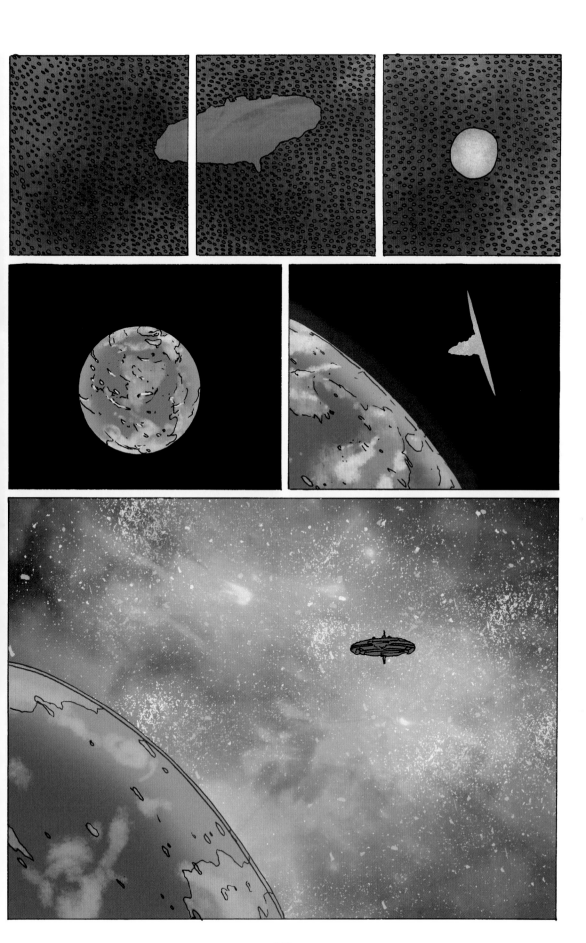

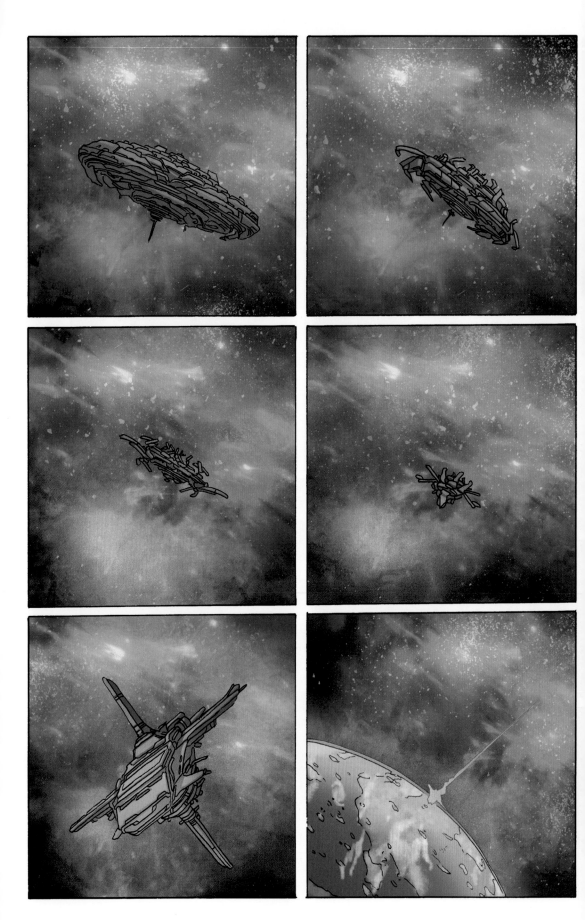

GODDAMN YOU, YOU CRAZY FUCKER.

AH, CLAUDIUS? I THINK YOU MIGHT WANT TO SEE THIS.

WHA--

WARHOL IS SHOWING THAT OUR COUNTERPARTS NATIVE TO THIS UNIVERSE ARE NEARBY. SHOULD WE MOVE TO NEUTRALIZE?

NO. OUR FIRST PRIORITY IS MAKING CONTACT WITH THE ASSET. BUT FIRST--

INITIATE GLOBAL MIDNIGHT.

YESSIR.

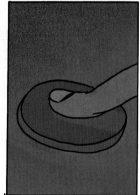

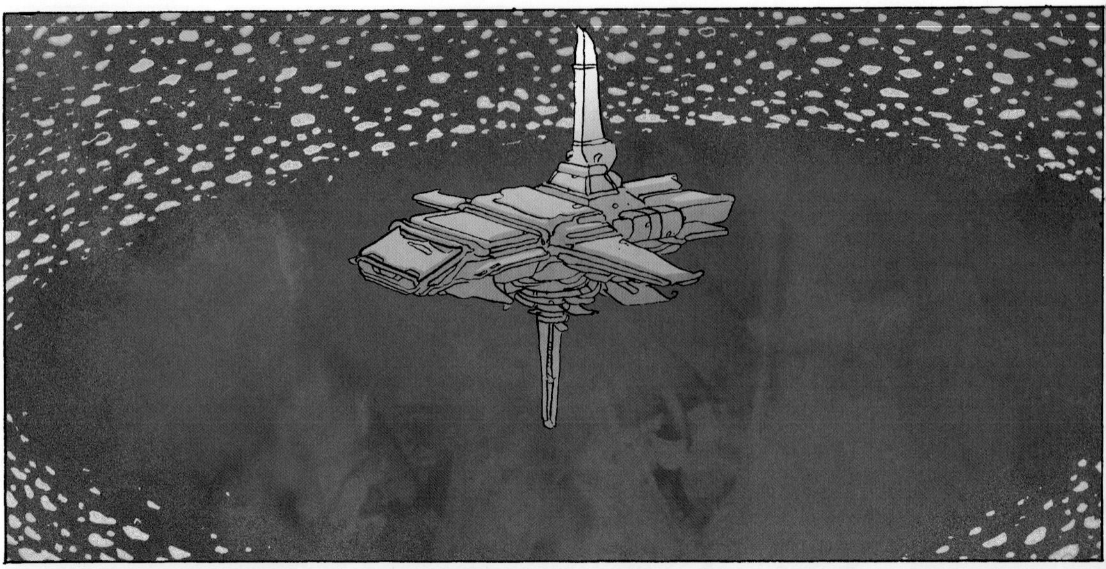

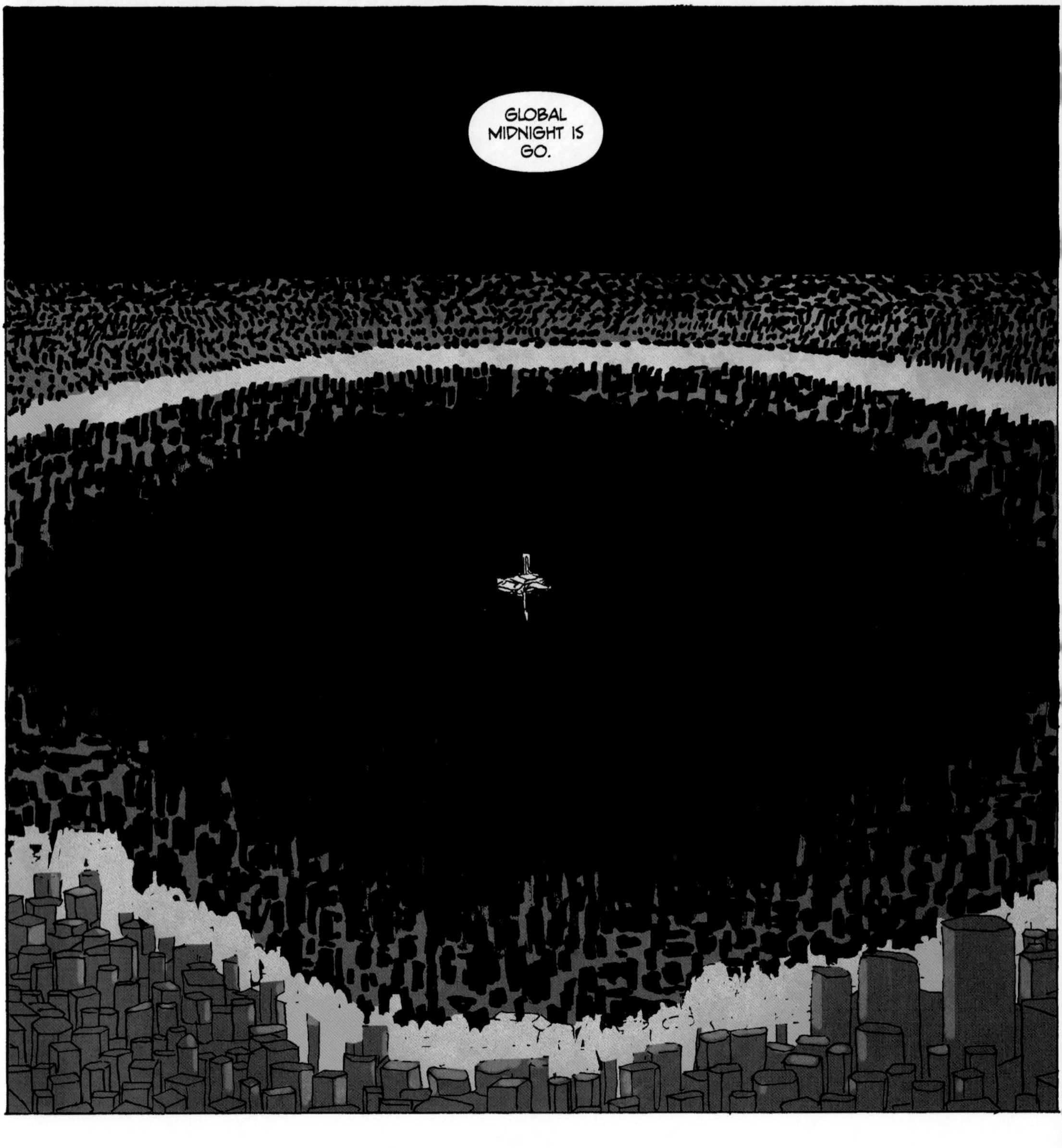
GLOBAL MIDNIGHT IS GO.

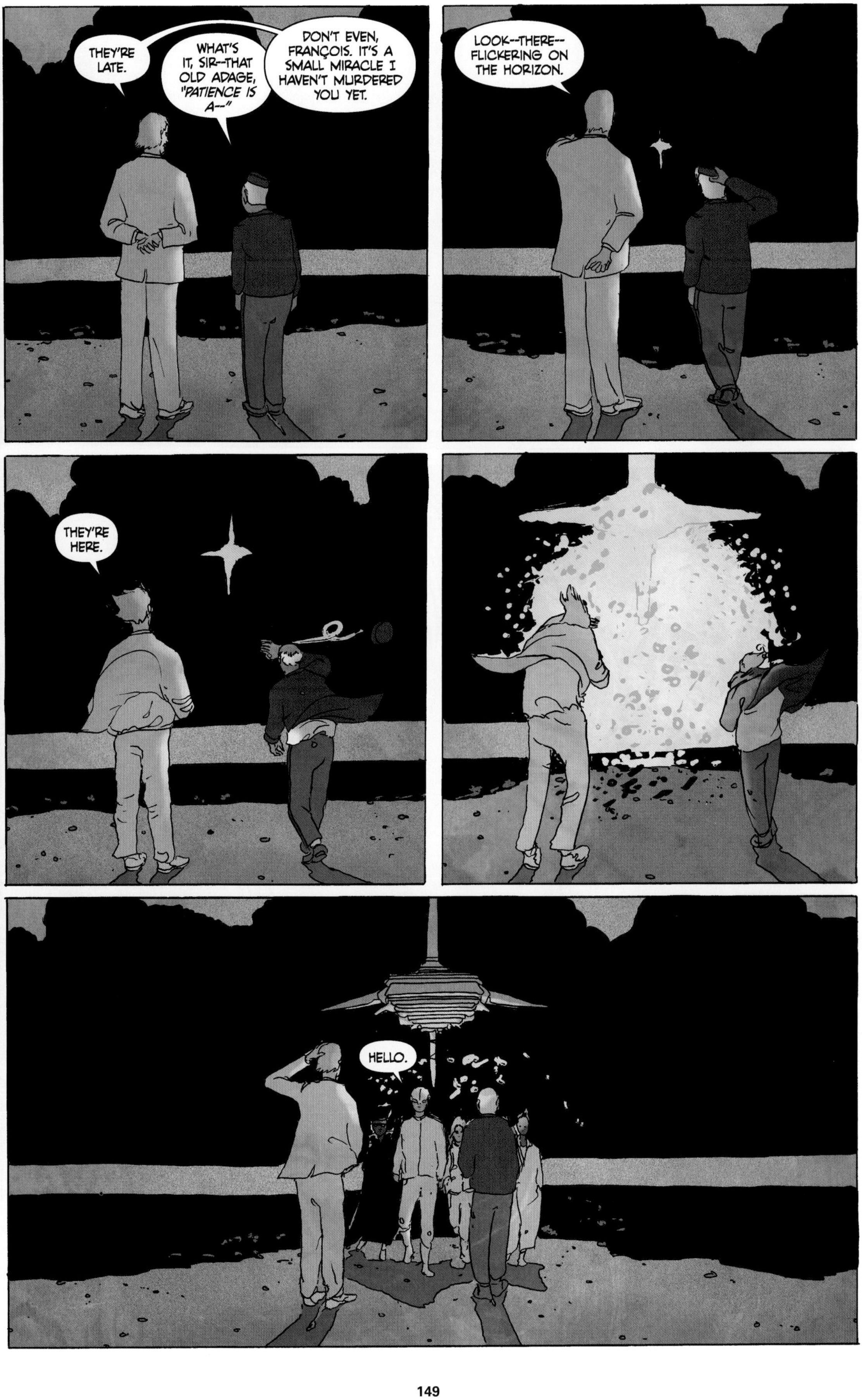
THEY'RE LATE.
WHAT'S IT, SIR--THAT OLD ADAGE, "PATIENCE IS A--"
DON'T EVEN, FRANÇOIS. IT'S A SMALL MIRACLE I HAVEN'T MURDERED YOU YET.
LOOK--THERE--FLICKERING ON THE HORIZON.
THEY'RE HERE.
HELLO.

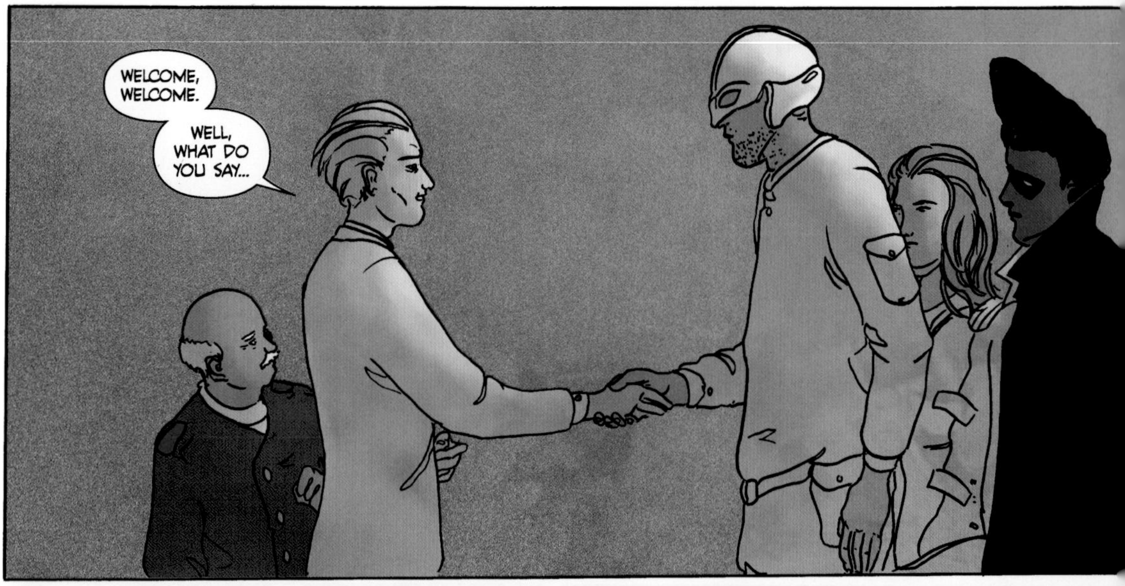
WELCOME, WELCOME.
WELL, WHAT DO YOU SAY...

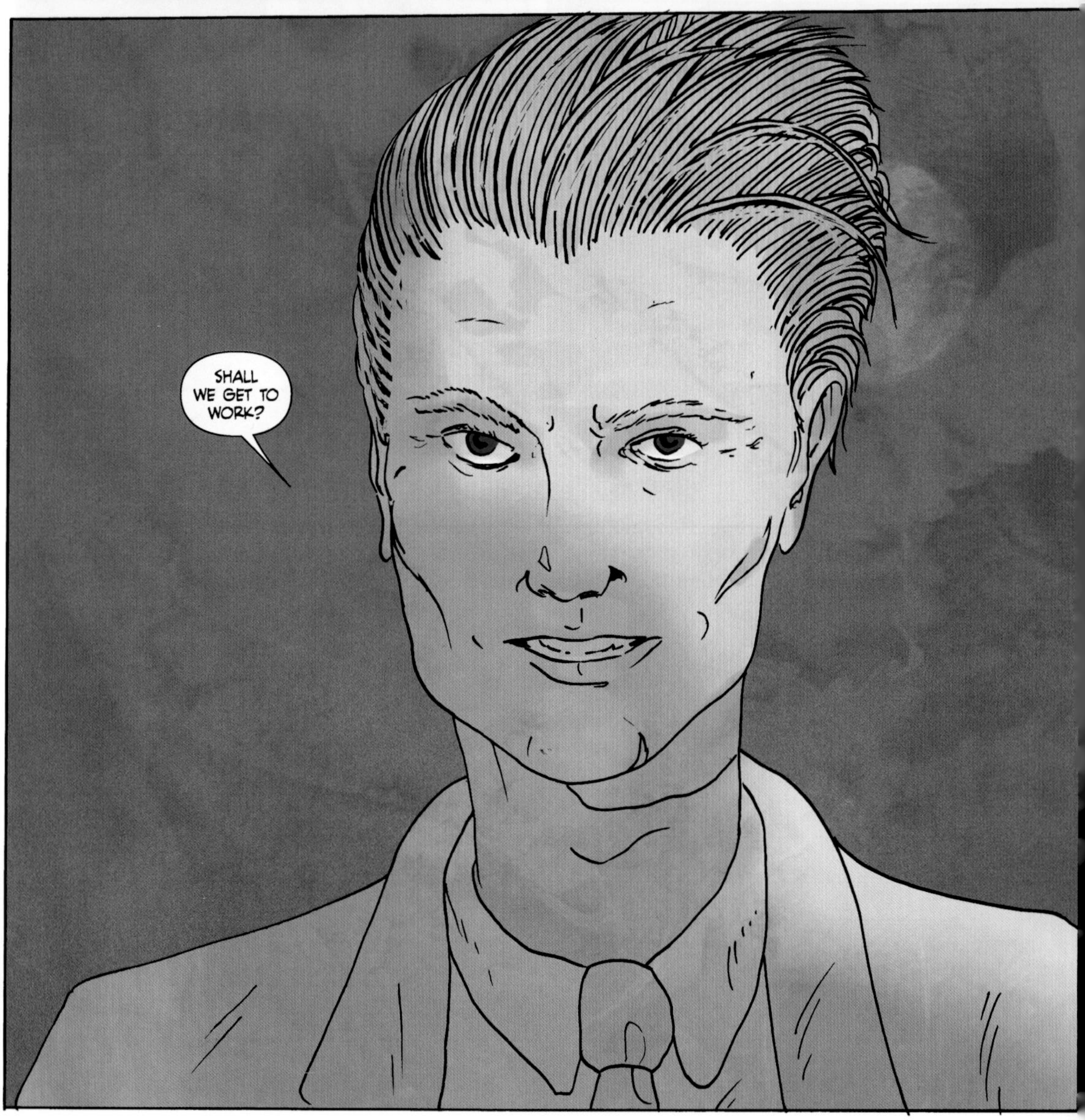
SHALL WE GET TO WORK?

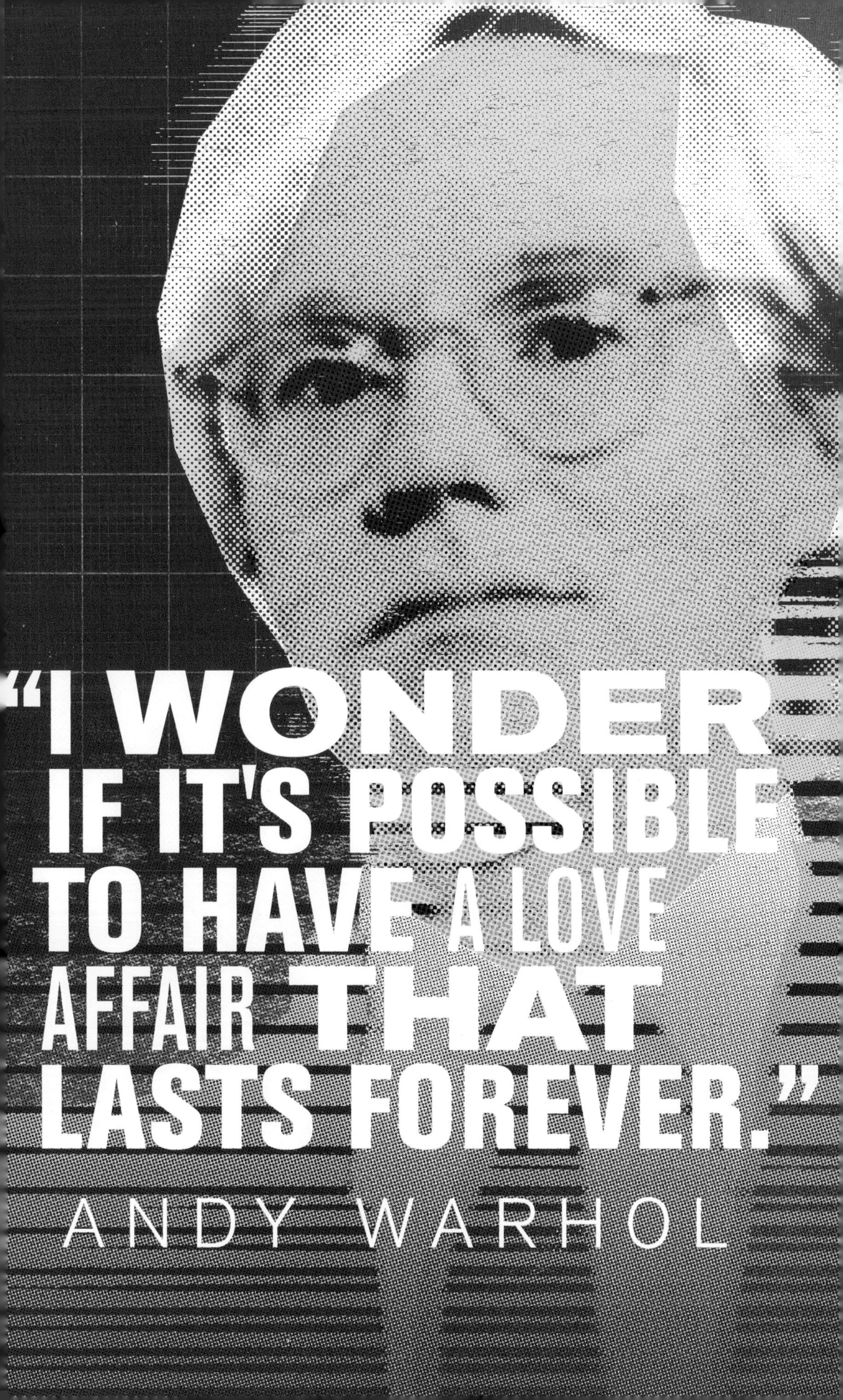
"I WONDER IF IT'S POSSIBLE TO HAVE A LOVE AFFAIR THAT LASTS FOREVER."
ANDY WARHOL

/// part six

# FINALE: CHILDREN OF THE BLACK HOLE

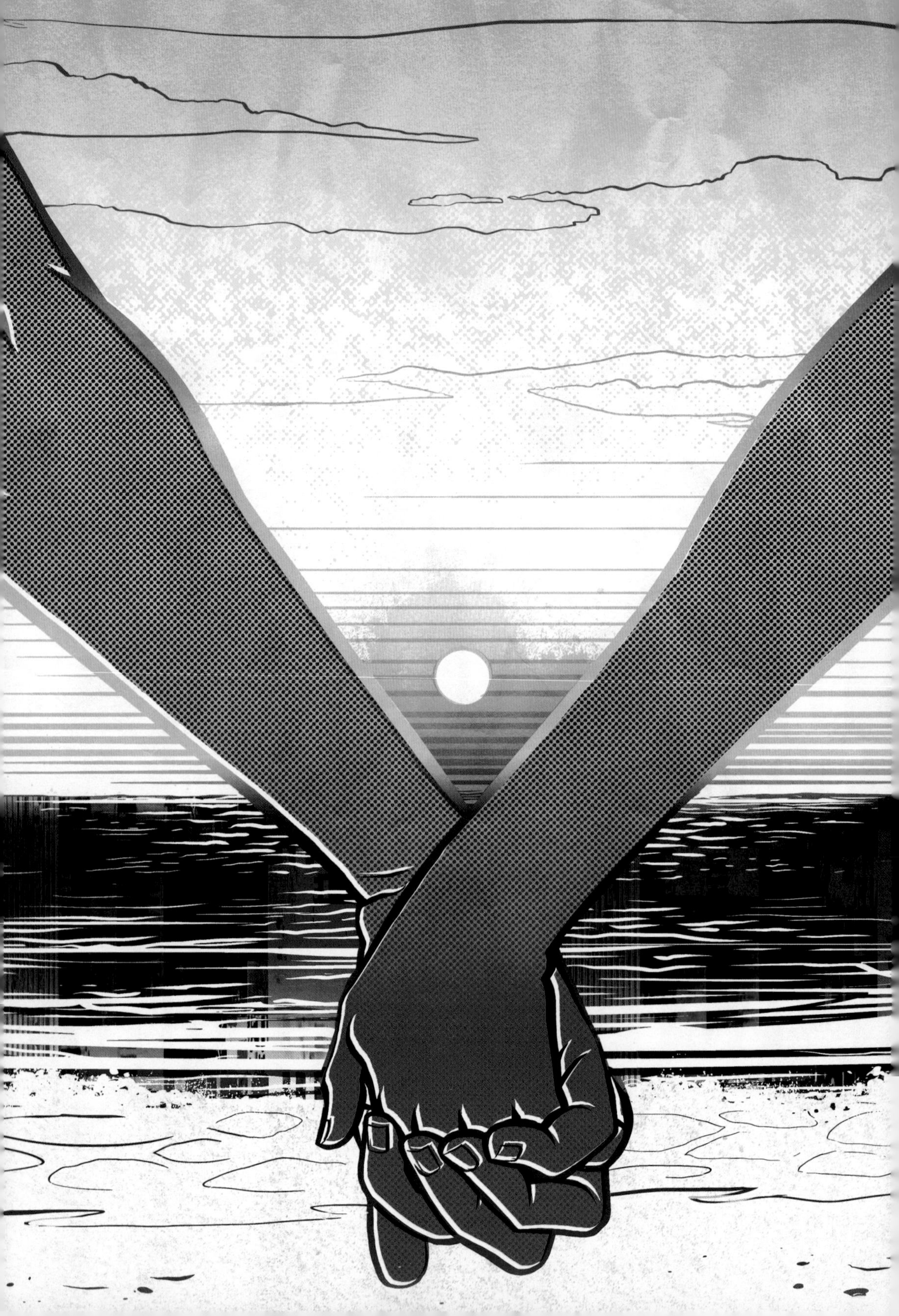

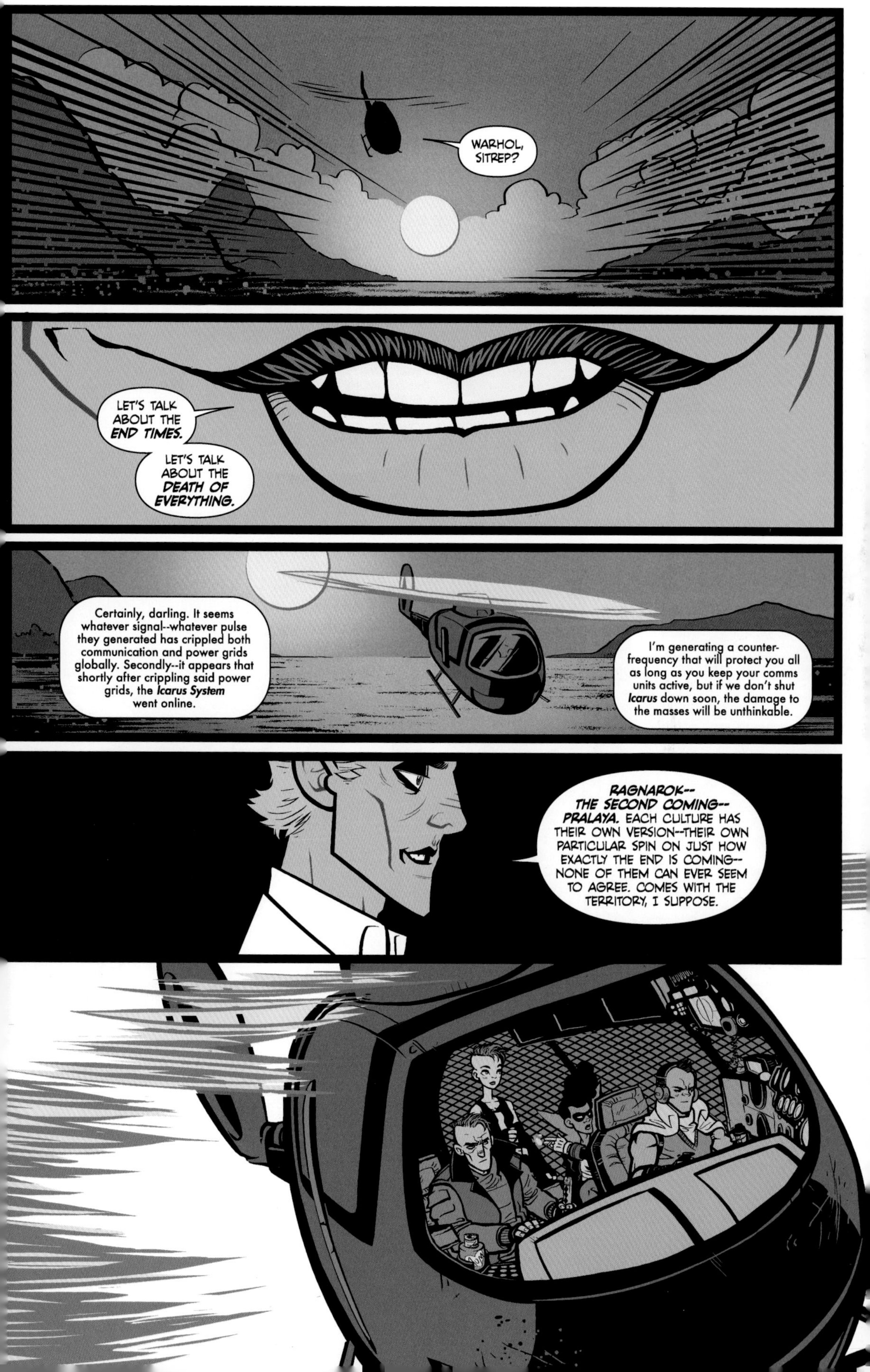
WARHOL, SITREP?
LET'S TALK ABOUT THE *END TIMES.*
LET'S TALK ABOUT THE *DEATH OF EVERYTHING.*
Certainly, darling. It seems whatever signal--whatever pulse they generated has crippled both communication and power grids globally. Secondly--it appears that shortly after crippling said power grids, the *Icarus System* went online.
I'm generating a counter-frequency that will protect you all as long as you keep your comms units active, but if we don't shut *Icarus* down soon, the damage to the masses will be unthinkable.
*RAGNAROK-- THE SECOND COMING-- PRALAYA.* EACH CULTURE HAS THEIR OWN VERSION--THEIR OWN PARTICULAR SPIN ON JUST HOW EXACTLY THE END IS COMING-- NONE OF THEM CAN EVER SEEM TO AGREE. COMES WITH THE TERRITORY, I SUPPOSE.

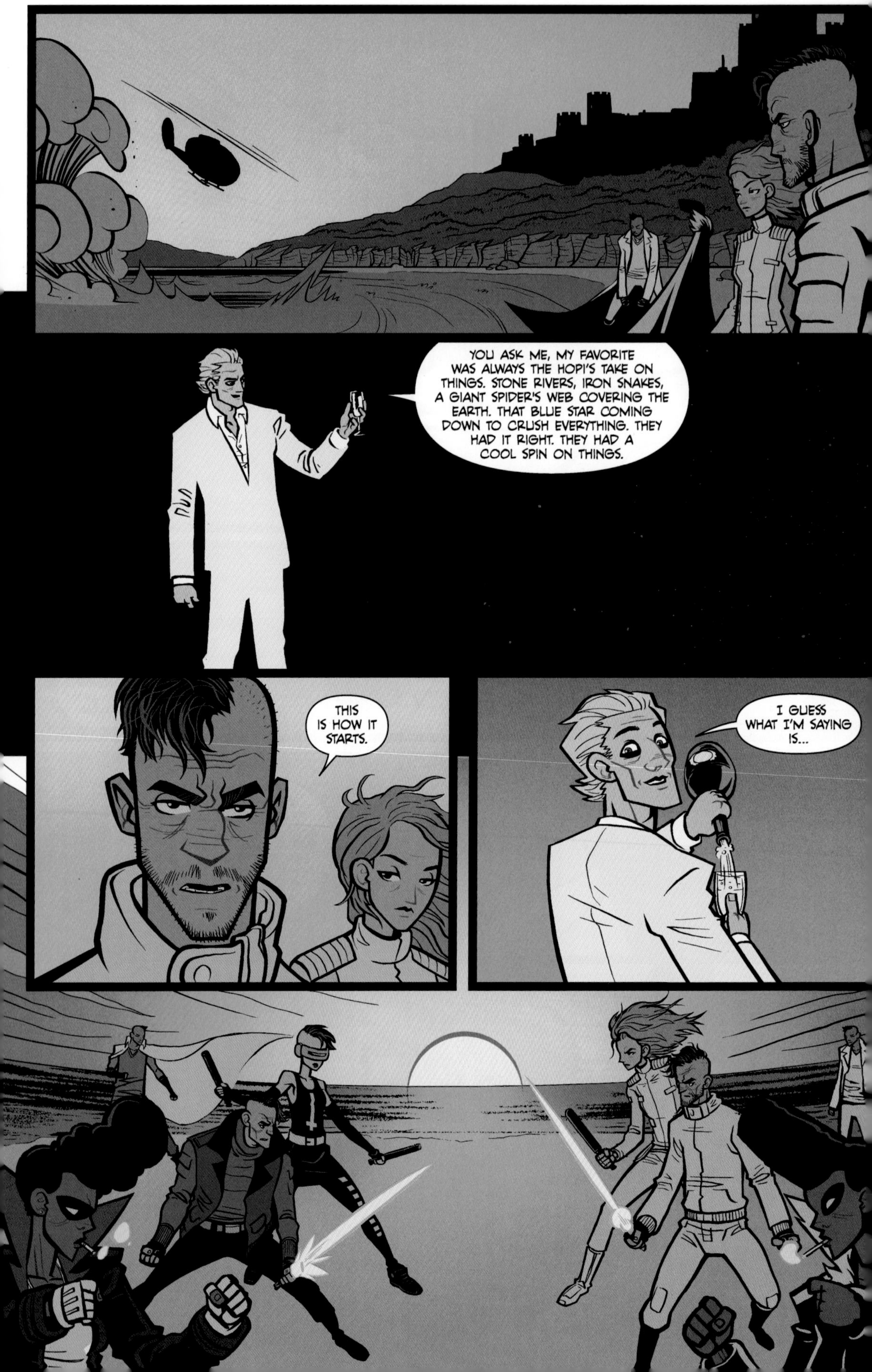
YOU ASK ME, MY FAVORITE WAS ALWAYS THE HOPI'S TAKE ON THINGS. STONE RIVERS, IRON SNAKES, A GIANT SPIDER'S WEB COVERING THE EARTH. THAT BLUE STAR COMING DOWN TO CRUSH EVERYTHING. THEY HAD IT RIGHT. THEY HAD A COOL SPIN ON THINGS.
THIS IS HOW IT STARTS.
I GUESS WHAT I'M SAYING IS...

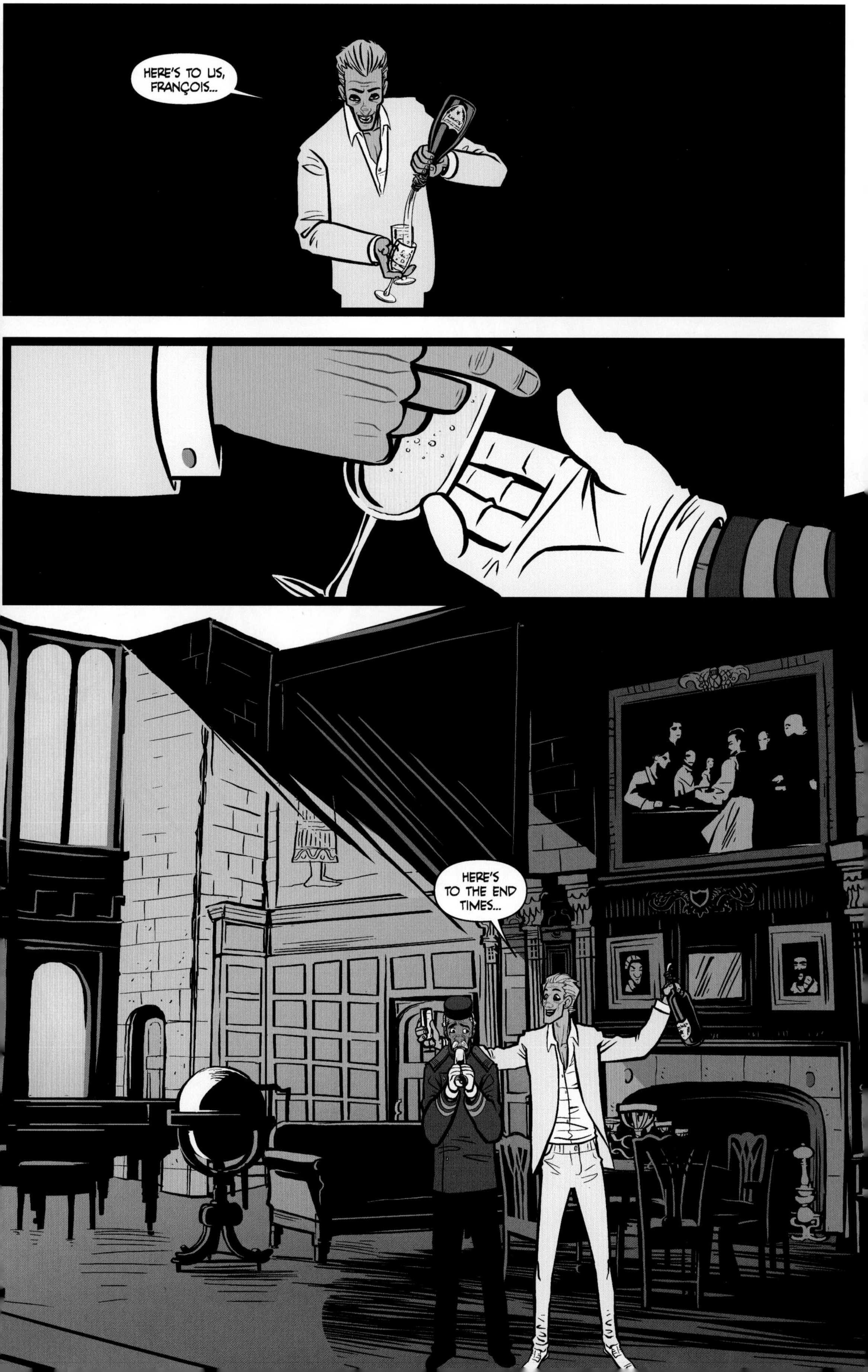
HERE'S TO US, FRANÇOIS...
HERE'S TO THE END TIMES...

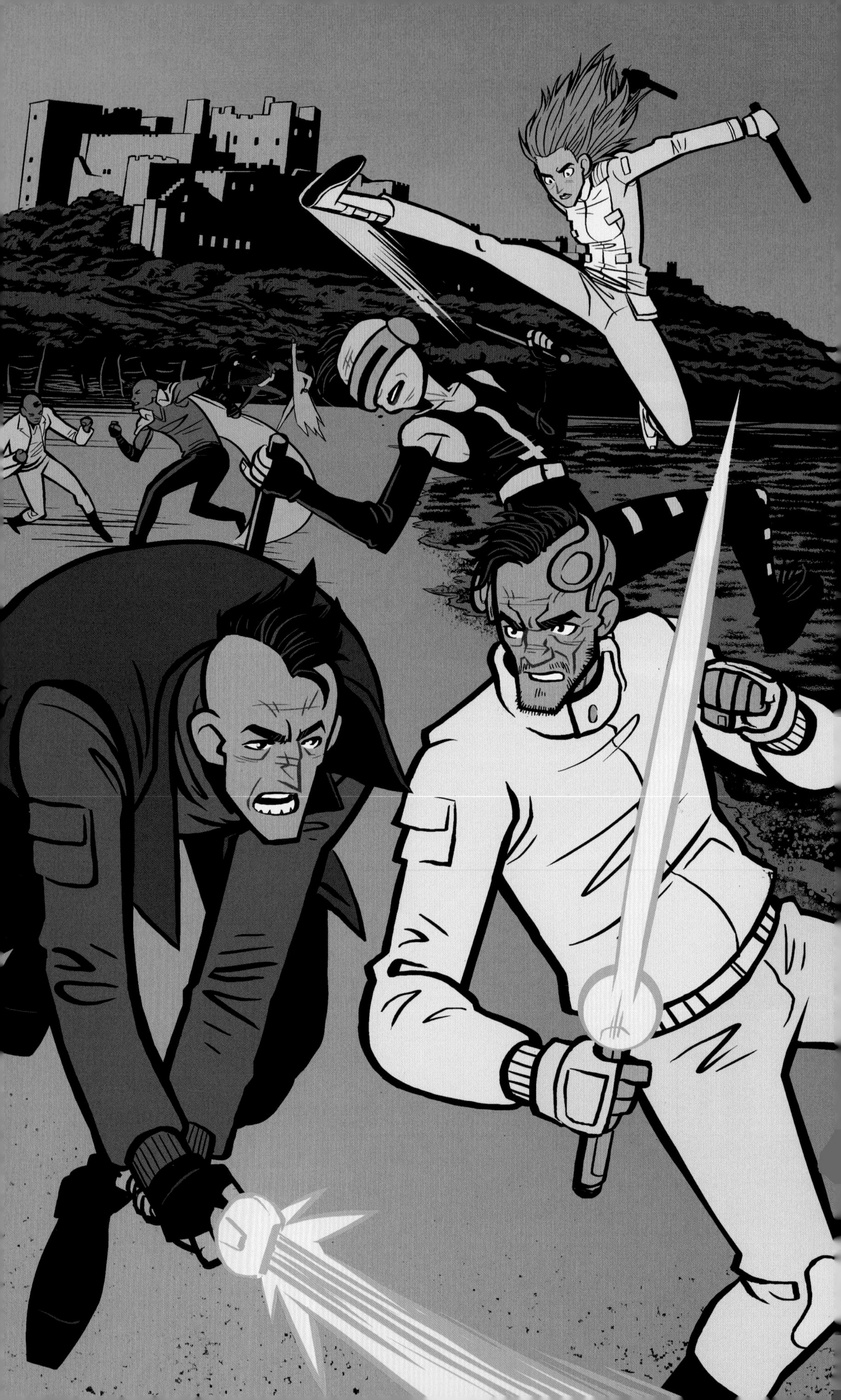

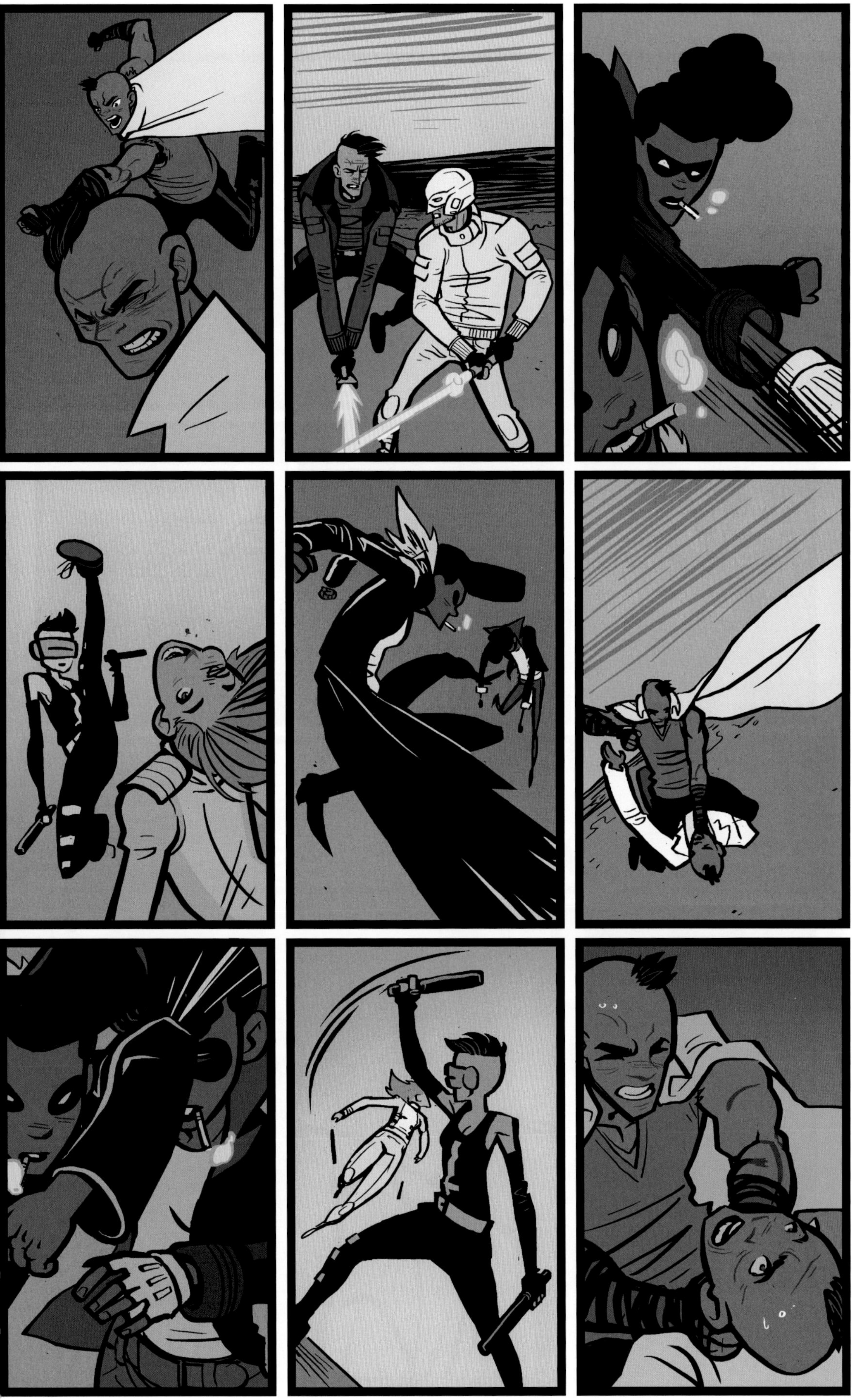

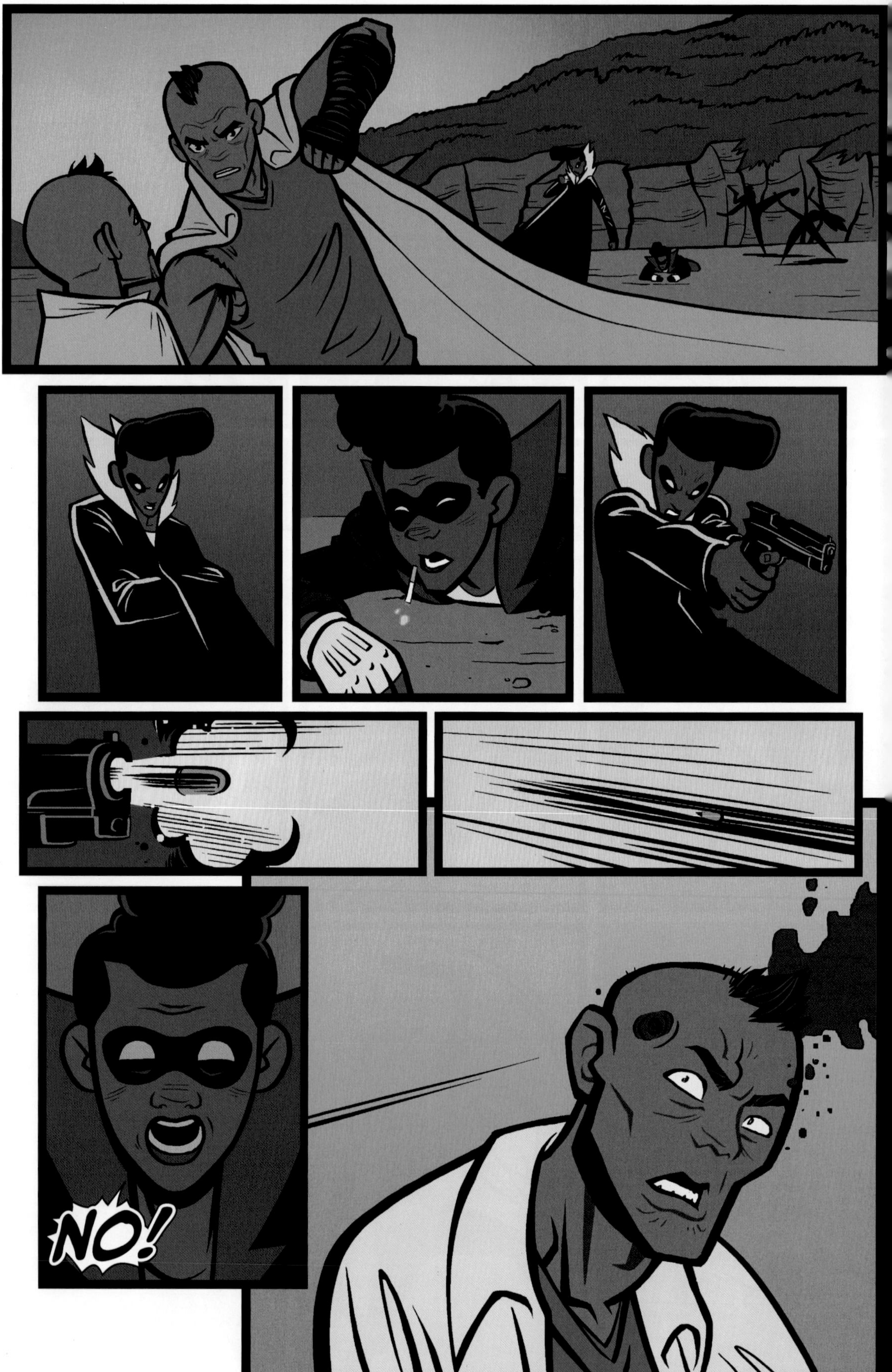
NO!

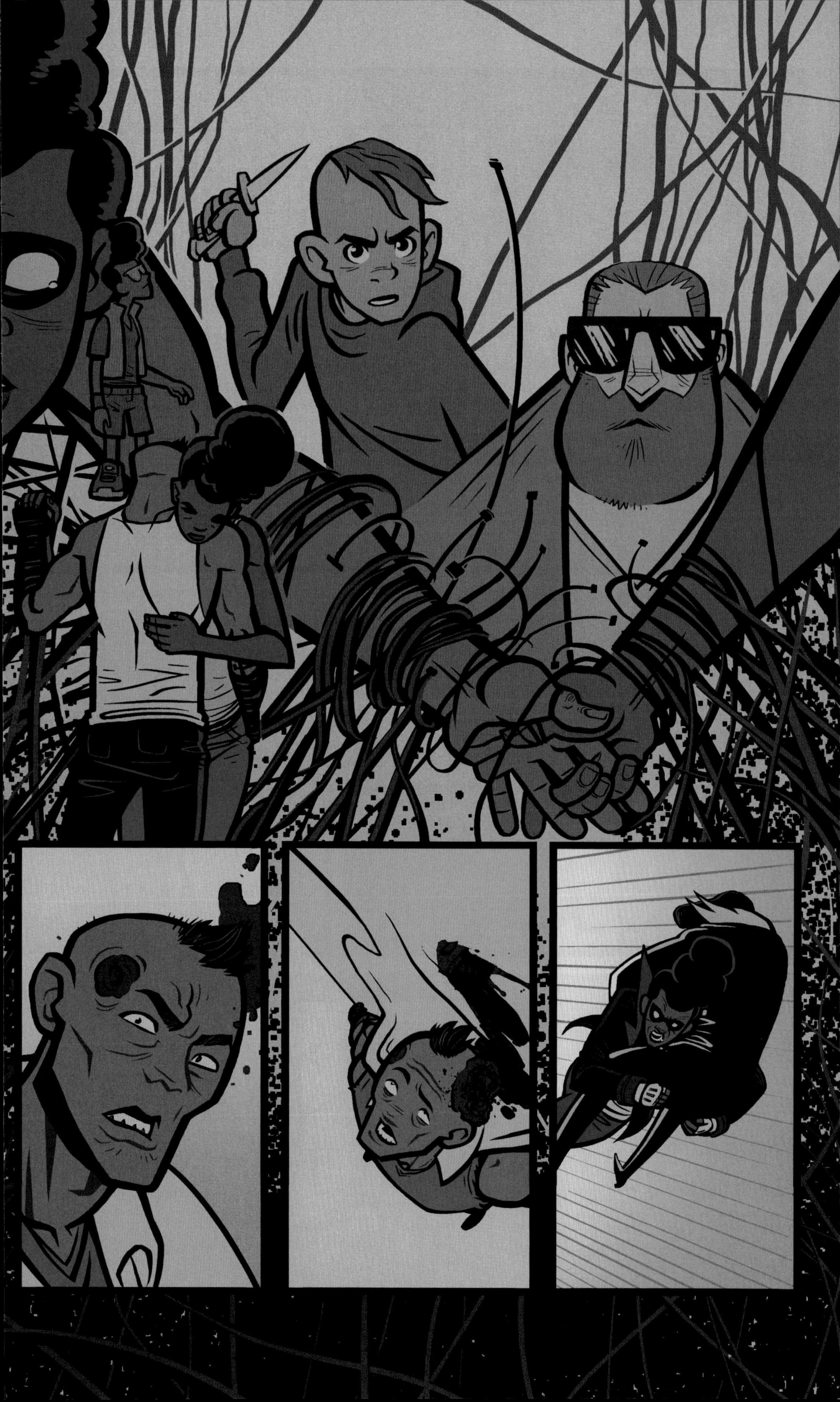

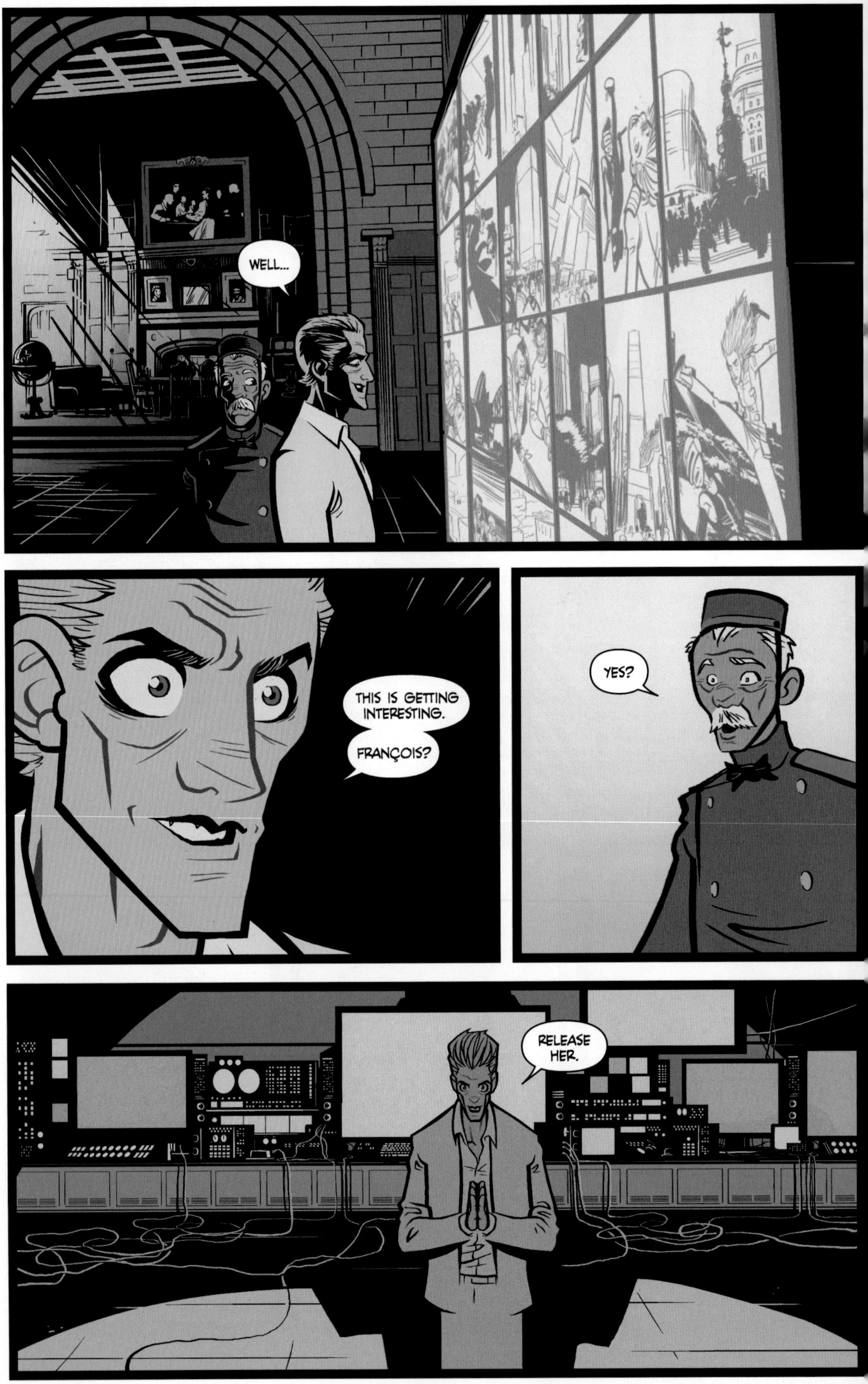

WELL...
THIS IS GETTING INTERESTING.
FRANÇOIS?
YES?
RELEASE HER.

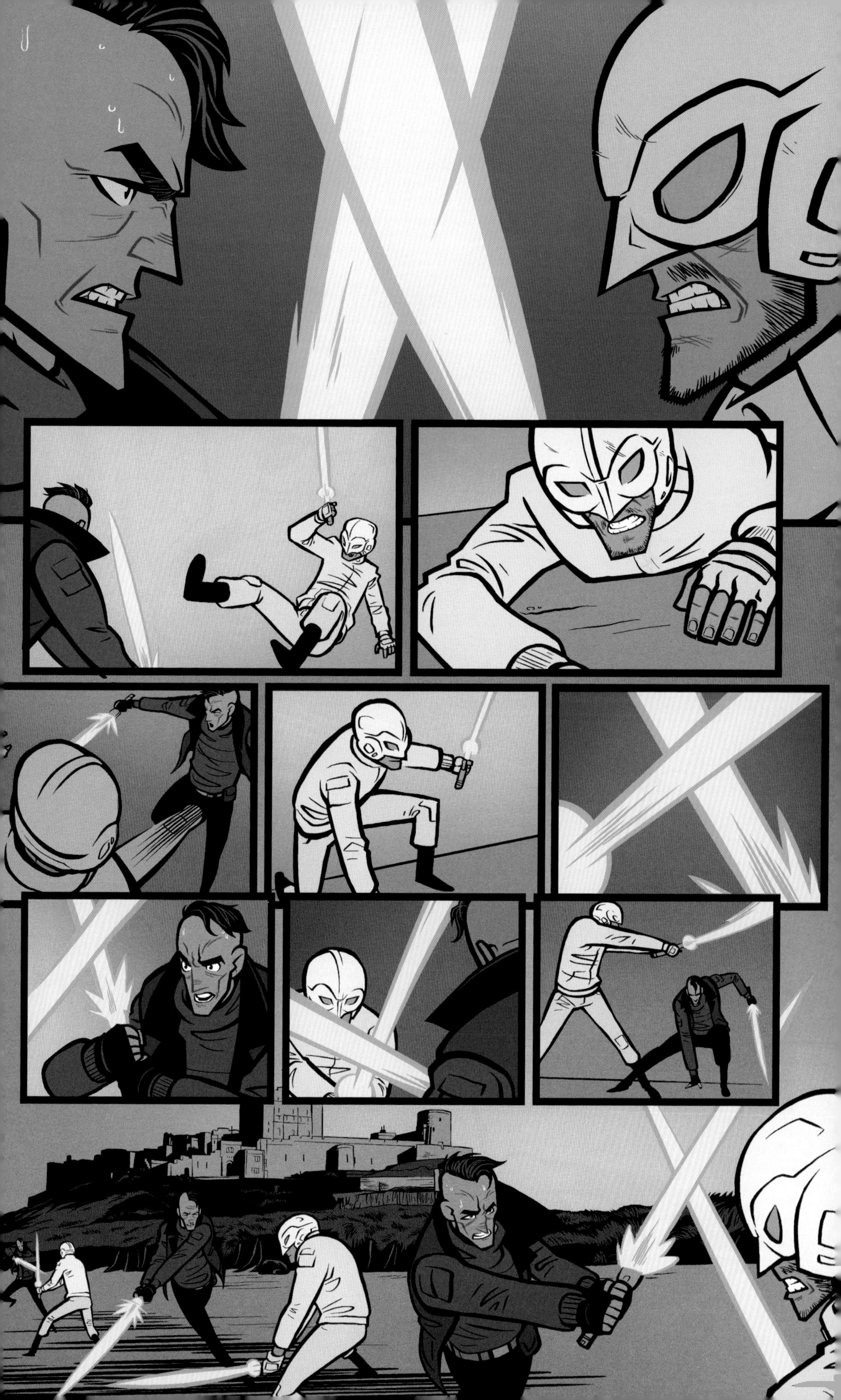

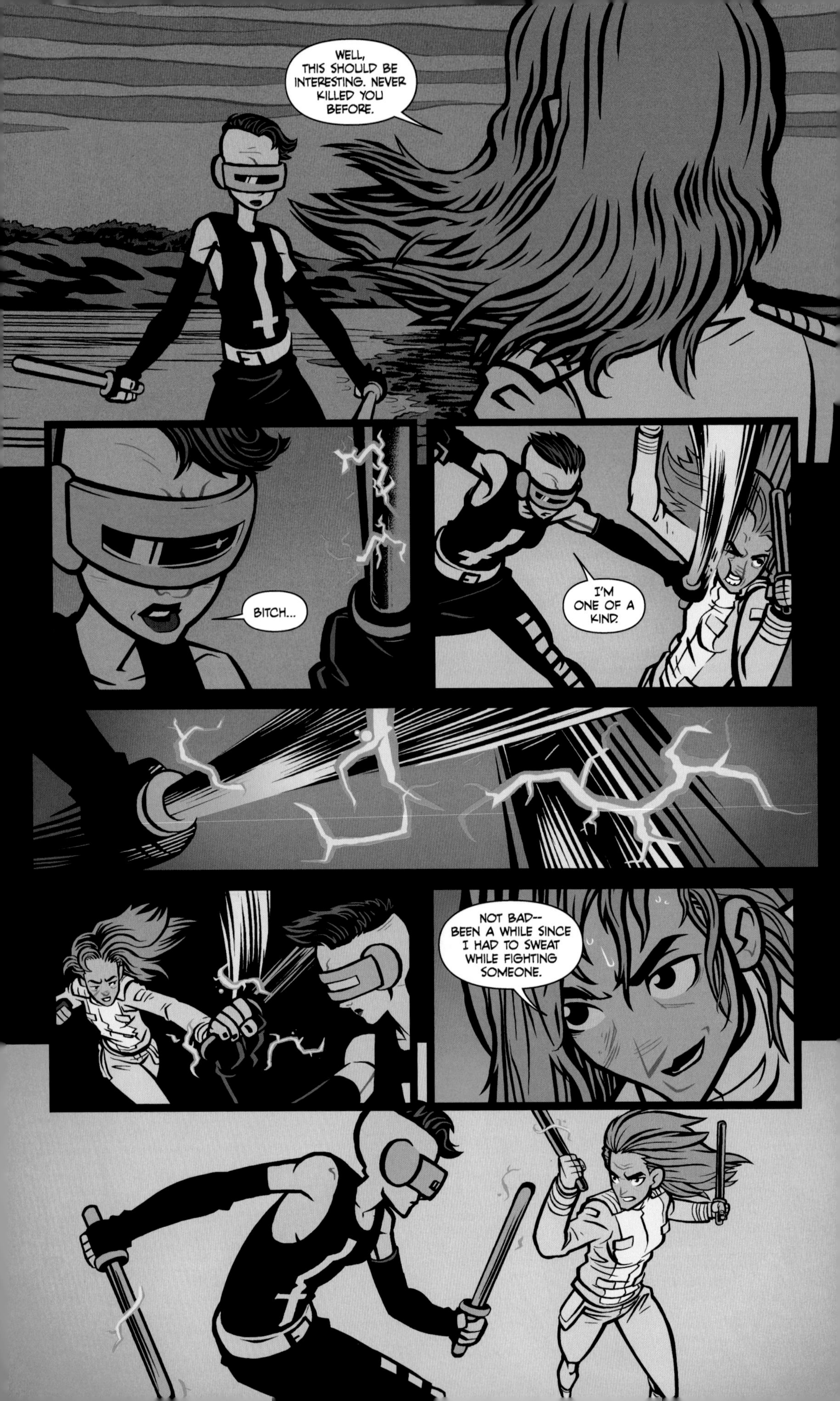
WELL, THIS SHOULD BE INTERESTING. NEVER KILLED YOU BEFORE.
BITCH...
I'M ONE OF A KIND.
NOT BAD-- BEEN A WHILE SINCE I HAD TO SWEAT WHILE FIGHTING SOMEONE.

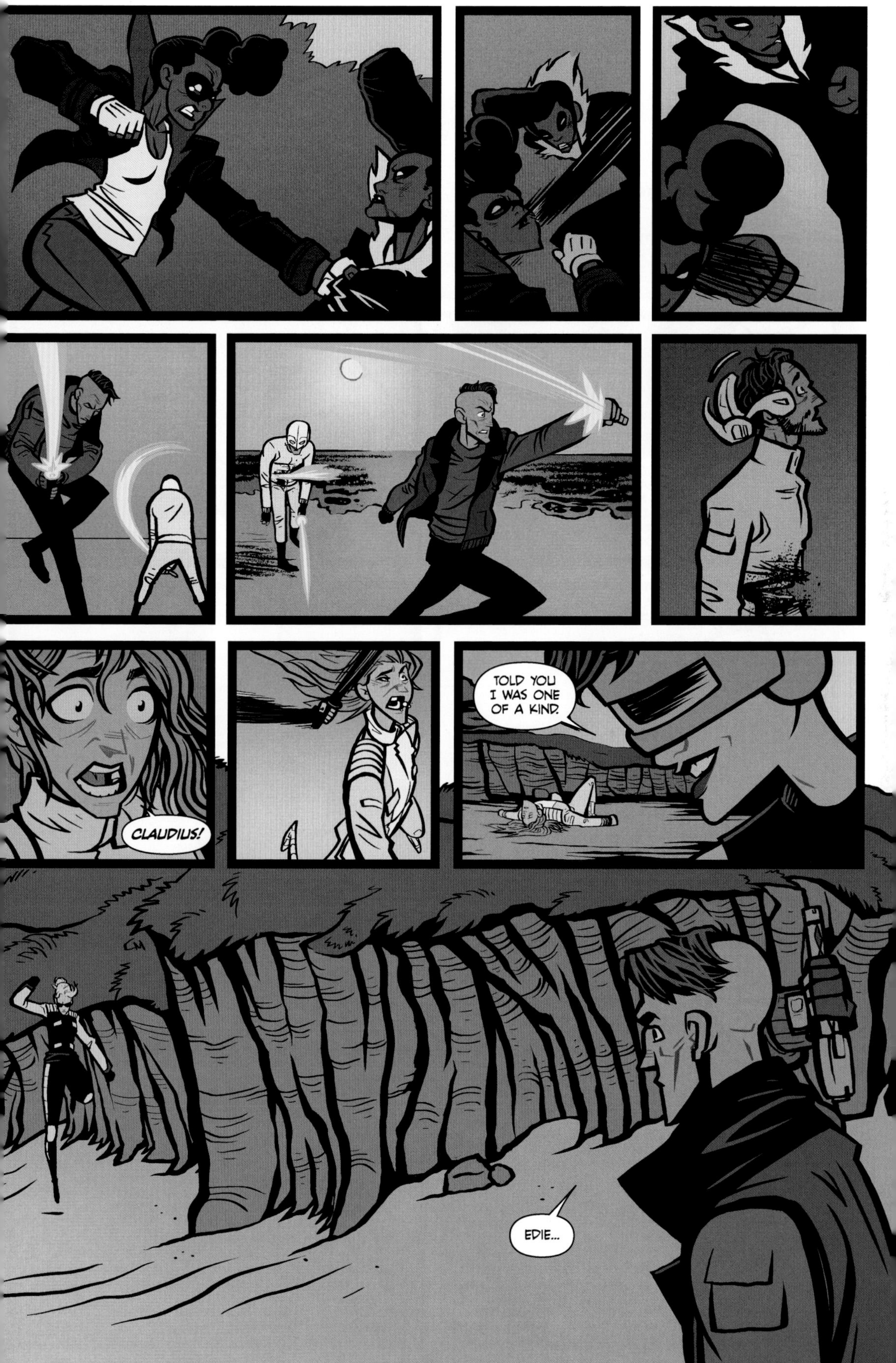
CLAUDIUS!
TOLD YOU I WAS ONE OF A KIND.
EDIE...

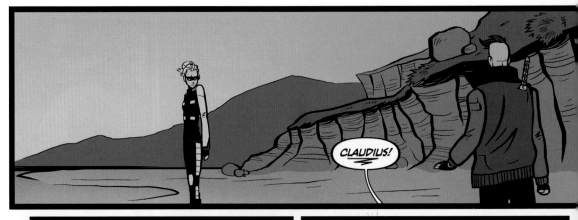

CLAUDIUS!

WHAT THE HELL ARE YOU DOING?

YOU GO AHEAD, SHUT IT DOWN. I'LL MEET YOU THERE. I'VE JUST GOT TO TAKE CARE OF THIS FIRST.

BUT...

TRUST ME, ZOEY. YOU'VE GOT THIS. YOU'RE READY.

OKAY. OKAY. I GOT THIS. YOU'RE RIGHT BEHIND ME THOUGH. NO BAILING.

NO BAILING.

HEY, CLAUDIUS?

YEAH?

THANKS.

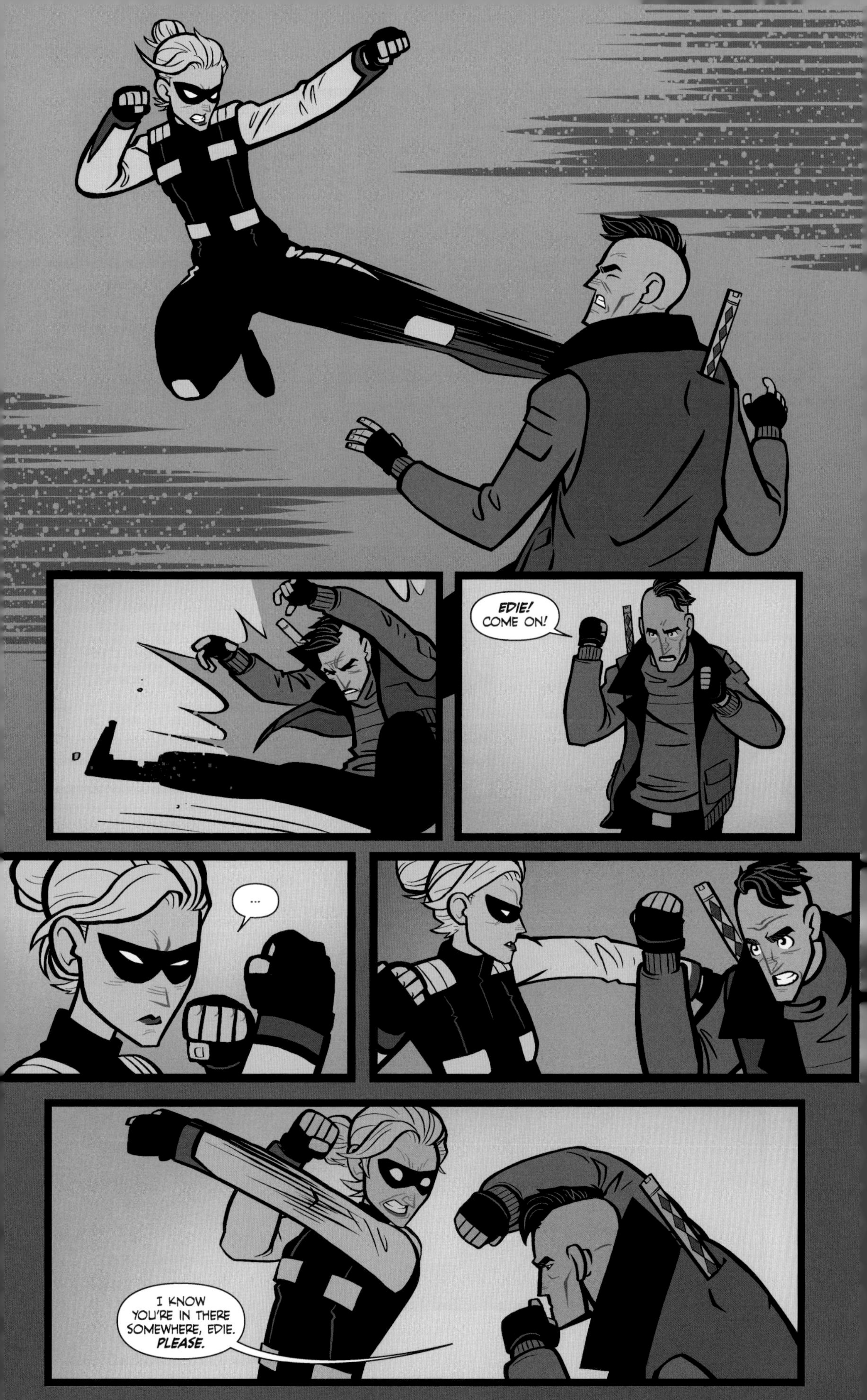
EDIE!
COME ON!
...
I KNOW YOU'RE IN THERE SOMEWHERE, EDIE. ***PLEASE.***

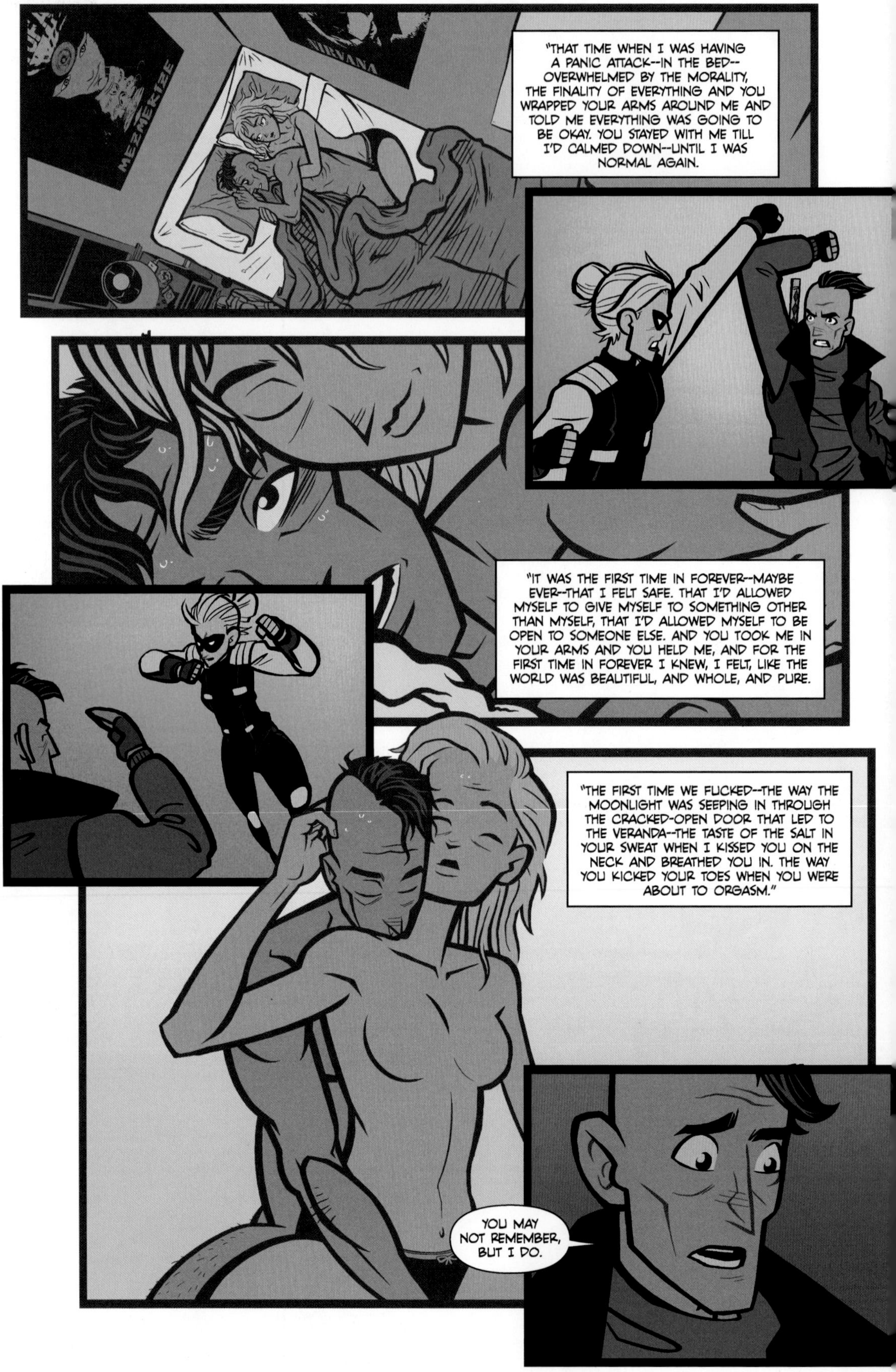
"THAT TIME WHEN I WAS HAVING A PANIC ATTACK--IN THE BED--OVERWHELMED BY THE MORALITY, THE FINALITY OF EVERYTHING AND YOU WRAPPED YOUR ARMS AROUND ME AND TOLD ME EVERYTHING WAS GOING TO BE OKAY. YOU STAYED WITH ME TILL I'D CALMED DOWN--UNTIL I WAS NORMAL AGAIN.
MEZMERIZE
NIRVANA
"IT WAS THE FIRST TIME IN FOREVER--MAYBE EVER--THAT I FELT SAFE. THAT I'D ALLOWED MYSELF TO GIVE MYSELF TO SOMETHING OTHER THAN MYSELF, THAT I'D ALLOWED MYSELF TO BE OPEN TO SOMEONE ELSE. AND YOU TOOK ME IN YOUR ARMS AND YOU HELD ME, AND FOR THE FIRST TIME IN FOREVER I KNEW, I FELT, LIKE THE WORLD WAS BEAUTIFUL, AND WHOLE, AND PURE.
"THE FIRST TIME WE FUCKED--THE WAY THE MOONLIGHT WAS SEEPING IN THROUGH THE CRACKED-OPEN DOOR THAT LED TO THE VERANDA--THE TASTE OF THE SALT IN YOUR SWEAT WHEN I KISSED YOU ON THE NECK AND BREATHED YOU IN. THE WAY YOU KICKED YOUR TOES WHEN YOU WERE ABOUT TO ORGASM."
YOU MAY NOT REMEMBER, BUT I DO.

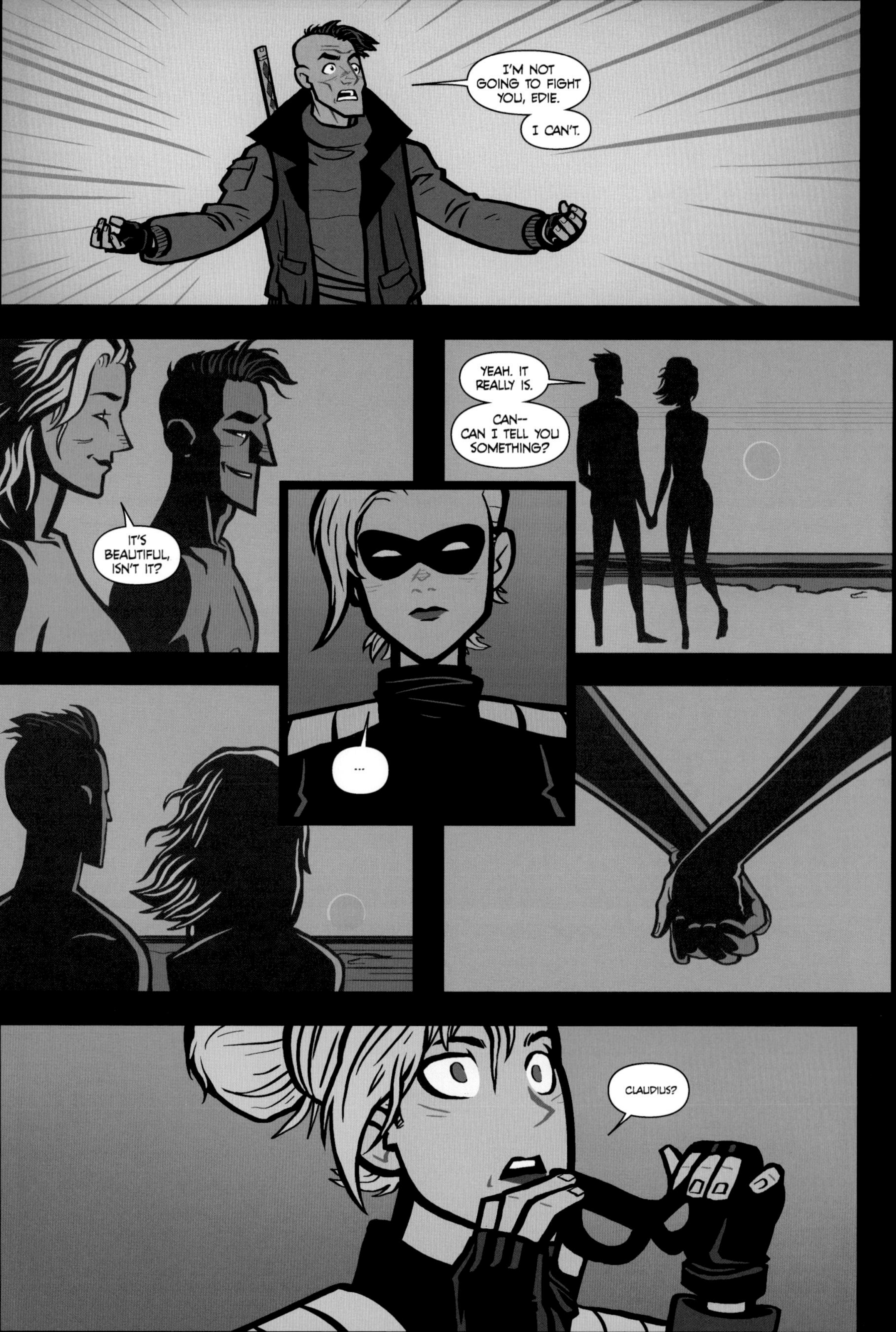

I'M NOT GOING TO FIGHT YOU, EDIE.
I CAN'T.
IT'S BEAUTIFUL, ISN'T IT?
YEAH. IT REALLY IS.
CAN-- CAN I TELL YOU SOMETHING?
...
CLAUDIUS?

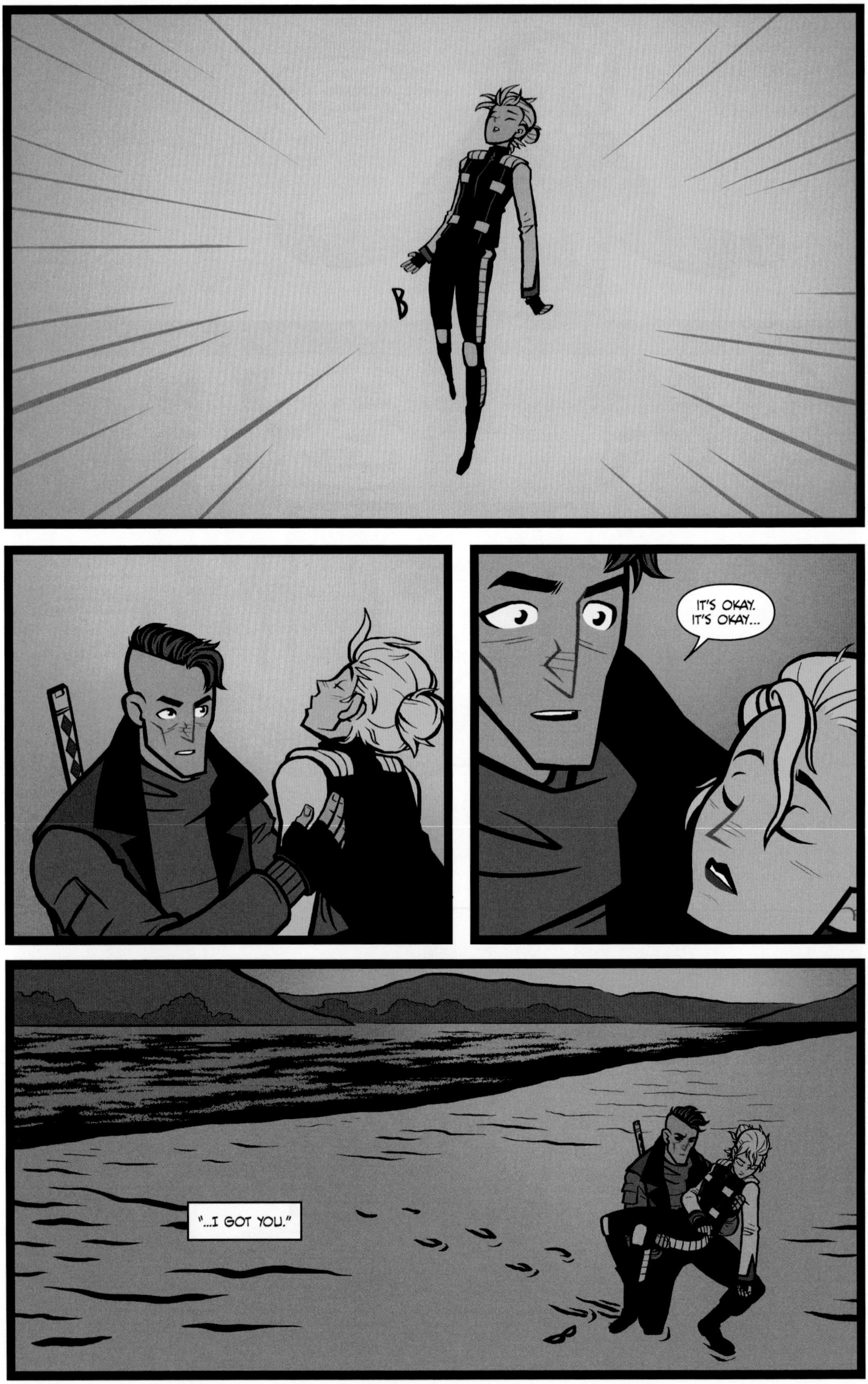
B
IT'S OKAY.
IT'S OKAY...
"...I GOT YOU."

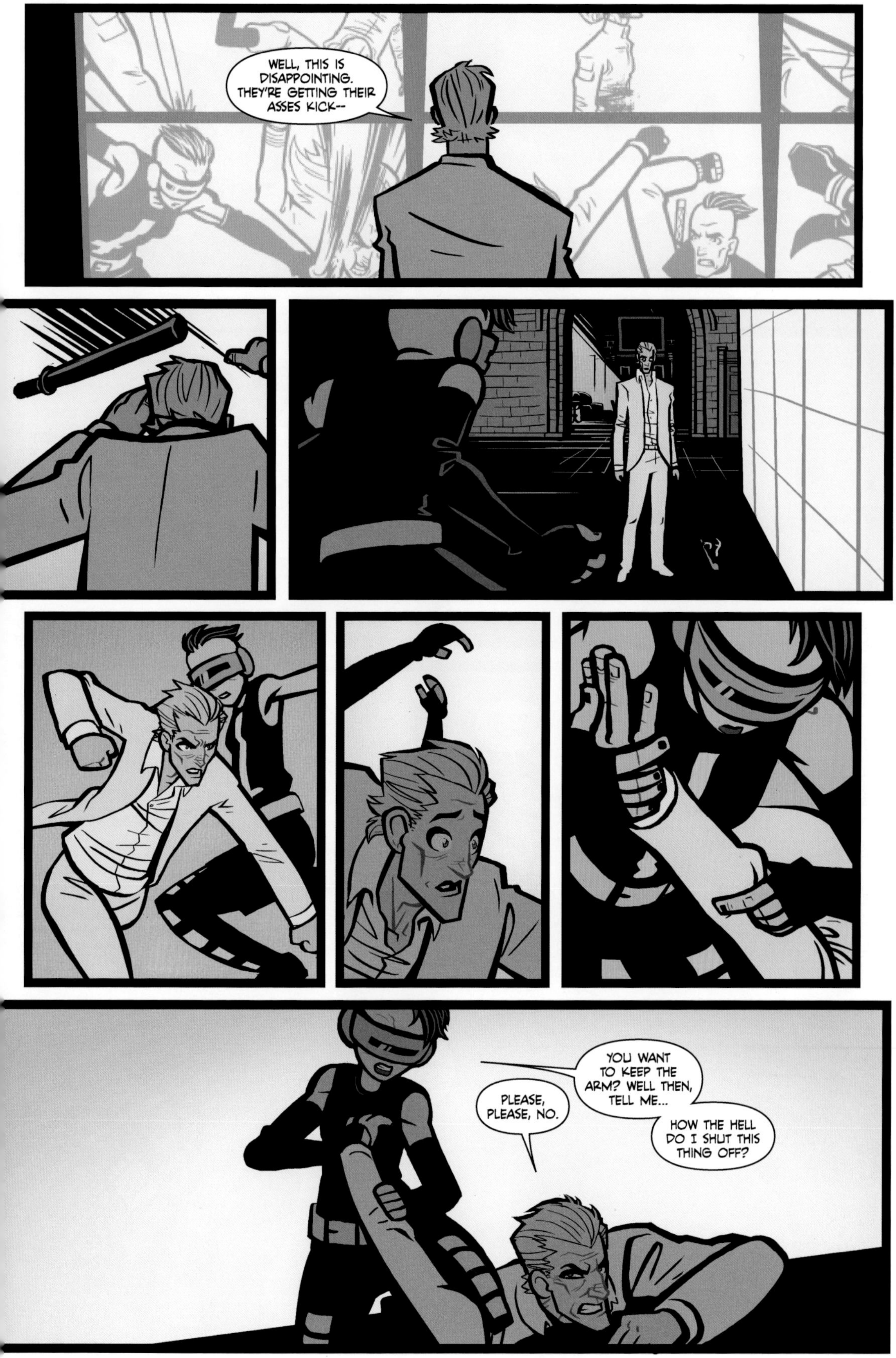
WELL, THIS IS DISAPPOINTING. THEY'RE GETTING THEIR ASSES KICK--
PLEASE, PLEASE, NO.
YOU WANT TO KEEP THE ARM? WELL THEN, TELL ME...
HOW THE HELL DO I SHUT THIS THING OFF?

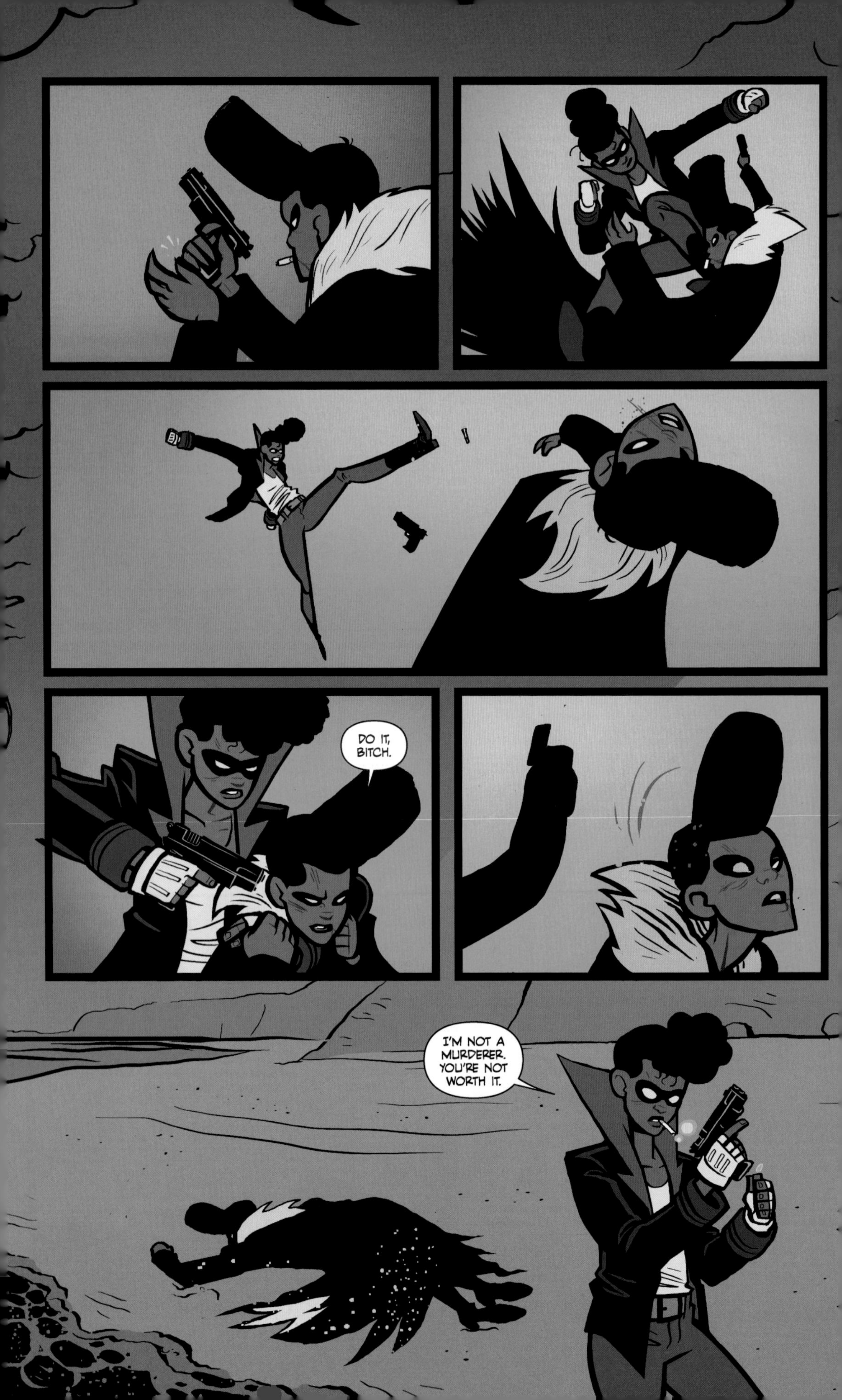

DO IT, BITCH.
I'M NOT A MURDERER. YOU'RE NOT WORTH IT.

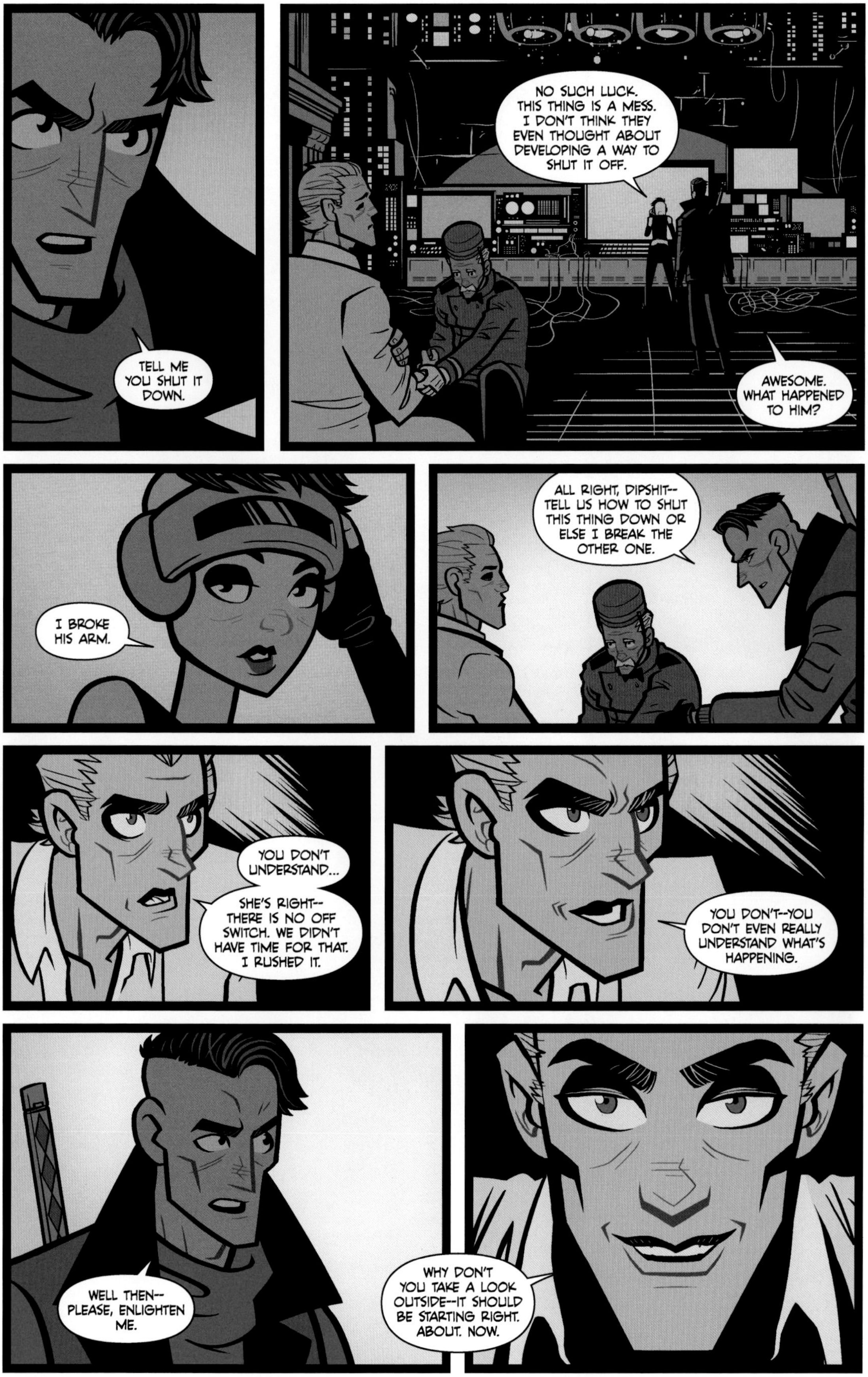
TELL ME YOU SHUT IT DOWN.
NO SUCH LUCK. THIS THING IS A MESS. I DON'T THINK THEY EVEN THOUGHT ABOUT DEVELOPING A WAY TO SHUT IT OFF.
AWESOME. WHAT HAPPENED TO HIM?
I BROKE HIS ARM.
ALL RIGHT, DIPSHIT-- TELL US HOW TO SHUT THIS THING DOWN OR ELSE I BREAK THE OTHER ONE.
YOU DON'T UNDERSTAND...
SHE'S RIGHT-- THERE IS NO OFF SWITCH. WE DIDN'T HAVE TIME FOR THAT. I RUSHED IT.
YOU DON'T--YOU DON'T EVEN REALLY UNDERSTAND WHAT'S HAPPENING.
WELL THEN-- PLEASE, ENLIGHTEN ME.
WHY DON'T YOU TAKE A LOOK OUTSIDE--IT SHOULD BE STARTING RIGHT. ABOUT. NOW.

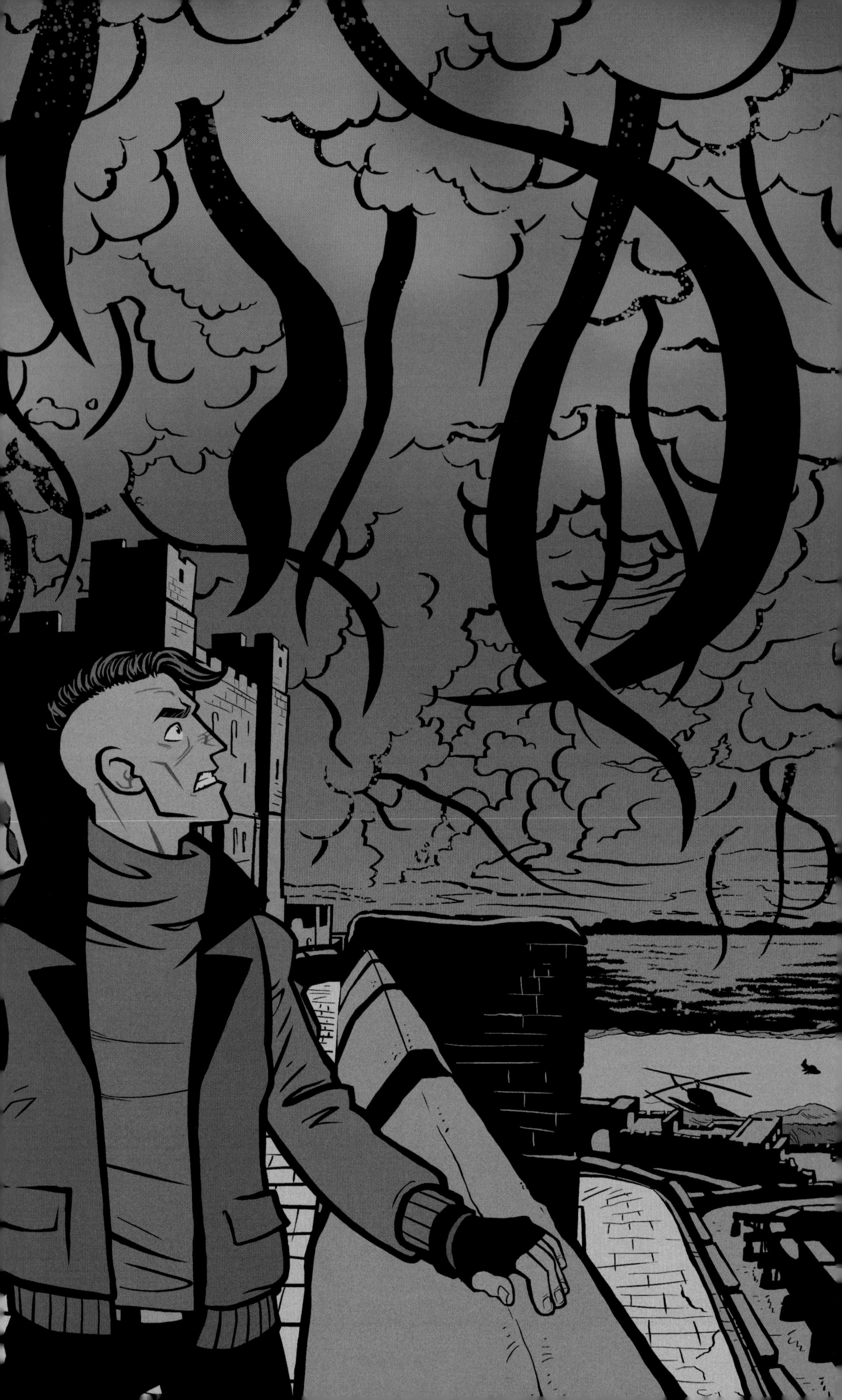

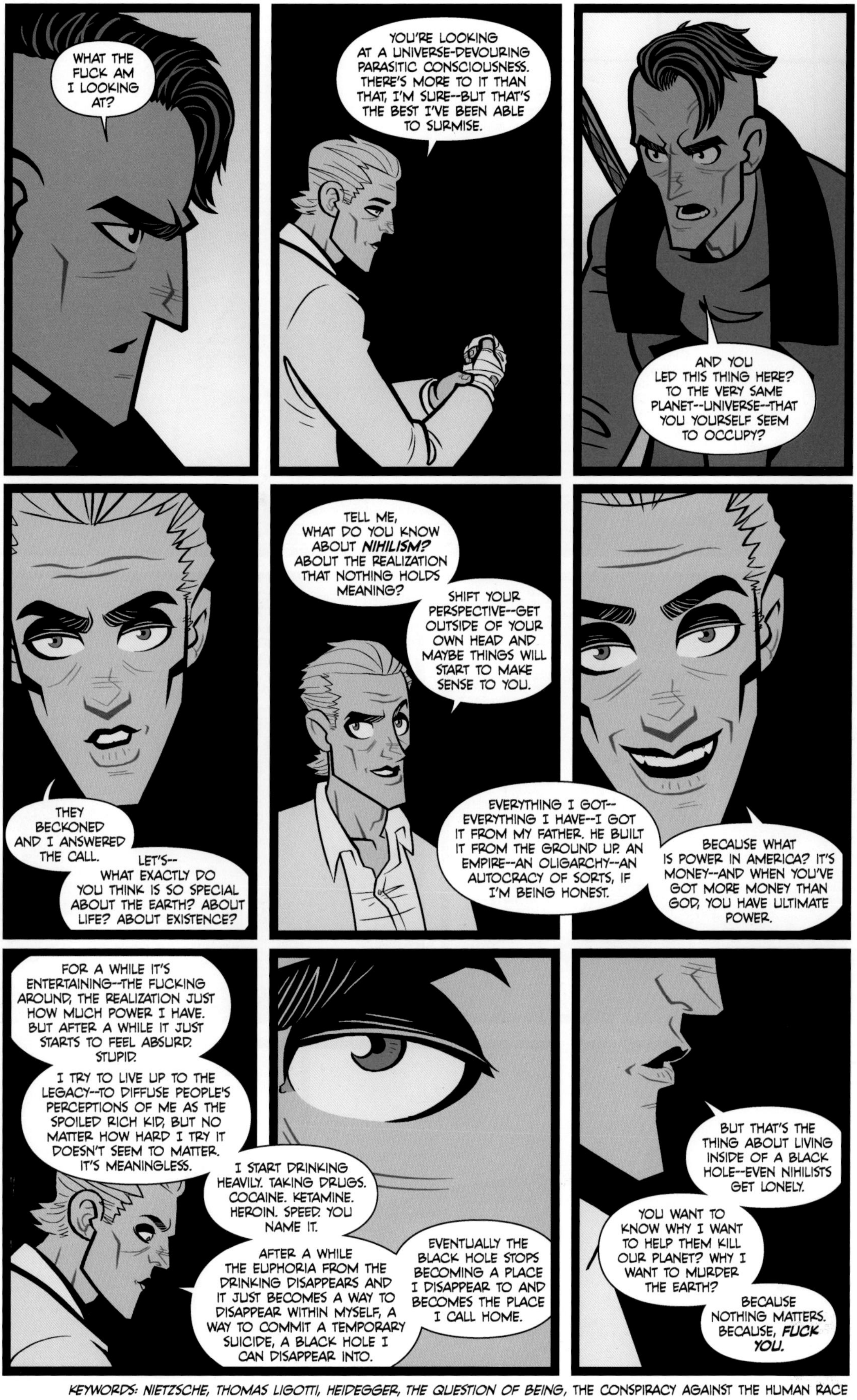
WHAT THE FUCK AM I LOOKING AT?
YOU'RE LOOKING AT A UNIVERSE-DEVOURING PARASITIC CONSCIOUSNESS. THERE'S MORE TO IT THAN THAT, I'M SURE--BUT THAT'S THE BEST I'VE BEEN ABLE TO SURMISE.
AND YOU LED THIS THING HERE? TO THE VERY SAME PLANET--UNIVERSE--THAT YOU YOURSELF SEEM TO OCCUPY?
THEY BECKONED AND I ANSWERED THE CALL.
LET'S-- WHAT EXACTLY DO YOU THINK IS SO SPECIAL ABOUT THE EARTH? ABOUT LIFE? ABOUT EXISTENCE?
TELL ME, WHAT DO YOU KNOW ABOUT NIHILISM? ABOUT THE REALIZATION THAT NOTHING HOLDS MEANING?
SHIFT YOUR PERSPECTIVE--GET OUTSIDE OF YOUR OWN HEAD AND MAYBE THINGS WILL START TO MAKE SENSE TO YOU.
EVERYTHING I GOT-- EVERYTHING I HAVE--I GOT IT FROM MY FATHER. HE BUILT IT FROM THE GROUND UP. AN EMPIRE--AN OLIGARCHY--AN AUTOCRACY OF SORTS, IF I'M BEING HONEST.
BECAUSE WHAT IS POWER IN AMERICA? IT'S MONEY--AND WHEN YOU'VE GOT MORE MONEY THAN GOD, YOU HAVE ULTIMATE POWER.
FOR A WHILE IT'S ENTERTAINING--THE FUCKING AROUND, THE REALIZATION JUST HOW MUCH POWER I HAVE. BUT AFTER A WHILE IT JUST STARTS TO FEEL ABSURD. STUPID.
I TRY TO LIVE UP TO THE LEGACY--TO DIFFUSE PEOPLE'S PERCEPTIONS OF ME AS THE SPOILED RICH KID, BUT NO MATTER HOW HARD I TRY IT DOESN'T SEEM TO MATTER. IT'S MEANINGLESS.
I START DRINKING HEAVILY. TAKING DRUGS. COCAINE. KETAMINE. HEROIN. SPEED. YOU NAME IT.
AFTER A WHILE THE EUPHORIA FROM THE DRINKING DISAPPEARS AND IT JUST BECOMES A WAY TO DISAPPEAR WITHIN MYSELF, A WAY TO COMMIT A TEMPORARY SUICIDE, A BLACK HOLE I CAN DISAPPEAR INTO.
EVENTUALLY THE BLACK HOLE STOPS BECOMING A PLACE I DISAPPEAR TO AND BECOMES THE PLACE I CALL HOME.
BUT THAT'S THE THING ABOUT LIVING INSIDE OF A BLACK HOLE--EVEN NIHILISTS GET LONELY.
YOU WANT TO KNOW WHY I WANT TO HELP THEM KILL OUR PLANET? WHY I WANT TO MURDER THE EARTH?
BECAUSE NOTHING MATTERS. BECAUSE, FUCK YOU.

*KEYWORDS: NIETZSCHE, THOMAS LIGOTTI, HEIDEGGER, THE QUESTION OF BEING,* THE CONSPIRACY AGAINST THE HUMAN RACE

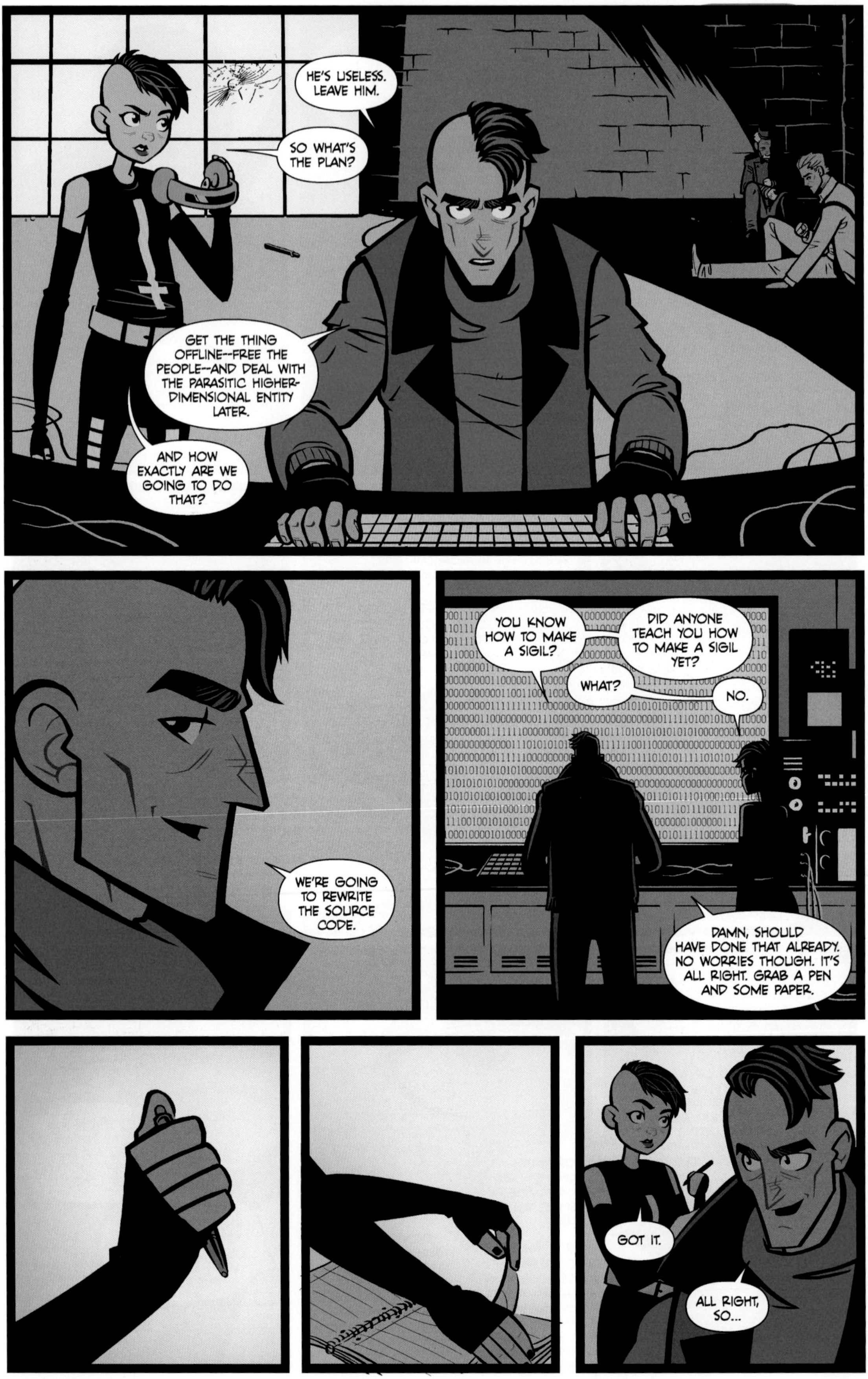
HE'S USELESS. LEAVE HIM.
SO WHAT'S THE PLAN?
GET THE THING OFFLINE--FREE THE PEOPLE--AND DEAL WITH THE PARASITIC HIGHER-DIMENSIONAL ENTITY LATER.
AND HOW EXACTLY ARE WE GOING TO DO THAT?
WE'RE GOING TO REWRITE THE SOURCE CODE.
YOU KNOW HOW TO MAKE A SIGIL?
DID ANYONE TEACH YOU HOW TO MAKE A SIGIL YET?
WHAT?
NO.
DAMN, SHOULD HAVE DONE THAT ALREADY. NO WORRIES THOUGH. IT'S ALL RIGHT. GRAB A PEN AND SOME PAPER.
GOT IT.
ALL RIGHT, SO...

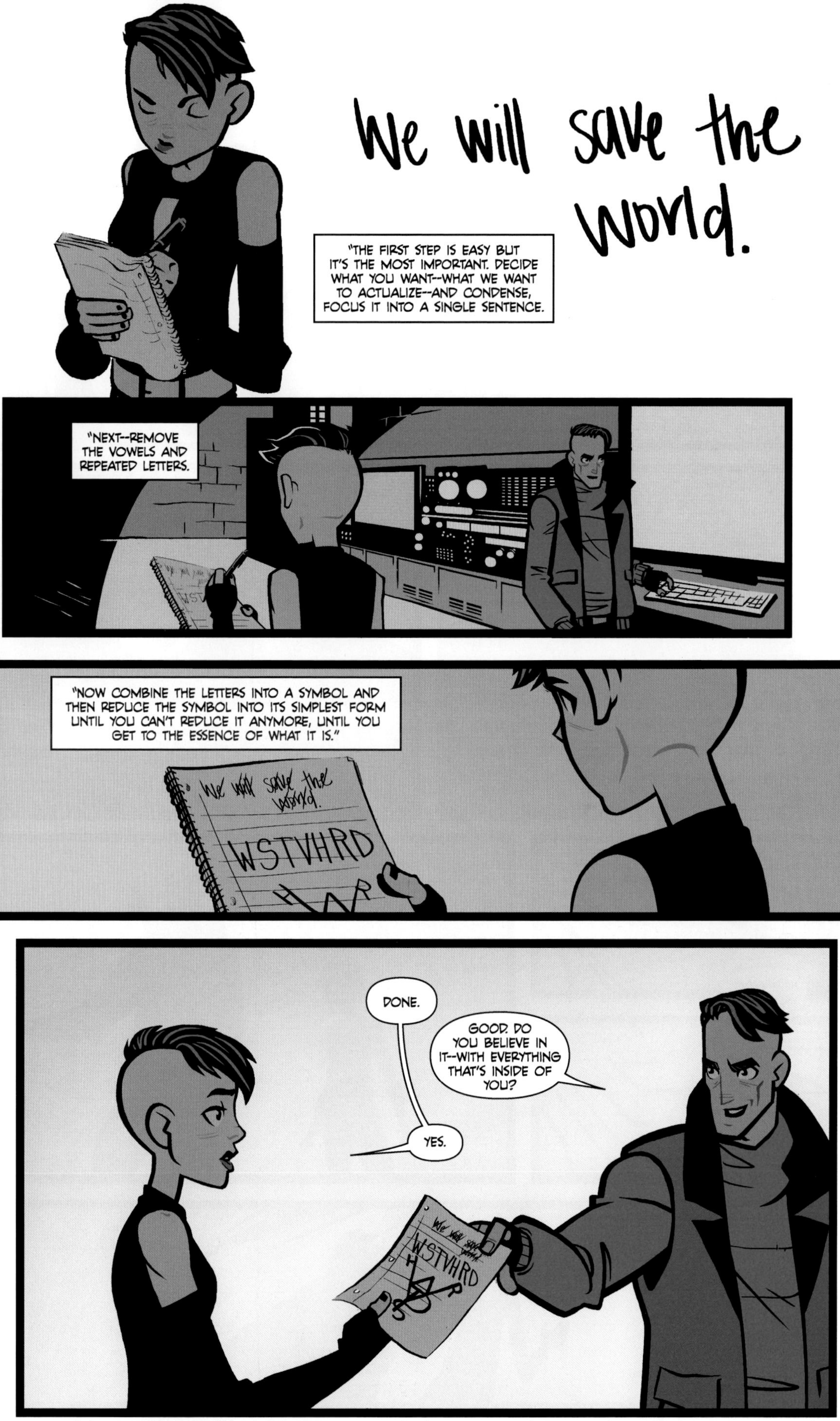
We will save the world.
"THE FIRST STEP IS EASY BUT IT'S THE MOST IMPORTANT. DECIDE WHAT YOU WANT--WHAT WE WANT TO ACTUALIZE--AND CONDENSE, FOCUS IT INTO A SINGLE SENTENCE.
"NEXT--REMOVE THE VOWELS AND REPEATED LETTERS.
"NOW COMBINE THE LETTERS INTO A SYMBOL AND THEN REDUCE THE SYMBOL INTO ITS SIMPLEST FORM UNTIL YOU CAN'T REDUCE IT ANYMORE, UNTIL YOU GET TO THE ESSENCE OF WHAT IT IS."
WSTVHRD
DONE.
GOOD. DO YOU BELIEVE IN IT--WITH EVERYTHING THAT'S INSIDE OF YOU?
YES.

*"MAGICK HAS MANY ASPECTS, BUT PRIMARILY IT ACTS AS A DRAMATIZED SYSTEM OF PSYCHOLOGY."--ROBERT ANTON WILSON*

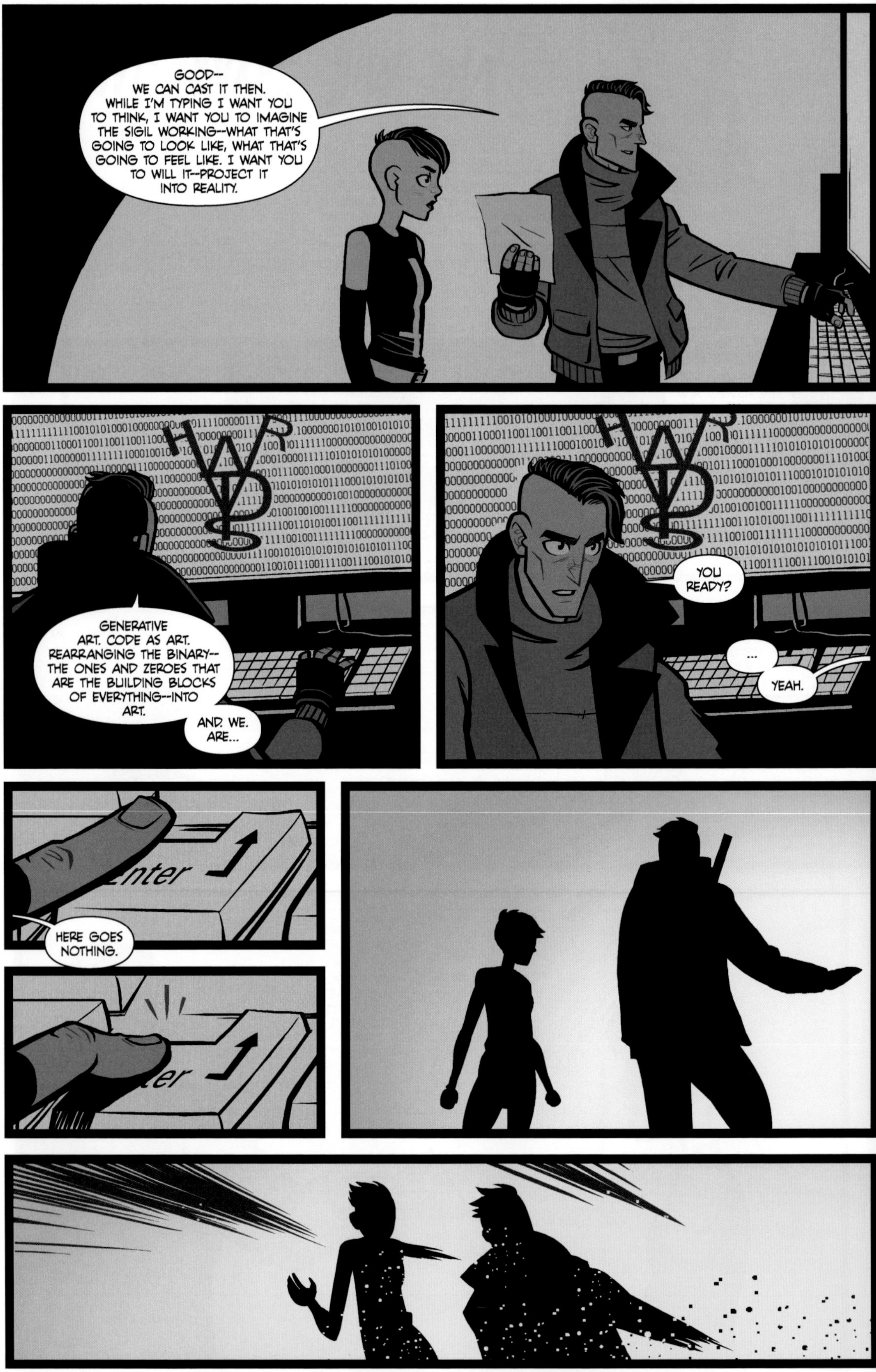
GOOD-- WE CAN CAST IT THEN. WHILE I'M TYPING I WANT YOU TO THINK, I WANT YOU TO IMAGINE THE SIGIL WORKING--WHAT THAT'S GOING TO LOOK LIKE, WHAT THAT'S GOING TO FEEL LIKE. I WANT YOU TO WILL IT--PROJECT IT INTO REALITY.
GENERATIVE ART. CODE AS ART. REARRANGING THE BINARY--THE ONES AND ZEROES THAT ARE THE BUILDING BLOCKS OF EVERYTHING--INTO ART.
AND. WE. ARE...
YOU READY?
...
YEAH.
Enter
HERE GOES NOTHING.

READ: HTTP://WWW.THEATLANTIC.COM/TECHNOLOGY/ARCHIVE/2010/08/CREATING-ART-WITH-CODE/61779/#SLIDE2

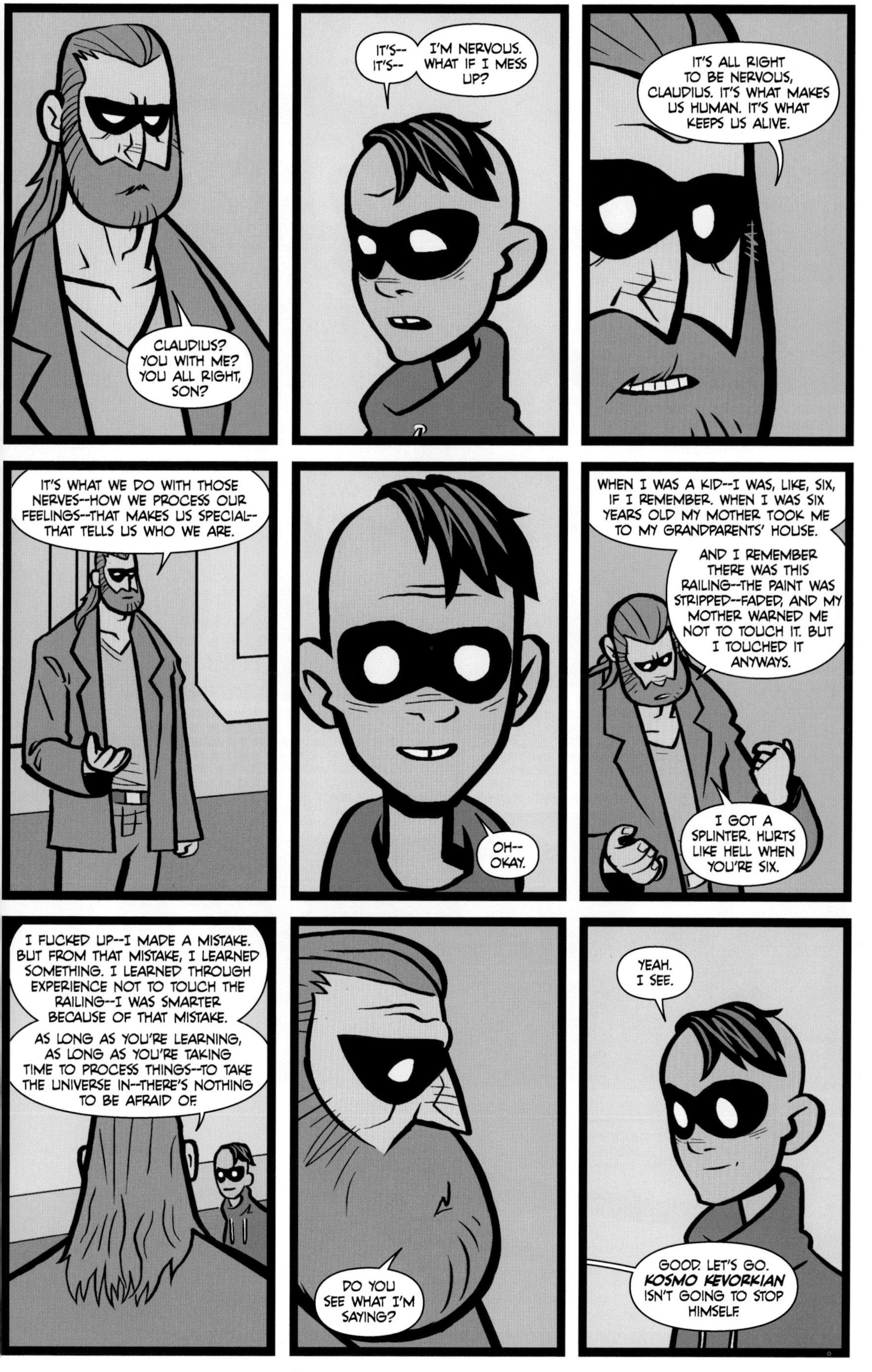
CLAUDIUS? YOU WITH ME? YOU ALL RIGHT, SON?
IT'S-- IT'S--
I'M NERVOUS. WHAT IF I MESS UP?
IT'S ALL RIGHT TO BE NERVOUS, CLAUDIUS. IT'S WHAT MAKES US HUMAN. IT'S WHAT KEEPS US ALIVE.
IT'S WHAT WE DO WITH THOSE NERVES--HOW WE PROCESS OUR FEELINGS--THAT MAKES US SPECIAL--THAT TELLS US WHO WE ARE.
OH-- OKAY.
WHEN I WAS A KID--I WAS, LIKE, SIX, IF I REMEMBER. WHEN I WAS SIX YEARS OLD MY MOTHER TOOK ME TO MY GRANDPARENTS' HOUSE.
AND I REMEMBER THERE WAS THIS RAILING--THE PAINT WAS STRIPPED--FADED, AND MY MOTHER WARNED ME NOT TO TOUCH IT. BUT I TOUCHED IT ANYWAYS.
I GOT A SPLINTER. HURTS LIKE HELL WHEN YOU'RE SIX.
I FUCKED UP--I MADE A MISTAKE. BUT FROM THAT MISTAKE, I LEARNED SOMETHING. I LEARNED THROUGH EXPERIENCE NOT TO TOUCH THE RAILING--I WAS SMARTER BECAUSE OF THAT MISTAKE.
AS LONG AS YOU'RE LEARNING, AS LONG AS YOU'RE TAKING TIME TO PROCESS THINGS--TO TAKE THE UNIVERSE IN--THERE'S NOTHING TO BE AFRAID OF.
DO YOU SEE WHAT I'M SAYING?
YEAH. I SEE.
GOOD. LET'S GO. *KOSMO KEVORKIAN* ISN'T GOING TO STOP HIMSELF.

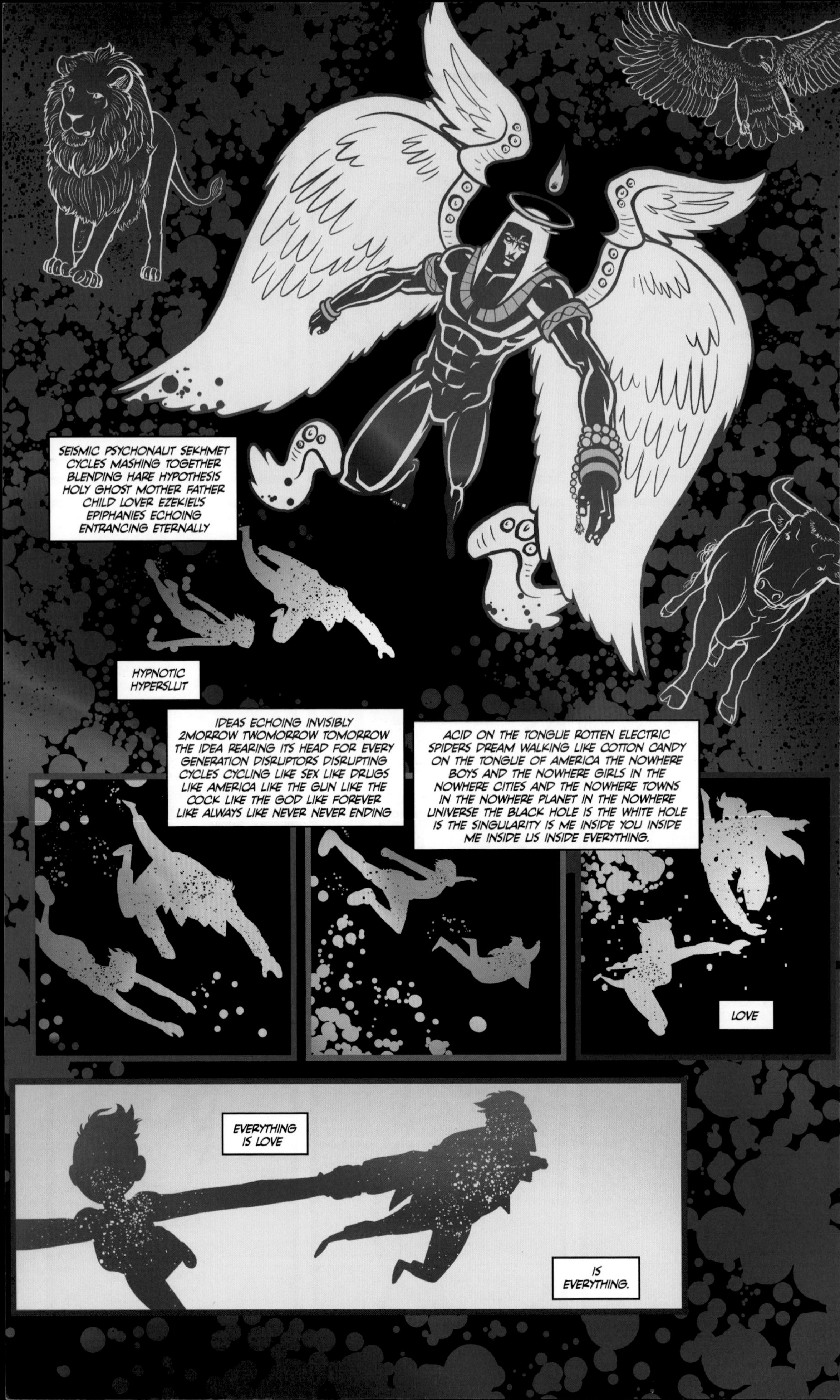
SEISMIC PSYCHONAUT SEKHMET CYCLES MASHING TOGETHER BLENDING HARE HYPOTHESIS HOLY GHOST MOTHER FATHER CHILD LOVER EZEKIEL'S EPIPHANIES ECHOING ENTRANCING ETERNALLY
HYPNOTIC HYPERSLUT
IDEAS ECHOING INVISIBLY 2MORROW TWOMORROW TOMORROW THE IDEA REARING ITS HEAD FOR EVERY GENERATION DISRUPTORS DISRUPTING CYCLES CYCLING LIKE SEX LIKE DRUGS LIKE AMERICA LIKE THE GUN LIKE THE COCK LIKE THE GOD LIKE FOREVER LIKE ALWAYS LIKE NEVER NEVER ENDING
ACID ON THE TONGUE ROTTEN ELECTRIC SPIDERS DREAM WALKING LIKE COTTON CANDY ON THE TONGUE OF AMERICA THE NOWHERE BOYS AND THE NOWHERE GIRLS IN THE NOWHERE CITIES AND THE NOWHERE TOWNS IN THE NOWHERE PLANET IN THE NOWHERE UNIVERSE THE BLACK HOLE IS THE WHITE HOLE IS THE SINGULARITY IS ME INSIDE YOU INSIDE ME INSIDE US INSIDE EVERYTHING.
LOVE
EVERYTHING IS LOVE
IS EVERYTHING.

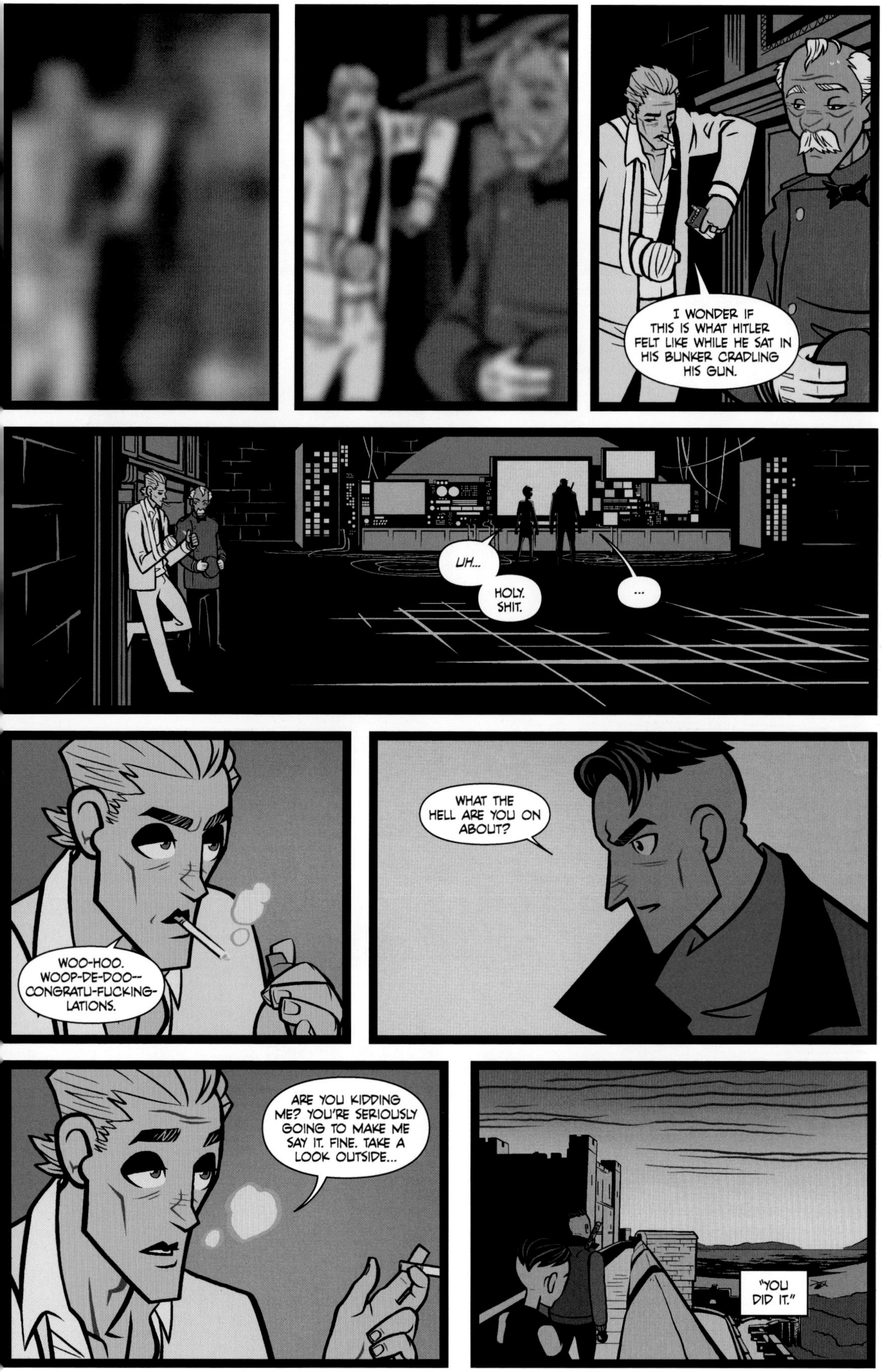
I WONDER IF THIS IS WHAT HITLER FELT LIKE WHILE HE SAT IN HIS BUNKER CRADLING HIS GUN.
UH...
HOLY. SHIT.
...
WOO-HOO. WOOP-DE-DOO-- CONGRATU-FUCKING-LATIONS.
WHAT THE HELL ARE YOU ON ABOUT?
ARE YOU KIDDING ME? YOU'RE SERIOUSLY GOING TO MAKE ME SAY IT. FINE. TAKE A LOOK OUTSIDE...
"YOU DID IT."

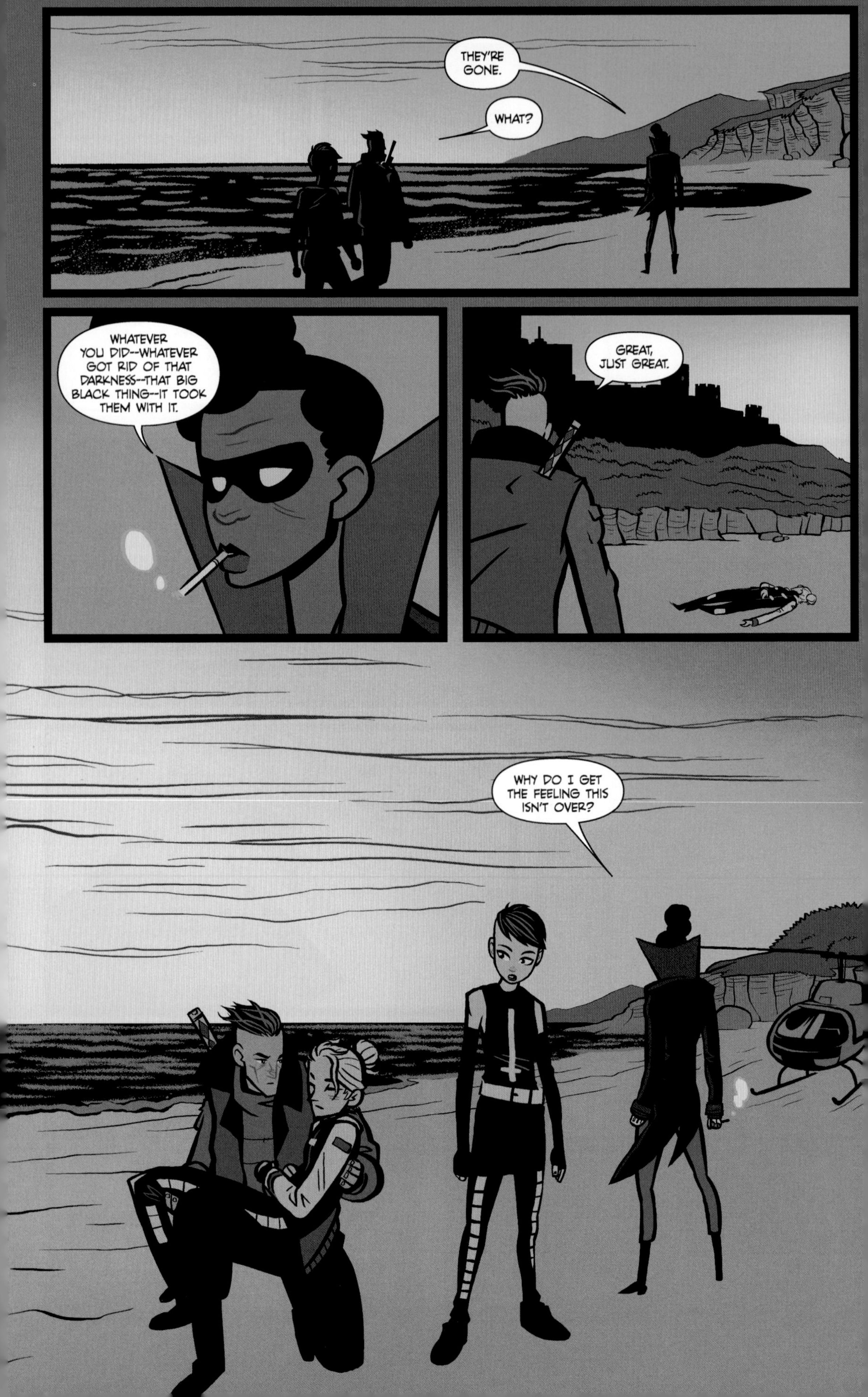
THEY'RE GONE.
WHAT?
WHATEVER YOU DID--WHATEVER GOT RID OF THAT DARKNESS--THAT BIG BLACK THING--IT TOOK THEM WITH IT.
GREAT, JUST GREAT.
WHY DO I GET THE FEELING THIS ISN'T OVER?

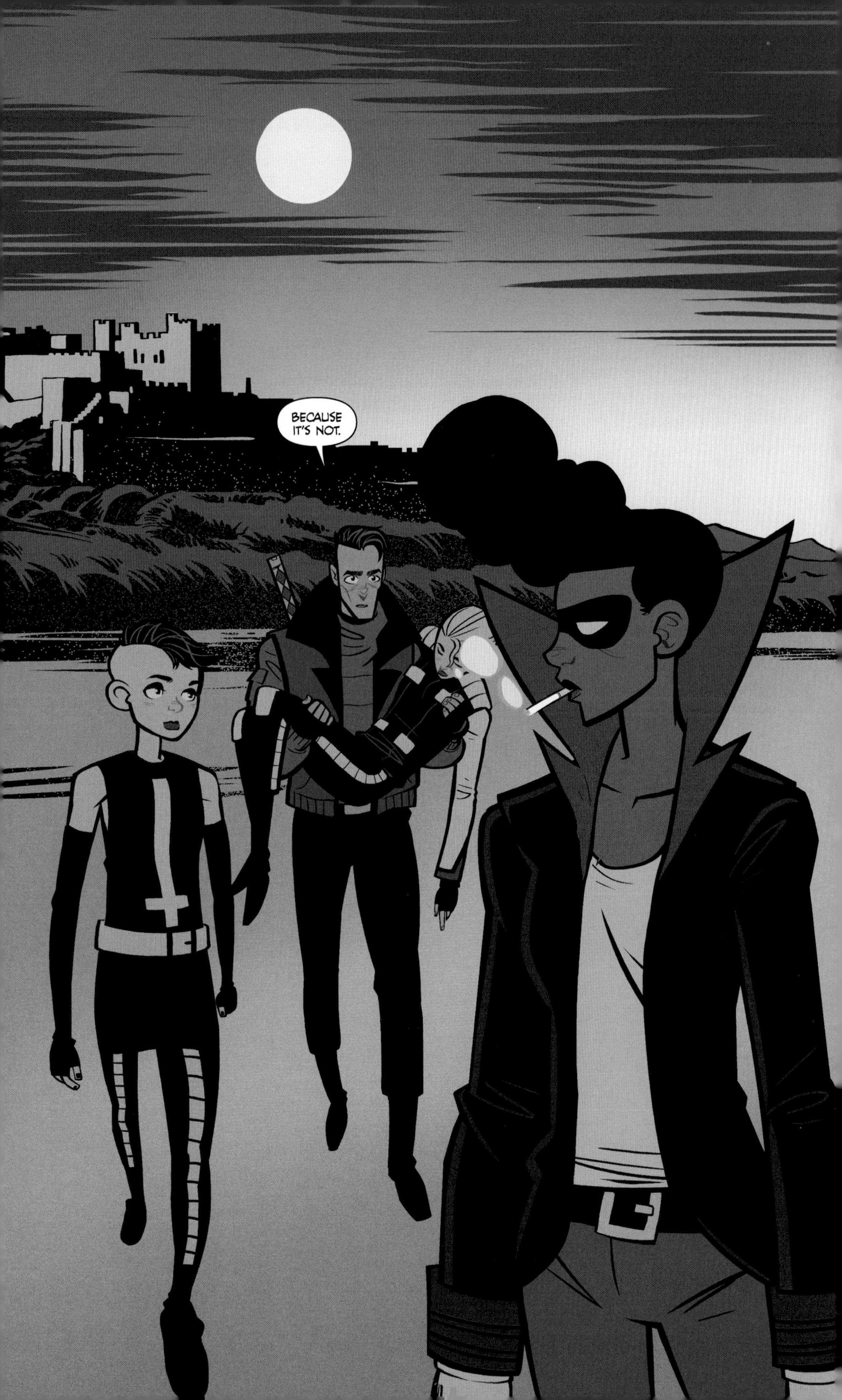
BECAUSE IT'S NOT.

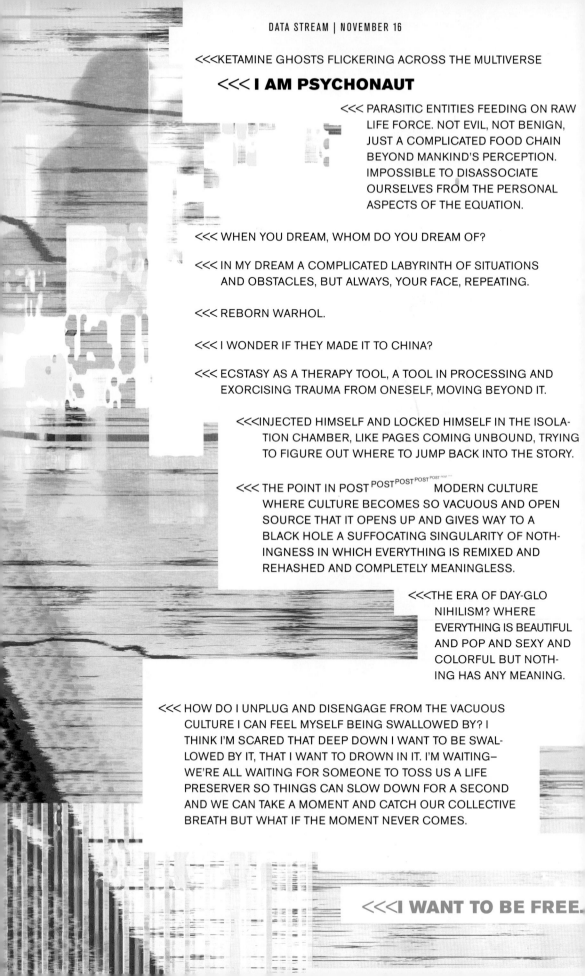

<<<KETAMINE GHOSTS FLICKERING ACROSS THE MULTIVERSE

## <<< I AM PSYCHONAUT

<<< PARASITIC ENTITIES FEEDING ON RAW LIFE FORCE. NOT EVIL, NOT BENIGN, JUST A COMPLICATED FOOD CHAIN BEYOND MANKIND'S PERCEPTION. IMPOSSIBLE TO DISASSOCIATE OURSELVES FROM THE PERSONAL ASPECTS OF THE EQUATION.

<<< WHEN YOU DREAM, WHOM DO YOU DREAM OF?

<<< IN MY DREAM A COMPLICATED LABYRINTH OF SITUATIONS AND OBSTACLES, BUT ALWAYS, YOUR FACE, REPEATING.

<<< REBORN WARHOL.

<<< I WONDER IF THEY MADE IT TO CHINA?

<<< ECSTASY AS A THERAPY TOOL, A TOOL IN PROCESSING AND EXORCISING TRAUMA FROM ONESELF, MOVING BEYOND IT.

<<<INJECTED HIMSELF AND LOCKED HIMSELF IN THE ISOLA-TION CHAMBER, LIKE PAGES COMING UNBOUND, TRYING TO FIGURE OUT WHERE TO JUMP BACK INTO THE STORY.

<<< THE POINT IN POST POSTPOSTPOST POST POST POST MODERN CULTURE WHERE CULTURE BECOMES SO VACUOUS AND OPEN SOURCE THAT IT OPENS UP AND GIVES WAY TO A BLACK HOLE A SUFFOCATING SINGULARITY OF NOTH-INGNESS IN WHICH EVERYTHING IS REMIXED AND REHASHED AND COMPLETELY MEANINGLESS.

<<<THE ERA OF DAY-GLO NIHILISM? WHERE EVERYTHING IS BEAUTIFUL AND POP AND SEXY AND COLORFUL BUT NOTH-ING HAS ANY MEANING.

<<< HOW DO I UNPLUG AND DISENGAGE FROM THE VACUOUS CULTURE I CAN FEEL MYSELF BEING SWALLOWED BY? I THINK I'M SCARED THAT DEEP DOWN I WANT TO BE SWAL-LOWED BY IT, THAT I WANT TO DROWN IN IT. I'M WAITING– WE'RE ALL WAITING FOR SOMEONE TO TOSS US A LIFE PRESERVER SO THINGS CAN SLOW DOWN FOR A SECOND AND WE CAN TAKE A MOMENT AND CATCH OUR COLLECTIVE BREATH BUT WHAT IF THE MOMENT NEVER COMES.

### <<<I WANT TO BE FREE.

Curt Pires writes and creates stories for comics, film, television, and more. He is the creator of POP, MAYDAY, THE FICTION, THE TOMORROWS, and the forthcoming series THE FOREVERS. He lives and writes on the edge of a fourth-dimensional singularity. That entire last sentence was a lie. Find him online at CurtPires.com and on Twitter: @CurtPires.

Jason Copland is a Vancouver-based comic book artist. He is currently drawing KILL ALL MONSTERS, a giant monster vs. giant robot OGN from Dark Horse Comics. He was the artist and cocreator of POP (also from Dark Horse Comics). His work has been published by Marvel, BOOM!, Image, IDW, and many others. More information about Jason can be found at JasonCopland.com or on Twitter: @JasonCopland.

Alexis Ziritt is originally from Venezuela but has lived in Florida for the past decade. He's been published by *Complex* magazine, Heavy Metal, BOOM! Studios, and Dark Horse Comics, among others. His kung fu is strong.

Ian MacEwan is the cocreator of THE YANKEE from Floating World Comics. He works as an illustrator on the side, in between watching Almodóvar films and episodes of *Herman's Head*, and talking about getting some sleep some day.

Andrew MacLean is the creator, writer, and artist of APOCALYPTIGIRL (Dark Horse Comics) and HEAD LOPPER (Image Comics).

Liam Cobb currently lives and works in London.

Kevin Zeigler, an awkward but beautiful man, is an artist born in the land of Hoosiers. He left his small hometown of Columbus, Indiana, to find his path in 2006. Raised in the ways of illustration and sequential arts by Savannah College of Art and Design, he has worked on AFTER HOUDINI and THE INSIDE. Armed only with his mustache and trusty pencil at his side, he continues to use his drawings to create marvelously magical myths that excite and inspire.

Adam Metcalfe was born in the Rocky Mountains during a summer snowstorm that endowed him with invincibility against freezing temperatures. While wearing T-shirts and shorts throughout Canadian winters, he's busy coloring comics at night and watching his two-year-old turn Super Saiyan during the day. Follow him on Twitter: @AdamGMetcalfe.

In addition to lettering comics for publishers such as Dark Horse Comics, Image Comics, and BOOM! Studios, Colin Bell is known for writing backups for Titan Comics' DOCTOR WHO: THE TWELFTH DOCTOR and being one of the creators of the SICBA Award–winning DUNGEON FUN, an all-ages comic published by his own imprint Dogooder Comics.